Artificial Intelligence
for CBSE Class IX

Reema Thareja

Assistant Professor
Shyama Prasad Mukherji College
University of Delhi

Universities Press

ARTIFICIAL INTELLIGENCE FOR CBSE CLASS IX

UNIVERSITIES PRESS (INDIA) PRIVATE LIMITED

Registered office
3-6-747/1/A & 3-6-754/1, Himayatnagar, Hyderabad 500 029, Telangana, India
info@universitiespress.com; www.universitiespress.com

Distributed by
Orient Blackswan Private Limited

Registered office
3-6-752 Himayatnagar, Hyderabad 500 029, Telangana, India

Other offices
Bengaluru, Chennai, Guwahati, Hyderabad, Kolkata,
Mumbai, New Delhi, Noida, Patna, Visakhapatnam

© Universities Press (India) Private Ltd 2023
First published 2023

ISBN: 978-81-954009-5-9

Cover and book design
© Universities Press (India) Private Ltd 2023

Typeset in Adobe Garamond Pro 10.5 *by*
SRS Publishing Services, Puducherry

Printed in India by
SS Colour Impression Pvt Ltd, Chennai 600 106

Published by
Universities Press (India) Private Limited
3-6-747/1/A & 3-6-754/1, Himayatnagar, Hyderabad 500 029, Telangana, India

Disclaimer
Care has been taken to confirm the accuracy of information printed in this book. The author and the publisher, however, cannot accept any responsibility for errors or omissions or for consequences from application of the information in this book and make no warranty, express or implied, with respect to its contents. This textbook does not constitute a standard, specification or regulation. The trademarks or manufacturers' names appear/are used in this book only because they are considered essential to the object of subject discussion and do not necessarily constitute endorsement of the product/ standard by the author or publisher. All products and company names are trademarks[TM] or registered[®] trademarks of their respective holders. Use of them does not imply any affiliation with or endorsement by them.

I dedicate this book to my family and my uncle Mr B L Thareja,
who is a well-known author himself.

ARTIFICIAL INTELLIGENCE (SUBJECT CODE 417)

CLASS – IX (SESSION 2022–2023)

Total Marks: 100 (Theory-50 + Practical-50)

	Units	Max. Marks for Theory and Practical	Refer Chapter No.
PART A	**Employability Skills**		
	Unit 1: Communication Skills-I*		1
	Unit 2: Self-management Skills-I	3	1
	Unit 3: ICT Skills-I	3	2
	Unit 4: Entrepreneurial Skills-I	4	1
	Unit 5: Green Skills-I*		1
	Total	**10**	
PART B	**Subject-specific Skills**		
	Unit 1: Introduction to Artificial Intelligence	10	3–7
	Unit 2: AI Project Cycle	10	8
	Unit 3: Neural Network	10	9
	Unit 4: Introduction to Python	10	10–14
	Total	**40**	
PART C	**Practical Work** Introduction to Python - Practical File with minimum 15 Programs	15	10–14
	Practical Examination • Simple programs using input and output function • Variables, arithmetic operators • Flow of control and conditions. • Lists *Any 3 programs based on the above topics	15	10–14
	Viva Voce	5	
	Total	**35**	
PART D	**Project Work / Field Visit / Practical File / Student Portfolio** * Relate it to sustainable development goals	15	5
	Total	**15**	
	GRAND TOTAL	**100**	

Note

Units marked with * are to be assessed through Internal Assessment/ Student Activities.
They are not to be assessed in Theory Exams.

Contents

| Chapter 3: | Introduction to Artificial Intelligence | 53 |

| Chapter 4: | Applications of Artificial Intelligence | 73 |

Preface

Artificial Intelligence (AI) is a niche technology that has been gaining significant importance over the past three decades. This is because, it provides solutions to a diverse variety of problems using big dataset in every industry. Hence, it is imperative for high-school students to understand AI and have the ability to use AI and big data to solve real-world problems.

Besides understanding the topics discussed in the AI curriculum, it is very important for the student to be aware of the ethics associated with the usage of AI to get maximum benefit. Students should know that they are already using AI in their day-to-day lives – from virtual assistance to the recommendation of videos on YouTube. Learning AI at school has the following benefits:

- It boosts creative thinking in students at an early age.
- It prepares children to lead in the future.
- It provides new strategies to effectively solve real-world problems.
- It improves the qualities of patience and perseverance among students.
- It helps students to learn by reasoning rather than by rote memory.

Hence, this book has been designed to introduce the basic concepts of AI to the student with focus on the subject syllabus prescribed by CBSE for Class IX. In addition, the book also covers Python, which is an open-source, excellent, easy, high-level, interpreted, interactive, object-oriented and a reliable language that uses English-like words. It is also a versatile language that supports development of a wide range of applications ranging from simple text processing to WWW browsers to games. Moreover, programmers can embed Python within their C, C++, COM, ActiveX, CORBA, and Java programs to give 'scripting' capabilities for users.

Python has a huge user base that is constantly growing. The strength of Python can be understood from the fact that this programming language is the most preferred language of companies like Nokia, Google, YouTube and even NASA for its easy syntax. The support for multiple programming paradigms, including object-oriented programming, functional Python programming, and parallel programming models makes it an ideal choice for the programmers.

However, no student can learn to program just by reading a book; rather it is a skill that must be developed by practice. So, after learning the rudiments of program-writing, students will find a number of examples and exercises that would help them to learn to design efficient programs. The book presents various programming examples that have already been implemented and tested using Python 3.8.3.

KEY FEATURES

This book is aimed at serving as a textbook for students enrolled in Class IX of CBSE. The objective of this book is to introduce the concepts of Communication, Entrepreneurship, Self-management, Sustainable Development, Green Technology, and the basics of Artificial Intelligence before introducing the Python Programming language as a multifaceted tool with diverse functions. Salient features of the book include:

Pictorial Approach: Well-labelled diagrams are provided throughout the text for clear understanding of the concepts.

Easy to understand: The book uses a very simple language to explain the concepts and breaks down technical jargons to simpler terms for the student's benefit.

Practical orientation: The book has numerous solved examples and chapter-end exercises in the form of objective type questions and review questions to help students face their exams with confidence.

Comprehensive Coverage: The book provides comprehensive coverage of all the topics prescribed by CBSE in its Class IX syllabus for Artificial Intelligence.

Glossary: A list of key terms included is provided at the end of each chapter to facilitate revision of important topics learned.

Informative Textboxes: Theory discussions are interspersed with ample hints and explanations given in well-placed textboxes for ease of understanding.

AI Lab Sessions and Activities at the end of all chapters to familiarize the student with the various AI-powered applications that are currently in use and to highlight the immense potential of this emerging technology.

Programmer's Zone examples are used in context to help the students understand the technique of programming.

Complementary App: Students can download the free mobile app Jruma from Google Play Store or Apple Store for additional learning resources. The app would help them to recapitulate and test their understanding of the concepts learnt, right from Class I. The app will also be useful for the students to hone their Computer Science (CS) and Logical Reasoning (LR) skills.

ACKNOWLEDGMENTS

The writing of this text book was a mammoth task for which a lot of help was required from many people. Fortunately, I have had the fine support of my family, friends and fellow members of the teaching staff at the Shyama Prasad Mukherji College.

My special thanks would always go to my father Late Sh. Janak Raj Thareja, my mother Smt. Usha Thareja, my brother Pallav and sisters Kimi and Rashi who were a source of abiding inspiration and are a divine blessing for me. I am especially indebted to my son Goransh, who has been very patient and cooperative in letting me realize my dreams. I am obliged to my uncle Mr B L Theraja for his inspiration and guidance in writing this book.

Last but not the least, my acknowledgements will always be incomplete if I do not thank the editorial team at Universities Press (India) Private Limited that gave me this brilliant opportunity to utilize my writing skills.

Reema Thareja
reema_thareja@yahoo.com

About the Author

Reema Thareja is Assistant Professor at Shyama Prasad Mukherji College, University of Delhi. She has over 17 years of experience, teaching computer science for various courses including BA, BSc, MSc, BBA, MBA, BCA and MCA. She has authored several books, including those on Computer Fundamentals, C Programming, OOPS with C++, Data Structures, Data Warehousing and Python Programming, which are well-accepted across the globe. She has also written books on Data Science and Machine Learning in R for the current academic session.

Dr Thareja has published more than 20 research papers in journals of national and international repute. A recipient of 64 Google Scholar Citations, she has launched a Computer Science Learning and Quizzing mobile app, Jruma, for both Android and iOS devices to promote incentive-based learning through quizzing.

A recipient of the Nobel Laureate Maria Goeppert–Mayer Inspiring Woman of the Year 2021 Award in the field of Computer Science by International Multi-disciplinary Research Foundation (IMRF), Dr Thareja was also among "India's Top 50 Women Leaders in the Education Industry" recognized by uLektz Wall of Fame for the year 2020. She has conducted several faculty development programs, student workshops and webinars in India and US, and participated in the International Dialogue on Empowered Future – Women's Role on the eve of International Women's Day 2021.

A member of the Computer Society of India and Editorial Board and Keynote Speaker of the IMRF Conference Board, Dr Thareja is a skilled motivator who helps students utilize their untapped skills and reinvent themselves. She was also conferred with the Knowledge Mobilization Award at the Seventh Annual Research Awards event organized by Shri Param Hans Education and Research Trust and was invited as a speaker at the Global Virtual Summit held recently in New York. She has received multiple awards and recognitions for her contributions in the field of education.

Communication, Self-management, Entrepreneurial and Green Skills

1

The chapter deals with concepts that help to improve the overall personality of an individual and broaden his/her outlook towards ideas pertaining to sustainable development. We will learn about:

- Effective communication skills
- Formal and informal communication and ways to improve them
- Self-management skills
- Developing and improving entrepreneurial skills
- Moving towards green technology

1.1 WHAT ARE COMMUNICATION SKILLS?

Communication skills of an individual refer to the abilities expressed while giving and receiving information. In a professional environment, we need to communicate new ideas, express our feelings, opinions or even share an update on a project.

Communication skills involve listening, speaking, observing and empathizing. They also help an individual to communicate in different modes through face-to-face interactions, telephonic conversations and digital communications like email and social media.

Active listening

Non-verbal communication

Clarity and conclusion

Friendliness

Confidence

Empathy

Open-mindedness

Respect

Feedback

Picking the right medium

Figure 1.1 Elements of effective communication

We need to learn and practice the skills for effective communication to become an able communicator (Fig. 1.1). An effective communicator has the following qualities:

Active listening: An active listener carefully listens to the speaker. Since this quality is difficult to develop and improve, people who are good listeners gain a lot of support and respect from their co-workers. To be an active listener, focus on the speaker, avoid distractions like cell phones, laptops or other projects. Also prepare questions, comments or ideas to thoughtfully respond.

Adapting communication style as per the audience: Our communication style must vary depending on the context in which we are communicating. Before communicating, we must consider the audience and accordingly decide the most effective way to communicate with them. For example, to communicate with a potential employer, send a formal email; to talk to your business heads, send a formal message or call them on the phone. Instead of writing long emails to multiple recipients, it is better to do a video conference.

Friendliness: Maintain healthy and friendly relationships at the workplace. Work with a positive attitude. Be honest and kind. Keep an open mind. Small gestures, such as asking someone how they are doing, smiling while listening to others, praising work that is well done and so on, will foster productive relationships with junior as well as senior colleagues.

Confidence: People get easily impressed and appreciate ideas that are presented with confidence. To exhibit confidence, make eye contact while talking to someone, and sit straight with shoulders open. Always prepare well before presenting or appearing for an interview.

Giving and receiving feedback: Strong communicators take critical feedback with dignity and give constructive feedback to others. During communication, they respond to answer questions, give solutions or to add additional information on the project or topic at hand.

Volume and clarity: Always be clear and audible. Adjust your voice so that you are heard easily. However, remember that speaking too loudly may be disrespectful or awkward in certain settings. Observe how other effective communicators speak and replicate their style when communicating with others.

Empathy: Understand and share the emotions of others. For example, if someone is angry or frustrated, empathy can help them acknowledge and diffuse their emotion. Similarly, if someone is feeling positive and enthusiastic then it becomes easy to gain his/her support for your ideas and projects.

Respect: Know when to initiate communication and respond. When working in a team or group setting, allow others to speak without interruption. While talking, stay on the topic, ask clear questions and respond fully to all queries.

Take care of nonverbal cues: A lot of communication takes place through nonverbal cues such as body language, facial expressions and eye contact. When listening to someone, pay attention to what they say verbally as well as through their nonverbal language. When speaking to others, keep a check on your body language to ensure that you are sending appropriate cues to others.

Responsiveness: A person who responds fast is more appreciated than the one who is slow to reply. So, always reply to a phone call, message or email at the earliest. If you are running short of time, then at least acknowledge the receipt of message/call and let the other person know you will respond in full later.

Clear and concise: The chances of being misunderstood become weak when dealing clear and concise messages. Instead of speaking in long, detailed sentences, talk briefly in full context. Provide context to your message and practice reducing your message to its core meaning.

1.1.1 How to Improve Your Communication Skills

We all develop and improve our communication skills with experience and practice. Identify your strengths and make them even stronger. You can also do the following:

- Request a close friend or colleague to give honest feedback and constructive criticism so that you can focus on your limitations and overcome them.
- Practice improving communication habits like making an eye contact, responding as fast as possible, accepting criticism with an open mind, etc.
- Join some workshops or classes for communication skills as they prepare you to effectively communicate with others.
- Look for opportunities to communicate. This will help you do away with stage fear
- Assert yourself. Be confident, especially when you are talking of getting a higher increment, seeking project opportunities or resisting an idea that may not be beneficial. Always observe the pitch and tone of your voice. You should always be respectful.
- Be calm and consistent, especially in case of any disagreement or conflict. Maintain a consistent body language to come to a conclusion peacefully and productively.

Figure 1.2 gives a few suggestions for improving your communication skills.

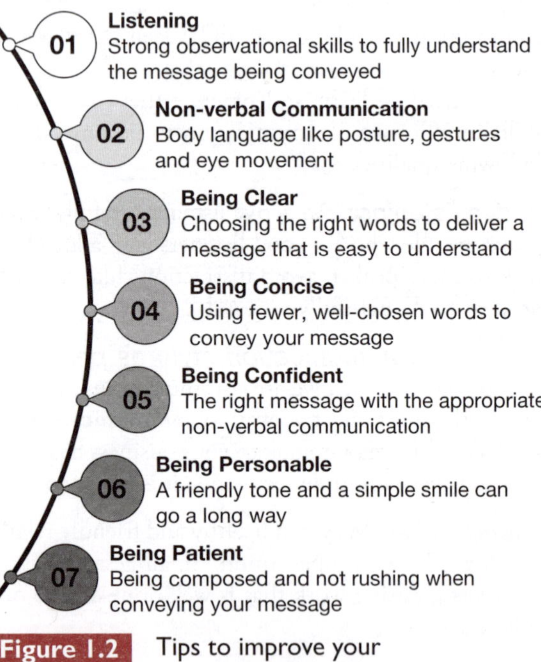

Figure 1.2   Tips to improve your communication skills

1.1.2 How to Highlight Communication Skills

We use communication skills everywhere – in school, college, office, home, when searching for a job, writing a CV or giving an interview for selection. Looking at the importance of these essential skills, let us discuss how you can highlight your communication skills to impress everyone around you.

Communication skills for resume A well-written resume demonstrates strong communication skills. The resume must be structured properly with no spelling or grammatical errors. It is always recommended to include some positive communication skills, especially if the job demands interacting with clients or management in the job description.

Communication skills for cover letter: Any cover letter that you write gives you an excellent opportunity to exhibit your communication skills. This letter is the first impression that you give to your employer/boss. Make your cover letter brief, well-written, clear, free of typos and spelling errors and customized with respect to the position you are applying for.

Communication skills for job interview: To prepare for an interview, first learn to present yourself. Go for the interview 10–15 minutes early and dress appropriately for the job you are applying for. Give due importance to non-verbal cues that you exhibit through your body language. Make sure that instead of looking into your phone during the interview, look at the interviewer, make eye contact with the interviewer, employ active listening skills and talk with full confidence.

Remember that your communication skills speak a lot about your personal as well as professional life. So, identify your strengths and weaknesses, practice good habits, improve how you connect and communicate with others.

1.2   TYPES OF COMMUNICATION SKILLS

Communication skills are essential to the success of any individual in any business. It is these communication skills that determine the effectiveness of any communication. We can broadly categorize communications as Verbal, Non-verbal and Visual (Fig. 1.3).

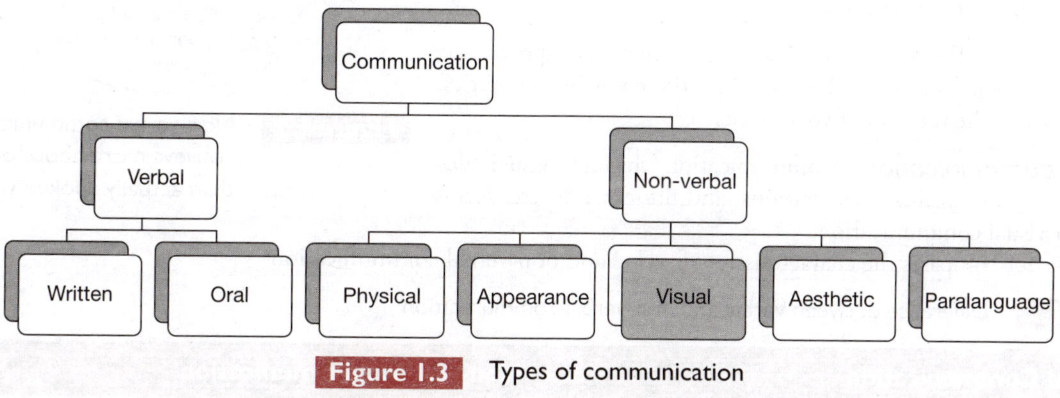

Figure 1.3   Types of communication

Verbal Communication   In a verbal communication, language is used to convey the intended message in the form of spoken words or in the written form.

Written communication: Written communication includes exchanging information in the written form. E-mails, letters, texts, reports, messages (SMS/Whatsapp), posts on social media, handbooks, posters, flyers, etc. are all examples of written communication.

Oral communication: This mode of communication uses spoken words using either a direct or indirect communication channel. This variant of verbal communication is made on a channel that transfers information in only one form – sound. You can converse face to face, over the phone, or via voice notes or chat rooms, etc.

Non-verbal Communication   In this mode of communication, messages are exchanged without transmitting any word(s). This type of communication is mainly used to aid wordless messages mainly through gestures, body language, symbols, and expressions.

Non-verbal communication is basically used to express one's mood or opinion or even to show a reaction to the messages that are being exchanged. Aspects of non-verbal communication vary across cultures. Awareness of the cultural norms in the given context will help us to communicate more effectively (Fig. 1.4). An individual's non-verbal actions often set the tone for the dialogue. This clearly means that you can bring the entire communication in your control by controlling and guiding the non-verbal communication. Some of the modes of non-verbal communication include:

Figure 1.4   Aspects of non-verbal communication

Physical non-verbal communication: This is the physically observable communication and includes facial expressions, posture, body language, hand gestures, tone of the voice, touch, gaze, etc.

It is believed that physical non-verbal communication constitutes about 65% of any individual's daily communications (Fig. 1.5). They convey a lot of information about your personality. For example, resting your head on your palms indicates that you are very disappointed or angry. Be very particular about what reaction you give to the presenter or to the audience.

Paralanguage: This is said to be the art of reading between the lines. It is related to the tone of one's voice and contributes to almost 38% of all the communication that we do daily. In addition to tone, the style of speaking, voice quality, stress, emotions, and intonation also form a part of paralanguage.

Aesthetic communication: In this form of communication, artwork including paintings, dance, music or other forms of art are used to covey the strongest messages. Even if we go back to our history, we would find that art has always been used as an effective tool for non-verbal communication.

Appearance: The first impression, that is, how you appear, sets the tone of communication. Your clothes, the color of the fabrics, etc. influences the reaction of your audience.

Visual communication: Communication through visual aids like drawings, playcards, presentations, and illustrations, etc. forms a part of visual communication.

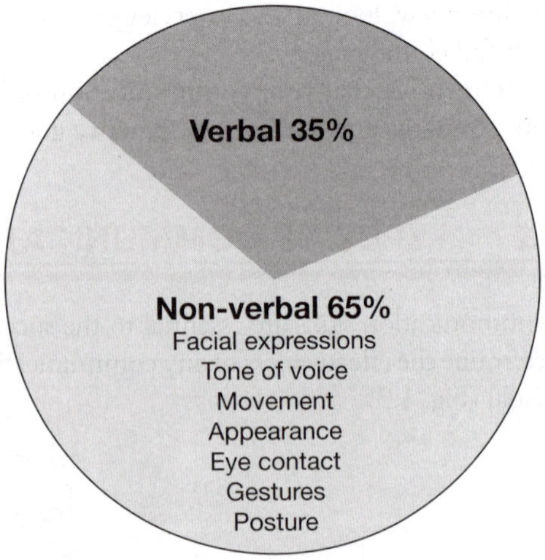

Table 1.1 compares the characteristics of verbal and non-verbal communication.

Figure 1.5   Non-verbal communication conveys more about ourselves than actually spoken words

Table 1.1   Difference between verbal and non-verbal communication

Verbal Communication	Non-verbal Communication
Uses words – said or written	No words are written or spoken
Easy to understand	Not so easy to understand
Highly structured form of expression	No formal structure
It is more consistent, so there is less possibility of distortion of information	Higher possibility of distortion of information as it is not at all consistent
We have limited words for a particular context	There are far more options to communicate without words
There may be a delay in getting feedback	There is less delay in getting feedback. Sometimes we get instant feedback
It has a legal and a documented reference	No such reference exists
Used extensively in business communications	Not used to convey business information

1.2.1 Formal and Informal Communication

In addition to the above types of communication, we can categorize communication as – formal and informal. We can broadly classify formal communication as,

Vertical: In this technique, information or data flows up and down the organizational structure.

Horizontal: This is type of communication takes place between two similar levels of the organization.

Diagonal: In this mode, communication is done across the functional levels of employees from various departments of the organization.

Informal: Informal or casual communication is the most general form of communication that happens randomly between people of the organization.

1.3 SELF-MANAGEMENT SKILLS

To be successful and productive, one must have strong self-management skills. Self-management skills are one's ability to regulate and control his/her actions, feelings, and thoughts. These skills help an individual to focus on his/her obligatory duties and responsibilities, set practical goals, and have more control over career, which eventually results in more exciting opportunities (Fig. 1.6).

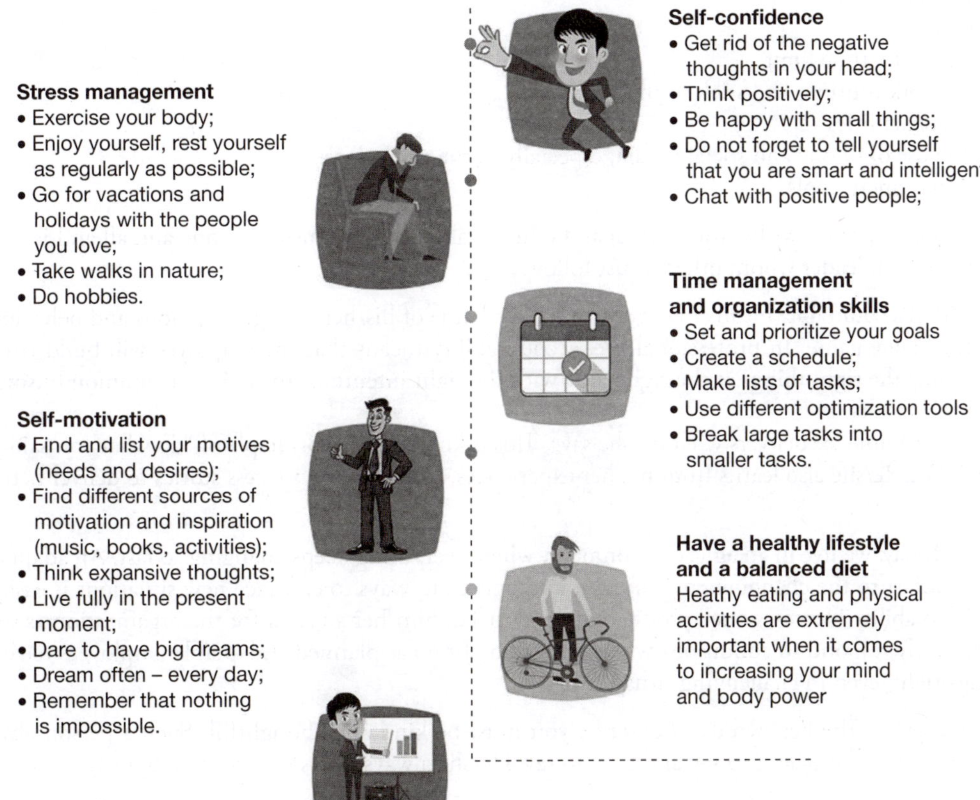

Figure 1.6 Self-management skills and tips

A person lacking self-management skills may be unpredictable, which can make an employer nervous. In contrast, a person who can manage himself/herself well will always be smart at work and maintain healthy relations at the workplace.

1.4   EXAMPLES OF SELF-MANAGEMENT SKILLS

An organization does extremely well when employees understand their responsibilities, goals, and actions that must be performed to achieve them. Some self-management skills that every employer yearns for include:

Reliability: Everybody can count on a reliable person. Such a person always keep promises made by him/her.

Stress management: A person who knows how to stay calm and manage even a highly tensed situation can attain great success in everything done by him/her. Stress is revealed, not just in our physical appearance but also in every work that we do. Excessive stress hampers our logical thinking and rational decision-making. Stressed employees cannot achieve their business goal as mental pressure lowers their productivity.

To cope up with strenuous situations, learn to self-manage your emotions by doing any or at best all of the following things.

* Get surrounded with highly motivated, calm people
* Learn to meditate for at least 5–10 minutes everyday
* Eat healthy food
* Make allowance for ample sleep with power naps after lunch.

Time management: The sky is the limit for a person who knows how to manage time, prioritize tasks, and get things done by others on time. Follow the steps given below for managing your time effectively:

* Note down the tasks to do
* Prioritize tasks
* For every task, set a time limit
* Design daily work routines and stick to them
* Delegate responsibilities
* Minimize the use of phone and social media, especially at the workplace
* Use time management tools.

Trustworthiness: A person with strong moral and ethical values can be trusted by one and all and is thus the best candidate to be an ideal leader whom others must follow.

Accountability: 'Accountable' means that a person takes charge of his/her thoughts, actions and behaviour. He/she will not play the blame game. In professional life, accountability means that the employee will build trust and stay committed to doing the right things at the right time with the right intention (to achieve a common business goal) to deliver exceptional results.

An accountable employee delivers what he/she says. This is known as the principle of "do what you said you would do" (DWYSYWD). He/she also learns from his/her experiences, mistakes and success stories to deliver better the next time.

Adaptability: Today, we live in an agile environment, where everything keeps changing so fast. An adaptable person who is quick to adjust to the changing environment and figure out ways to embrace new situations is easily accepted by everyone. Adaptability increases one's productivity and makes him/her an asset for the organization as such an employee can effectively respond to conditions when things do not go as planned. Adaptable employees have the power to set the things right, even in challenging situations.

Conscientiousness: The best words to describe you must be kind and thoughtful. Such a person always knows what to say, where to say, to whom to say and how to say. He/she always treats others with dignity.

Self-motivation: Self-motivation is the ability to encourage oneself to achieve a goal even in the most challenging times. The happiness of goal achievement gives a sense of satisfaction and pride. Self-motivated people have a strong desire to excel and are thus not distracted by external factors. When such people get promotions and appreciations, they build trusting relationships with colleagues. To self-motivate yourself, you must,

* Set practical goals that can be realized
* Plan to achieve that goal
* Think of the reward that you will give to yourself if that goal is achieved
* Learn new things

- Be an optimist
- Stay in the company of motivated and high-spirited people
- Come out of your comfort zone.

Align to the right level of engagement: In an organization, there is a continuum from strategy to execution that moves from "why" to "what" to "how". A self-managed employee will have focus on the right point appropriate for his role. For example, as a middle manager, the focus would be on the "why" part of the strategy and on "what" or "how" part of it.

1.5   IMPORTANCE OF SELF-MANAGEMENT SKILLS

Everyone needs to learn self-management skills sooner or later but learning them sooner is always beneficial because of the following reasons:

- It speeds up one's career graph.
- It helps one to become organized.
- It enhances one's confidence and self-control.
- It increases accountability.
- It makes one responsible.
- It prepares one to face any difficult situation at home or at work.
- It motivates one to set goals, prioritize tasks and track progress, even in the smallest things.

1.6   ENTREPRENEUR SKILLS: DEFINITION AND EXAMPLES

An entrepreneur is a person who builds or operates a business. If everything goes well, the entrepreneur can earn huge profits, but there is always a risk involved in doing business. These risks can be financial, emotional or career-related. To mitigate these risks, the entrepreneur must possess certain skill-sets and must be able to effectively communicate, sell, focus, learn, and strategize (Fig. 1.7).

A successful entrepreneur possesses certain hard (like accounting, marketing, business management, economics, financial planning) and soft skills (like communication, problem-solving and decision-making). While hard skills are critical for running and managing a business, promoting innovation and staying competitive, soft skills on the other hand, help an individual to scale up the business. Having a good command over these

Figure 1.7   Skill-sets for successful entrepreneurship

skills requires practice and a dedicated learning plan. To be a successful entrepreneur, we need to not only learn these skills but also develop risk-taking skills.

Business management skills (BMS): These skills are necessary to run a business and ensure that all business goals are met. Entrepreneurs with BM skills can easily look after the work of different departments as they possess a good understanding of each function. BMS includes multitasking, delegating responsibilities and making critical business decisions.

Communication and active listening skills: Entrepreneurs must be able to communicate effectively with clients, employees, investors, customers, creditors, peers, and mentors.

They need excellent verbal communication skills during meetings, presentations and effective writing skills when writing emails and summarizing business reports. In addition to this, entrepreneurs must be excellent listeners to understand the project's requirements and facts or ideas shared during project meetings. A good entrepreneur learns to master all forms of communication, including one-on-one and in-person conversations and group conversations.

Risk-taking skills: An entrepreneur must be able to calculate and analyze risks that may harm the project. However, they never run away from taking those risks because they take the risks as an opportunity to learn and grow their business.

Networking skills: Networking means building and managing business relationships to foster the speed of growth. Entrepreneurs having effective networking skills can easily establish their business as a big brand, thereby opening the gates of more opportunities. Through networking, entrepreneurs can meet like-minded professionals, build future teams and get updated about fast-changing technology. It is one of the most desirable skills as entrepreneurs can exploit their network to meet professionals for funding their ideas, providing business expertise and getting feedback on their new venture or idea.

Professional network may also include:

- Ex and current co-workers
- Alumni from your educational institutions
- Ex teaching faculty
- Industry leaders
- Keynote speakers
- Ex and current clients
- Friends and family members.

Critical thinking skills: Critical thinking allows an entrepreneur to analyze the data, draw useful trends and patterns, build strategies for business growth, scrutinize information, understand the problem (if any) and come up with a logical solution.

Problem-solving skills: Problems, risks, losses, and handling challenging and unexpected situations are a part of every entrepreneur's life. For example, a venture capitalist may stop further funding or a team member may leave the organization. To cope up well with such unforeseen circumstances, an entrepreneur must be an excellent problem-solver.

Creative thinking skills: Creativity is a valuable, yet underappreciated skill in the digital world. Creative thinking is the backbone for innovation and it forces employees to think differently. Entrepreneurs with creative thinking skills are never hesitant to try solutions that others may overlook because of fear of failure. Such people think out-of-the-box and always seek input from professionals in a different field for understanding a new perspective. It is one of the most sought-after entrepreneur skills because it allows them to see patterns (even when there are no patterns) and develop innovative ways to solve business issues.

Customer service skills: Providing timely support to customers promotes the brand and increases its loyalty.

Financial skills: To maximize cost cutting and generating profits, an entrepreneur must optimize the use of business resources. For this, he/she must assess investments, calculate ROI, and keep track of all the financial processes by using accounting and budgeting software tools.

A successful entrepreneur mobilizes the revenue of the organization properly, utilizes human resources in a cost-efficient manner and provides channels of further economic growth in the organization.

Leadership skills: A successful entrepreneur inspires colleagues, empowers the workforce and leads by setting examples. Entrepreneurs with leadership skills motivate their employees to attain business goals, manage operations efficiently and delegate tasks to run the business smoothly.

Time management and organizational skills: To enhance productivity, an entrepreneur masters time management. He/she knows how to delegate tasks, prioritize tasks, avoid procrastination, set deadlines, track progress at milestones and use technology to organize flow of information in the workspace.

Technical skills: Technical skills are hard skills that are required to have a good understanding of the tools for planning, marketing, budgeting, managing project, tracking sales and analyzing key data.

Sales: If an entrepreneur is an effective communicator, then he/she can effectively sell ideas and physical products.

Focus: Every business faces ups and downs. A successful entrepreneur therefore needs to be highly focused, especially when the going gets tough. He/she needs to keep an unwavering eye on the end goal and pursue it wholeheartedly to achieve it. Figure 1.8 shows the key qualities needed for a successful entrepreneur.

Ability to Learn: An entrepreneur is never shy to learn. He/she has the ability and desire to learn even in the worst situation. He/she understands that failures help expand one's knowledge and understanding of the business.

Strategy: An entrepreneur must have an impressive business strategy based on sound business principles.

Optimism: Optimism is an asset, especially for being an entrepreneur. Such a quality helps one to get through tough times.

Negotiation: An entrepreneur is a good negotiator. He not only knows how to negotiate favorable prices, but is also able to resolve differences between people in a positive, mutually beneficial way.

Ethics: A good entrepreneur should have high ethical values. When dealing with people, he/she always values qualities like respect, integrity, fairness and trust to build a happy and productive business.

Figure 1.8   Entrepreneurship: What it takes to succeed

1.7   IMPROVING ENTREPRENEUR SKILLS

To learn or excel in entrepreneur skills, one can read books, take a course or attend seminars as discussed below.

- ***Read business books*** to know more about effective business strategies.
- ***Enroll*** in a management, marketing or finance course to sharpen your skill set.
- ***Attend workshops*** and other networking events. You will get an opportunity to listen to and interact with experienced business owners as speakers. This would help you to gain valuable insights on how to run your business to success.
- ***Listen*** to podcasts of successful entrepreneurs to learn how different entrepreneurs use technology to speed up their business growth.
- ***Hire*** an experienced business mentor to develop the skills that you are lacking. You can even work under a successful business owner for some time to understand how to manage a business.

All these techniques, in turn, improve our cognitive ability, increase our decision-making capability and make us learn from the failure of others. Figure 1.9 presents a list of successful entrepreneurs in India.

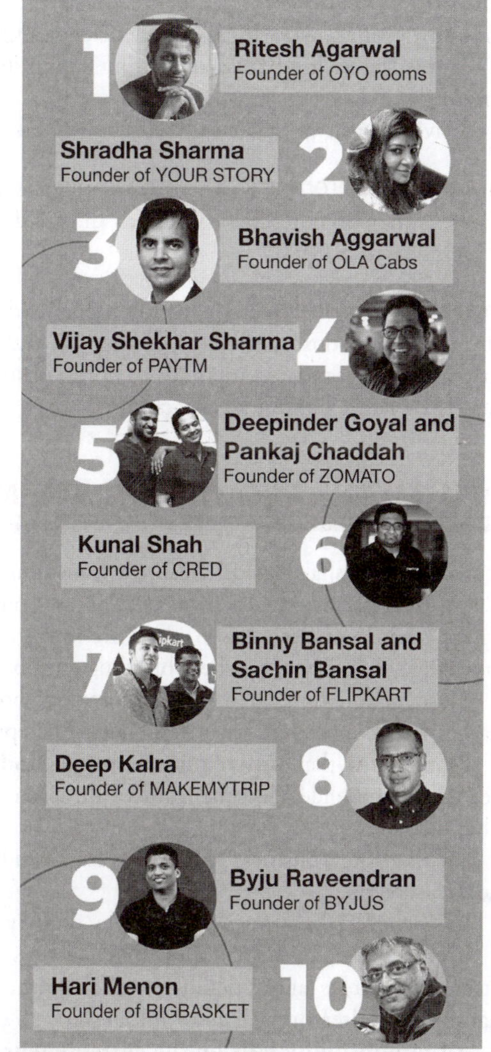

Figure 1.9   Successful Indian entrepreneurs

1.8   TYPES OF ENTREPRENEURS

We can categorize an entrepreneur as innovative, imitating, Fabian or Drone entrepreneur depending on his/her working relationship with the business environment he/she is functioning in.

Innovative Entrepreneurs are always interested in introducing some new ideas. To lead innovation, they invest a lot of time and money in doing research and development.

Examples: Satyajeet Mohanty and Ronak Kumar Samatray, started Bolt to develop the world's first small mobile phone charger for motorbikes. This helped users to quickly charge their phones while riding. They also created a Bolt Riders App to track the entire ride, total distance covered, average speed, etc. Bolt devices have a unique detachable design which prevents theft or any misuse of the device. Its devices are very popular on ecommerce platforms such as Flipkart and Amazon.

Chaayos was started in November 2012 to explore India's everlasting love for tea. At present there are more than 53 cafes operating in six cities. The startup caters to Indian taste buds with lip smacking snacks that are usually taken with tea.

UrbanClap is India's first online service platform. The app provides on-demand services across six cities and. It was difficult to find reliable service providers (like carpenters, plumbers etc) for home, But with Urban Clap they can be contacted in no time.

Imitating Entrepreneurs are often referred to as 'copy cats' because they consider an existing successful system and just improve it by removing all the deficiencies while retaining its efficiencies.

Examples: Sachin Bansal and Binny Bansal started Flipkart in 2007 as the Indian version of US e-commerce giant, Amazon.

Bhavish Aggarwal started Ola in 2010 to take on Uber, the US taxi aggregator.

Fabian Entrepreneurs These entrepreneurs are very careful in their approaches and cautious in adopting any changes. They do not believe in taking drastic decisions and avoid the use of any innovation or change that does not fit their narrative.

Drone Entrepreneurs These entrepreneurs do not like a change. They prefer to do business using their own traditional or orthodox methods of production and systems. Such people feel proud to be tagged as 'traditional' or even with labels like 'outdated methods of doing business'. For example, tobacco-making industry is still making tobaccos entirely by hand without any machinery.

1.9   MYTHS ABOUT ENTREPRENEURSHIP

According to Vishal Trivedi (Business Consultant, Founder and CEO of Horizon Unlimited), approximately one in every 18 people worldwide owns a business. Some start a company to exploit an opportunity, others do it to earn a living. Whatever be the reason, there are many myths and misconceptions that surround entrepreneurship. Having a knowledge about these can help budding entrepreneurs to achieve success.

Many people think that **businessmen are born** to be entrepreneurs with certain natural talents. But the truth is that anyone can become an entrepreneur. Entrepreneurism is a learned skill, not a natural-born ability.

People think that **only requirement is a good idea**. But it is not true. You just need proper execution of an existing idea to make the idea become reality. Entrepreneurs need planning, talent, leadership, communication, and a host of other factors.

Starting a new business **guarantees freedom** but the fact is that with a startup, you may need to work even beyond the 9–5 schedule.

It is believed that starting a company quickly leads to **wealth,** but that is not always true.

It is a commonly held notion that businesses can either **flourish or fail**. However, in reality, the outcome of a business venture is far less definitive. It takes time and lot of patience for businesses to get established. Some companies that initially falter, or have a low initial start, go on to achieve healthy growth.

All responsibility falls on the entrepreneur. However, the fact is that success depends on collaboration and the art of delegation. No one can do it all alone.

There is no secret, "silver bullet" **key to success.** This is just a myth. There is no hard and fast rule to attain success. Many successful entrepreneurs create a notion that they have found the key to success. However, they hide the previous ideas that failed; the hard work and patience with which they had worked to build a strong company (Fig. 1.10).

Businesses need someone with a **formal MBA degree.** This is, however, not true. Some startup owners have no formal degree but have high technical knowledge.

Quitting is for losers is believed to be true but it is not actually so. An entrepreneur should know when to walk away and move on to the next idea.

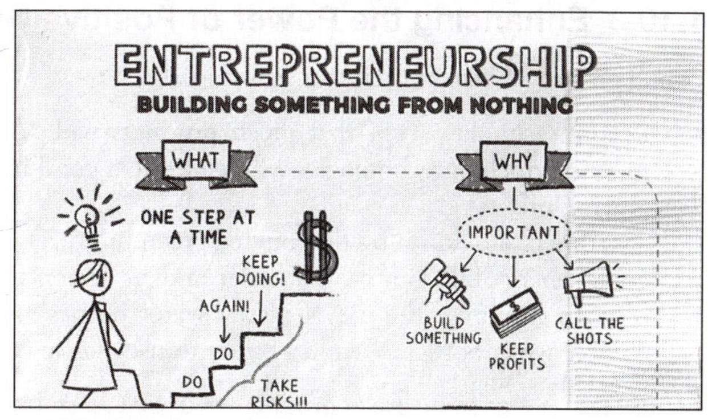

Figure 1.10 Building a business is step-by-step work

1.10 GREEN TECHNOLOGY

Technology means application of knowledge and the term "green technology" therefore refers to sustainable technology that considers the long- and short-term impact of something on the environment. Green products are environmentally friendly, energy efficient, recyclable, safe, and use renewable resources.

The goals of developing green products must be:

Sustainable, meeting the needs of society in such a way that they can be used even in the future without damaging or depleting natural resources. This would ensure that green products would meet present needs without compromising on the ability of future generations to meet their own needs.

Reusable, so that the manufactured products can be fully reclaimed or re-used.

Waste reduction, to reduce waste and pollution by changing the way they are produced and consumed.

Innovative, by developing alternatives to existing technologies. For example, to a technology that uses fossil fuels, there can be an alternative that uses some chemical that causes less/no damage to health and the environment.

1.10.1 Green Technology Subject Areas

Let us consider certain areas where green technology is used:

Green building is very particularly designed by considering even minute details like what material has been used to construct it, where the building is located, etc.

Green chemistry includes the invention, design and application of chemical products and processes that either reduce or eliminate the use and generation of harmful substances.

1.10.2 Go Green or Face Extinction?

Our planet and its environment have been adversely affected, right from the day when the steam engine was invented. Severe droughts, excessive rainfall, melting of glaciers, rapid depletion of groundwater, seawater acidification, rising seawater levels, rapid spread of diseases and extinction of species are some changes that are irreversible. For example, household batteries and electronic gadgets have dangerous chemicals that pollute soil and groundwater. These chemicals cannot be removed from drinking water supply. They also enter the human body with food crops that are grown on the contaminated soil and through livestock that feeds on fodder from degraded soil.

Plastic pollutants are another big cause for the destruction of ocean habitats of sea creatures around the world. It has resulted in killing of fish, birds, and countless other species. In such a worsening situation, green technology is the only hope to counteract the effects of climate change and pollution, at least to a certain extent. We need to understand that the world has a fixed amount of natural resources, some of which have already been depleted or ruined.

1.10.3 Enhancing the Power of Positive Green Thinking

Going green will benefit everyone. For this,

- Inventors should accept that green products will be the future. Investing in clean technologies will fetch them good business with growing profits.
- Consumers should realize that buying green products will not only reduce energy bills but are also safer and healthier. For example, we must minimize the use of plastic water bottles and switch to reusable water bottles. We must refuse to use plastic straws.

Let us learn about some green products that we can start using in our daily lives.

Figure 1.11 Using LED bulbs consumes lesser electricity and helps reduce energy bills

LED lighting: By using LED bulbs instead of incandescent lights, we can make efficient use of energy (Fig. 1.11).

Solar panels: Low-cost solar panels coupled with monetary incentives such as tax credits have resulted in their widespread use. Using solar energy drastically reduces energy use and thus, electricity bills. New inventions in solar panel design facilitate the production of both electricity and heat.

Moreover, researchers and scientists have been able to design solar panels that could collect energy, irrespective of whether it is sunny or raining. These panels, known as all-weather solar panels, can be used just anywhere an ordinary solar panel is used. During rainfall, these panels generate electricity from the force of the rain falling on their surface.

Wind energy: Harnessing wind power in huge wind farms is used as green tech for providing steady, reliable and clean energy.

Composting: It is one of the best and easiest green technology that is incredibly simple. Worm bins can be used in a home, and many cities have even initiated composting programs.

Electric vehicles: Navigant Research (https://www.greencarreports.com/news/1093560_1-2-billion-vehicles-on-worlds-roads-now-2-billion-by-2035-report) states that there are now more than 1.2 billion vehicles on the road, and with rapid economic growth, this number is set to increase drastically. Can you imagine how much pollution and strain it would put on the environment?

In such a scenario, using an electric vehicle can only help. Although the price of EVs is too high, there are continuous advances in EV technology. Better gas mileage and zero emissions make it a better alternative than a petroleum-powered car. EV is undoubtedly the future of the automotive industry.

Programmable thermostats: It is a low-cost green technology solution that can be set to automatically adjust the temperature of the house when you are at home. This not only saves energy but also money. You can easily schedule a thermostat for more flexibility, monitor its working and change the temperature remotely.

Vertical farming: Vertical farming is an eco-friendly technology in which small plants are grown in stacked vertical layers. Such a configuration does not require soil, and uses very less water. The concept of vertical farming can solve our food production problems, especially in over-crowded cities and at the same time cut greenhouse gas emissions by eliminating the need to transport the produce over long distances.

Water purification: We are using water extensively in our day-to-day lives and also, unfortunately, wasting this precious resource. *The Earth naturally recycles its water, but adopting new technologies can speed up this process.*

The United Nations water agency (UN Water) estimates that more than 80 percent of the wastewater generated by society flows back into the ecosystem without being treated or reused.

Therefore, techniques like membrane filtration, microbial fuel cells, nanotechnology, development of biological treatments and natural treatment systems such as wetlands can be used to reduce pollutants and even make the water fit for drinking.

Recycling and waste management: *New advancements in green technology are being used to better manage and recycle waste material. For example, in Demark,* unsorted household waste is divided into plastic fractions for recycling and for obtaining a liquid from which the nutrient waste has been dissolved. This liquid is then used to make biogas.

Even chemical recycling is an innovative process that breaks down chemicals into their valuable components that can be then be used as fuel or re-converted into new plastic products.

Tidal energy: Waves, tides and ocean currents are already being used to generate energy. An Australian company uses underwater buoys to convert sea waves into zero emission energy and desalinated water.

1.11 GREEN ECONOMY

We have seen that green skills are the knowledge, abilities, values and attitudes that are required to develop a sustainable and resource-efficient society. The need of the hour is to switch to new ways of production and consumption that are environmentally sustainable.

The transition to a low-carbon, resource-efficient economy requires systemic changes that will result not only in new products and services but also changes in production processes and business models. This greening of the economy is also referred to as green economy.

1.11.1 Skills Required for a Green Economy

A green economy completely changes the skills required to do a particular task. New economic activity creates new occupations, which, in turn, require an entirely new skill-set, qualification and training framework. Structural changes are also inevitable as the demand for some tasks will increase and for others, it may decrease.

Tasks that are especially important for green occupations include:

Engineering and technical skills: This includes all the hard skills like the design and construction of eco-friendly buildings, assessing and enhancing the use of renewable energy and doing extensive energy-efficient projects (Fig. 1.12). These skills are usually mastered by engineers and technicians.

Science skills: Skills in Biology, Physics and other science-related subjects are in high demand in each stage of value chains and also in the utility sector for providing basic amenities like clean water, sewage services and green electricity.

Lighting
Expand the use of LED bulbs, LED tube lights, and solar lamps to improve efficiency of electricity consumption and reduce expense

Cooling
Expand the use of efficient fans and cool roofs to increase thermal comfort, improve efficiency of electricity consumption, and reduce expense

Irrigation
Advance the use of solar pumps – to reduce costs and air pollution – and micro-irrigation practices to improve water-use efficiency

Household Cooking and Key Livelihood Opportunities
Cleaner cooking options to reduce indoor air pollution and drudgery; and for livelihoods – promote electric three-wheelers and solar-based appliaces such as driers and milk chillers

Community-level Interventions
Install solar street lights and develop green schools and green health care centres (multiple appliances) to provide reliable and clean energy services and build awareness

Figure 1.12 Steps for sustainable green economy

Operation management skills: These skills require knowledge related to organizational structure to support green activities. For example, activities supporting life-cycle management, production and co-ordination with customers and other stakeholders come under this category. Such skills are usually required for sales engineers, climate change analysts, sustainability specialists and transportation planners.

Monitoring skills: These skills are required to assess how well the projects address the technical and legal aspects of business activities. For example, environmental compliance inspectors are needed to see that the product/service is in line with green technology specifications.

However, in addition to these skills, soft skills also need to be acquired. For example, skills related to design thinking, creativity, adaptability, resilience, and empathy come in this domain.

To help developing and emerging economies to swiftly move on the path of becoming a green economy, the United Nations Industrial Development Organization (UNIDO) is promoting industrial skills development through its programme, Learning and Knowledge Development Facility (LKDF). This program is based on Public Private Development Partnerships (PPDP) in which both public and private sectors make a joint investment to establish and upgrade local industrial training institutions. For example, the H2O Maghreb project, implemented by UNIDO with support from the Government of Morocco, is trying to improve water management practices in the country. For this, a training centre has been established to provide market-oriented training in wastewater treatment and water management.

1.11.2 Towards a Green Economy

As stated earlier, a green economy indicates a low-carbon, resource-efficient and socially inclusive economy, in which public and private players invest into economic activities. Both public and private sector can contribute to develop infrastructure and assets that facilitate reduced carbon emissions and pollution, enhanced energy and resource efficiency, and prevention of the loss of biodiversity and ecosystem services. All this is done through targeted public expenditure, policy reforms and changes in taxation and regulation.

UN Environment promotes a development path (Fig. 1.13), especially for poor people whose livelihoods depend on natural resources.

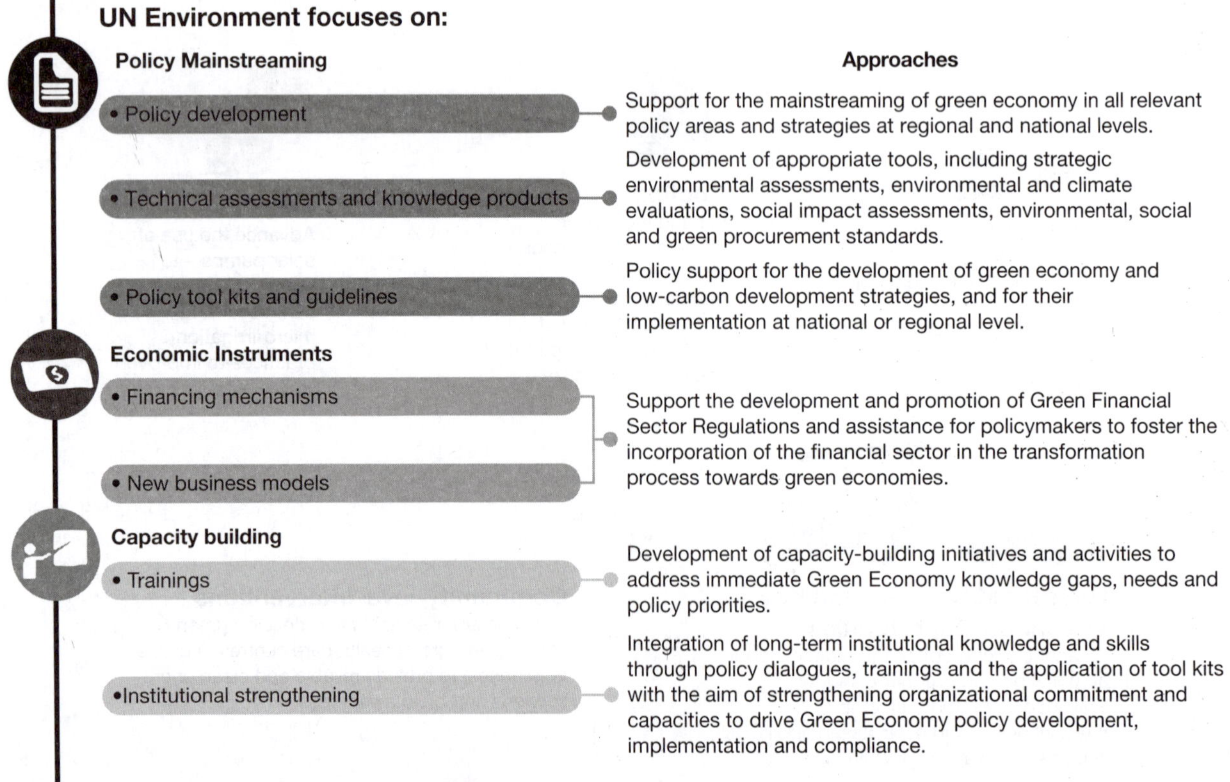

Figure 1.13   UN Environment program

A Green Economy that supports sustainable consumption and production of energy-efficient products reduces resource consumption, waste generation and emissions across the full life-cycle of processes and products.

1.11.3 How Green Is the Economy of Delhi?

According to a report on climate-change mitigation compiled by the International Labour Organization (ILO) which is part of the United Nations, in February 2018, 7.5% of electricity came from renewable sources in India. This is expected to be as high as 40% by 2030 and around 3 million new jobs will be created in India by the scaling down of carbon-intensive and resource-intensive industries and adoption of sustainable practices. The report also stated that all the sectors in the economy, except the mining industry, will see more employment by 2030.

The Indian government has committed to the Paris Climate Agreement 2015 to install 175 GW of renewable power capacity by 2022. This is enough to power a hundred million light-bulbs, 100 Watts each, for an hour.

Realizing the fact that jobs rely heavily on a healthy environment, green economy can help millions of people to overcome poverty. In India, public employment program like Mahatma Gandhi National Rural Employment Guarantee Act (MGNREGA), will be an important policy tool. For example, in 2012, almost 60% of the work hours provided through MGNREGA were used for water conservation and 12% to look after irrigation facilities.

India has experienced several natural disasters caused or exacerbated by human activities. Such disasters result in an average loss of 5.7 working life-years per person every year. In addition to this, heat stress would be another common reason for reduced working hours of the workforce. The worst affected community would be agriculture workers who would lose 64% of hours in 2030. If we look globally, by 2030, 5.3% of total hours of work will be lost resulting in a productivity loss equivalent to 30.8 million full-time jobs. It is predicted that global temperature would increase by 1.5 °C by the end of the 21st century and we cannot even imagine how adverse the effects would be.

1.11.4 Green Skill Development Programme

India needs crores of new workforces in various sectors. Skill development is therefore required to meet the demand (Fig. 1.14). For example, expertise on wildlife conservation, nurseries, horticulture etc. is essential for the Department of Environment and Forests.

The Green Skill Development Programme emphasizes on training young minds who could not complete their higher education due to different financial or social constraints but have an urge to learn new things and do something fruitful. The green-skilled workforce has technical knowledge as well as the commitment to achieve sustainable development. Thus, green skill is mandatory for transiting from an energy and emission-intensive economy to one that is cleaner and greener.

Figure 1.14   Green skill development

For example, the Indian government, as a part of Green Skill Development Program, conducted a pilot project in the year 2017. Following this, the ministry has now taken the following steps to expand the Green Skill Development Programme:

- Budget allocation for conducting training courses under the Green Skill Development Programme has been increased.
- Number of people to be trained has been increased.
- The government has recognized 35 courses under this programme. These courses include pollution monitoring (air/water/noise/soil), effluent treatment plant operation, forest management, water budgeting, etc.

Key Terms

Communication skills: Skills of an individual that one uses to express while giving and receiving information.

Verbal communication: A type of communication in which language is used to convey the intended message in the form of spoken words or in the written form.

Non-verbal communication: In this mode of communication, messages are exchanged without transmitting any word(s).

Vertical communication: Communication in which information or data flows up and down the organizational structure.

Horizontal communication: Communication in which information exchange takes place between two similar levels of the organization.

Diagonal communication: Communication in which information exchange is done across the functional levels of employees from various departments of the organization.

Self-management skills: One's ability to regulate and control his/her actions, feelings, and thoughts.

Self-motivation: The ability to encourage oneself to achieve a goal, even in most challenging times.

Entrepreneur: A person who builds or operates a business.

Innovative entrepreneurs: Entrepreneurs who are always interested in introducing some new ideas.

Imitating entrepreneurs: Entrepreneurs who consider an existing successful system and improve on it by removing all the deficiencies while retaining its efficiencies.

Fabian entrepreneurs: Entrepreneurs who do not believe in taking drastic decisions and avoid the use of any innovation or change that does not fit their narrative.

Drone entrepreneurs: Entrepreneurs who do not like a change. They prefer to do business using their own traditional or orthodox methods of production and systems.

Technology: Application of knowledge.

Green technology: Sustainable technology that considers the long-term and short-term impact of something on the environment.

Chapter Highlights

- Informal communication happens randomly between people in an organization.
- An accountable person delivers on what he/she says. This is known as the principle of "do what you said you would do" (DWYSYWD). He/she also learns from his/her experiences, mistakes and success stories to deliver better the next time.
- An entrepreneur can face financial, emotional or career-related risks. To mitigate them, the entrepreneur must possess certain skill-sets that include the ability to effectively communicate, sell, focus, learn, and strategize.
- Critical thinking allows an entrepreneur to analyze the data, draw useful trends and patterns, build strategies for business growth, scrutinize information, understand the problem (if any) and come up with a logical solution.
- Green chemistry includes the invention, design and application of chemical products and processes that either reduce or eliminate the use and generation of harmful substances.
- Vertical farming is an eco-friendly technology in which small plants are grown in stacked vertical layers. Such a configuration does not require soil, and uses very less water.
- A Green Economy supports sustainable consumption and production of energy-efficient products, and reduces resource consumption, waste generation and emissions across the full life-cycle of processes and products.

Review Questions

1. What are communication skills? Why do you need them?
2. Imagine that your friend Sarah has started on her first job last week. Tomorrow, she has been asked to give a very important business presentation. Tell her some points that she should keep in her mind during her presentation.
3. Tanu is writing a resume for a new job. Suggest any three points she should be very careful of.
4. Mahip has cleared the entrance test for MBA and has been shortlisted for a group discussion round. Imagine that you are the judge of the event. Write any five points that you will look for in a candidate.
5. Differentiate between verbal and non-verbal communication.
6. Imagine that you are a middle-school teacher. How will you deduce whether students have understood the lesson taught by you, using non-verbal communication techniques?

7. Assume that you are hiring professionals for your team. Candidate A has scored little better than Candidate B in the written test but in the interview, he was nervous, under stress and lacked motivation. On the contrary, candidate B was calm, composed and better managed his time to fluently answer all the questions asked. Which candidate will you recruit? Justify your answer.

8. What tips will you give to your younger brother so that he can manage his time in a better way during his examination?

9. Brainstorm ideas to jot down points illustrating what should be your level of engagement as a student and as a son/daughter.

10. List any five skills possessed by a successful entrepreneur.

11. Your best friend wants to start a new business venture. What will you suggest him to do before actually starting the business?

Fill in the Blanks

1. Voice notes or chat rooms are examples of _________ communication.

2. In ___________ mode of communication, messages are exchanged without transmitting any word(s).

3. _________ (Horizontal/Vertical) communication exchanges information between a project manager and his team member.

4. An __________ person will not play the blame game.

5. _________ is the ability to encourage oneself to achieve a goal, even in the most challenging times.

6. _____ skills are required to calculate ROI and utilize human resources in a cost-efficient manner.

7. Before becoming an __________, one must read business books, attend workshops, hire a mentor, enroll in a course and listen to the interviews of successful businessmen.

8. _________ Entrepreneurs are always interested in introducing some new ideas.

9. ___________ Entrepreneurs are often referred to as 'copy cats'.

10. Sustainable technology that considers the long-term and short-term impact something has on the environment is often referred to as _________.

11. Green _________ includes the invention, design and application of chemical products and processes that either reduces or eliminates the use and generation of harmful substances.

12. _________ can solve our food production problems, especially in over-crowded cities.

13. A ________ Economy supports sustainable consumption and production of energy-efficient products, and reduces resource consumption, waste generation and emissions across the full life-cycle of processes and products.

State True or False

1. Communication skills are required to just give information.

2. Posts on social media, handbooks, posters, flyers, etc. are examples of physical non-verbal communication.

3. Non-verbal communication has a legal binding.

4. Verbal communication has a formal structure of expression.

5. Formal communication happens randomly between people in organizations.

6. A person who knows how to stay calm and manage even a highly tensed situation, can attain great success in everything done by him/her.

7. Communication, problem-solving and decision-making are examples of hard skills of a successful entrepreneur.

8. Innovative entrepreneurs do not like a change.

9. To start a new business, you must first take an MBA degree.

10. All-weather solar panels can be used to collect energy from both the rain and sun.

11. Electric vehicles have better mileage and zero emissions.

12. The Earth naturally recycles its water.

13. According to a report by ILO, around 3 million jobs will be lost in India by the adoption of sustainable practices.

14. Climate change is responsible for reduced working life-years per person every year.

Multiple Choice Questions

1. Communication skills are not important for _______.
   a. empathizing
   b. social media
   c. sharing an update on a project
   d. None of these.

2. When speaking in a conference, it is not acceptable to
   a. see the time left in your phone again and again.
   b. look into audienece eyes.
   c. collect feedback.
   d. respond fully to all queries.

3. When attending a meeting you must not
   a. sit straight.
   b. acknowledge the receipt of message.
   c. observe the body language of others.
   d. interrupt the speaker.

4. Identify oral communication technique from the following:
   a. Whatsapp
   b. E-mails
   c. Voice notes
   d. Flyers

5. Gestures, body language, symbols, and expressions are a part of _______ communication.
   a. oral
   b. written
   c. non-verbal
   d. aesthetic

6. Paintings, dance, music are examples of _______ communication technique.
   a. paralanguage
   b. aesthetic
   c. visual
   d. oral

7. _______ communication exchanges information across the functional levels of employees from various departments of the organization.
   a. Vertical
   b. Horizontal
   c. Diagonal
   d. Spiral

8. _______ skills help an individual to focus on his/her obligatory duties and responsibilities, set practical goals, and have more control over career.
   a. Communication
   b. Self-management
   c. ICT
   d. Green

9. Which of the following will not help you to deal with stress in your life?
   a. Get surrounded with highly motivated, calm people.
   b. Take drugs/cigarettes/alcohol.
   c. Eat healthy food.
   d. Have ample sleep with power naps after lunch.

10. Identify the incorrect statement related to time management.
    a. Prioritize tasks.
    b. Set a time limit.
    c. Do not delegate your task to others.
    d. Design daily work routines.

11. A/An _______ person is quick to adjust to the changing environment and figure out ways to embrace new situations and is easily accepted by everyone.
    a. accountable
    b. adaptable
    c. trustworthy
    d. reliable

12. Which of the following is not a hard skill required by a successful entrepreneur?
    a. Communication
    b. Accounting
    c. Marketing
    d. Financial planning

13. An entrepreneur needs _______ skills to meet professionals for funding their ideas, providing business expertise and getting feedback on their new venture or idea.

    a. business management   b. risk-taking
    c. networking   d. active listening

14. __________ allows an entrepreneur to analyze the data, draw useful trends and patterns, build strategies for business growth, scrutinize information, understand the problem and come up with a logical solution.
    a. Financial skill   b. Critical thinking   c. Risk-taking   d. Leadership

15. An entrepreneur must not __________.
    a. be an optimist   b. be focused   c. be ethical   d. None of these.

16. Which type of entrepreneurs do business using their own traditional or orthodox methods of production and systems?
    a. Innovative   b. Imitating   c. Drone   d. Fabian

17. Identify the correct sttaement about entrepreneurship.
    a. Just anyone can become an entrpreneur.
    b. You just need a good idea to start a new business
    c. You must start a buisness to enjoy your own working schedule
    d. A startup gives you more money than your current job.

18. Green products are __________.
    a. environmentally friendly   b. energy-efficient
    c. recyclable   d. All of these.

19. __________ products meet present needs without compromising the ability of future generations to meet their own needs.
    a. Reusable   b. Sustainable   c. Recyclable   d. Innovative

Group Discussion

1. How is climate change affecting us?
2. Elaborate on some common body language errors.
3. Discuss the products that can be used to promote green technology in our everyday lives.

Role Play

1. Assume that you are Mr. Sartaj Singh Sodhi from Punjab who has gone on a world tour. 1. You can communicate well in Punjabi but can understand Hindi. Now, how will you communicate in countries where neither language is spoken and understood?
2. Imagine that you are the captain of the Indian Cricket Team. Give a three-minute speech that you will give during a press conference after winning the World Cup.

Class Activity

1. Ask the students to introduce themselves to their classmates (say at least 10 lines).
   Hint: Highlight your strengths, weakness, fears and hobbies.
2. Ask the students to write a 100-line paragraph sharing their experiences on the last field-trip they had.
3. Make a PowerPoint presentation about your favorite entrepreneur, giving details about how he/she succeeded in establishing a business in his/her chosen segment.

Project Work

1. Collect information illustrating the hard work done by JRD Tata.
2. Make a presentation on the Green Skill Development Program.

Use words from the list as well as any others you can think of to describe these pictures

bored, uninterested, frightened, angry, sad, happy annoyed, disgusted, joyful, pleased, elated, excited surprised, welcoming, pleased

This person is:

This person is:

This person is:

This person is:

This person is:

This person is:

This person is:

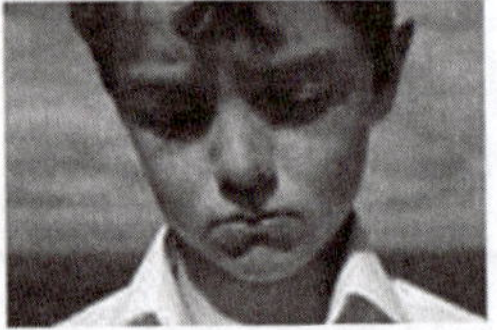

This person is:

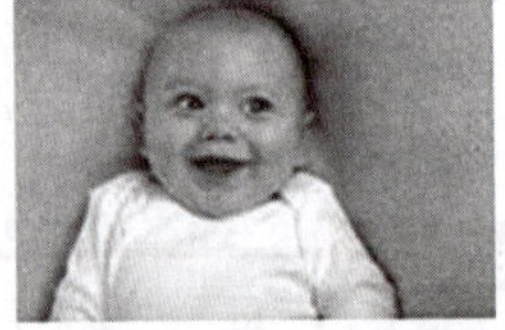

This person is:

Answers

Fill in the Blanks

1. oral
2. non-verbal
3. Vertical
4. accountable
5. Self-motivation
6. Financial
7. Entrepreneur
8. Innovative
9. Imitating
10. Green Technology
11. chemistry
12. Vertical Farming
13. Green

State True or False

1. False
2. False
3. False
4. True
5. False
6. True
7. False
8. False
9. False
10. True
11. True
12. True
13. False
14. True

Multiple Choice Questions

1. d
2. a
3. d
4. c
5. c
6. b
7. c
8. b
9. b
10. c
11. b
12. a
13. c
14. b
15. d
16. c
17. a
18. d
19. b

Computer Systems and Organization

2

Before delving into Artificial Intelligence, let us first recapitulate the concepts about computer systems. For this purpose, following topics will be discussed in this chapter:

- Computer, its organization and components
- Input, output and storage devices
- Operating system
- Internet and its applications
- Social media
- Key web terminology

We all have seen computers being used in our homes, schools, offices, and in fact every other place we visit. The smartphone that we have in our hands is also an example of a small computer. Today, it is just impossible to think of our lives without this machine.

2.1 WHAT IS A COMPUTER?

A computer is an electronic machine that takes data and instructions as input and performs computations on data based on the specified instructions.

Before going in to details, let us learn some key terms that are frequently used in computers.

Data: Data is a collection of raw facts or figures.

Information: Information comprises of processed data to provides answers to *"who"*, *"what"*, *"where"* and *"when"* type of questions.

Knowledge: Knowledge is the application of data and information to answer the *"how"* part of the question. (Refer Fig. 2.1)

Instructions: Commands given to the computer that tells what it has to do.

Programs: A set of instructions in computer language is called a program.

Software: A set of programs is called software.

Hardware: Computer and all its physical parts are known as hardware.

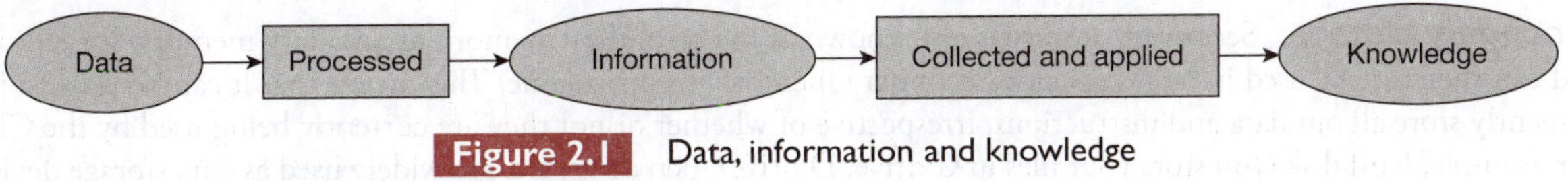

Figure 2.1   Data, information and knowledge

2.2   BASIC COMPUTER ORGANIZATION

A computer performs five major operations, which can be listed as follows:

1. It accepts data or instructions (input).
2. It stores data.
3. It processes data.
4. It displays results (output).
5. It controls and co-ordinates all operations inside a computer.

To perform these functions, different parts of a computer interact with each other as shown in the Fig. 2.2.

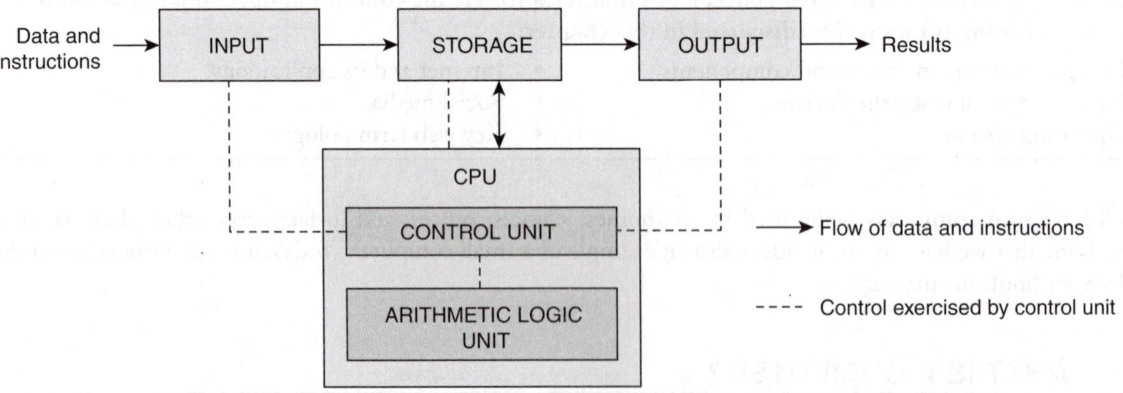

Figure 2.2   Interaction between different parts of a computer system

Input: The process of entering data and instructions into the computer system is known as input. Users can provide input to the computer using different input devices like keyboard, mouse, scanner, trackball, etc.

Storage: Storage is the process of saving data, instructions and results of processing in the computer's memory for future use. Once our work is stored in the computer, we can use it at any time as required. A computer has two types of storage areas:

> The computer understands binary language, which consists of only two symbols (0s and 1s), so it is the responsibility of the input devices to convert the input data into binary codes.

Primary storage: Primary storage or the main memory is that storage area of the computer which is directly accessible by the CPU at a very fast speed. It can be used to store data, instructions and recently generated results of processing. The primary storage is very expensive and therefore limited in capacity. Another drawback of main memory is that it is volatile in nature, that is, as soon as the computer is switched off, the information stored in it gets erased. Hence, it cannot be used as a permanent storage of useful data and programs for future use. Example, RAM (Random Access Memory).

Secondary storage: Secondary storage is also known as the secondary memory or auxiliary memory. It is cheaper and can therefore be used in large capacity. Secondary memory is non-volatile. This means that it can be used to permanently store all our data and instructions, irrespective of whether or not they are currently being used by the CPU. For example, hard disk (you store your files in C drive, D drive), pen drive, etc. are widely used as data storage devices. Table 2.1 shows the difference between the two types of storage.

Table 2.1   Difference between primary and secondary memory

Primary Memory	Secondary Memory
• It is more expensive	• It is cheaper
• It is faster to access	• It is slower to access
• Directly accessed by the CPU	• Cannot be accessed directly by the CPU
• It is volatile in nature	• It is non-volatile in nature
• Storage capacity is limited	• Large storage capacity
• Consumes less power	• Consumes more power
• Stores data temporarily	• Stores data permanently
• Holds instructions and data when a program is executing.	• Holds data and programs that not currently being executed by the CPU.

Output: Output is the reverse of input. It is the process of presenting the result of data processing to the outside world (external to the computer system). The results are given through output devices like monitor, printer, etc. Since the computer accepts data only in binary form and the result of processing is also in the binary form, the result cannot be directly given to the user. The output devices therefore convert the results available in binary codes into a human-readable language before displaying it to the user.

Central Processing Unit (CPU): Processing means performing operations on the data as per the instructions specified by the user. Data is processed in the CPU. For this, the CPU takes data and instructions from the primary memory. The data and instructions are then transferred to the *Arithmetic and Logical Unit (ALU),* which performs all sorts of operations. When the data is completely processed, the final result is then transferred to the main memory.

The *control unit* inside the CPU is the central nervous system of the entire computer system. It manages and controls all the components of the computer system. It is the control unit which decides the order in which the instructions will be executed and the operations that will be performed by the ALU.

CPU (Central Processing Unit) is a combination of the ALU and the Control Unit. It is known as the brain of the computer system as the entire processing of data is done with the help of ALU and the control unit. While the entire processing of data is done in the ALU, CU on the other hand, activates and monitors the operations of other units (such as input, output, and storage) of the computer system. The two units of the CPU are detailed as follows.

Arithmetic and logic unit: The ALU performs all kinds of calculations, such as arithmetic (add, subtract, multiply, divide, etc.), comparison (less than, greater than, or equal to), and other operations. The intermediate results of processing may be stored in the main memory, as they might be required again. When the processing completes, the final result is then transferred to the main memory. Hence, the data may move from main memory to the ALU multiple times before the processing is over.

Control unit: The main function of the CU is to direct and coordinate the computer operations. It interprets the instructions (program) and initiates action to execute them. The CU controls the flow of data through the computer system and directs the ALU, input/output (I/O) devices and other units. It is therefore called the central nervous system of the computer system. In addition, the CU is responsible for fetching, decoding, executing instructions and storing results.

2.3   INPUT DEVICES

We have read that data and instructions that we enter into the computer are called ***input.*** And devices that help us to give input to the computer are called ***input devices.***

Some commonly used input devices are keyboard, mouse, microphone, web camera, scanner, joystick, etc.

2.3.1 Keyboard

A keyboard (Fig. 2.3) is the main input device for computers. With a keyboard, a user can type a document, use keystroke shortcuts, access menus, play games, and perform numerous other tasks. Most keyboards have between 80 and 110 keys, which include the following:

Alphabetic keys include the letters of the English alphabet. The layout of the keyboard is known as QWERTY for its first six letters. The QWERTY pattern has been a standard right from the time computer keyboards were introduced.

Numeric keys include Arabic numerals (0–9), arranged in the same configuration found on calculators to speed up data entry of numbers. When the Num Lock key is set to ON, the user can type numbers, dot, or input the symbols such as /, *, –, and +. When the Num Lock key is set to OFF, the numeric keys can be used to move the cursor on the screen. A set of numeric keys are also present at the top of alphabet keys.

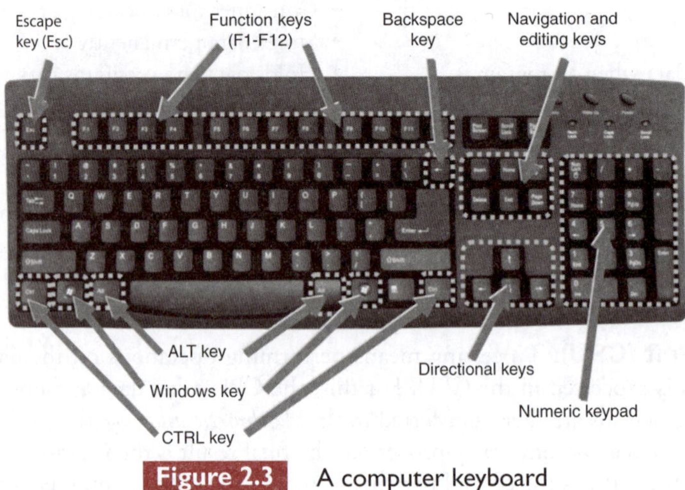

Figure 2.3   A computer keyboard

Function keys are used by computer programs (or software) and operating systems to input specific commands. They are often placed on the top of the keyboard in a single row. Function keys can be programmed so that their functionality varies from one program to another. For example, the ALT and F4 keys when pressed together will close the current window.

Arrow keys are arranged in an inverted *T*-type fashion between the alphabetic and the numeric keys, and are used to move the cursor on the screen in small increments.

Home and End keys are used to move the cursor to the beginning and end of the current line, respectively.

PageUp and PageDown move the cursor up and down by one screen at a time, respectively.

Insert key is used to enter a character between two existing characters.

Delete key deletes a character at the cursor position.

Shortcut key is used to access the options available by pressing the right mouse button.

Esc key cancels the selected option.

Pause key suspends a command/process in progress.

Print Screen key captures everything on the screen as an image. The image can be pasted into any document.

Wireless Keyboard: can be operated without connecting it to the computer through a physical wire. It is powered by a battery and allows users to work up to 10 feet from its receiver. This is especially desirable when we want to keep our desk uncluttered without wires. However, on the downside, greater the distance between the wireless keyboard and the receiver monitor, more is the delay in receiving the keystrokes.

Bluetooth wireless keyboard Bluetooth is one of the most popular methods of syncing a wireless keyboard with a computer. Such a keyboard is well-suited for offices as it creates a reliable connection without cluttering the desk.

> Keys such as Shift, Ctrl, and Alt are called *modifier keys* because they are used to modify the normal function of a key. For example, Shift + character (lower case) makes the computer display the character in upper case.

> Many a time, a few keystrokes get dropped from the input.

2.3.2 Mouse

Mouse is an input device that was invented by Douglas Engelbart in 1963. It is the key input device used in a graphical user interface (GUI). The mouse can be used to handle the pointer on the screen to perform various functions such as opening an application or a file. With the mouse, users no longer need to memorize commands, which was earlier a necessity when working with text-based command line environments like MS-DOS. A mouse is shown in Fig. 2.4.

A mouse has two buttons and a scroll wheel. It can be held in the hand and easily moved, without lifting, along a hard, flat surface to move the cursor to the desired location—up, down, left, or right. Once the mouse is placed at an appropriate position, a user may perform the following operations:

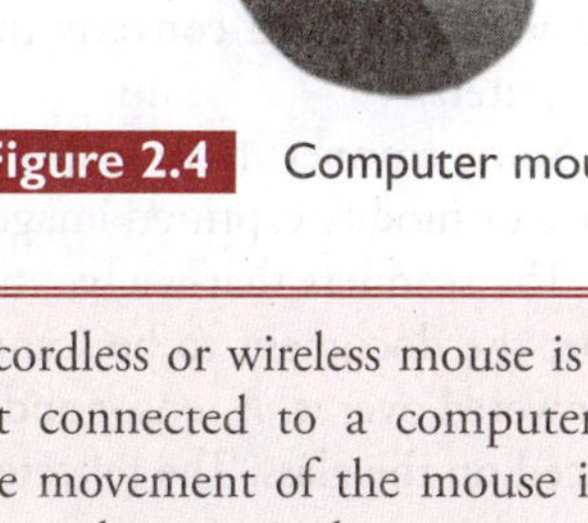

Figure 2.4   Computer mouse

Point Placing the pointer over a word or an object on the screen by moving the mouse on the desk is termed as pointing.

Click Pressing either the left or the right button of the mouse is known as clicking. Clicking a mouse button initiates some action; for example, when we click the right button by pointing the mouse on a word, a menu pops up on the screen. When we move the pointer over the icon of an application, say Internet Explorer, and double-click on it, then it opens that application for us.

A cordless or wireless mouse is not connected to a computer. The movement of the mouse is detected using radio waves or infrared light waves.

Drag Dragging means pointing to a desired location and pulling the mouse while pressing the left button.

Scroll The scroll wheel, which is placed in between the left and right buttons of the mouse, is used to vertically scroll through long documents.

2.3.3 Touchpad

Touchpad or a trackpad, as shown in Fig. 2.5, is a small, flat, rectangular stationary pointing device with a sensitive surface of 1.5–2 square inches. A user has to slide his or her fingertips across the surface of the pad to point to a specific object on the screen. The surface translates the motion and position of the user's fingers to a relative position on the screen.

Figure 2.5   Touchpad

2.3.4 Joystick

Joystick is a cursor control device widely used in computer games and computer-aided design (CAD)/computer- aided manufacturing (CAM) applications. It consists of a hand-held lever that pivots on one end and transmits its coordinates to a computer (Fig. 2.6).

The joystick has one or more push buttons, called switches, whose position can also be read by the computer. The lever of a joystick moves in all directions to control the movement of the pointer on the computer screen. A joystick is similar to a mouse, but with the mouse, the cursor stops moving as soon as we stop moving the mouse. However, in the case of the joystick, the pointer continues moving in the direction to which the joystick is pointing. To stop the pointer, the user must return the joystick to its upright position.

Figure 2.6   Joystick

2.3.4 Touchscreen

Touchscreen (shown in Fig. 2.7) is a display screen that can identify the occurrence and position of a touch inside the display region. A user can touch the screen by using either a finger or a stylus. Such touchscreen displays are available on computers, laptops, PDAs, and mobile phones.

Touchscreen monitors are an easy way of entering information into computers (or mobile phones). They have become more and more commonplace as their prices have steadily dropped over the past decade. These days,

Figure 2.7   Touchscreen

touchscreen monitors are widely used in different applications including point-of-sale (POS) cash registers, automated teller machines (ATMs), car navigation screens, mobile phones, gaming consoles, and any other type of appliance that requires users to input and receive information instantly.

2.3.5 Image Scanner

Image Scanner (shown in Fig. 2.8) is a device that captures images, printed text, and handwritten text, from different sources such as photographic prints, posters, and magazines and converts them into digital images for editing and display on computers.

Some scanners have graphics software such as Adobe Photoshop to help users resize or modify captured images.

The scanners that we see in our colleges or offices are flatbed scanners. In this type, the document to be scanned is placed on a glass pane and an opaque cover is lowered over it. A sensor and light move along the pane, reflecting off the image placed on the glass. The reflected image is scanned onto a computer for further processing.

Figure 2.8   Image scanner

Advantages
- Any printed or handwritten document can be scanned and stored in a computer for further processing.
- The scanned and stored document will never deteriorate in quality with time. The document can be displayed and printed whenever required.
- There is no fear of loss of documents. Users can scan important documents and store them permanently in the computer.

Disadvantages
- Scanners are usually costlier than other input devices.
- The documents that are scanned and stored as images are bigger in size as compared to other equivalent text files.

Text documents are scanned and stored as images. Therefore, they occupy more space and are also un-editable because computers cannot interpret individual characters in images. To make these documents occupy lesser space, the scanned document can be passed through optical character recognition (OCR) software (see Fig. 2.9) where the images of individual characters are recognised and stored as a doc file. However, this method cannot be used for documents where illustrations or mathematical equations are present.

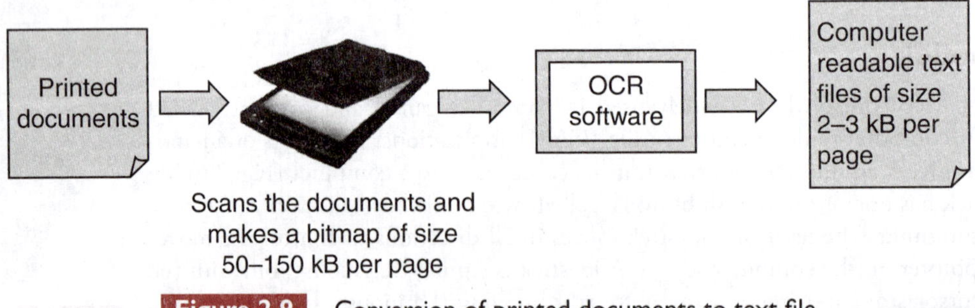

Figure 2.9   Conversion of printed documents to text file

2.3.6 Stylus

Stylus is a pen-shaped input device used to enter information or write on the touchscreen of a handheld device (Fig. 2.10). It is a small stick that can also be used to draw lines on a surface as input into a device, choose an option from a menu, move the cursor to another location on the screen, take notes, and create short messages. The stylus usually slides into a slot built into the device for that purpose.

Figure 2.10   Stylus

2.3.7 Barcode Reader

Barcode Reader (also price scanner or POS scanner), as shown in Fig. 2.11, is a handheld input device that is used to capture and read information stored in a barcode. It consists of a scanner, a decoder, and a cable used to connect the reader to a computer. The function of the barcode reader is to capture and translate the barcode into numerals and/or alphabets. It is connected to a computer for further processing of the captured information.

A barcode reader works by directing a beam of light across the barcode and measuring the amount of light that is reflected back.

The scanner converts this light energy into electrical energy. The decoder then converts these signals into data and sends it to the computer for processing. These days, barcode readers are widely used in following areas:

- Supermarkets and retail stores as POS devices
- To take inventory in retail stores
- To check out books from a library
- To track manufacturing and shipping movement
- To keep track of employee login
- To identify hospital patients
- To tabulate the results of direct mail marketing returns
- To tag honeybees used in research.

Advantages
- Barcode readers are cheap.
- They are portable.
- They are handy and easy to use.

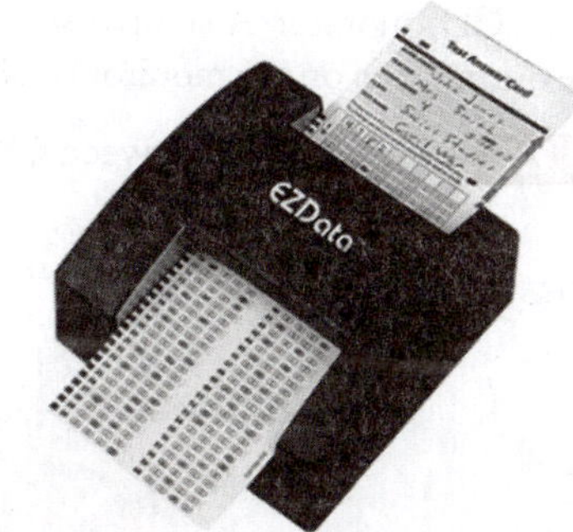

Figure 2.11 Bar code reader

Disadvantages
- Barcode readers must be handled with care. If they develop a scratch, the user may not be able to read the code.
- They can interpret information using a limited series of thin and wide bars. To interpret other unique identifiers, the bar display area must be widened.

2.3.8 Optical Mark Recognition (OMR)

OMR is the process of electronically extracting data from marked fields, such as checkboxes and fill-in fields, on printed forms. The optical mark reader, as shown in Fig. 2.12, is fed with an OMR sheet that has pen or pencil marks in pre-defined positions to indicate each selected response (such as answers for multiple-choice questions in an entrance examination).

The OMR sheet is scanned by the reader to detect the presence of a mark by measuring the reflected light levels. The dark or the marked areas reflect less light than the unmarked ones. The OM reader interprets this pattern marks and spaces, and stores the interpreted data in a computer for storage, analysis, and reporting. The error rate for OMR technology is less than 1%. For this reason, OMR is widely used for applications in which large numbers of hand-filled forms have to be quickly processed with great accuracy, such as surveys, reply cards, questionnaires, ballots, or sheets for multiple-choice questions.

Figure 2.12 Optical mark recognition

Advantage
Optical mark readers work at very high speeds. They can read up to 9,000 forms per hour.

Disadvantages
- It is difficult to gather large amounts of information using an OMR.
- Some data may be missing in the scanned document.
- It is a sensitive device that rejects the OMR sheet if it is folded, torn, or crushed.

2.3.9 Magnetic Ink Character Reader (MICR)

MICR is used to verify the legitimacy of paper documents, especially bank checques. It consists of magnetic ink printed characters that can be recognized by high-speed magnetic recognition devices (refer Fig. 2.13). The printed characters provide important information (such as checque number, bank IFSC code, customer account number, and, in some cases, the amount on the cheque) for processing to the receiving party.

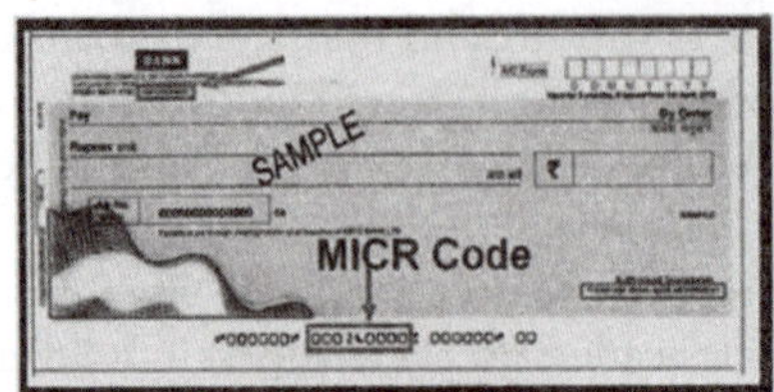
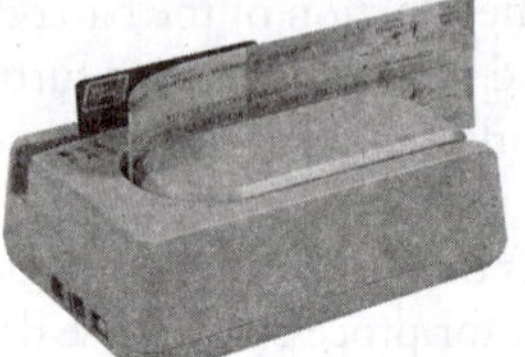

Figure 2.13   MICR code and MICR reader

2.3.10 Digital Camera

Digital camera (Fig. 2.14) is used to click photographs and record videos. These pictures and videos are stored in a small memory chip placed inside the camera. To transfer all the pictures and videos to the computer, you simply need to connect the digital camera with the computer.

Figure 2.14   Digital camera

2.4   OUTPUT DEVICES

Devices that give the output are called ***output devices.*** Some commonly used output devices are monitor, printer, speakers, headphone, etc.

2.4.1 Monitor or VDU (Visual Display Unit)

The computer monitor looks like a TV screen. Whatever we type on the keyboard can be seen on the monitor as output. Monitors are available in different sizes like 15, 17, 21 inches. You must use a bigger size monitor as it causes less strain to your eyes. There are two types of monitors – Cathode Ray Tube (CRT) monitor and Liquid Crystal Display (LCD) monitor. A comparison between CRT and LCD screens is given in Table 2.2.

The output seen on the monitor is called ***soft copy*** output because we can see it for the time computer is switched on.

Table 2.2   Comparison between CRT and LCD screens

Cathode Ray Tube (CRT) Monitor	Liquid Crystal Display (LCD) Monitor
Very big in size	Light weight
Difficult to carry from one place to another	Easy to carry from one place to another
Consumes more electricity	Consumes less electricity

Plasma monitors are thin and flat monitors widely used in televisions and computers (Fig. 2.15). The plasma display contains two glass plates that have hundreds of thousands of tiny cells filled with xenon and neon gases.

Advantages
- The technology used in plasma monitors allows producing a very wide screen using extremely thin materials.
- Very bright images are formed which look good from almost every angle.
- These monitors are not heavy and are thus easily portable.

Figure 2.15   Plasma monitors

Disadvantages
- These monitors are very expensive.
- They have high power consumption.
- Since the images are phosphor-based, at times, they may suffer from flicker.

2.4.2 Speakers

Speakers help us to listen to music. Other sounds from the computer can also be heard from speakers (Fig. 2.16 (a)). For example, when you switch on your computer, a welcome sound is heard. Usually two speakers are attached to a computer.

> These days, monitors also have a speaker fitted inside them.

2.4.3 Headphone

Headphones are used to listen to music from a computer. We can also use headphones while chatting with our friends through computer. With speakers, users can enjoy music, movie, or a game, and the voice will be spread through the entire room (Fig. 2.16 (b)). With good-quality speakers, the voice will also be audible even to people sitting in another room or even to neighbours!

However, in case the user wants to enjoy loud music without disturbing the people nearby, a *headphone* can be used. Headphones are small devices that fit in or on the ear, and give about the same quality and power of the sound as speakers, only to the listener. Most of today's headphones feature some noise-cancelling technologies, so that the listener may listen to only the sound from the speakers and not anything else from the surrounding environment.

Users often use headphones to chat with people over the Internet. With headphones, they are assured that the conversation is heard only by them. However, in addition to the headphones, they are also required to use a separate microphone to talk to the other person. Hence, another device called the *headset* was developed to allow users to talk and listen at the same time, using the same device. Headsets are widely used in call-centres and other telephone-intensive jobs, and for personal use on the computer to facilitate comfortable simultaneous conversation and typing.

2.4.4 Printer

A printer is a device that takes the text and graphics information from a computer and prints it on to a paper (Fig. 2.16 (c)). Printers are available in the market in various sizes, speeds, sophistication, and costs. Usually, more expensive printers are used for higher-resolution colour printing.

Colour printers are used for presentations, maps, and other pages where colour is part of the information. Colour printers can also be set to print only in monochrome. These printers are more expensive, so if the users do not have a specific need for colour and usually take lot of printouts, they will find a black-and-white printer cheaper to operate.

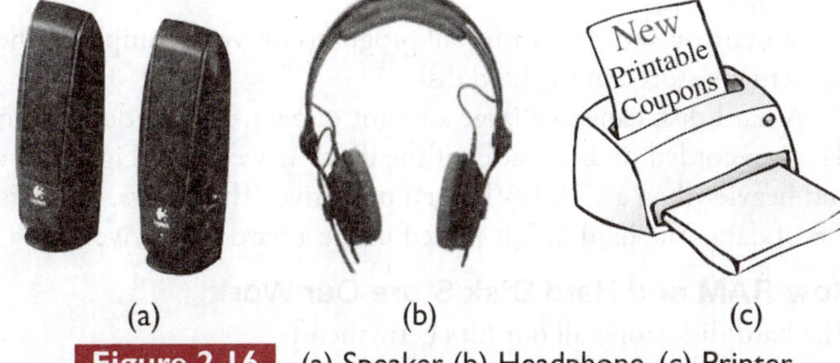

(a)   (b)   (c)

Figure 2.16   (a) Speaker, (b) Headphone, (c) Printer

2.4.5 Projector

A projector (Fig. 2.17) is a device that takes an image from a video source and projects it onto a screen or another surface. These days, projectors are used for a wide range of applications, varying from home theatre systems for projecting movies and television programs onto a screen much larger than even the biggest available television, to organizations for projecting information and presentations onto screens large enough for rooms filled with many people.

Projectors also allow users to change/adjust some features of the image such as brightness, sharpness, and colour settings, similar to the

Figure 2.17   Projector

features available in a standard television. Projectors are now available in a variety of different shapes and sizes, and are produced by many different companies.

Projectors can be broadly classified into two categories, depending on the technology they use.

LCD Projector makes use of its own light to display the image on the screen/wall. These projectors are based on LCD technology. To use these projectors, the room must be first darkened, else the image formed will be blurred.

Digital Light Processing (DLP) Projector uses a number of mirrors to reflect the light. When using the DLP projector, the room may or may not be darkened because it displays a clear image in both situations.

2.4.6 Plotter

A plotter (Fig. 2.18) is a printing device that is usually used to print vector graphics with high print quality. They are widely used to draw maps, in scientific applications, and in CAD, CAM, and computer-aided engineering (CAE).

Architects use plotters to draw blueprints of the structures they are working on. A plotter is basically a printer that interprets commands from a computer to make line drawings on paper with one or more automated pens. Since plotters are much more expensive than printers, they are used only for specialized applications.

Hewlett–Packard is the leading vendor of plotters worldwide.

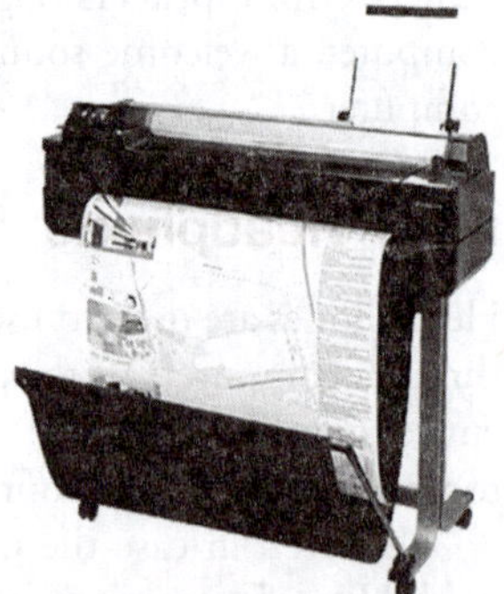

Figure 2.18   Plotter

2.5   STORAGE DEVICES

Storage devices are secondary memory devices. They are used to store large amounts of data permanently (until the user explicitly deletes them). Secondary storage devices are necessary because the main memory (or primary storage) loses its data when the computer is turned off. To retain the data for a longer time, we must have secondary storage in our computer.

Some examples of secondary memory storage devices are hard disk, flash disk, memory cards and optical disks (like CD, DVD, etc).

2.5.1 Hard Disk

Hard disk is the main secondary storage device of the computer. It is placed inside the CPU Box.

When you save data or install programs on your computer, the data and programs are actually stored in the hard disk.

A hard disk can store large amount of data. It is made up of multiple disks where data is recorded on both sides of the disk. As we see in Fig. 2.19, a hard disk is bigger and heavier than a CD, DVD, or a pen drive. These days, hard disks can store up to 5 TB of data. The hard disk is placed inside a hard disk drive.

How RAM and Hard Disk Store Our Work

The hard disk stores all our files permanently.

Figure 2.19   Hard disk

- Whenever we open a file, it is copied into RAM from the hard disk.
- Now, while working with the opened file, i.e., whenever we make changes in the file and save it, the file is copied from the RAM to the hard disk.
- Finally, when we close the file, the file is removed from the RAM but is still present in the hard disk.

> When you double click on Computer icon, all the drives C: Drive, D: Drive, etc. are actually a part of the hard disk. All our data is stored on the hard disk.

2.5.2 CD (Compact Disc)

The full-form of CD is Compact Disc. It is circular in shape and can store up to 700 MB of data. Because of its light weight and small size, we can easily carry a CD from one place to another.

CDs are extensively used to take back up of data (store a copy of data from the computer so that it is not lost or damaged). CDs are also used to record songs, movies and software. There are two types of CD. While CD-R can is read-only, the CD-RW on the other hand, can be read as well as written on.

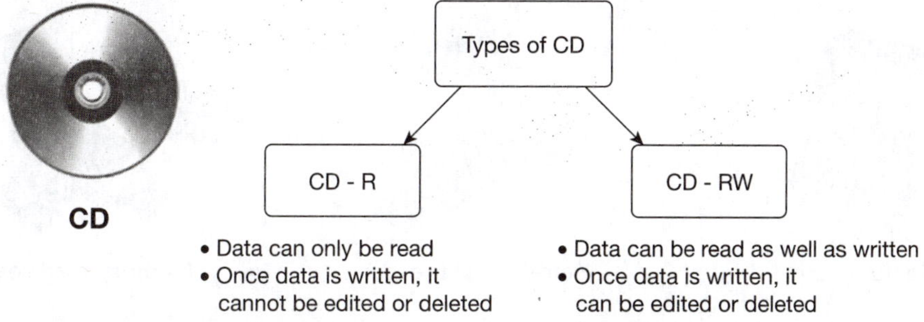

2.5.3 DVD (Digital Versatile Disc)

The full-form of DVD is Digital Versatile Disc. Like CD, a DVD is also circular in shape. Although a DVD resembles a CD, it is smaller (in size) than a CD.

A DVD can store data either on one side or both sides of the disc. It can store more data than a CD. Usually, a DVD on which data can be written on a single side can store up to 4.7 GB of data and a DVD that write data on both sides of the disc can store 17 GB of data.

We can easily carry a DVD from one place to another. Like CDs, DVDs are also used to take data back-up and record songs or movies with high video and sound quality.

To use a DVD you must have a DVD drive in your computer. A DVD drive can play both – CD as well as a DVD.

DVD

CDs and DVDs are optical storage devices because they store data using light (laser beams).

2.5.4 Blu-ray Disc

A Blu-ray disc is an optical disc which is replacing the DVD. It is similar to a CD/DVD but can store data up to 25 GB on its single side and 50 GB on both sides. The disc is called a Blu-ray disc because a blue laser is used to read/write on the disc

A computer needs a Blu-ray reader to read the Blu-ray disc. Such discs are used to store high-quality sound, games and movies.

A Blu-ray player can play a CD, DVD or a Blu-ray disc but a CD/DVD player cannot play a Blu-ray disc.

Blu-ray disc

2.5.5 USB Flash (or Pen) Drive

A pen drive is used to store our work for future use, move the data from one computer to another and also to take data back-up.

Pen drive is a very small, light-weight, removable drive which can be easily taken from one place to another. Since they can be attached to the computer and removed at any time, they are also known as *plug-and-play devices.*

A pen drive can store more data as compared to a CD or a DVD. These days, pen drives can store up to 1 TB of data.

Since a pen drive is attached to USB port of a computer, it is also known as a **USB drive**.

2.5.6 Multimedia Card

A multimedia card is also known as a **memory card**. It is used as a storage medium for portable devices (devices that can be carried from one place to another) like mobile phones, digital cameras, music players, etc.

A hard disk is fitted inside the computer but all other secondary storage devices like CD, DVD, Blu-ray, pen drive and memory card are attached externally to the computer.

A memory card is very small in size, almost of the size of a postage stamp. Data from a memory card is transferred to the computer using a multimedia card reader which is connected to the computer through a USB port.

Most of the laptops come with in-built card readers. These days, multimedia cards can store up to 128 GB of data.

Memory card

Memory card reader

Memory card reader

2.6   OPERATING SYSTEM – THE MANAGER OF COMPUTER'S RESOURCES

The Operating System (OS) is the most important system software in our computer. Once it is loaded in the RAM, it performs the following functions:

- The operating system *manages all computer's hardware devices* including the main memory and other storage devices.
- The operating system acts as an *intermediary between the application software and the computer hardware*. This means that users can use the hardware and other system software only through the operating system (Fig. 2.20).
- The operating system *manages application software* and other system software in the computer.
- *Makes computer easier to use.* A computer system comprises of one or more CPU, memory and I/O devices like disks, tapes, printers, terminals, etc. Writing programs to correctly and efficiently use the computer is an extremely challenging job and requires in-depth knowledge of functioning of these resources. So, to make computers easy to use and manage, the operating system is added as a layer in between the application programs and computer hardware to shield the users and programmers from the complexities of the underlying hardware.
- *Share resources* with all applications that are currently being run by the user. The operating system controls and efficiently utilizes hardware components like CPU, memory and I/O devices. It also

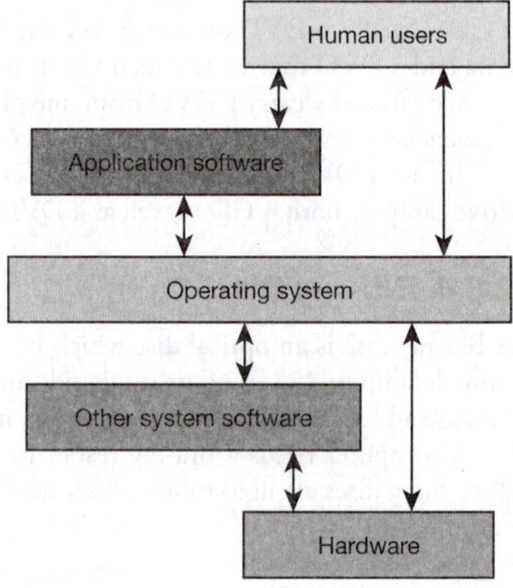

Figure 2.20   Operating system as an intermediary

facilitates sharing of CPU time amongst different user applications. Usually, users run different applications simultaneously (like creating a word document, sending email and listening to music) and each application constantly compete for the CPU's time, memory, and use of input/output devices until they finish their execution. The operating system, therefore, ensures that each application gets the necessary resources it needs. For this, the operating system decides when the CPU will execute which program, the programs that will be present in memory at any given time, when a given program will use the I/O device, etc.

- Every application running in the computer needs CPU, RAM and storage. In this scenario, the operating system keeps a *track of which user is using which resource and for how long.* It ensures that every user gets an equal chance to use the computer's resources (like files, memory and devices).

The operating system manages and keeps a *track of the primary memory* (Fig. 2.21). That is, what part of it is in use by whom, what part is not in use, etc. and reserves memory when a program requests it.

- The operating system allows users to *create and manage their files.* Users can arrange their files in folders and easily move, copy, delete and rename these files and folders.

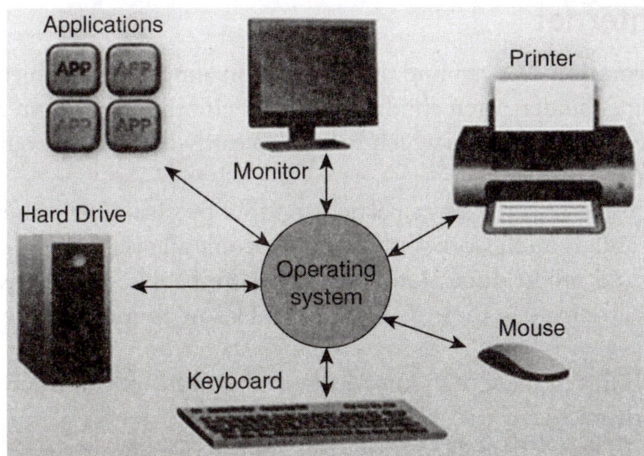

Figure 2.21 Operating system managing resources

- The operating system *monitors the performance* of the computer. It continuously checks how busy the CPU is, how fast data is being read from the hard drive, Internet speed and so many other things.
- The operating system not only allows users to access the computer but also provides *protection* of one user's files from other users through one or more security mechanisms (like password protection).
- The operating system allows users to *create, copy, delete, move and rename a file*. The operating system also keeps a track of location, access time, modified time, and other details of files and directories (folders) saved on the secondary storage devices. Users can even restrict access of their files by other users.
- The operating system provides a *consistent application interface* that ensures the programmers that the applications developed on one computer will also run on other computers with same or different hardware configuration. The operating system can easily manage hardware from the thousands of vendors manufacturing computer equipment. For example, in Windows, the steps to add a new printer will be the same irrespective of whether the printer was manufactured by HP, Cannon or some other company.

2.6.1 How an Operating System Runs a Program

Step 1: Users double click on an icon or type an instruction to open a program or file.
Step 2: The operating system searches for that file or program on the secondary storage device.
Step 3: The operating system reserves a part of RAM and loads the file or program into it.
Step 4: The operating system schedules the process and instructs the CPU to start executing the program from the beginning.

2.7 THE INTERNET – AN OCEAN OF INFORMATION AND OPPORTUNITIES

The Internet is a great invention that has opened the world to people by stripping away geographical barriers and sharing information instantly. The number of people using Internet is on constant rise. The graph given in Fig. 2.22 clearly shows that number of Internet users in India have increased manifold in the last few years and will continue to grow in the coming years. To understand the reason behind this sharp increase, we will need to know the advantages of the Internet.

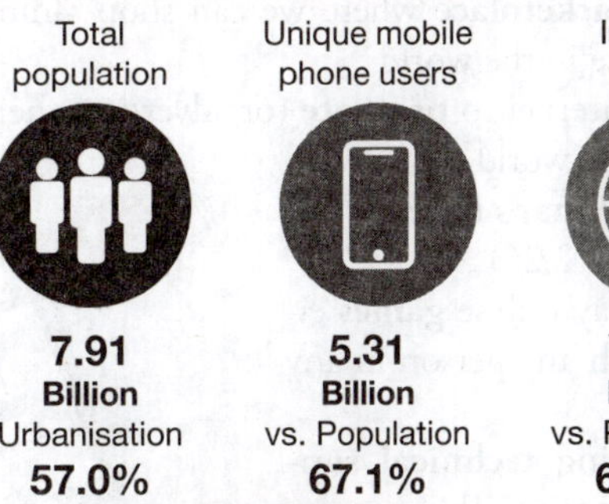

Figure 2.22 Number of Internet users

Source: https://datareportal.com/global-digital-overview

2.7.1 Advantages of Internet

- Internet is an ocean of **information**. We can find information on almost every subject and suitable for all age-groups (kindergarten children to senior citizens) on the Internet. There are many powerful search engines which help us to easily find out relevant information from the Internet.

  Anybody can conduct extensive research on a particular topic by sitting at home. There are numerous articles and research works published by people all over the world.

- There are **message boards** and group discussion websites where people can discuss ideas on any topic. We can participate in those discussions and know about everyone's opinions on that subject.

  People can use blogging websites to share their knowledge and experiences on a particular topic with other people having a similar interest in that topic.

- The Internet offers free **email** service that allows users to send their emails instantly to people located anywhere in the world.

- We can watch breaking **news** and live sports or other live events on the Internet. So even at places where we cannot carry our TV set, Internet on computer or smartphone can help.

- We can watch **movies** and listen to songs on the Internet. We can even download them for free.

- Using Skype or other programs with video calling features, we can hold a video conference with anyone in the world (Fig. 2.23).

- We can make **friends** over the Internet and can get connected with our friends and relatives living in any part of the world. Internet is an easy, cheap and fast way to connect with people worldwide (Fig. 2.24).

- **Matrimonial** sites like shaadi.com, jeevansati.com, etc., have helped people to find suitable match for themselves.

- **Jobs** sites like MonsterIndia have helped people to find a suitable job for themselves.

- Many universities are offering **online courses** on the Internet. Anyone from any part of the world can enroll in those courses, attend online lectures, submit online assignments and take online tests to get themselves evaluated to get the completion certificate. Imagine yourself doing a course from the prestigious Stanford University in US or from IITs in India while sitting at home.

- Websites like MakeMyTrip help us to plan an entire **trip** on the Internet. We can see pictures of many places, decide on a destination, book tickets, book hotels, cabs and everything using the Internet.

- With Internet **banking**, we can perform all sorts of banking operations like deposit or transfer money, know our balance, or pay bills while sitting at home.

- Internet offers 24*7 **marketplace** where we can shop almost anything, at any time and from anywhere in the world.

- Companies are using Internet to **promote** (or advertise) their products at much cheaper rates in the entire world (Fig. 2.25).

- People are using Google **maps** to reach unknown destinations (Fig. 2.26).

- Internet allows us to play online **games** either individually or with any person in any part of the world.

- Companies are providing **technical support** for their products online. They are also using Internet to get their customers' feedback. This helps the companies to directly get in touch with their customers and improve their products.

Figure 2.23 Video conferencing

Figure 2.24 Social networking sites

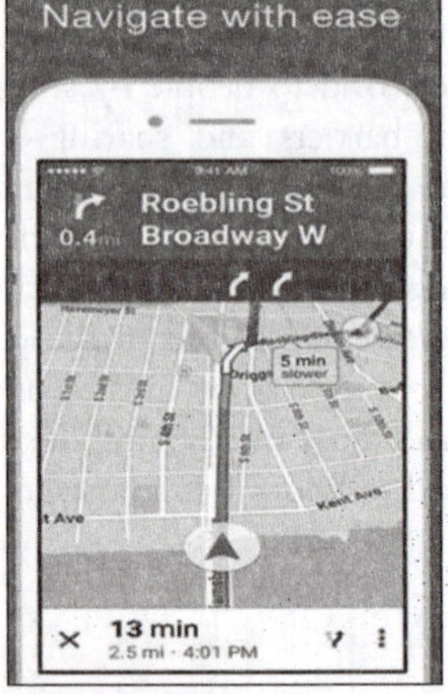

Figure 2.26 Google Maps

Figure 2.25 Online shopping

- Images from safety camera installed in banks and other places are transferred to the control room using Internet.
- Before buying any product or booking a hotel, we can read the reviews written by other users. This helps us to make an informed decision (Fig. 2.27).
- Internet allows even a common man to **sell** his products (even a second-hand product).
- Students who also work as bloggers are earning incomes by writing blogs. Blogging websites give a platform to those students who are interested in media and want to be a writer in the future. Blogging helps to increase their professional skills, which would enable them have a great future.

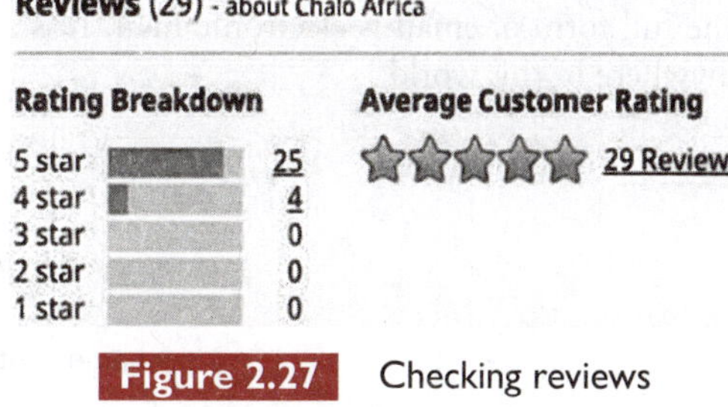

Figure 2.27   Checking reviews

2.7.2 Disadvantages of Internet

The Internet has revolutionized our lives and made it very convenient. However, it has an ugly side also. The following are some disadvantages of the Internet.

- Though there is lot of information on the Internet, there is no guarantee that the information is 100% accurate. This is because anybody from anywhere can post information. Do you know that even you can post information on Wikipedia? Find out how!
- On social networking sites, many people or rather **cheats** are on the lookout for making friendship with innocent people to take full advantage of their innocence. Many people get addicted to the Internet. They become less active in their interactions with real-world friends and loved ones and therefore risk losing them.
- **Pornographic** websites are easily viewed by children. Children are also watching action and other stuff that is not appropriate for their age.
- People who are fond of net surfing spend hours together going from one website to another. This adds to their **sedentary lifestyles** and makes them prone to problems like obesity, hypertension, constant pain in the neck and shoulders, strain on eyes, etc. (Figure 2.28)
- People and even students are **copying information** from the Internet to complete their work. This reduces their ability to think and be creative. They may even unknowingly use copyrighted material and thus lead themselves in troubles.
- Some people offer easy loans, enticing business offers, free holiday packages, etc., to fool innocent people and **extract money** from them.
- Some malicious users create **viruses** and other malware to intentionally harm computers or steal information about other people.
- There are many online games that contain violence and it negatively influences the children. Children who play a lot of online games often become **violent** about small things.
- Many people are deliberately connecting with children to **extract personal information** from them. They use this information to arrange a theft or even kidnap the children.

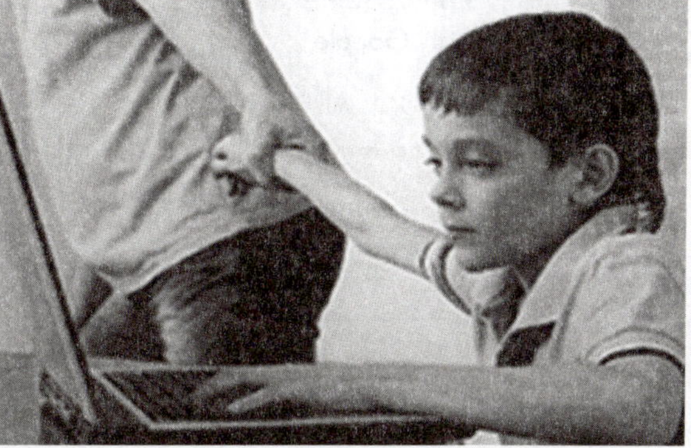

Figure 2.28   Side effects of Internet: No time for personal relationships and Internet addiction

2.8 ELECTRONIC MAIL (EMAIL)

The full form of email is electronic mail. It is a fast and easy way to send letters (mails) to other people who may be anywhere in this world

Anyone who wants to send or receive emails must have an email address. Everyone on the Internet has a unique email address.

Advantages of an Email

- Emails can be exchanged very fast – in a few seconds.
- Emails can be sent to a user in any part of the world.
- You can send text, pictures, audio, video, file etc. through an email.
- Email service is provided free of cost by many websites like Yahoo, Gmail, Hotmail, etc.
- One email can be sent to many users at the same time.

Activity: Let Us Create an Email Account on www.gmail.com

Step 1: Open any Web browser like Internet Explorer, Google Chrome or Mozilla Firefox.

Step 2: In the address bar, type www.gmail.com.

Step 3: Click on "Create an account".

Step 4: Fill your details in the form provided and click on "Next Step".

Step 5: Your account will be created and a welcome page would be displayed. Click on Continue to Gmail button.

Step 6: Your mailbox will be displayed. Now you can send emails, photographs, files or any other document to your friend.

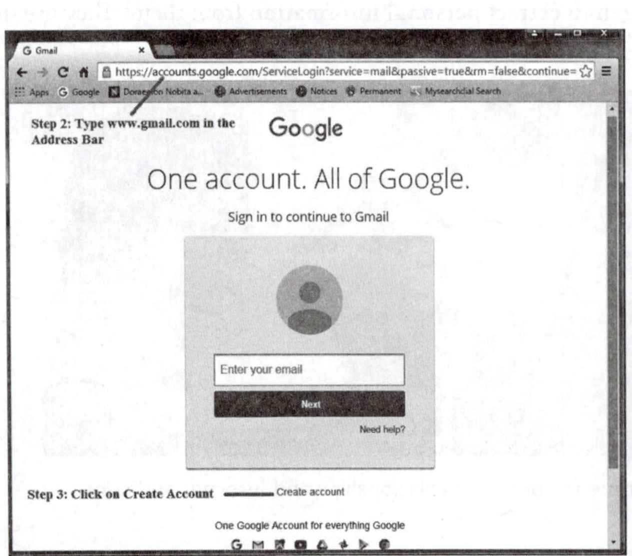

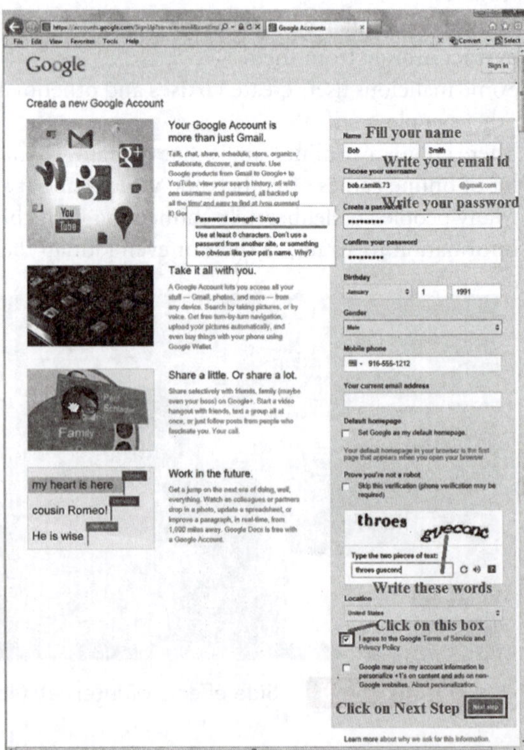

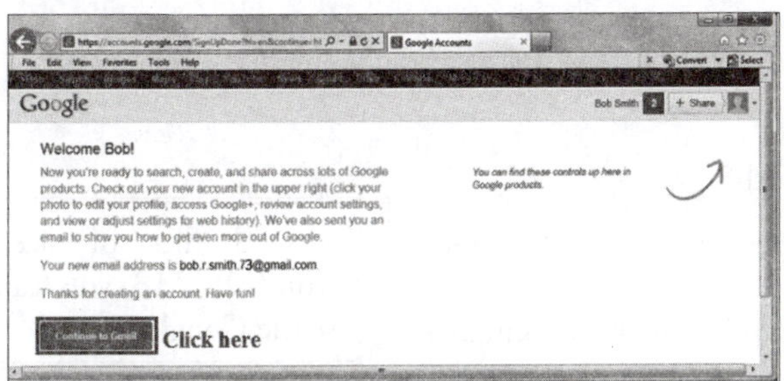

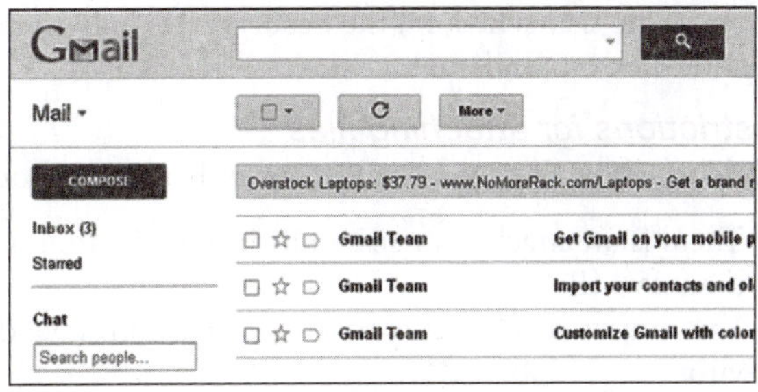

Activity: Let Us Read Our Emails on Our Gmail Account

Step 1: Open any Web browser like Internet Explorer, Google Chrome or Mozilla Firefox.

Step 2: In the address bar, type www.gmail.com

Step 3: Enter your username and password. Then click on Sign In.

Step 4: Your mail box will be displayed.

Step 5: All the unread emails are shown in Bold. Click on the email you want to read.

> After reading/writing mails you must Logout from your email account. To logout click on the arrow just next to your email address on the top right corner of email window and select logout.

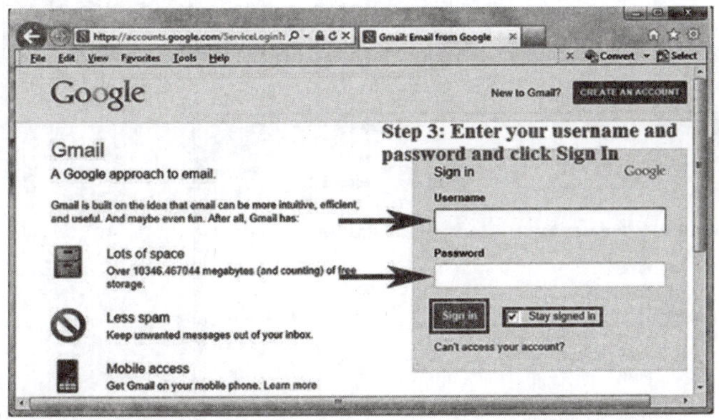

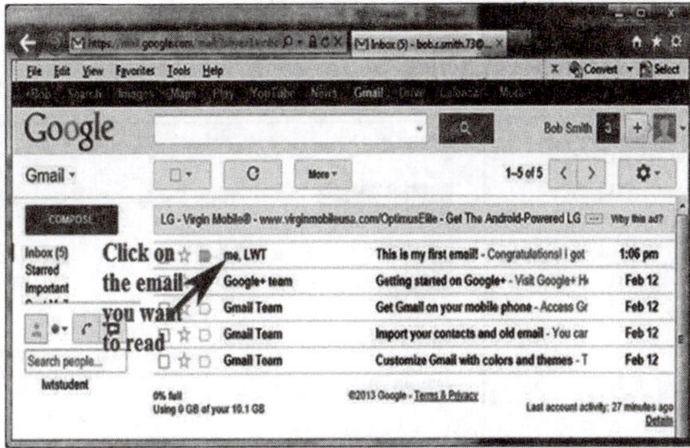

Activity: Let Us Compose (or Write) and Send an Email Through Gmail Account

Step 1: Open any Web browser like Internet Explorer, Google Chrome or Mozilla Firefox.

Step 2: In the address bar, type www.gmail.com.

Step 3: Enter your username and password. Then click on Sign In

Step 4: Your mail box will be displayed. Click on Compose.

Step 5: In the To field, enter your friend's email id, in the subject field write "My first email", in message field write whatever you want

Step 6: Click on Send.

> The Subject field is a brief description of the message that is displayed in the recipient's in box before they open the message.

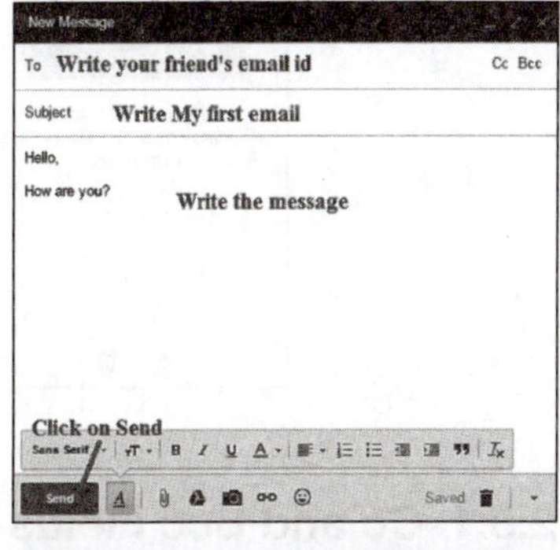

Activity: Let Us Attach a File in the Email

You can send attachments, like files, videos, and photos in your emails.

Step 1: Open your Gmail account.

Step 2: Click on Compose.

Step 3: Click on Attach.

Step 4: Browse and select the file to be attached. Click on Open to upload the file.

> You can also add an image either by dragging and dropping it into the message body of the Compose window or simply by copying it and pasting it in the Message body field.

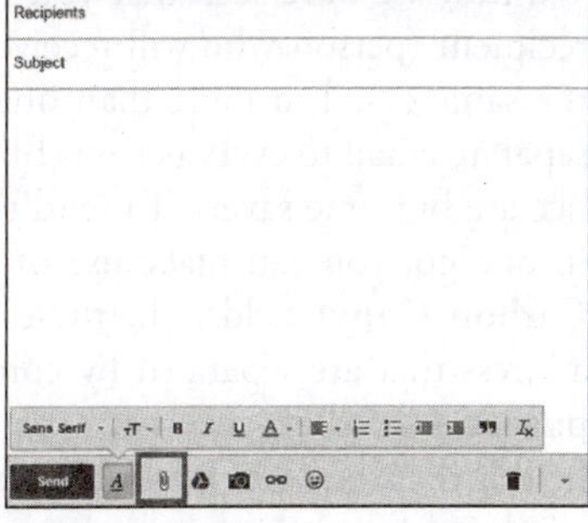

Once the file is attached, fill the details in To, Subject and Message body fields.
Step 5: Click on Send.

Restrictions for attaching files

While attaching files, you need to remember two important things.

- There is an attachment size limit in Gmail. Your attached files cannot be larger than 25 MB.
- You cannot attach files with a .exe extension since this type of file may contain a virus.

> To send files of size beyond 25 MB you can use the Google Drive.

Activity: Let Us Forward an Email Message

Forwarding a message means passing a received email to a person(s) other than the sender. Follow the steps given below to forward an email message:

Step 1: Open the email. Click on Forward at the bottom of the message. You can also select Forward by clicking on the small arrow next to the Reply arrow button (from the More drop-down menu).

Step 2: Enter the recipient's email address (or addresses if you want to forward the message to more than one person) in the To: field.

Step 3: If you want to type any message, do it in the textbox (also called Body of the message).

Step 4: Click on Send.

> Type the Subject carefully. Typing an irrelevant subject or leaving the subject line blank could result in your message getting into the recipient's Spam folder.

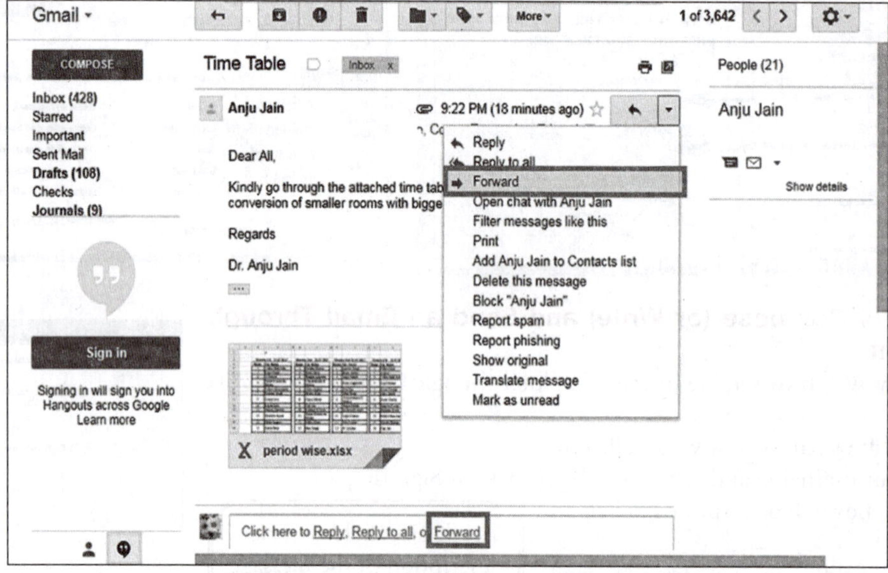

2.8.1 Cc and Bcc Fields

Till now we have seen that you were sending the email message to only one recipient (person who will receive the message). What if you wanted to send the same email to more than one person? One way is to individually send a separate email to every person. But this is not a good idea. In such cases cc and bcc are big time savers. To send the same email message to multiple receivers in one go, you can make use of the **To, Cc (Carbon Copy)** or **Bcc (Blind Carbon Copy)** fields. In these fields, you can enter more than one email address that are separated by commas. Though all the fields serves the same purpose, the difference with the email addresses that are written in the bcc field is that they are not visible (cannot be seen) to other recipients.

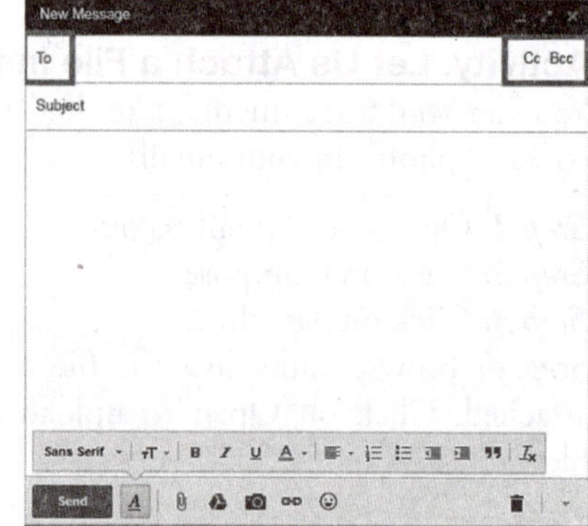

To enter the email address in Cc and Bcc field, just click on them. Type the email address just next to Cc and Bcc.

Tips while using Cc and Bcc

- Use the Cc field when you don't care if recipients get to know each other.
- Bcc should be used when the email addresses of the recipients should be kept secret.
- The best thing is to enter the recipient's email address in the To field and other email addresses in the bcc field. This is mainly important because nobody likes his email address to be exposed to everyone, especially strangers. Moreover, this may go in hands of a fraudster.

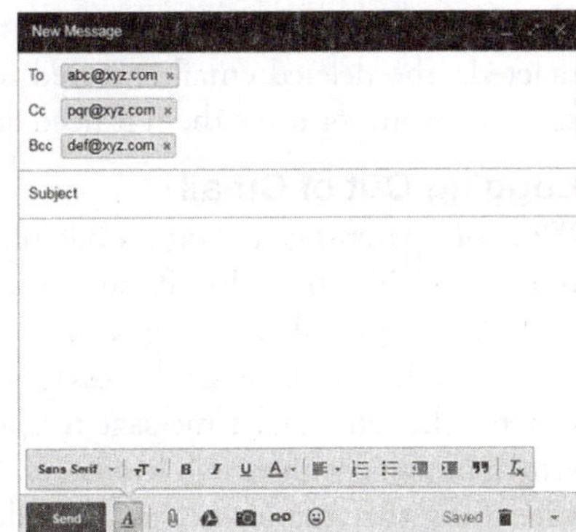

The addresses written in the To and Cc field can be seen by every recipient.

The To field cannot be left empty. You have to fill at least one email address in this field.

2.8.2 Mailbox: Inbox and Outbox

Every email address or account has a mailbox. Mailbox is the container that stores all the emails that are sent and received using that email account. For this it has a few folders like Inbox, Outbox, Spam and Trash.

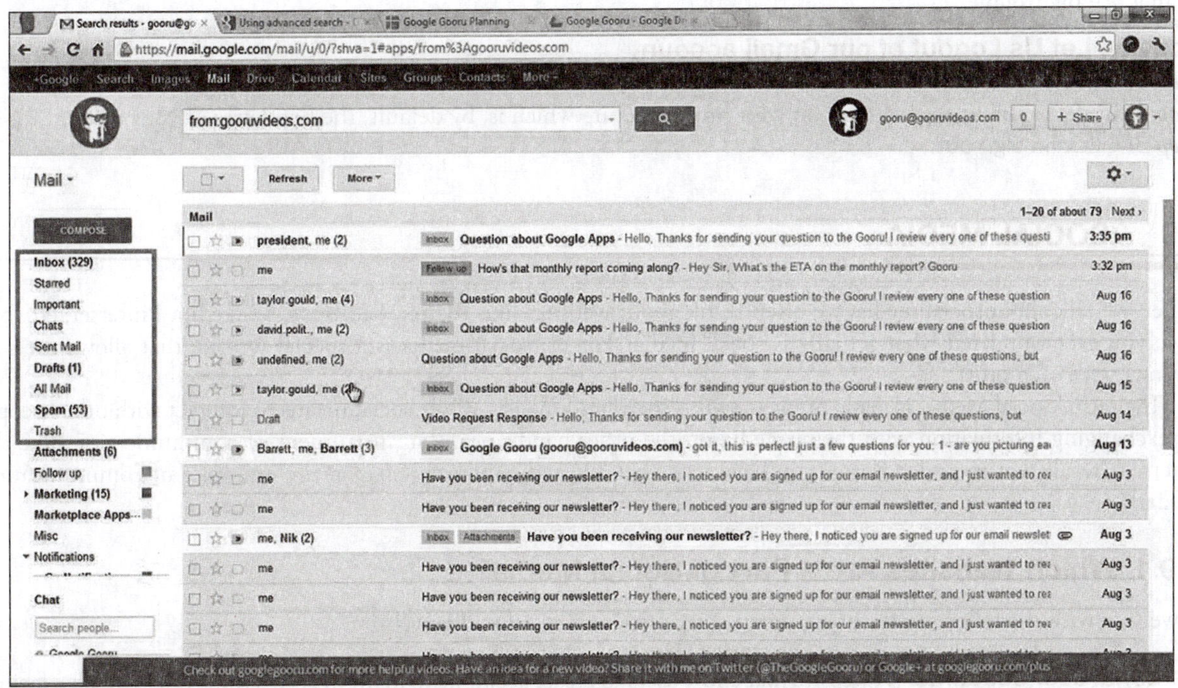

Inbox: It is the folder in which all the incoming emails (emails that are received) are stored. All the messages are displayed sorted according to the date in descending order.

Outbox or Sent Items: It is the folder that stores all the email messages that were successfully delivered.

Draft: It is the folder in which email messages that are composed (or written) but not sent are stored. For example, you may write an email to a friend but could not send it because of a power outage. In that case, the email will be saved for future use in the Drafts folder.

Spam: It is the folder in which all fake and spam email messages are stored. Such messages may contain virus, malware, spyware, or code to steal data. The email application analyzes all the received emails and then stores the legitimate emails in Inbox and others that look like spams in the Spam folder.

Change the password of your email at least once every month. Also keep it a secret. Do not tell your password even to your best friend.

Trash: It is the folder that stores all the email messages that have been deleted. The deleted email is stored for some time so that you can reuse, send, forward, or print them if need arises.

> To remove an attachment from the email message, just click X to the right of the attachment name.

Logging Out of Gmail

Will your parents give their mobile phone to just any-one to use? No? But why? Because it may be misused. Someone, especially a stranger, may take their phone and make fake calls or send messages that may harm others (like send a false message to spread a rumor or send a message with virus). Moreover, a phone is a pri-vate thing that cannot be just shared with everyone. Same is the case with an email account. Your email address is a personal thing. It must not be shared with others as it may be misused.

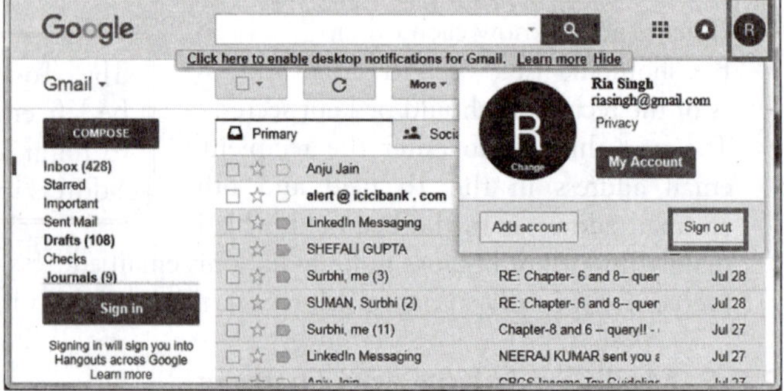

Therefore, when you have finished reading and writing emails, you must always Logout or Sign Out of your email. If you leave your email open and someone else sits at the computer, then he/she can use your email account to send messages to others that may be fake and contain some malware. In that case, you will be caught and be in a real big trouble.

Activity: Let Us Logout of our Gmail account

Step 1: Open your Gmail account.
Step 2: In the top right corner, click on your profile picture which is, by default, the first letter of your name.
Step 3: Click on Sign out.

2.9   SOCIAL MEDIA

When we talk about social media, we often think about websites like Twitter, Facebook, Linkedin, Pinterset, etc. but have you ever wondered what actually is social media? For us, social media is a special website that allows users to interact with each other.

The term 'Social Media' is made of two terms – social and media. While social means to interact with other people by exchanging information with them, media on the other hand, means an instrument of communication, like the Internet (recall that in junior classes you have read that TV, radio, and newspapers are examples of communication media).

2.9.1 Which Websites Are a Part of Social Media?

A website with the following features is often considered as a social media website.

Personal user accounts: A website that allow users to create accounts to login to access the services. Such a facility indicates that you would be having some kind of personal interaction with other users.

Profile pages: A profile page is one that allows users to present them as their own brand. Users can fill information about them like their name, DOB, profile photo, bio, website, interests and likings. Others can even see recent posts, recommendations, recent activity and know more about the user through his profile page.

Friends, followers, groups, hashtags and so on: A social media website allows a user to connect with other users and subscribe to their page to get information about them.

Personalization: Social media sites allow users to customize their account's settings, manage the information they get to see and even give feedback on what they do not want to see.

Notifications: A website that notifies users about others' activities is a prominent feature of a social media. However, users can choose to receive the types of notifications that they want.

Managing information: A social media website allows its users to post a message, write a textual message, upload a photo/GIF/sticker/link or just any other thing to express themselves or share some information.

Like buttons and comment sections: A user can interact on social media by writing comments, pressing the like, dislike and other reaction buttons.

Review or rate: On a social media website, users can write a review, rate a product/service and cast their vote to express their opinion about something.

Hence, we can say that social media is a collective term for websites and applications that facilitate communication, interaction, content-sharing and collaboration.

Examples of Social Media Some commonly used social media websites are:

Facebook that allow users to register themselves, create profiles, upload photos and video, send messages and keep in touch with friends, family and colleagues. Users can create stories and read news about topics they are interested in.

LinkedIn is used by professionals and business community to create a network of people they know and trust professionally.

Pinterest allow users to share and categorize images found online. Clicking on an image will take a user to its original source.

Reddit is a social news website and forum where its registered members (known as redditors) can create and promote stories. The site has a large number of subreddits (or sub-communities) where each subreddit has a specific topic like technology, politics or music. Redditors can submit content that members vote on. This is specifically done to bring all well-regarded stories to the top of the site's main page.

Twitter is a free micro-blogging service where registered members can broadcast short posts called tweets.

Wikipedia is a free open-content encyclopedia created through a collaborative community. Anyone registered on this website create publish an article. Users can even edit the articles (without prior registration).

Tumblr/Medium/WordPress/Blogger Blogs are one of the oldest forms of social media. Users can write a review on a particular thing, comment on someone else's article and share their opinion.

Snapchat is a social media website that allows users to share updates with friends and followers to see. Users can share posts with specific people only at specific times.

2.9.2 Issues with Social Media

Not everything is good about social media. It is rather a channel that has several challenges.

Spam: Social media provides enough opportunities to spammers (including people and bots) to bombard other people with lots of useless content.

Cyberbullying/Cyberstalking: This is very common among children and teenagers. Users keep an eye on others' online activity (cyber-stalking). Of course, they may misuse any information they get anytime for any reason. Some users also criticize, mock and shame other users on social media (cyber bully). But one must not forget that such mischiefs can cost someone's life and it is a cybercrime to get involved in such type of activities.

Self-image manipulation: Not everything posted on social media is true. Some users who are actually fed up in their real lives create an image on social media that casts them as the happiest person on this planet.

Information overload: Some users are active on multiple social media websites and have hundreds of followers. They may also be following hundreds of other users. In such a scenario, it becomes very hectic for the users to keep up with the posted content, resulting in an additional stress.

Fake news: Fake news spread like wildfire on social media. People read an article of their interest and then share it with other users without thinking about the authenticity of the content.

Privacy/Security: Data privacy and security takes the back seat when users start sharing information about themselves – where they go for having dinner/last vacation/places they often visit, etc.

Stress: The stress of getting/reading/replying to unlimited messages, and managing hundreds of followers, is a burden of social media. The pressure of garnering tons of likes and comments on social media posts and becoming a celebrity also disturbs our real life. Moreover, overuse of social media can create an addiction that can affect one's mental health very badly.

Productivity concerns. Excessive social activity, online or in person, is distracting and adversely affects our productivity.

2.9.3 Benefits of Social Media

Every coin has two sides and so does social media. Apart from utilizing social media to communicate, collaborate and interact with others, it is also used by businesses to market and promote their products and track customer concerns. Business groups analyze their performance as well as that of their competitors by reading the reviews and feedback written by the customers about products and services offered by them. Even new customers can be easily acquired through social media.

Social media is also used as a crowdsourcing platform to pool knowledge, money, goods or services. For example, companies use crowdsourcing to get ideas from employees, customers and the general public for improving products or developing future products or services. Table 2.3 given below shows which social media website is being used for what purpose.

Companies are also use social media websites like Linkedin to recruit suitable candidates as their employees and to develop connections with people who share similar interests or activities.

Table 2.3 Popular social media sites

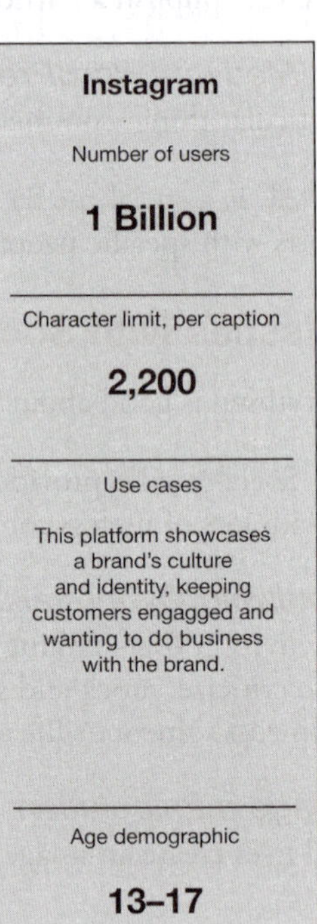

	Facebook	LinkedIn	Twitter	Instagram
Number of users	2.3 Billion	630 Billion	330 Billion	1 Billion
Character limit	63,206 (per post)	700 (per update)	280 (per post)	2,200 (per caption)
Use cases	B2C companies and nonprofits can build communities through targeted advertising and promoting events.	A B2B platform where industry leaders and buyers spend their time. Users can create their own forums to start conversations, which promote thought leadership, and share industry knowledge.	Thought leadership, information-seeking individuals and media outlets. Writers and blogger's use this as a search engine to find real-time information. Provides brand awarness for companies and shines light on different topics.	This platform showcases a brand's culture and identity, keeping customers engaged and wanting to do business with the brand.
Age demographic	All ages	30–49	18–29	13–17

2.9.4 Social Media Best Practices

In today's scenario, it has become very important for companies to have a social media strategy and establish social media goals to build trust, educate their employees on what and how to respond, create brand awareness and connect with their customers. A few crucial best practices when working on social media are discussed below.

- Establishing social media policies sets expectations for appropriate employee social behavior. Employees should not expose the company to legal problems or cause any type of public embarrassment. Clear instructions should be stated for employees to create a brand image of their company and they should therefore share any information with great responsibility.
- Every social media campaign must be based around the customer's expectations.
- Use social media metrics to track market trend and customer interests so that appealing audio/visual content can be shared on social media to enhance customer engagement.
- Use short, clear, simple sentences while interacting with customers
- Accept posts from employees and customers that talk positively about the organization and repost that content.

2.10 WEBSITE

- A website is a collection of related web pages. It contains one or more web pages. In fact, a website may even have thousands of web pages.
- To access a website, we must enter its URL in the address bar of the web browser. When no particular web page is mentioned in the URL, by default, the home page or the index page which stored as index.htm is displayed on the screen. If you remember, home page is the first page or the starting page of a website.
- However, to refer to a particular web page on a website, the user must enter the complete path of the web page.
- For example, if we write www.abc.com, then the index.htm page on the abc website is displayed. But if we write www.abc.com/contacts/customer.htm, then the customer.htm web page stored in the contacts folder is displayed.

> Any business, government, or person can create a website on the Internet. Today, there are billions of websites on the Internet that have been created by billions of different people.

- A website is stored on a web server (Fig. 2.29). A very large website may be spread over a number of servers in different geographic locations. For example, the website of IBM consists of thousands of files and its web pages are spread out over many servers across the globe. However, one web server can also store the files and web pages of several small websites.

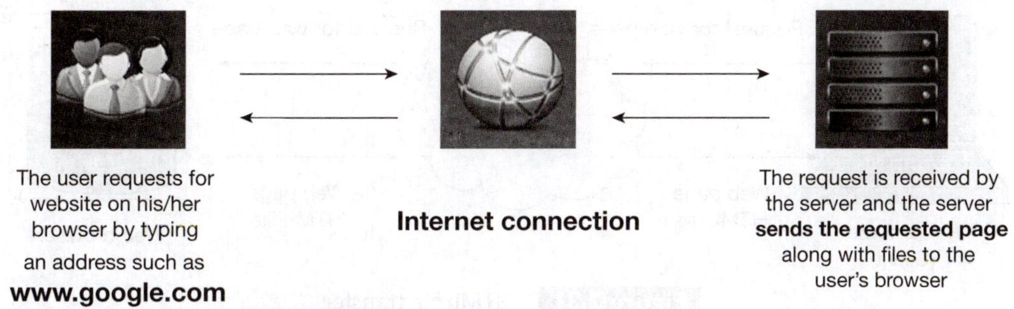

Figure 2.29   Accessing a website across Internet

- All websites hosted through the Internet constitute the World Wide Web (WWW). To be useful, a website must have well-structured information presented in a user-friendly look and feel.

> Multiple pages of a large website can be stored on several servers. In contrast, a single server can host pages of several small websites.

2.10.1 HTTP (Hypertext Transfer Protocol)

HTTP is the most commonly used protocol on the Internet. It specifies a set of rules for transferring web pages that include text, graphic images, sound, video, etc. and other multimedia files) on the World Wide Web. Whenever a user types the URL in the address bar of the web browser, he is indirectly using HTTP.

Since most web browsers use HTTP as the default protocol, even if you type the domain name like google.com, the web browser will automatically insert "http://" and the complete URL will then be read as, www.google.com.

> HTTP, hypertext and hyperlink lays the foundation of data communication for the World Wide Web.

HTTP uses a request–response model in which the client makes a request and the server sends the response containing the requested information.

URL: The full form of URL is Uniform Resource Locator. URL means the address of the web page. We know that each web page has a unique address. This address is known as the URL of the web page.

Web Pages: A web page is a document available on the World Wide Web (www). A web page may contain text, graphics, audio, video and hyperlinks (links to other web pages).

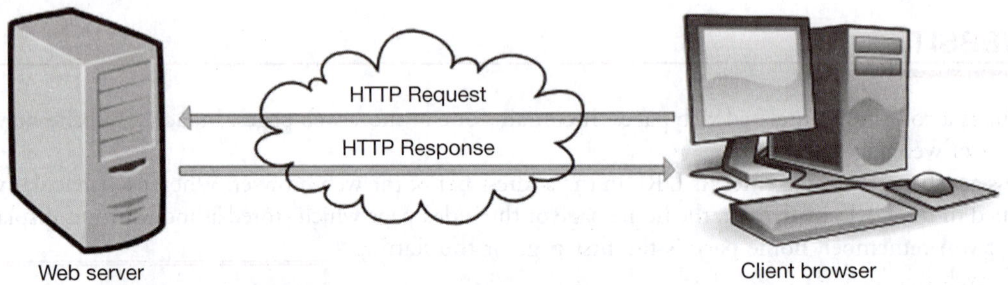

Figure 2.30   Interaction between web browser and web server

Web pages are stored on a web server and can be viewed using a web browser (Fig. 2.30). To view a web page on the web browser, you just need to enter its URL address in the Address Bar. When you enter the URL in the Address Bar, the following sequence of activities takes place.

- When we enter the URL in the web browser, the browser requests for that page from the web server through the Internet.
- On receiving the request, the web server sends that page to the web browser through the Internet as Hyper Text Markup Language (HTML).
- The web browser displays the page received from the web server (Figure 2.31).

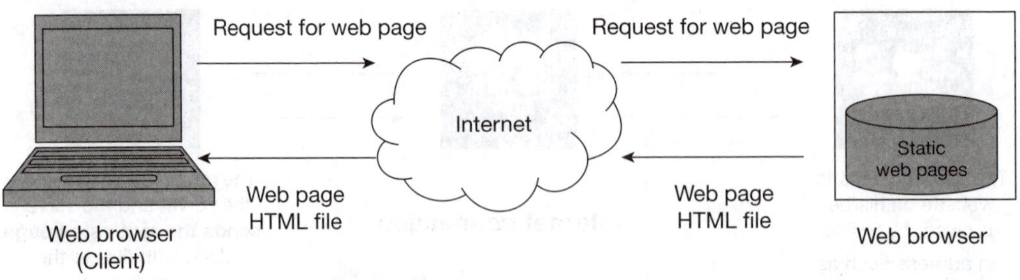

Figure 2.31   HTML file transfer

Website: A website is a group of connected pages on the World Wide Web containing information on a particular subject. Each website has a unique address (or the URL). Examples of website are www.google.com, www.discoverykids.com, etc.

> The web pages of a website are stored on a web server. For example, all web pages of website www.yahoo.com are stored on yahoo web server.

When we open a website, its home page is displayed. The homepage may contain hyperlinks to other pages on the same or other website(s).

Home Page: Home page is the first web page displayed when a user opens a particular website. The URL (or the address) of a Web site is actually the address of its home page. The home page acts as the starting point of website. For example, visiting http://discoverykids.com will display the Discovery Kids home page.

The home page usually contains hyperlinks to other pages on the website.

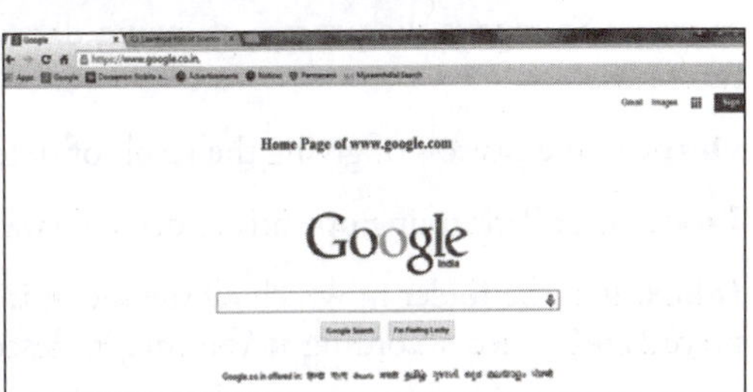

Links/ Hyperlinks/Hotlink: Hyperlink is a link that connects one page to another. They help users to move or navigate to different web pages of the same as well as of a different website.

Hyperlinks can be in the form of word or a picture. Whenever, the mouse pointer is moved over a hyperlink, the pointer changes to the hand symbol.

The moment you click on a hyperlink you move to another page on the www.

> Hyperlink is a clickable area on a web page.

World Wide Web (WWW): WWW is a collection of all the websites. There are millions of web pages on the www that contains information on a wide range of topics.

Pages on the www can be accessed by users in any part of the world. Whenever you search for any information on the Internet, the web browser searches for it on the World Wide Web.

Many people often get confused between the terms Internet and the www. While the Internet is a huge network of computers, www on the other hand, is a massive collection of information that can be accessed through the Internet.

> The www was invented by Tim Berners Lee. He gave the concept of hyperlinks which formed the backbone of www.

Net Surfing or Web Browsing: Web browsing means seeing different web pages on the Internet. Browsing the Internet is also known as Net surfing.

For example, moving from one website or web page to another to search for some information on the World Wide Web (WWW) is called as Net surfing.

> A web browser gets information from the web server (computer on which all the pages of a website are stored) and displays it on the screen.

Key Terms

Computer: An electronic machine that takes data and instructions as input and performs computations on data based on the specified instructions.

Data: Data is a collection of raw facts or figures.

Information: Information comprises of processed data to provide answers to the *"who"*, *"what"*, *"where"* and *"when"* type of questions.

Knowledge: Knowledge is the application of data and information to answer the *"how"* part of the question.

Instructions: Commands given to the computer that tells what it has to do.

Programs: A set of instructions in computer language is called a program.

Software: A set of programs is called software.

Hardware: Computer and all its physical parts are known as hardware.

Input: The process of entering data and instructions in to the computer system is known as input.

Storage: Storage is the process of saving data, instructions and results of processing in the computer's memory for future use

Output: The process of giving the result of data processing to the outside world (external to the computer system).

Processing: Performing operations on the data as per the instructions specified by the user.

Inbox: It is the folder in which all the incoming emails (emails that are received) are stored. All the messages are displayed and sorted according to the date in descending order.

Outbox or Sent Items: Email folder that stores all the email messages that were successfully delivered.

Draft: Email folder in which email messages that are composed but not sent are stored.

Spam: Email folder in which all fake and spam email messages are stored.

Trash: Folder that stores all the email messages that have been deleted.

Website: A collection of related web pages.

Chapter Highlights

- A computer is an electronic machine that takes data and instructions as input and performs computations on data based on the specified instructions.

- Storage is the process of saving data, instructions and results of processing in the computer's memory for future use.

- A computer has two types of storage areas: Primary storage or main memory and Secondary storage or auxiliary memory

- The process of entering data and instructions into the computer system is known as input.

- Output is the process of presenting the result of data processing to the outside world (external to the computer system).

- CPU (Central Processing Unit) is a combination of the ALU and the Control Unit. It is known as the brain of the computer system

- The ALU performs all kinds of calculations in the CPU while the Control Unit directs and coordinates the computer operations

- Devices that help us to give input to the computer are called ***input devices.***

- A keyboard is the main input device for computers. Most keyboards have between 80 and 110 keys.

- A wireless keyboard can be operated without connecting it to the computer through a physical wire.

- An image scanner captures images, printed text and handwritten text from different sources such as photographic prints, posters, and magazines and converts them into digital images for editing and display on computers.

- MICR consists of magnetic ink printed characters and can be used to verify the legitimacy of paper documents, especially bank cheques.

- A printer takes the text and graphics information from a computer and prints it on to a paper.

- Hard disk is the main secondary storage device of the computer. It is placed inside the CPU Box. When you save data or install programs on your computer, the data and programs are actually stored in the hard disk.

- The operating system manages all hardware devices of the computer including the main memory and other storage devices. It acts as an intermediary between the application software and the computer hardware.

- HTTP is the most commonly used protocol on the Internet. It specifies a set of rules for transferring web pages that include text, graphic images, sound, video, etc. and other multimedia files) on the World Wide Web. Whenever a user types the URL in the address bar of the web browser, he is indirectly using HTTP.

Review Questions

1. Explain the basic organization of a computer system.

2. Write a short note on any three input devices.

3. What are output devices? Explain any two output devices that are frequently used by you.

4. Explain the role of operating system in a computer.

5. Imagine that your younger sister is very active on social media websites. Is it a matter of concern for you? If yes, why and how will you make her understand these issues?

6. Mention any three websites on social media. Also write for what purpose they are used the most.

Differentiate Between the Following

1. Data and information

2. Primary and secondary storage

3. CD-R and CD-RW

4. Traditional mail and an email

5. Cc and bcc

6. An ordinary website and a social media website

7. Web page and a website

Fill in the Blanks

1. Computer and all its physical parts are known as ___________.

2. _________ is the process of saving data, instructions and results of processing in the computer's memory for future use.

3. _________ (RAM/ROM) can be used as a permanent storage of useful data and programs for future use.

4. Data is processed in the __________.

5. CPU takes __________ and __________ from the primary memory.

6. Two data values are compared in the __________ component of the CPU.

7. __________ captures everything on the screen as an image. The image can be pasted into any document.

8. __________ is a small, flat, rectangular stationary pointing device with a sensitive surface of 1.5–2 square inches.

9. __________ is a pen-shaped input device used to enter information or write on the touchscreen of a handheld device.

10. __________ is the process of electronically extracting data from marked fields, such as checkboxes and fill-in fields on printed forms.

11. A combination of headphone and microphone is known as a __________.

12. A double-sided DVD can store __________ GB of data.

13. A pen drive is attached to the __________ port of a computer.

14. An __________ acts as an intermediary between the application software and the computer hardware.

15. All the incoming emails are stored in __________.

16. __________ means users keep an eye on others' online activity.

17. To access a website, enter its __________ in the address bar of the web browser.

18. A page on a website is known as __________.

19. A website is stored on a __________.

20. __________ specifies a set of rules for transferring web pages that include text, graphic images, sound, video, etc. and other multimedia files on the World Wide Web.

21. __________ page is the first web page displayed when a user opens a particular website.

22. The home page usually contains __________ to other pages on the website.

State True or False

1. A set of programs is called software.

2. The process of entering data and instructions in to the computer system is known as output.

3. Secondary storage is directly accessible by the CPU at a very fast speed.

4. Secondary memory is non-volatile.

5. The output devices therefore convert the results available in binary codes into a human readable language before displaying it to the user.

6. ALU is responsible for fetching, decoding, executing instructions, and storing results.

7. Touchscreens are used as input as well as output devices.

8. Optical mark readers can read up to 9,000 forms per hour with an error rate of less than 1%.

9. Image scanner consists of magnetic ink printed characters and can be used to verify the legitimacy of paper documents, especially bank cheques.

10. To view a presentation on a big screen, you will use a plotter.

11. Blu-ray disk can store more data than a hard disk.

12. Outbox/Sent folder stores all the email messages that were successfully delivered.

13. In cyber bullying, a person criticizes, mocks and shames other users on social media.

14. HTTP uses a request–response model.

15. Two web pages can have the same address.

Multiple Choice Questions

1. ________ are the commands given to the computer that tells what it has to do.
   a. Software
   b. Instructions
   c. Program
   d. Hardware

2. Knowledge is the application of data and information to answer the _______ part of the question.
   a. What
   b. Where
   c. How
   d. When

3. The process of giving the result of data processing to the outside world is _______.
   a. Input
   b. Output
   c. Storage
   d. Processing

4. The _____ component of CPU manages and controls all the components of the computer system.
   a. ALU
   b. Memory Unit
   c. Control Unit
   d. Input Unit

5. ________ keys are used to move the cursor to the beginning and end of the current line, respectively.
   a. HOME and END
   b. PAGEUP and PAGEDOWN
   c. ARROW
   d. ESC and PAUSE

6. ________ captures images, printed text and handwritten text from different sources such as photographic prints, posters, and magazines and converts them into digital images for editing and display on computers.
   a. Keyboards
   b. Barcode Reader
   c. MICR device
   d. Image Scanner

7. Identify the odd one out.
   a. Microphone
   b. Monitor
   c. Speaker
   d. Plotter

8. To draw maps, in scientific applications and in CAD, CAM, and computer aided engineering (CAE), you will use a ________.
   a. Printer
   b. Plotter
   c. Projector
   d. Touchscreen.

9. All the programs installed by us on the computer are actually stored in the _____.
   a. RAM
   b. ROM
   c. Hard Disk
   d. Pen Drive

10. Identify the storage device which is circular in shape and can store up to 700 MB of data.
    a. CD
    b. DVD
    c. BD
    d. Memory Card

11. Mobile phones, digital cameras, music players have _______ as its storage device.
  a. Pen Drive
  b. USB Drive
  c. Flash Drive
  d. Memory Card

12. Identify the incorrect statement.
  a. System software manages the operating system and application software.
  b. The operating system manages memory and CPU.
  c. Operating system manages user files and folders.
  d. Users will not be able to work on the computer if any operating system is not installed in it.

13. Which field cannot be left empty in an email?
  a. To
  b. CC
  c. BCC
  d. All of these.

14. _________ is the email folder in which email messages that are composed but not sent, are stored.
  a. Sent
  b. Outbox
  c. Draft
  d. Inbox

15. All websites hosted through the Internet constitute the _______.
  a. Web Page
  b. Web Server
  c. World Wide Web (WWW)
  d. Network

16. A web page cannot contain _________.
  a. Text
  b. Graphics
  c. Audio
  d. None of these.

17. Which software helps users to view web pages?
  a. Word Processor
  b. Web Server
  c. Web Browser
  d. WordPress

Give a Website for Each

1. Find jobs _____________

2. Find information for a project _____________

3. To book hotels for a three-day vacation ___________

4. To buy a book _________

5. To see a movie ___________

6. To watch a web series ____________

7. To do an online course ___________

8. To make a creative cover page of a book _____________

9. To buy a used car ___________

10. To buy a property _______________

11. To keep in touch with friends, family and colleagues ____________

12. To create a network of people whom you trust professionally _____________

13. Social news website _____________

14. Microblogging _______________

15. Free open content encyclopedia _____________

Group Discussion

- Discuss the applications of Internet.
- What difference do you find in Netflix series and a daily soap relayed on a Doordarshan/Zee/Sony channel? Which one do you prefer and why?
- What would you prefer – shop online or offline? Justify your answer.
- How active are you on social media?

Role Play

Assume that you are a class teacher. Your student has told you that her classmate reads all her social media posts and writes sarcastic comments on them to insult her. What action(s) will you take?

Class Activity

Design a poster inviting students from classes VI–VIII in your school to participate in an IT Quiz. Email this poster to class monitors of all the sections.

Project Work

Collect information about what steps can be taken to protect our data while working on the Internet.

Topic for Debate

Are Traditional Media also Social Media?

Hint: Traditional media are just broader examples of media such as the TV, radio, and newspapers. These are not a part of social media, at least not quite yet, entirely. The line drawn between the two is slowly thinning as each continues to evolve.

Social media does not just give you information, but interacts with you while giving you the information. This interaction can be as simple as asking for your comments or letting you vote on an article, or it can be as complex as Vudu recommending movies to you based on the ratings of other people with similar interests.

Think of regular media as a one-way street where you can read a newspaper or listen to a report on television, but you have very limited ability to give your thoughts on the matter. Social media, on the other hand, is a two-way street that gives you the ability to communicate too.

Answers

Fill in the Blanks

1. hardware	**9.** Stylus	**17.** URL
2. Storage	**10.** OMR	**18.** webpage
3. RAM	**11.** headset	**19.** web server
4. CPU	**12.** 17	**20.** HTTP
5. data and instructions	**13.** USB	**21.** Home/Index
6. ALU	**14.** operating system	**22.** hyperlinks
7. Print Screen key	**15.** inbox	
8. Touchpad or a trackpad	**16.** Cyber-stalking	

State True or False

1. True
2. False
3. False
4. True
5. True
6. False
7. True
8. True
9. False
10. False
11. False
12. True
13. True
14. True
15. False

Multiple Choice Questions

1. b
2. c
3. b
4. c
5. a
6. d
7. a
8. b
9. c
10. a
11. d
12. a
13. a
14. c
15. c
16. d
17. c

Introduction to Artificial Intelligence 3

The chapter gives a brief introduction to Artificial Intelligence which is the buzzword today and our topic of study. We will read about:

- History and types of AI systems
- Techniques used in AI
- Advantages and limitations of the technology
- Human–Machine interaction
- The AI waves

3.1   WHAT IS ARTIFICIAL INTELLIGENCE?

From a layman's view, Artificial Intelligence (AI), simply means the intelligence demonstrated by machines that help them to mimic the actions of humans. AI simulates natural intelligence in machines that are programmed to learn from experiences, adjust to new inputs and perform human-like tasks.

> Most AI examples, from chess-playing computers to self-driving cars, heavily depend on deep learning and natural language processing techniques.

From a researcher's view, AI is a set of algorithms that generates results without having to be explicitly instructed to do so, thereby making machines capable of thinking and acting rationally and humanely.

AI applications perform specialized tasks by processing large amounts of data and recognizing patterns in it. Besides learning from experience, AI applications can recognize objects, understand and respond to language and make decisions to solve real-world problems.

3.2   HISTORY OF ARTIFICIAL INTELLIGENCE

You must have observed that today, when we type a word in WhatsApp or Gmail, the application automatically gives us suggestions for the next word. When we are using Google Maps, Google automatically knows where we are and suggests to us the shortest/fastest route to our destination. Whenever we surf the Internet, we are recommended to buy certain products in which we may actually be interested. Every time we use Facebook, we get a list of Suggested Friends we may know or a list of pages in which we may be interested in. All this happens because of one technology – **AI**.

Did you ever wonder why all this is happening all of a sudden; why not decades before? Basically, this surge in using AI is possibly because of the following factors:

- availability of large amounts of data
- widespread use of computers
- improvements in computing power and storage
- advanced algorithms to process large amounts of data.

Let us understand the history of AI by looking at the timeline given in Fig. 3.1:

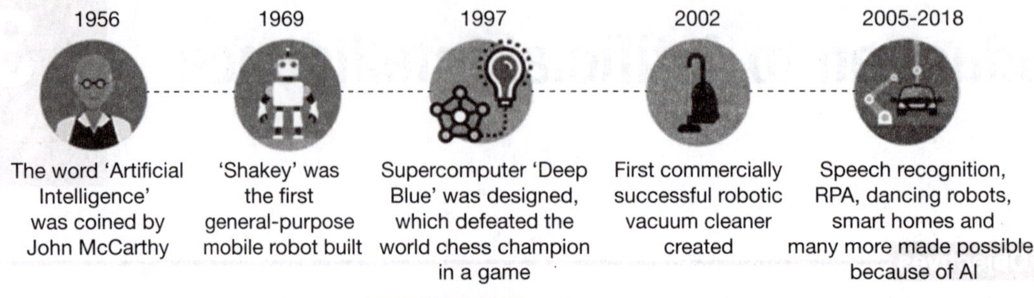

Figure 3.1   AI timeline–1

To visualize developments in AI in the period 2007 – 2019, you can refer to Fig. 3.2.

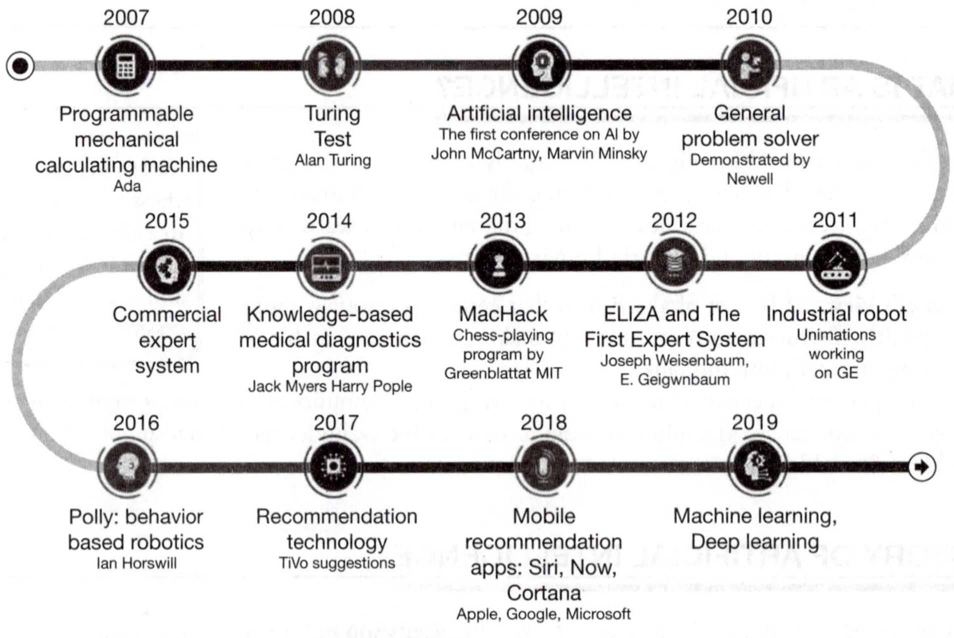

Figure 3.2   AI timeline–2

Thus, we see that the term 'artificial intelligence' was first coined in 1956. In the 1960s, the US Department of Defense started training computers to mimic basic human reasoning. In the 1970s, the Defense Advanced Research Projects Agency (DARPA) completed street mapping projects and in 2003, produced intelligent personal assistants. Later, Siri, Alexa or Cortana became household names in the US.

Since then, automation and formal reasoning with decision support systems and smart search systems that complement and augment human abilities are commonly used in computers today.

Many Hollywood movies and science fiction novels depict AI as human-like robots that take over the world. But that is not true. The current state of AI technologies is not that devastating.

3.3 TYPES OF ARTIFICIAL INTELLIGENCE

We can categorize artificial intelligence applications into two broad categories based on capabilities and functionality as shown in Fig. 3.3

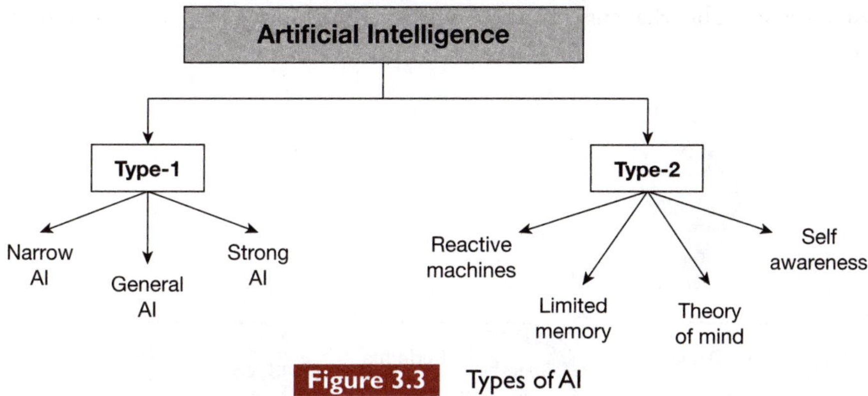

Figure 3.3 Types of AI

3.3.1 AI Type-1: Based on Capabilities

Based on capabilities, AI applications can be classified as Weak AI (or Narrow AI), General AI and Strong AI (or Super AI).

Narrow AI

It is the most commonly used type of AI these days. Narrow or Weak AI, performs a dedicated task with intelligence. But it cannot perform any other task as it is specifically trained for specific tasks only.

Narrow AI does not mimic or replicate human intelligence. It just simulates human behaviour based on a narrow range of parameters and contexts. Narrow AI are close to human functioning but in very specific contexts, and can even surpass them many times. However, narrow AI works well only in very controlled environments with a limited set of parameters.

Examples of Weak AI include,

- Virtual assistants like Siri by Apple, Alexa by Amazon, Cortana by Microsoft that use narrow AI as they work with a limited pre-defined range of functions.
- IBM's Watson supercomputer, which is an Expert system that combines machine learning and natural language processing techniques.
- AI systems used in medicine to diagnose cancer and other diseases with great accuracy by using cognition and reasoning techniques.
- Chatbots that use NLP to interpret human language and interact with human beings.
- Other examples are playing chess, purchasing suggestions on e-commerce site, self-driving cars, speech recognition, and image/facial recognition. Moreover, manufacturing robots, drones, email spam filters, social media monitoring tools and marketing content recommendations based on watch/listen/purchase behaviour also make use of narrow AI to perform their specified task.

General AI

It performs intellectual tasks with human-like efficiency. General AI makes smart decisions without human intervention. As of now, there is no system that falls under this category as there is no machine that can perform any task as perfect as a human. But researchers worldwide are actively working to develop machines with General AI.

A general AI system has a human-level of cognitive function across a wide variety of domains such as language processing, image processing, computational functioning and reasoning and so on.

Super AI

Super AI or Strong AI is a level of intelligence of systems at which machines could surpass human intelligence. The main aim here is to make machines use their cognitive properties to perform any task better than humans.

Super AI systems have the ability to think, reason, solve a puzzle, make judgments, plan, learn, and communicate on their own. However, like General AI, even Super AI is a hypothetical concept of Artificial Intelligence and development of such systems is still a big challenge. Figure 3.4 projects the future of AI and shows the relative level up to which it has currently evolved.

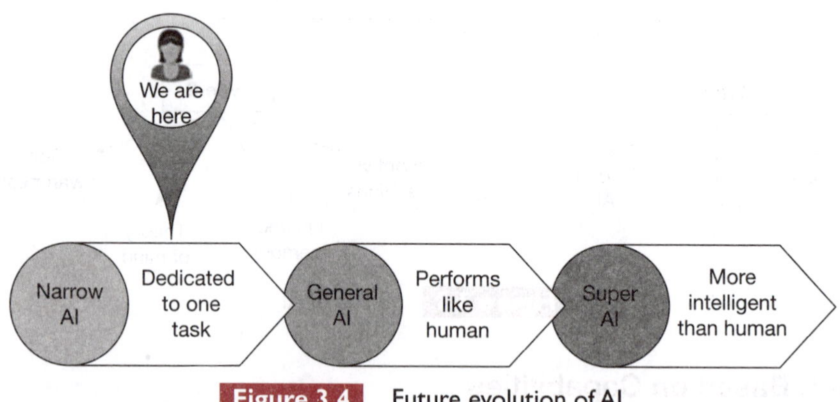

Figure 3.4   Future evolution of AI

The difference between Weak AI and Strong AI is summarized in Table 3.1.

Table 3.1   Comparison of weak and strong AI

Weak AI	Strong AI
It supports a narrow range of applications with a limited scope.	It supports a wider range of applications with a broad scope.
This application is good at specific tasks.	This application has incredible human-level intelligence.
It uses supervised and unsupervised learning to process data.	It uses clustering and association techniques to process data.
Example: Siri, Alexa.	Example: Advanced robotics

3.3.2 Artificial Intelligence Type-2: Based on Functionality

Based on functionality, AI can be classified as reactive machines, limited theory, theory of mind and self-awareness.

Reactive Machines

Reactive machines are the most basic type of Artificial Intelligence machines. As the name indicates, such systems focus on current scenarios and react on it in the best possible way. They do not store past experiences for future actions. Examples of such AI systems are: IBM's Deep Blue system and Google's AlphaGo.

IBM's Deep Blue (Fig. 3.5) defeated chess grandmaster Garry Kasparov. It is a reactive machine that sees the chessboard pieces and reacts to them. It has no way to refer to any of its prior experiences so that it can improve its performance. It just identifies the pieces on a chessboard and tries to predict its opponent's as well as its own next moves.

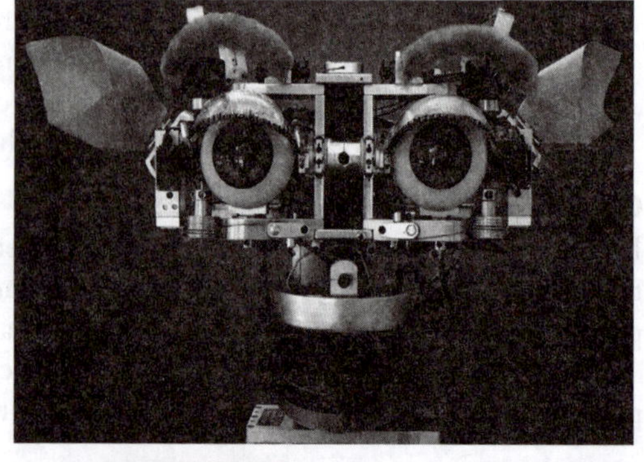

Figure 3.5   IBM's Deep Blue

Limited Memory

As evident from the name, such AI systems have a memory, though limited in size, to store past experiences or some data for a short period of time. Self-driving cars are one of the best examples of such AI systems. These cars store recent speed of nearby cars, the distance of other cars, speed limit, and other vital information that is necessary to navigate the road.

Theory of Mind

These are AI systems that can understand human emotions, people beliefs, and be able to interact socially like humans. Though researchers are aggressively working on such systems, they are still not developed yet.

One real-world example of the theory of mind AI is Kismet, which is a robot head made in the late 90s by a Massachusetts Institute of Technology (MIT) researcher. The robot mimics human emotions and recognizes them. However, it can still not follow gazes or convey attention to humans.

Another robot Sophia (Fig. 3.6), applies the theory-of-mind AI. Cameras are fitted inside Sophia's eyes. Pictures taken by the camera, when processed with AI algorithms, allow her to see, sustain eye contact, recognize individuals, and follow faces.

Self-awareness: As of today, self-awareness AI systems are a hypothetical concept. But such systems are said to be the future of AI systems. These machines will be super-intelligent, have their own consciousness, sentiments, and self-awareness. Such machines are expected to be much smarter than the human mind.

> Theory-of-mind level AI is not about replication or simulation; it is about training machines to truly understand humans.

> Strong AI uses a theory-of-mind AI framework to ensure that robots possess the capability to discern needs, emotions, beliefs and thought processes of other intelligent entities.

Figure 3.6 Sophia applies the theory of mind

3.4 ADVANTAGES AND DISADVANTAGES OF ARTIFICIAL INTELLIGENCE

We have seen that AI has made our life better by making recommendations, mapping directions and preventing fraud. But there are always two sides to a coin, and that holds true even with AI. Let us look into some advantages as well as disadvantages of this technology (Table 3.2).

Table 3.2 Advantages and disadvantages of AI

Advantages of AI	Disadvantages of AI
• Reduction in human error • Available 24 × 7 • Helps in tirelessly performing repetitive work • Faster and accurate decisions • Improved security • Efficient communication, also provides digital assistance • AI robots reduce human risks by performing all hazardous tasks. For example, robots are used in places like coal mines, exploring the deepest parts of the ocean, sewage treatment, and nuclear power plants to avoid any disaster involving precious human life.	• AI systems are expensive as compared to their traditional counterpart. • Less talent available in this area. • Can lead to disaster if misused. • AI systems do not make decisions based on emotions, compassion, and empathy.

3.5   HOW ARTIFICIAL INTELLIGENCE WORKS

Building an AI system is a process of reverse-engineering human traits and capabilities in a machine. AI is a broad field of study that includes many theories, methods and technologies. To understand how Artificial Intelligence actually works, we must look into its various sub-domains (Fig. 3.7). All these domains have one thing in common. They process large amounts of data with fast and intelligent algorithms to allow the software to learn automatically from patterns or features in the data. These sub-domains are:

Artificial Intelligence

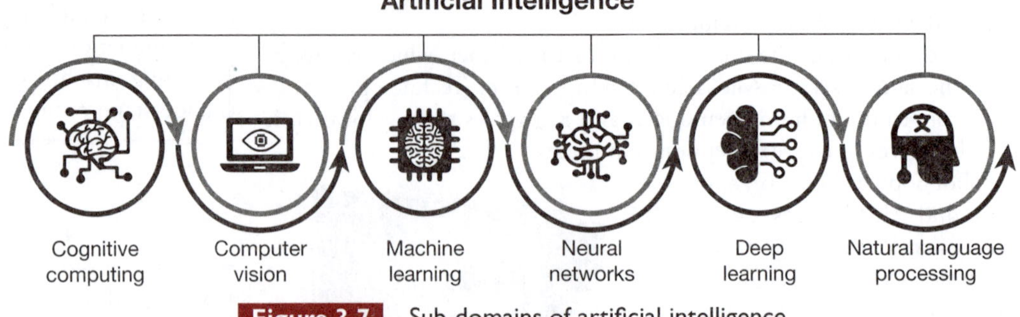

Figure 3.7   Sub-domains of artificial intelligence

3.5.1   Neural Networks

Neural Networks work in the same way as Human Neural (brain) cells. A series of nodes capture the relationship between various underlying variables and processes the data. Every node (or neuron) processes information by responding to external inputs and relaying information between each unit. The entire process of learning requires multiple passes at the data to derive meaning from undefined data (refer Fig. 3.8).

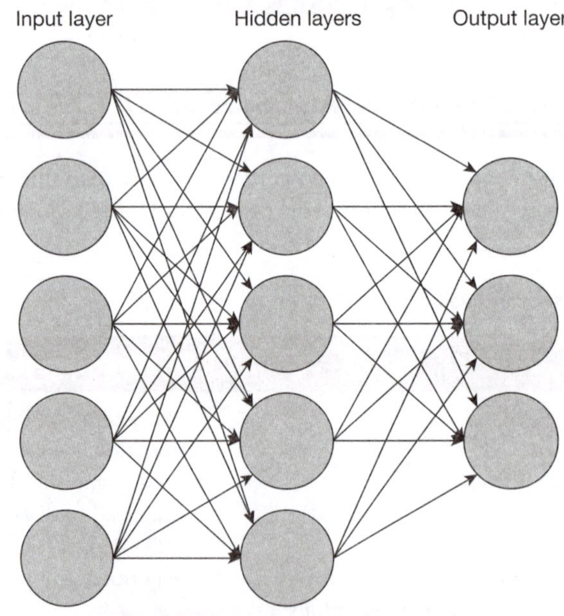

Figure 3.8   Basic neural network

Note that even the most basic neural network consists of the following layers:

An ***input layer***, which is the layer from where data enters the network.

At least one ***hidden layer***, where machine learning algorithms process the inputs. Weights, biases and thresholds are applied to the received inputs and the results of processing are passed to the output layer.

An ***output layer***, which is the layer that gives the final result to be displayed.

3.5.2 Machine Learning

Machine Learning (ML) is a branch of artificial intelligence (Fig. 3.9) that analyzes data and identifies patterns to teach a machine to deduce results and make decisions without any human intervention. ML algorithms learn from experiences rather than instructions. They automatically learn and improve by learning from their output. For this, humans do not have to write instructions for them to produce the desired output. They learn by analyzing data sets and comparing the final output. In case of any error, they repeat the learning process until the accuracy of the outputs improve.

This automation not only saves human time and effort but also makes better decisions.

Machine-learning algorithms can be categorized as supervised or unsupervised.

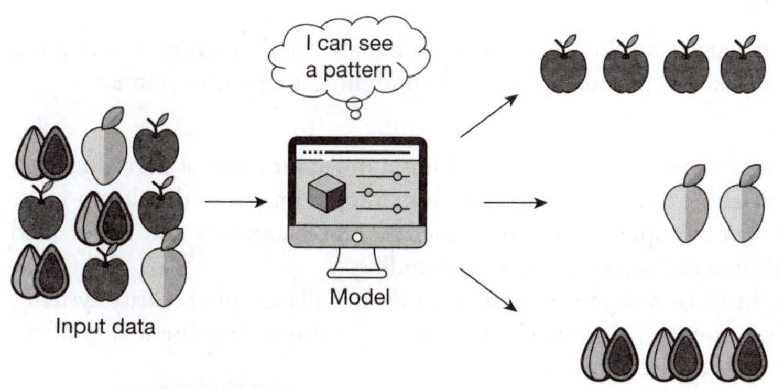

Figure 3.9 Sub-divisions of AI

Supervised Learning: Supervised machine-learning algorithms, as the name indicates, have a supervisor as teacher. These algorithms apply learning from past data (or experiences) to new data using labeled examples.

> Supervised learning should be used when output of data in the training set is known.

These algorithms start with analyzing a known training dataset to produce an inferred function that can be used to predict future data values. The learning algorithm then compares the predicted output with actual output to find errors and modify the model accordingly.

For example, if you have a basket filled with different variety of fruits, then the first step is to train the machine to identify a fruit. Once our machine is trained, it can easily identify whether the new fruit in hand is an apple, banana, grapes or any other. It will clearly know that a red colored round fruit is an apple, and so on.

Unsupervised Learning: Unsupervised learning trains the machine using information that is neither classified nor labeled. In this case, the machine learning algorithm works on that information without any guidance. The unsorted information is grouped based on similarities, patterns and differences without any prior training of data. For example, if we give an image of mango and an orange, then initially the machine has no idea about how a mango looks and how the orange looks.

Unsupervised machine learning algorithm learns through observation and finding structures in the data. That is, the model automatically finds patterns and relationships in the dataset by creating clusters in it. For example, if given a dataset of pictures of both mangoes and oranges, the algorithm can make two clusters – one containing only pictures of oranges and the other of mangoes (Fig. 3.10). What an unsupervised machine learning cannot do is specifying labels to the clusters. That is, it can only segregate the pictures but cannot tell that this is a real-world orange and that is a mango.

> Semi-supervised machine learning algorithms fall somewhere between supervised and unsupervised algorithms since they use both labelled and unlabeled data for training. These algorithms improve accuracy.

Figure 3.10 Unsupervised machine learning

Deep Learning

Deep Learning (DL) is an ML technique that teaches a machine to process inputs through layers to more accurately classify, infer and predict the outcome. DL creates huge neural networks with several layers of processing units to take full advantage of advances in computing power and improved training techniques. This helps the algorithm to learn complex patterns in large amounts of data. Some applications of DL include image and speech recognition.

Deep learning models are based on *deep neural networks,* that is, neural networks with multiple hidden layers (Fig. 3.11). In such a network, each hidden layer further processes the temporary outputs received from the previous layer. This movement of computations through the hidden layers to the output layer is known as ***forward propagation***.

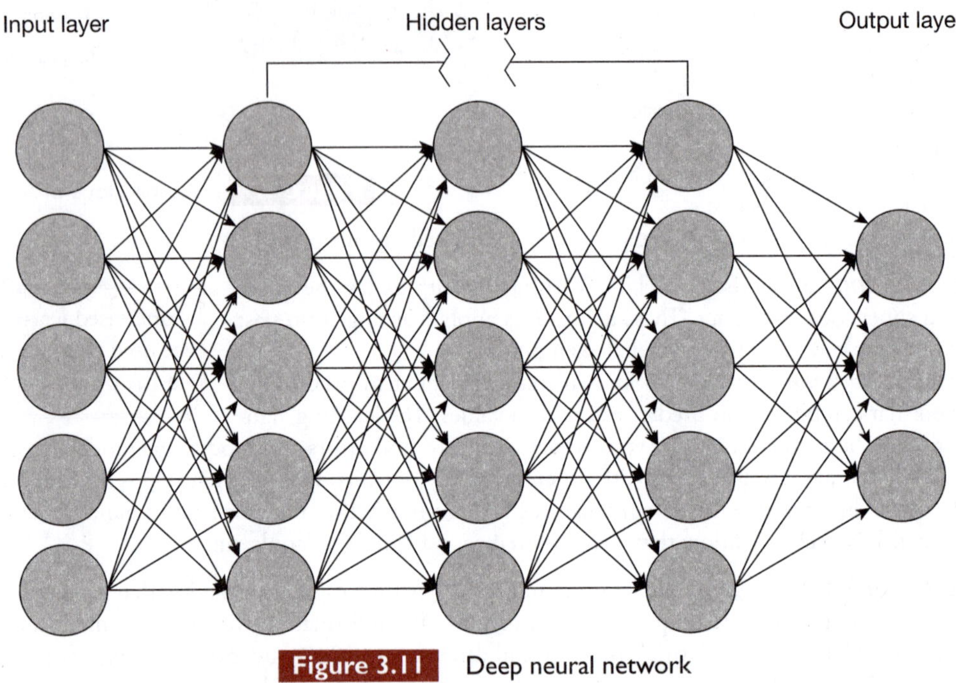

Figure 3.11   Deep neural network

Once the final result is produced by the output layer, its accuracy is calculated. In case of unsatisfactory results, the errors are identified, weights assigned to each node are updated, and pushed back to the previous layers to refine or train the model. This process of moving backward to update weights of all nodes is known as ***backward propagation***.

Deep learning models can work with labeled as well as unlabeled data. This means that deep learning supports both *supervised* and *unsupervised learning.*

3.5.3 Natural Language Processing

Natural Language Processing (NLP) is a science in which a machine is made to read, understand, interpret and respond to a human language. This is specifically done to make the machine capable of communicating with a human.

Computer Vision

Computer vision is a branch of AI that tries to understand an image by breaking it down into several parts and then studying each part of the image. This helps the machine to classify and learn from a set of images so that it can make better decisions based on previous observations. For example, when a machine can process, analyze and understand images, they can capture images or videos in real time and interpret their surroundings.

Computer vision techniques are used today for facial recognition that helps in surveillance and security systems, autonomous vehicles, retail stores for tracking inventory and customers, in medicine for diagnosing diseases, in financial institutions to prevent fraud, and in several other applications.

Cognitive Computing

Cognitive computing algorithms try to mimic a human brain by analyzing text, speech, images or objects in the same way to give the desired output. It is basically a subfield of AI that is used to provide a natural, human-like interaction with machines. The ultimate goal of using cognitive computing is to make the machine speak coherently in response to a human.

Apart from the above-mentioned techniques, some additional technologies that enable and support AI include:

Graphical processing units that provide heavy computing power required for iterative processing and training neural networks.

Internet of Things to generate massive amounts of data from connected devices. Usually, this data remains unanalyzed. Automating models with AI helps to analyze this data and extract useful information from it. Advanced algorithms can be used to analyze data faster at multiple levels to identify and predict rare events, understand complex systems and optimize unique scenarios.

3.6   AI DOMAINS FOR HUMAN–MACHINE INTERACTIONS

Humans interact with computers while working on them to perform a specific task or operation. In human–machine interactions, hardware and software both play a vital role in communication. The interface of such an interaction should be very user-friendly. In AI, human–machine interactions are done using the following domains (Fig. 3.12):

1. Data
2. Computer Vision (CV)
3. Natural Language Processing (NLP)

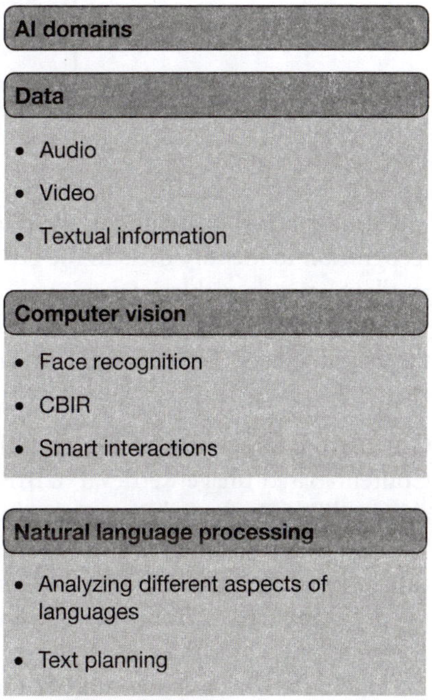

3.6.1 Data

Today, data is everywhere in abundance. Did you ever notice that the attendance taken by your teacher on a daily basis generates a huge amount of weekly/ monthly/ yearly data?

Data is the backbone of any AI system. In fact, an AI system learns using the underlying data. As the system development grows, processing of data also increases.

This data can be in any form – text, audio, video, images or big data for predictions, insights, forecasts, decision making, etc. For example, a computer program can be written to play the game **Rock–Paper–Scissor** with the user.

Figure 3.12   AI domains

3.6.2 Computer Vision (CV)

Computer vision is a field of science that helps computers gain a high level of understanding from digital images or videos. It is done by acquiring images, processing them, analyzing them and finally understanding the information they are conveying.

Once the images are understood, computer vision is then used in the following areas.

Facial Recognition

Facial recognition systems to recognize faces in images and videos. Applications like Google Photos, spam chat, Facebook, Instagram, etc., use facial recognition system to identify people (Fig. 3.13).

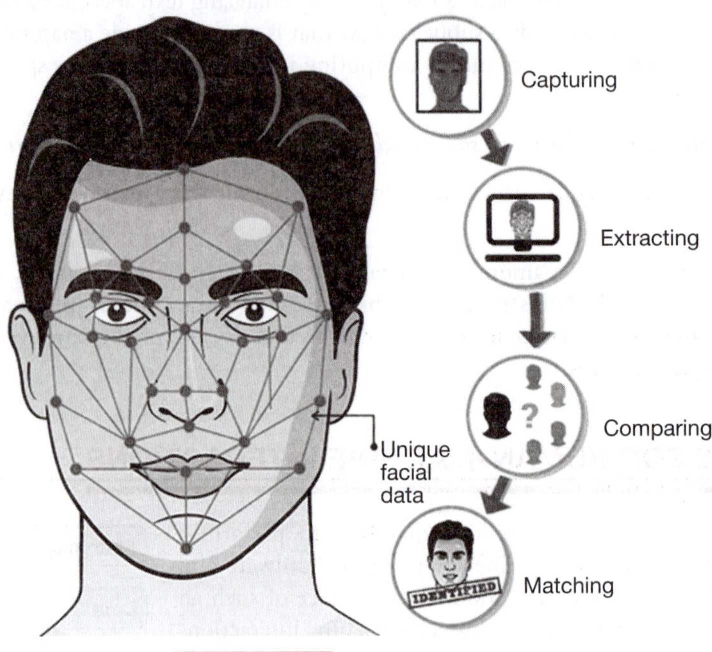

Figure 3.13   Facial recognition

Almost every smart phone these days use facial-recognition algorithms to unlock phones. Facebook uses facial recognition to identify users in the posted pictures. In China, this technology is integrated with **payment technology** to allow users do cashless payment.

Some government agencies in different countries are also using facial technology for **surveillance**. Though use of this has raised concerns among rights and privacy advocates, facial recognition technique applications are on a constant rise.

Content-Based Image Retrieval Systems

Content-Based Image Retrieval (CBIR) systems identify image properties like composition, color, texture etc. Search engines like Google and Bing and software analyzing CT scans and MRIs in hospitals, etc. use CBIR systems.

Computer Vision is extensively used in smart interactions to give input to computers. This is especially helpful in case of **gaming software** and in systems designed for differently abled individuals.

Software used in **home security systems**, office security systems, drone-based surveillance systems, etc., also use computer vision techniques.

Computer vision is the heart of **augmented reality apps** that detect physical objects in real-time to place virtual objects within the physical environment. For example, when you use apps like Snapchat, you can place your image on any background, you can put any hair-style, facial features (eyes, lips, ears, etc), accessories (earings, hairbands, lipstick, etc) and a lot more.

Many agricultural organizations use computer vision techniques to **monitor the harvest** (Fig. 3.14) and solve common agricultural problems including weed emergence or nutrient deficiency. Images collected from satellites, drones, or planes are processed by computer vision algorithms to **detect potential problems** in the early phase, thereby avoiding unnecessary losses at a later stage.

Self-driving cars (like Tesla) use computer vision to learn from their surroundings. Every smart vehicle

Figure 3.14   Use of computer vision for crop harvesting

has cameras to capture videos from different angles. These videos act as an input to the computer vision software that processes them to detect objects like road marking, pedestrians or other cars, traffic lights, etc.

Websites like Facebook perform **content moderation** using computer vision techniques. Billions of posts by users every day are reviewed and any images/videos that contain violence, extremism or pornography are immediately removed.

Ninety percent of medical data is present in the form of images. So, most of the diseases can be easily diagnosed by processing images available in the form of **X-rays, MRI, mammography**, etc. For example, computer vision algorithms can detect diabetic retinopathy (Fig. 3.15), which is the most prevalent cause of blindness. Going further, these algorithms can also process pictures of the back of the eye, detect diseases (if any) and rate their severity. Computer vision algorithms can even detect cancer with much higher precision than human doctors.

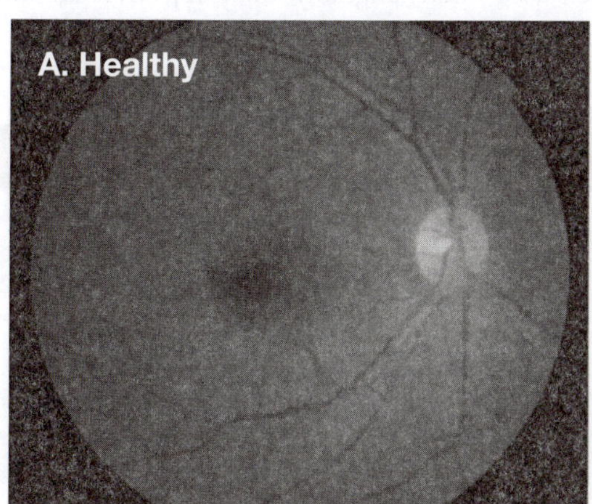

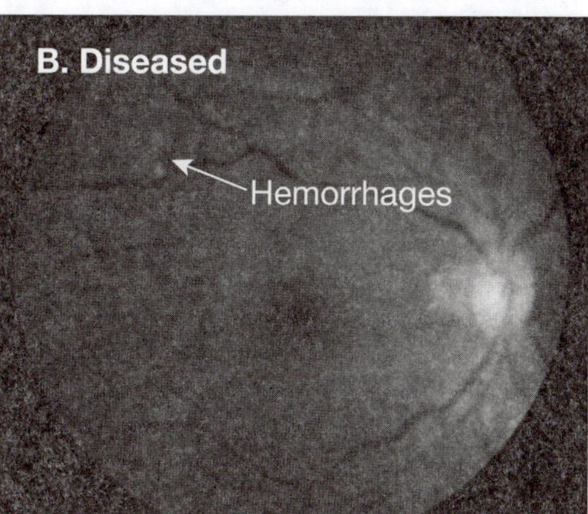

Figure 3.15   Use of computer vision software in medical imaging

How Computer Vision Algorithms Work

Computer vision applications recognize things in photographs by using the following techniques.

Object Classification to identify the broad category of object in the photograph. (For example, a human or an animal)

Object Identification to classify the type of a given object in the photograph. (For example, a cat or a dog).

Object Verification to confirm the presence of object in the photograph. (For example, to detect whether any dog is there in an image or not).

Object Detection to locate the objects in the photograph. (For example, if a dog is present, then the position at which it is present).

Object Landmark Detection to understand the key points for the object in the photograph. (For example, to identify the main features of the dog).

Object Segmentation to enumerate the pixels that belong to the object in the image.

Object Recognition identifies objects and their position/location in the photograph. It is a combination of object identification and detection techniques.

To better realize the application of computer vision, play the game **Emoji Scavenger Hunt.**

3.6.3 Natural Language Processing (NLP)

Every computer programming language has its own syntax, semantics and keywords. However, the aim of NLP is to develop systems that work on natural human language. For this, every NLP system has two main components:

Natural Language Understanding (NLU) is used to analyze different aspects of language. For this, the connection between spoken or written language and natural language is understood to know what the words represent.

Natural Language Generation (NLG) that helps users to produce meaningful phrases and sentences along with Text Planning, Sentence Planning, and Text Realization.

Example: The movie is not that good.

The movie is too good to be seen on a small screen.

Note that in both the sentences word 'good' is used for the movie, but in an altogether different context. While the first sentence conveys a negative review, the second portrays a positive feedback. So, the same word(s) can be used in multiple contexts and NLP system must differentiate between the contexts to understand the true meaning behind an input given in natural language.

Speech and Voice Recognition

The power of NLP lies in its ability to perform speech and voice recognition. Both these recognition techniques are extensively used in robotics. Though the two terms are often used interchangeably, their objectives are different, as illustrated in Table 3.3.

Table 3.3   Difference between speech and voice recognition

Speech Recognition	Voice Recognition
Aims to understand and comprehend **WHAT** was spoken.	Aims to recognize **WHO** is speaking.
Used in hands-free computing or in navigating through a map or menu.	Used to identify a person by analyzing the tone, voice pitch, and accent, etc.
Speech recognition system is speaker independent.	Voice recognition system is speaker dependent.
Such systems are difficult to develop.	These systems are comparatively easy to develop.

Despite the underlying differences, both speech and voice recognition systems take input from a microphone that goes to sound card of the system. The sound card converts analog signal into its equivalent digital signal for processing. A database is used to compare sound patterns to recognize the words, which are then passed as input to the Translation Engine, to be finally converted into the target language (Fig. 3.16).

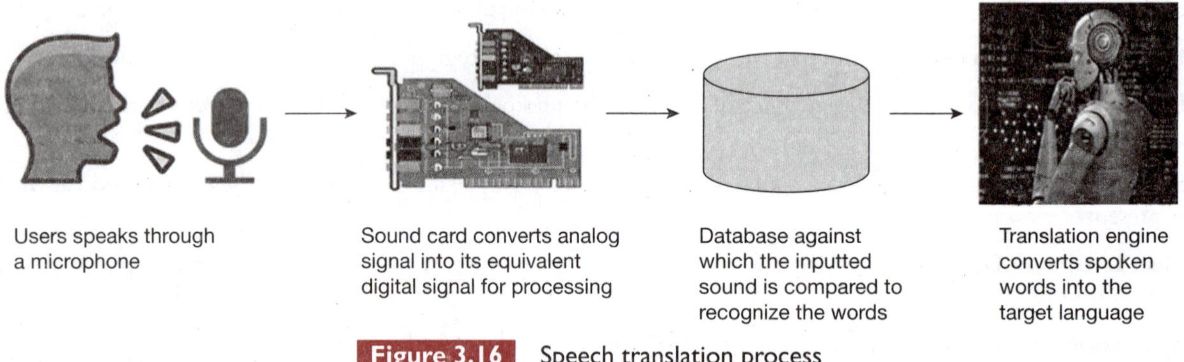

Figure 3.16   Speech translation process

To understand NLP, play the game **Mystery Animals**. To visualize how NLP systems understand, play **Go** game. To anticipate how NLP systems generate and translate language, play Chess and **Checkers** game respectively.

3.7   WAVES OF ARTIFICIAL INTELLIGENCE

The chronology of AI can be better understood by looking at the four waves that mark the beginning of a new area in the field of artificial intelligence (Fig. 3.17). The first three waves have been described by DARPA's John Launchbury and refers to the state of artificial intelligence capabilities in the past, present and in future. We have added another wave as the fourth wave to account for what, many believe, will be the ultimate phase of AI.

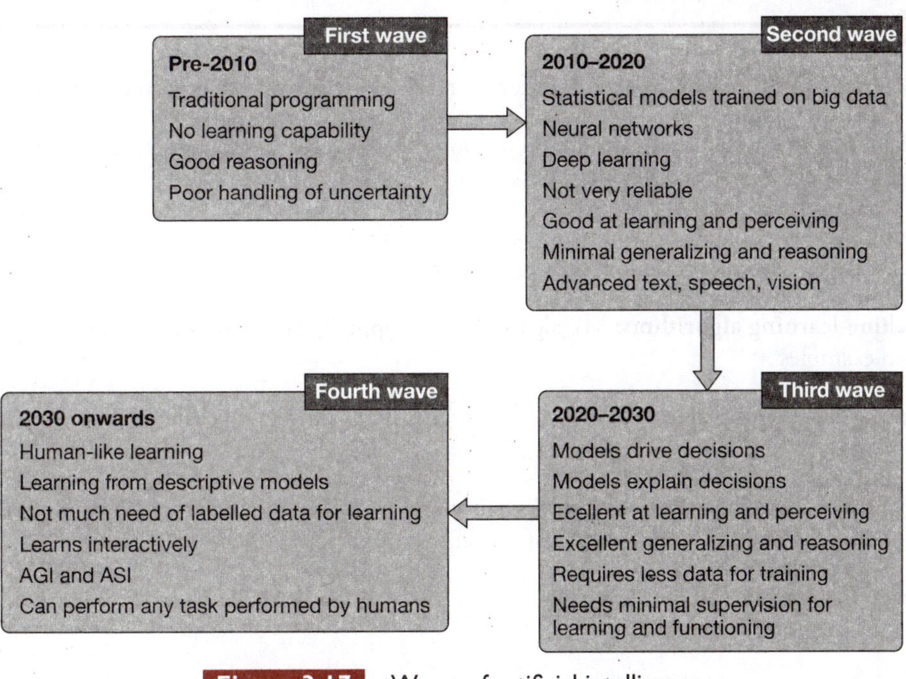

Figure 3.17   Waves of artificial intelligence

First Wave: In the first wave, traditional programming was used to program computers. Data and programs were fed to get the desirable output. At this time, machines had no IQ to learn by themselves.

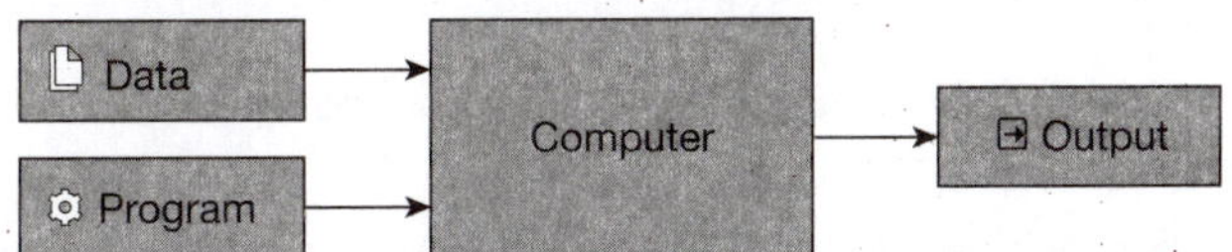

Second Wave: In this wave, statistical learning models were used on enormous amount of data to make the machines learn, create clusters of similar data, predict values and make decisions. In this phase, neural networks and deep learning techniques, advanced text, speech and vision technology were used to make the machines good at reasoning and perceiving details. For this, data and output were fed into the computer and the underlying program to generate the given output was produced by the computer.

Third Wave: This phase talks about the present era. It constantly tries to make machines understand and perceive the world on its own without relying entirely on data to learn from it. Intelligent machines in this era would be excellent at learning, reasoning, generalizing, perceiving and explaining decisions. The computer will be given a goal and the AI will generate the entire program to achieve that goal.

Fourth Wave: The Fourth Wave of AI can be thought of as an advancement of the third wave that has common sense and understands ethics to make decisions based on ethics, regulations, and law to avoid its misuse.

Key Terms

Artificial Intelligence (AI): Intelligence demonstrated by machines that help them to mimic the actions of humans.

Neural network: A series of nodes that capture the relationship between various underlying variables to process the data and give the final output.

Machine Learning (ML): A branch of computer science that analyzes data and identifies patterns to teach a machine to deduce results and make decisions without any human intervention.

Supervised machine-learning algorithms: ML algorithms that apply learning from past data (or experiences) to new data using labeled examples

Unsupervised machine-learning algorithms: ML Algorithms that train the machine using information that is neither classified nor labeled

Deep Learning (DL): An ML technique that teaches a machine to process inputs through a huge neural network with several layers of processing units to accurately classify, infer and predict the outcome.

Natural Language Processing (NLP): A science in which a machine is made to read, understand, interpret and respond to a human language.

Computer Vision: A branch of AI that tries to understand an image by breaking it down into several parts and then studying each part of the image.

Chapter Highlights

- Narrow or Weak AI performs a dedicated task with intelligence. But it cannot perform any other task as it is specifically trained for that specific task only.

- General AI takes smart decisions without human intervention. As of now, there is no system that falls under this category.

- Super AI or Strong AI is a level of intelligence of systems at which machines could surpass human intelligence. The main aim here is to make machines use their cognitive properties to perform any task better than humans

- Reactive machines focus on current scenarios and react on it in the best possible way.

Review Questions

1. Define Artificial Intelligence.

2. List some factors that have caused tremendous surge in AI applications.

3. Differentiate between the following:

   a. Narrow AI and Strong AI.

   b. Supervised and Unsupervised Learning

   c. Speech Recognition and Voice Recognition

4. Give some advantages and disadvantages of using AI systems.

5. What is a neural network?

6. Explain the significance of machine learning in context of AI applications.

7. Why is deep learning better than machine learning?

8. What do you understand by the term 'computer vision'? How is it useful?

9. Write a short note on waves of AI.

10. Identify the domain of AI used in the following applications:

    a. Number plate detection ____

    b. Email spam filter   ____

    c. Google translator   ____

    d. Google photos   ____

    e. Emoji scavenger hunt   ____

Fill in the Blanks

1. AI applications process large amounts of data to identify ________ in it.

2. ________ AI performs a dedicated task with intelligence.

3. ________ layer in a neural network applies weights, biases and thresholds.

4. ML algorithms learn from __________ rather than __________.

5. Unsupervised learning finds patterns and relationships in the dataset by creating __________.

6. In __________ propagation, output from the previous input layer is processed and the results are passed to the next hidden layer.

7. __________ is a branch of AI that tries to understand an image by breaking it down into several parts and then studying each part of the image.

8. ________ processing units provide heavy computing power required for iterative processing and training neural networks.

9. ________ generate massive amounts of data from connected devices.

10. ______ is the backbone of any AI system.

11. ________ recognition technique is used in hands-free computing or in navigating through a map or menu.

12. Both speech and voice recognition systems take input from a ________ that goes to the __________ of the system.

13. "Give the goal and AI system will give you program" is a feature of the ______ wave of AI.

State True or False

1. AI simulates natural intelligence in machines.

2. Strong AI can perform only a specific task.

3. IBM's Deep Blue that defeated Garry Kasparov is a reactive machine.

4. AI systems do not make decisions based on emotions, compassion and empathy.

5. Supervised learning should be used when output of data in the training set is known.

6. In forward propagation, the weights assigned to each node is updated and passed to the previous layer.

7. *Manan is too smart to do that theft*, creates a positive image about him.

8. Speech recognition aims to recognize WHO is speaking.

9. In the first wave of AI, statistical learning models were used on enormous amount of data to make the machines learn, create clusters of similar data, predict values and make decisions.

10. Machine Learning and NLP are sub-domains of Artificial Intelligence.

11. You must acquire advanced skills to create AI applications.

12. Open-ended AI systems do not exist, so far.

13. AI is a sub-field of Robotics.

14. We can expect a large number of IoT devices to be used worldwide due to increased use of 4G internet.

15. Narrow AI is still in the R&D stage.

16. Weak AI systems mimic human intelligence.

17. It is easier to analyze unstructured data than analyzing structured data.

Multiple Choice Questions

1. AI applications can __________.
   a. recognize objects
   b. understand human language
   c. solve real-world problems
   d. All of these.

2. Which of the following statements about Strong AI is correct?
   a. It works with a limited pre-defined range of functions.
   b. The best example of Strong AI is an NLP based chatbot.
   c. As of now, there is no strong AI application.
   d. Siri and Alexa are based on strong AI.

3. Manufacturing robots, drones, email spam filters, social media monitoring tools, all use ______ AI.
   a. Strong
   b. Weak
   c. General
   d. All of these.

4. ______ machines focus on current scenarios and react on it in the best possible way.
   a. Reactive
   b. Theory-of-mind
   c. Limited Memory
   d. Self-awareness

5. Self-driving cars use __________ AI.
   a. Reactive
   b. Theory-of-mind
   c. Limited Memory
   d. Self-awareness

6. A neural network can have any number of ________ layers.
   a. input
   b. output
   c. hidden
   d. neural

7. Deep learning works with __________ learning.
   a. supervised
   b. unsupervised
   c. Both of these.
   d. None of these.

8. _______________ involves acquiring images, processing them, analyzing them and finally understanding the information they are conveying.
   a. NLP
   b. Machine Learning
   c. Image Analysis
   d. Computer Vision

9. Which of the following company produces self-driving cars?
   a. Tesla   b. Amazon
   c. Adobe   d. Microsoft

10. Face recognition uses __________ techniques.
    a. Speech Recognition   b. Voice Recognition
    c. Image Processing   d. Computer Vision

11. Object ____________ locates the objects in the photograph.
    a. Identification   b. Detection
    c. Verification   d. Classification

12. Sheena is exaggerative, but not a liar, creates a __________ image about her.
    a. positive   b. negative
    c. Both of these.   d. Difficult to say.

13. Data- and program-generated output is a characteristic of which wave of AI?
    a. First   b. Second
    c. Third   d. Fourth

14. Which of the following is not a sub-domain of AI?
    a. Machine Learning   b. Deep Learning
    c. Neural Networks   d. Python Programming

15. ________ will surpass human intelligence.
    a. Narrow AI   b. Strong AI
    c. Super Intelligent Systems   d. Robots

16. A Weak AI system cannot work with which type of data?
    a. Audio   b. Video
    c. Image   d. None of these.

Identify the Applications that Use Artificial Intelligence

1. An information retrieval system that searches 1000 pages and highlights all the words on which search was made.

2. An information retrieval system that can searches 1000 pages and summarizes the content in just 10 pages.

3. CCTV cameras that records an important event in an eminent monument of historical importance.

4. A video camera-based security system that captures videos and performs automated identification of people based on their face.

5. A smart attendance system that records students' attendance using their biometric features, stores the attendance for the entire month and makes it available to be viewed any time by the teacher.

6. An attendance system that predicts student's performance and attendance based on data of the past few months.

7. WordPad that allows users to type letters and other important documents.

8. Gmail that notifies users about an incorrect spelling(s) or grammatical mistake(s) and suggests correction(s) and text that can be typed next.

Fun Activity – Emoji Scavenger Hunt

Identify emojis in the real world with your phone's camera. Use the following link to go to the website https://experiments.withgoogle.com/emoji-scavenger. Emoji Scavenger Hunt is an experiment that leverages the power of neural networks and your phone's camera to identify the real-world versions of the emojis we use every day.

The AI Game – Rock, Paper, Scissors

In the game of Rock, Paper, Scissors, each player picks one of the three objects. The challenge of the game is to guess what the opponent has selected and then pick an object to beat him/her. To beat the opponent, remember the following points.

Several rounds of the game are played. Usually, people use previous choices to guess what their opponent will do next. It is hard for humans to pick up a sequence of perfectly random choices, so any pattern that a player develops could be learned by the opponent and used to win the game.

For example, if out of 10, 7 times the opponent selected paper, then it is likely that the opponent will be using paper more frequently.

Paper wraps (beats) Rock   **Scissors cut (beat) Paper**   **Rock blunts (beats) Scissors**

You can visualize the playing of this game on the link given below. http://www.cs.stir.ac.uk/~kms/schools/rps/index.php

The computer keeps track of the choices the user makes and always picks the action to beat the one that the user is most likely to pick.

The AI Game – Mystery Animal

Mystery Animal Game is a very interesting game in which the computer pretends to be an animal and the user tries to guess it by using his/her voice.

Rule 1: Users can only ask Yes-No questions such as 'Are you a reptile?" or 'Do you have feathers?', "Can you swim?", "Are you a carnivore?", "Are you a mammal"

Rule 2: Users have to guess the animal in 20 questions.

Visit the link to play the game. https://mysteryanimal.withgoogle.com/

Project Work

Write down about any five software that makes extensive use of AI.

Role Play Activity

1. Choose an AI or any sub-domain of AI and then speak for at least 5 minutes in front of the class highlighting the selected topic's relevance in real-world.

2. Choose any AI-powered device and then introduce its capabilities to other students.

AI Lab Session – Talk to Transformer

AI text generator tool, **Talk to Transformer** is used to create human-like text by predicting the next word from the 40 GB Internet data (around 8 million web pages). The tool extensively uses Neural Network and NLP techniques (more specifically NLG) by learning from the data and by predicting the context of the previous data. Users just have to type a single line of text and the tool will in turn generate multiple results based on the prediction of what is already written.

Visit the URL, https://app.inferkit.com/demo. Select a topic by clicking the down arrow and see the multiple results you get. Just read the story. You will feel as if it had been written by humans only.

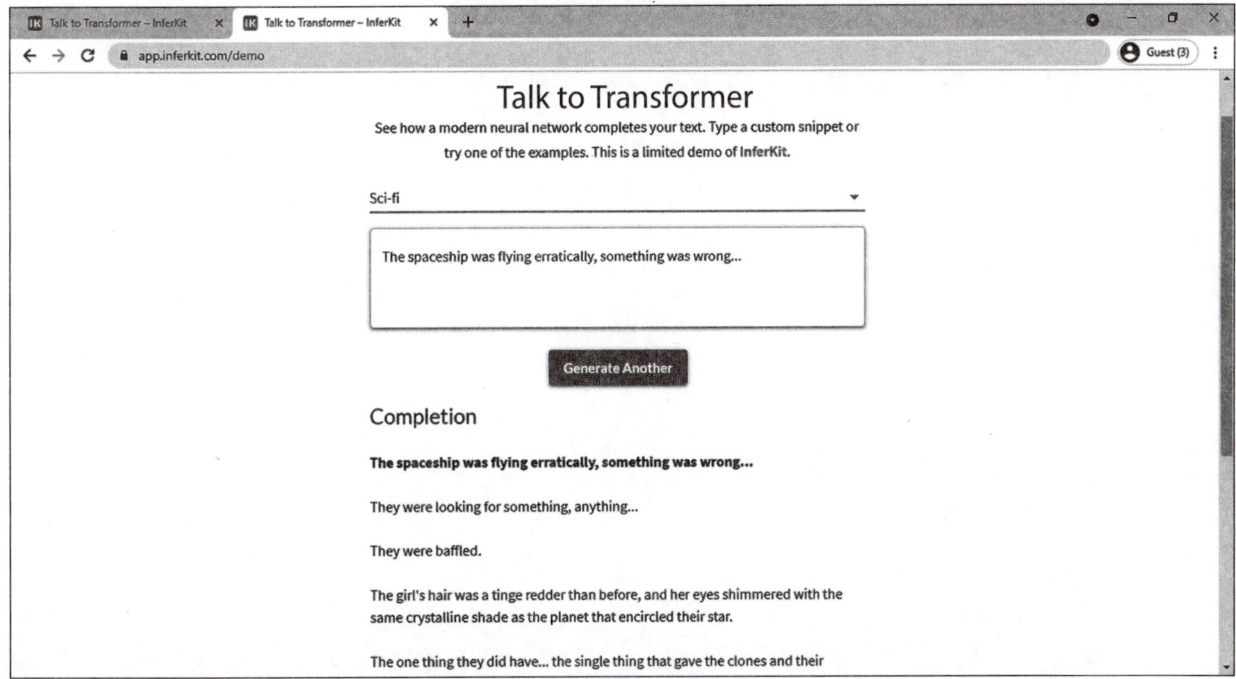

Answers

Fill in the Blanks

1. patterns
2. Narrow or Weak
3. Hidden
4. experiences, instructions
5. clusters
6. forward
7. Computer Vision
8. Graphical
9. Internet of Things
10. Data
11. Speech
12. microphone, sound card
13. third

State True or False

1. True
2. False
3. True
4. True
5. True
6. False
7. False
8. False
9. False
10. True
11. True
12. True
13. False
14. False
15. False
16. True
17. False

Multiple Choice Questions

1. d
2. c
3. b
4. a
5. c
6. c
7. c
8. d
9. a
10. d
11. b
12. d
13. a
14. d
15. c
16. d

Identify the Applications that Use Artificial Intelligence

1. No AI
2. AI
3. No AI
4. AI
5. No AI
6. AI
7. No AI
8. AI

Applications of Artificial Intelligence   4

Now that we have familiarized ourselves with Artificial Intelligence, let us now take a closer look at how this technology is being used in today's world. AI is being widely used in:

- Health care systems
- Fraud detection
- Identifying fake news
- Automatic stock trading
- Face, voice, hand-writing recognition
- Education, robotics and military applications
- Building smart cities
- Flying drones

4.1   UTILIZATION OF ARTIFICIAL INTELLIGENCE

Artificial Intelligence is widely being used by companies to improve their process efficiencies, automate resource-heavy tasks, and to make business predictions by analyzing data. Today, data is all around us. Especially with the Internet of Things (IoT) and sensors collecting every bit of data and possessing the ability to harness that data, artificial intelligence (AI) can be extensively used to learn interesting patterns in the data and automate tasks for a variety of business benefits. Some of them are discussed below.

Automating Repetitive Tasks

AI automates repetitive learning and discovery through data. But AI is different from hardware-driven, robotic automation. While a robot automates manual tasks, AI can be used to perform frequent, high-volume, computerized tasks reliably without fatigue. In such a system, human intervention is still required to set up the system.

Adding Intelligence to Existing Products

AI is not usually sold as an individual application; rather, it is used within existing products to improve their capabilities. For example, Siri was added as a feature to a new generation of Apple products. Automation, bots and smart machines can be used at home and in the workplace for anything ranging from security intelligence to investment analysis.

Example: Consider an AI-based application that predicts a student's marks in the final exams based on certain facts. Such a system can help the student to know how much more hard work needs to be put in to get the expected results (Fig. 4.1).

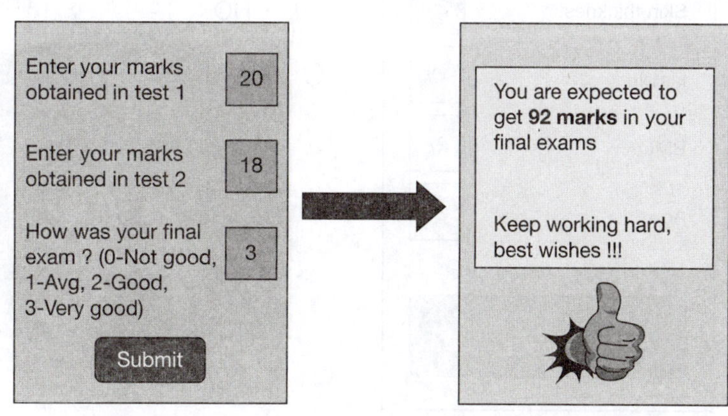

A simple AI application that asks a student to enter marks obtained in two class tests and how he/she did his/her final exam to predict the marks that can be expected in the final exam.

Figure 4.1   AI-based application to predict a student's marks in the final exams

Fraud Detection

AI analyzes tons of data using neural networks and deep neural networks with multiple hidden layers to detect fraud and other unwanted activity. The more data you feed to an AI system, the more accurate they become (Fig. 4.2).

AI systems do all their work with incredible accuracy using deep neural networks. For example, your interactions with Alexa, Google Search and Google Photos are all based on deep learning. In the medical field, deep learning, image classification and object recognition, which are all part of AI techniques, are used to find cancer on MRIs with the same accuracy as highly trained radiologists.

AI Gets the Most Out of Data

When we use self-learning techniques, the data itself becomes intellectual property. Huge volumes of data are rigorously analyzed to extract otherwise hidden useful information and create a competitive advantage. In any industry, a company having best data wins despite tough competition.

Healthcare

In the healthcare industry, AI systems are used to analyze the patient's information efficiently. They are also used in non-emergency situations in which patients can use AI systems to analyze their symptoms and assess if there is a need for medical attention (Fig. 4.3). This not only helps the patient but also reduces the pressure on medical professionals by forwarding only critical cases to them.

Assisted Diagnosis

Using techniques like computer vision and neural networks, AI systems can easily interpret information from MRI scan reports to check for tumors and other malignant growths, with almost same accuracy but at a much faster pace than a radiologist.

Figure 4.2   Data analysis using AI for fraud detection

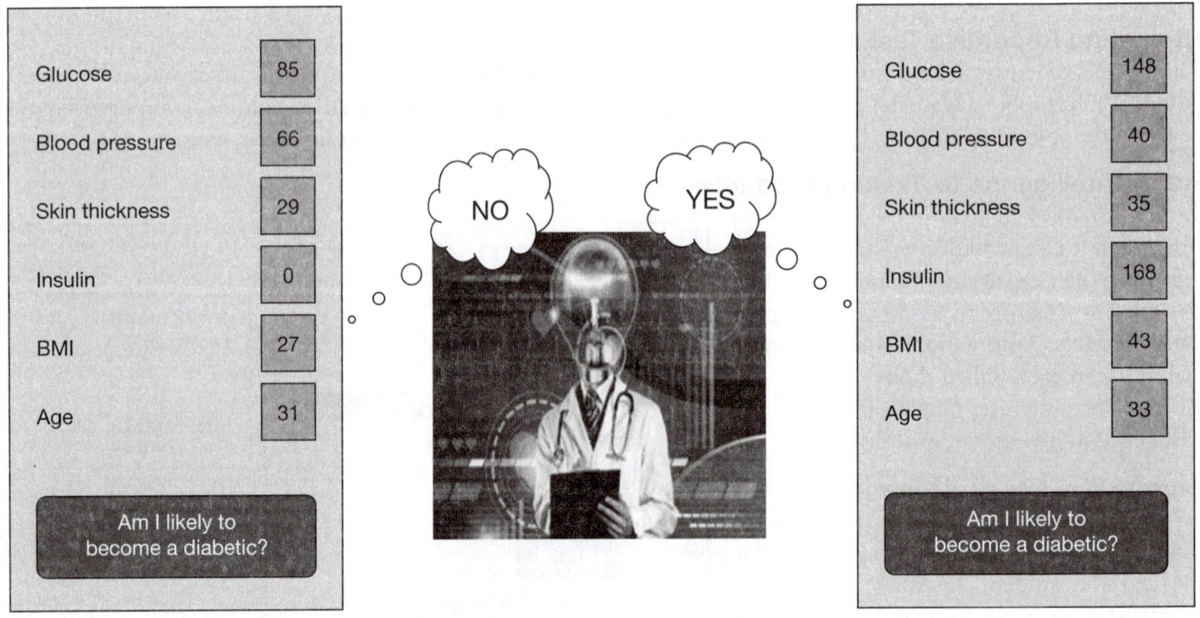

Figure 4.3   AI systems in healthcare

Robot-assisted Surgery

Robots, when used for doing surgeries, can perform their task very precisely with negligible margin of error round-the-clock without getting tired. Robotic surgeries not only reduce the time to conduct a surgery but also reduce the amount of time spent by patients to recover after a surgery.

Wearable Health-monitoring Gadgets

A person's state of health is an ongoing process, and it needs to be continuously monitored. For this, wearable devices that are continuously collecting and analyzing this data are available on the market. They can predict health fluctuations even before the patient is aware about some serious illness within his/her body and can even save lives in critical cases.

E-commerce

In e-commerce, AI techniques are extensively used for recommending products/services. Even social networking sites use it to recommend friends or useful connections to a user. Companies are also using AI to predict demand for different products at different times of the year so that companies can efficiently manage their stocks to meet the demand. They also use AI to create targeted recruitment ads and predict an applicant's suitability to the company. AI-powered employment services help job seekers to explore the opportunities available in various avenues (Fig. 4.4).

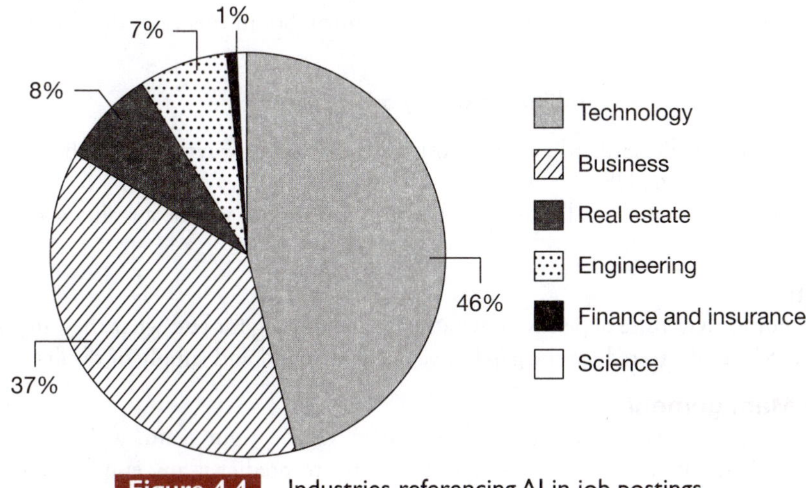

Figure 4.4   Industries referencing AI in job postings

Chatbots

You must have noticed that these days almost every website has an assistant program that greets the user and prompts for help. These AI-based systems are known as chatbots. Chatbots are specifically embedded to serve customers during odd-hours and peak hours, thereby reducing the workload of limited human resources.

Filtering Spam and Fake Reviews

Websites like Amazon get a very high number of reviews and some of them may be fakes and thus need to be filtered. At times, it is impossible for humans to do this job. But using NLP, AI systems can scan these reviews to identify suspicious activities and filter them to provide a better buyer experience.

Today's virus and spam detection software also use deep neural networks to detect new types of virus and spam with great speed and high accuracy.

Speech Recognition

Also known as speech-to-text (STT), this AI technology recognizes spoken words and converts them to digitized text. Such software is used in computer dictation apps, TV voice remotes, voice-enabled text messaging, GPS, and voice-driven phone-answering menus.

Automated Stock Trading

AI is used to optimize stock portfolios. An AI system can make thousands or even millions of trades per day without human intervention.

Ride-share Services

Uber, Lyft, and other ride-share services use AI techniques to help passengers collaborate with drivers to minimize wait times and even eliminate the need for surge pricing during peak hours.

Autopilot Technology

Autopilot technology using AI is being used for flying commercial and military aircraft. Autopilot aircrafts use sensors, GPS technology, image recognition techniques, collision avoidance technology, robotics, and natural language processing to guide an aircraft safely through the skies.

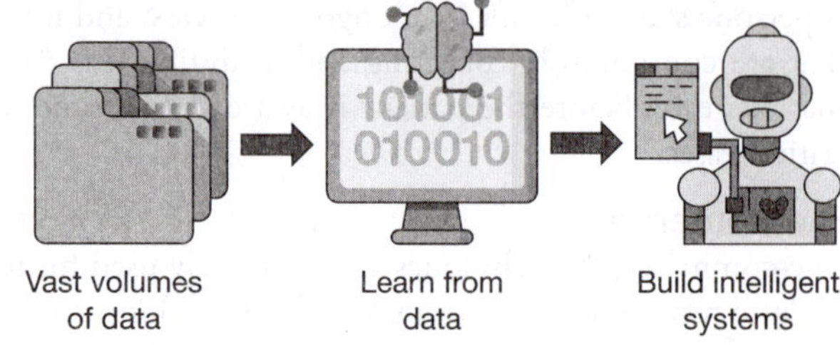

Advanced navigation systems not only save time but also adapt to the changing conditions in the ocean, which might be dangerous for cargo ships.

Automated Transportation

In automated transportation many options are available to the users. For example, AI can be used to drive the car in the absence of a driver. **Tesla's AutoPilot** and **Nissan's ProPilot,** both provide the steering, acceleration and braking systems. However, in case of failure, the driver needs to take control. So, in this case, the driver needs to be alert and keep an eye on the road.

Audi's A8L can take up full driving responsibility in slow-moving traffic.

Fully self-driven cars can drive independently without any driver. Google's Waymo project has come up with one such car, which is already operating in the US.

Autonomous transportation requiring absolutely no human interaction will be a reality soon. **Robotic taxi** is one such project.

Optimizing Search

The success of any e-commerce website depends on what users are looking for and what they are able to find. AI techniques can optimize search results to reduce the gap between the demand and supply of results.

Human Resource Management

AI is used to analyze employee data to place the right talent in the right team, assign projects based on their competencies, collect feedback about the workplace, and even try to predict if any employee is thinking of quitting the company.

Using NLP, an AI system can easily scan thousands of CVs in just few seconds to shortlist really good candidates. This can be done without any human errors or biases thereby shortening the length of hiring cycles.

Robotics

AI has helped man to innovate and improve the design and capabilities of robots. Robots in AI have found applications across verticals and industries in the manufacturing and packaging industries. For example, robots are now used for the following jobs:

> Speedfactory is an entirely robot-enabled manufacturing plant. It aims to reduce errors in manufacturing and shipping time. Companies like Faulhaber MICROMO, USA, have even started working on robots that could diffuse bombs.

In Assembly-related Jobs: AI along with computer vision techniques are used to make the robots learn which path is best for a certain process while it is performing its operation.

Robots providing **Customer Service** use NLP to interact with customers just like humans.

AI enabled robots are used in **Packaging Industry** to enable quicker, cheaper, and more accurate packaging. Movements of robots to do a particular task can be optimized to achieve best performance.

Bitmojis and Criminal Identification

A bitmoji is a personalized cartoon avatar that is created to look just like the user. The bitmoji app translates an image to a cartoon that has similar properties to the image (Fig. 4.5). When working with this app, you can either choose to use your or any other person's face photo to translate it into an emoji or can choose only the eyes, nose, lips, etc.

This technique has also been proved useful in criminal identification. The eyewitnesses or policemen can create an avatar of the criminal. This is far simpler and more accurate than creating regular sketches. Moreover, with this technique any cartoon avatar can be translated into a photo again, which looks closely like the face.

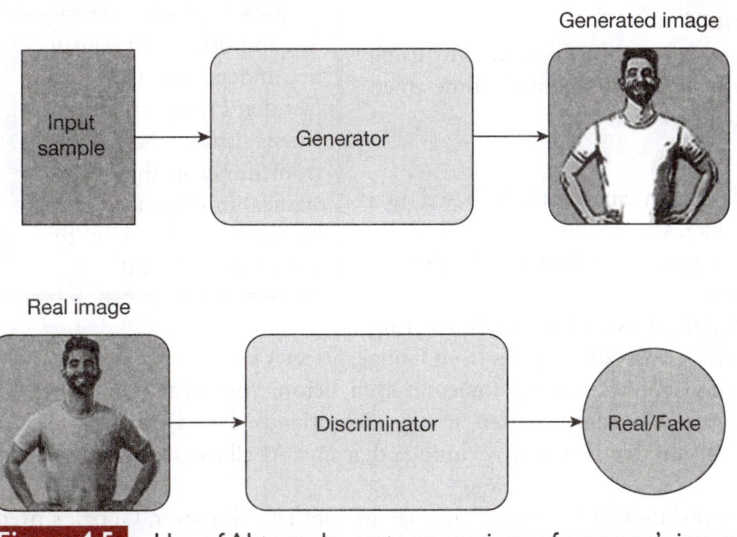

Figure 4.5   Use of AI to make cartoon versions of a person's image

Battlefield Surveillance

AI can be used to get updated information about hostile zones for a military response, especially when getting such updates are difficult owing to high danger. For example, AI-operated drones are already used to provide instant alerts when they notice an anomaly or even to conduct pre-emptive strikes.

Movie Industry

Science fiction movies use Artificial Intelligence to a great extent (Fig. 4.6). The first movie portraying AI as a movie character was a German movie Metropolis released in 1927. Since then, AI characters like HAL: 9000 from 2001: A Space Odyssey (1968), the Skynet from the Terminator series or Ultron from Avengers: Age of Ultron (2015) have been raising concerns of people regarding this technology.

Figure 4.6   AI in science fiction movies

However, some AI characters loved by people for their mannerisms, helpful nature, good deeds and pleasing personalities include R2-D2 and C-3PO from the Star Wars series and WALL-E from the movie WALL-E (2008).

Ghost in a Shell, an animated movie released in 1995 having fictional characters changed how people viewed AI and their possible synergy with humans. Similarly, I, Robot, released in 2005, showed billions of AI-operated robots acting as personal and public servants. Though these robots were built on the 'three principles of AI' that prevented them from harming humans, the outcome was not what was perceived.

Education

These days, students can be educated by AI teacher robots. Such a technology has proved very beneficial for visually challenged students, who can learn using voice assistants.

AI techniques can be used to monitor a student's performance at regular intervals and also recommend content based on past experience.

Disaster Management

The havoc created by disasters can be minimized by using AI to get constant alarm alerts right from the time when even a minute potential risk is detected.

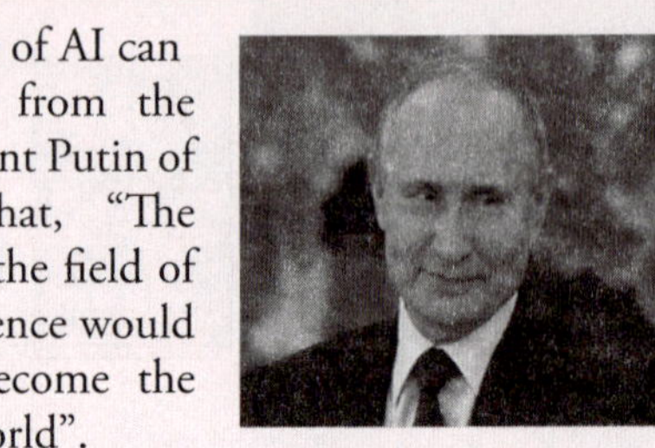

The importance of AI can be understood from the fact that President Putin of Russia said that, "The fronttunner in the field of artifical intelligence would be likely to become the leader of the world".

Besides this,

- Robots are used to perform **custom tasks**, based on a specific application like, say, small-scale agriculture
- Smart computer systems can easily **detect forgery** as compared to humans.
- Researchers from Stanford use AI to **predict voting behavior** in elections by analyzing images from Google Street View.
- Facebook knows when you are dating someone even before you write something about it on the platform. Facebook also automatically suggests users to tag their friends, based on their facial features in their images. Similarly, Amazon's **predictive shipping** technique that uses AI allows it to send you a package before you know you want it.
- Google uses AI to **translate text** from one language to another. Moreover, Google's **predictive search algorithm** keeps a track of data entered by a user in the past to predict what the user would type next in the search bar. Similarly, Netflix uses past data to recommend what movie a user might want to see next. This knowledge helps the website to hook the user onto the platform to increase watch time.
- Even **plagiarism checkers and tools** use AI to identify text that is taken from other websites, books or any other sources.
- Scientists use AI to design robots that can provide **medical care to senior citizens**.

4.2   ROBOTICS – AN APPLICATION OF AI

Robotics is a branch of engineering that involves the conception, design, manufacture, and operation of robots. It is an inter-disciplinary field that includes the study of electronics, computer science, artificial intelligence, mechatronics, nanotechnology and bioengineering.

Science-fiction author Isaac Asimov, had first used the term robotics in the year 1940s. According to him, robots must,

Rule 1: Never harm humans.
Rule 2: Always follow instructions from humans without violating rule 1.
Rule 3: Protect themselves without violating the other rules.

Some important aspects of robot include:

- They have electrical components for providing power and controlling the machinery.
- They have mechanical construction and their shape or design depends on the task they are intended to accomplish.
- They are programmed. Instructions fed to them help them to determine what, when and how it would do something.

These days, robots are being extensively designed as bots that explore Earth's harshest conditions and assist in almost every facet of healthcare. Though the robotics industry is still evolving, we already have robots that work in regions from the deepest depths of our oceans to the highest reaches of outer space. They are being used to do everything that humans, in the recent past, could not dream of doing.

4.2.1 Types of Robots

Pre-programmed Robots operate in a controlled environment to perform simple, monotonous tasks. For example, a mechanical arm on an automotive assembly line that is used to weld a door, or insert a certain part into the engine. This type of robot can perform repetitive tasks for long hours, faster and more efficiently than a human.

Humanoid Robots look like humans and/or mimic human behaviour. They can perform human-like activities (like running, jumping and carrying objects). Sophia and Atlas are two popular examples of humanoid robots.

Autonomous Robots operate without human operators. They are designed to perform tasks in open environments that do not require human supervision. For example, the Roomba vacuum cleaner uses sensors to roam freely throughout a home to clean it.

> Robots are also used for tasks varying from diffusing bombs to performing surgeries. VR Robots are also becoming popular these days.

Tele-operated Robots are mechanical bots controlled by humans. They are used in extreme geographical conditions, weather circumstances, etc. For example, human-controlled submarines used to fix underwater pipe leaks during the BP oil spill or drones used to detect landmines on a battlefield are examples of tele-operated robots.

Augmenting Robots either enhance current human capabilities or replace the capabilities a human may have lost. Robotic prosthetic limbs or exoskeletons used to lift hefty weights are examples of such robots.

4.2.2 Applications of Robotics

* Helping fight forest fires
* Assisting humans in manufacturing plants (known as co-bots)
* Provide companionship to elderly people
* Work as surgical assistants
* Deliver food order or other packages
* Perform household tasks like vacuuming and mowing the grass
* Locate and transfer items in warehouses
* Perform search-and-rescue missions after natural disasters
* Landmine detectors in war zones

Industry-wise applications can be given as, Manufacturing industry is amongst the first well-known user of robots. They use robots and co-bots (bots that work alongside humans) to efficiently test and assemble products like cars and industrial machinery.

Logistics **companies** use robots in their warehouses to perform tasks like shipping, handling goods and ensuring quality control. Robots are supposed to take items off the shelves, transport them across the warehouse floor and package them. They are now also used for last-mile delivery of packages for faster and efficient delivery.

Self-driving cars are a result of integrating data science with robotics. Automakers, like Tesla, Ford, Waymo, Volkswagen and BMW, are all working to provide users an ultimate experience of travel that will let them sit back, relax and enjoy the ride. Companies such as Uber and Lyft are also developing autonomous rideshare vehicles that will be operated without humans.

Healthcare industry uses robots to perform complicated surgeries, and deliver everything from medicines to clean linens.

Space Agencies like NASA uses robots in different ways. Robotic arms on spacecraft can move large objects in space. Robotic spacecraft can visit other worlds like the moon or Mars. For example, Mars rovers Spirit and Opportunity are robots. Cassini studies Saturn and its moons and rings. Robots like The Voyager and Pioneer spacecraft are now traveling beyond our solar system. People on earth use computers to send messages to the spacecraft. The robots have antennas that pick up the message commands and work as per the instructions given to it.

Robotic airplanes can fly without a pilot aboard. NASA is also developing robotic astronauts (robonaut) to help people in space (Fig. 4.7). The upper body of robonauts looks like a person. It has a chest, head and arms. They can work outside a spacecraft and work like an astronaut on a spacewalk.

Figure 4.7 Robots used by NASA

NASA is also working on robots that might help an astronaut in an emergency. For example, when an astronaut is seriously hurt, a doctor on Earth could use the robotic arm to perform surgery. This technology can help doctors on Earth, as well. Doctors can help people in faraway places where there are no surgeons to perform complicated surgeries.

Robots are also used as **scouts** to check out new areas to be explored. They take photographs, measure the terrain, look for dangers and find the best places to walk, drive or stop. This not only helps scientists and engineers make better plans for exploring but also helps astronauts to work more safely and quickly. Figure 4.8 shows some poplar robots.

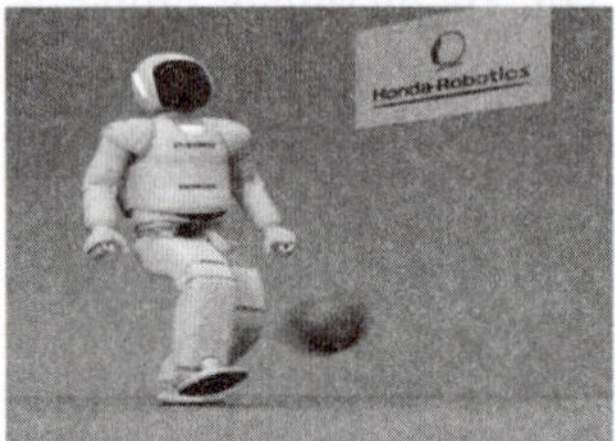

ASIMO is a humanoid that has the ability to recognize moving objects, postures, gestures, understand its environment, and interact with humans.

Pepper is the world's first robot capable of recognizing human emotions. It is social, can converse with people, give them directions and even dance with them.

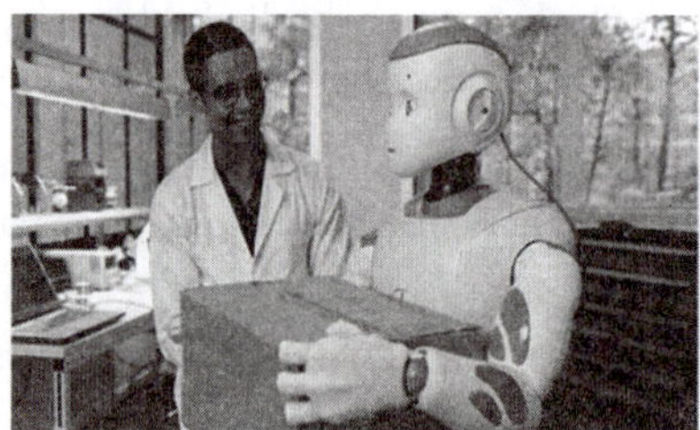

Romeo helps with everyday tasks, assists when people have fallen over, makes conversations and plays games.

Buddy is designed to entertain the family, help you with your everyday activities, offer reminders, provide recipes in the kitchen, make video calls, keep an eye on your home while you are not at home, connect all your smart home devices together and even help your children learn.

Panasonic Robot Egg uses NLP to communicate with you. It's an intelligent assistant that can be controlled by your voice, play video footage via a built-in projector and even engage in interactive games. This robot is Wi-Fi connected and promises software updates in future to improve it further.

REEM is a full-size humanoid service robot that can act as a receptionist, provide entertainment for guests, make presentations and give speeches in different languages and help with a variety of different chores. REEM is able to self-navigate, interact with people it encounters and keep on working for up to eight hours.

Figure 4.8   Present-day robots use Artificial Intelligence to make our lives easier

4.3   DRONES USING AI

The term "drone" generally means any unpiloted aircraft that operates using a combination of technologies including computer vision, artificial intelligence, object avoidance tech, and others. Also known as "Unmanned Aerial Vehicles" (UAVs), these drones can be as large as an aircraft or as small as the palm of your hand (Fig. 4.9). With drones becoming readily accessible, they are now increasingly being used for the most dangerous and high-paying jobs that are discussed below.

Figure 4.9   Drones provide an aerial view of the targeted area and are used for a wide range of applications

Emergency Response: Drones outfitted with thermal imaging cameras are used by emergency response teams to identify victims who are difficult to spot with the naked eye.

Humanitarian Aid and Disaster Relief: During times of natural disaster, drones are used to assess damage, locate victims, and deliver aid (Fig. 4.10). In addition to this, they are also used to prevent disasters altogether.

Surveillance: Drones outfitted with thermal imaging cameras can be used to monitor and combat forest fires. Thermal cameras can measure and detect abnormal forest temperatures. This information can then be used to identify areas that are more prone to forest fires or identify fires just minutes after they begin.

Conservation: Poaching and related activities result in climate change that adversely affects wildlife worldwide. In

Figure 4.10   Use of drones for relief aid

fact, according to the World Wildlife Fund, thousands of species are estimated to become extinct each year. To help combat this trend, conservationists are extensively using drones for geospatial imagery to monitor and track animals to protect our biological ecosystem.

Disease Control: Many infectious diseases spread through animals. In such a scenario, drones can be used to capture and test mosquitoes for infectious disease. This initiative can not only protect local residents, but also prevent epidemics before they begin.

Moreover, drones are also being used in remote areas to provide quick access to vital drugs, medicines and medical equipment. All these initiatives have a profound impact on preventing disease, increasing life expectancy, and raising the general standards of living.

Bomb Detection: Small-sized drones fitted with effective cameras can easily penetrate into constricted spaces to detect live bombs and save lives of thousands of people.

Air Strikes: Drones are used for conducting air strikes. Former US President Barack Obama used drones regularly to attack militants in the tribal areas of Pakistan. While being controlled by the defense personnel, drones can be made to fly around suspected areas to fulfill military operations (Fig. 4.11). However, use of drones for military operations has also raised numerous moral and ethical concerns as they lack accountability and failure to fully grasp the consequences of actions.

Agriculture: Farmers in some advanced countries are extensively using drones to gather data, automate and eliminate redundant processes, and improve efficiency to reduce costs and expand yields. Drones also help farmers to predict their potential harvest.

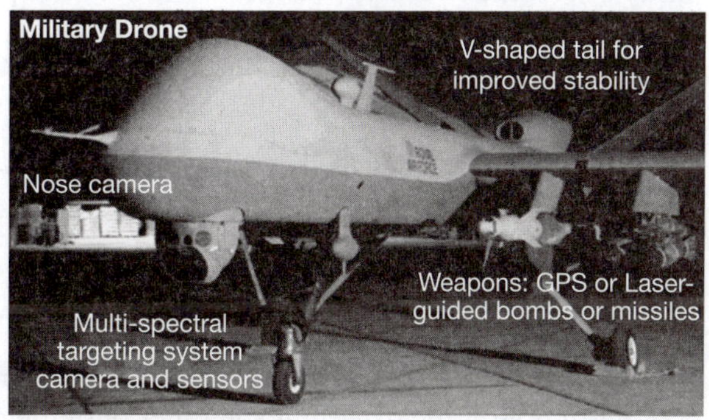

Figure 4.11   Drones in military operations

Weather Forecasting: Scientists are using drones to collect data about temperature, humidity, wind speed and other climatic parameters that could help them to accurately predict future changes to global weather systems. Drones used as autonomous sailboat are used to collect oceanic and atmospheric data from the ocean surface.

Maritime: Drones are used to inspect ships above the surface as well as hulls from below. Countries like the Netherlands, Denmark, and Norway are already using drones to identify ships committing emission infractions.

Waste Management: Drones are being used to clean oceans, collect waste in ports and harbors, and maintain systems for wastewater management.

Energy: Drones are used by energy-generating companies to set up new sites for the production of energy. For this, the drones are made to survey areas and gather topographic detail that can be used to help oil and gas companies identify new drill sites. Drones are also used to extract, refine, and transport oil and gas while ensuring compliance with regulations and standards.

Drones fitted with specialized thermal sensors can detect leaks faster than a human inspector. Even companies generating solar energy can use drones to design configurations for new arrays.

Mining: Mining activities require constant measurement and assessment of stockpiles of ore or rock or minerals. Drones fitted with unique cameras can capture large amounts of data from the air, thereby reducing the risks associated with having surveyors on the ground.

> Drones are being used by the Indian government to deliver COVID vaccine even in the remotest areas.

Construction Planning: Drones are used to improve construction planning, enhance project monitoring and site management. Cameras fitted in these drones monitor buildings and gauge topography and soil type throughout the construction lifecycle (Fig. 4.12).

Urban Planning: With increasing urbanization, cities are overburdened to accommodate more people in the already congested spaces. In such a scenario, urban planning is being done with drones to implement data-driven improvements. For example, drones are used to gather data in populated areas. This data, when analyzed using ML algorithms, can suggest areas that may get benefited from green space or classify the different types of structures and regions on the map.

Personal Transportation: China-based EHANG, was started as an autonomous aerial vehicle (AAV) that operates with 4 rotors (quadcopter) for vertical takeoff. The vehicle is

Figure 4.12   Drones for construction planning

used to help passengers reach their destinations. Such a vehicle is especially very useful in an urban environment with plenty of obstacles. Personal transportation drones require minimal inputs from the passenger and aims to allow safe landings even in case of engine failure or a collision.

Big companies like Uber, Airbus, Boeing, and Rolls-Royce are working on developing flying drones (robotaxis) for ferrying passengers around.

Space: Drones are being used in space science. For example, NASA used drone-like helicopter in its Mars 2020 mission to help look for signs of life on Mars and gather data about the planet's terrain and survey areas the rover cannot reach.

NASA is also using a nuclear-powered drone for exploring Titan — one of Saturn's moons. The drone will arrive on Titan by 2034, autonomously traverse the planet for about 2 years, taking photos and sending data back for analysis.

Telecommunications: Telecommunication towers must be inspected frequently to ensure service reliability. However, this process is too dangerous and time-consuming to do manually. In such a scenario, drones are able to quickly assess damage to help guide repair teams in restoring service.

Internet: Drones are being used to provide Internet access in remote areas and over irregular landforms. For example, Facebook has designed a solar-powered drone called Aquila, to provide Internet access to rural parts of the world. However, in 2018 Facebook halted the use of Aquila and uses only third-party drones instead.

Even SoftBank, in collaboration with the drone manufacturer AeroVironment, is planning to develop drones that will operate in the stratosphere to serve as "floating cell towers" to provide Internet service to customers.

Outdoors: Drones are used outdoors to perform aerial landscape photography and extreme sports footage and map the entire mountain face to help climbers and skiers to better understand the terrain.

Tourism and Hospitality: These days, flying drones providing luxury accommodations can be used to travel to new locations on demand or to remote and traditionally inaccessible locations for guests. They are also being used to deliver packages and room service quickly.

Live Entertainment: Drones are already being used by Disney for entertainment through synchronized light shows, floating projection screens, and as drone puppeteers.

Journalism and News Coverage: News companies are using drones to gather news, especially from areas that are difficult to visit due to safety issues, high costs, or physical barriers. For example, drones are used to get aerial footage of the aftermath of hurricanes and wildfires, and assess flood-ridden areas in many countries.

Food Services: Drones are being used by online food ordering and delivery services for faster and cheaper delivery. This helps restaurants to downsize their physical locations and lower real-estate expenses.

4.4   SMART CITIES

A smart city is a framework that makes extensive use of Information and Communication Technologies (ICT), to develop, deploy, and promote sustainable development practices to cater to growing urbanization issues. ICT increases operational efficiency, shares information with the public and improves both the quality of government services and citizen welfare. This ICT framework is basically an intelligent network of connected objects and machines that transmit data using wireless technology over the cloud.

Cloud-based IoT applications receive, analyze, and manage data in real-time to help municipalities, companies and citizens make better decisions that improve quality of life.

In a smart city, citizens are connected using smartphones, mobile devices, smart cars and smart homes. Sharing data with a city's physical infrastructure and services can help service providers improve energy distribution, streamline trash collection, decrease traffic congestion, and improve air quality. The primary goal of a smart city is to create an urban environment that provides its citizens a high quality of life while also generating overall economic growth. Smart city technologies aim at optimizing infrastructure, mobility, public services, and utilities. For example,

- Connected **traffic lights** receive data from sensors and cars (adjusting light cadence and timing to respond to real-time traffic) to reduce congestion on roads.
- Connected **cars** can share data with parking meters and electric vehicle (EV) charging docks and direct drivers to the nearest available spot.
- Smart **garbage cans** send data to waste management companies so that they can schedule a pick-up.
- Citizens can use their smartphone to store their driver's license and other digital credentials to speed-up and simplify access to the city and local **government services**.
- Smart city initiatives also address **environmental concerns** such as climate change and air pollution.
- Sensors are used to measure water parameters and guarantee the quality of drinking water. A smart city also has proper **wastewater removal** and drainage system.
- Smart city improves **public safety** by monitoring areas of high crime through sensors. Sensors can also be used to issue an early warning before droughts, floods, landslides or hurricanes.
- **Smart buildings** with sensors monitor the structural health of buildings. They can detect wear and tear and notify officials when repairs are needed.
- Sensors are used to **detect leaks** in water mains and other pipe systems. This reduces costs and improves the efficiency of public workers.
- Smart city also provides **efficiency** to tasks related to urban manufacturing, urban farming, including job creation, energy efficiency and space management.

4.4.1 Need for Smart Cities

Today, 54% of people across the globe live in cities. According to the UN Department of Economic and Social Affairs, by the year 2050, this number would reach to 66%. This means that considering the overall population growth and movement of people from rural to urban areas, another 2.5 billion people will move to cities over the next three decades. In such a scenario, environmental, social, and economic sustainability has to be ensured to deal with rapid urbanization. Smart city is one such initiative in this direction.

Secured wireless connectivity and IoT technology have transformed our cities (Fig. 4.13). For example, streetlights have become intelligent lighting systems that work on solar power and connect to a cloud-based central control system. Their high-power embedded LEDs alert commuters about traffic woes, provide severe weather warnings, detect free parking spaces and even work as EV charging docks.

With the introduction of 5G technology, smart cities project will get a boost due to more and better connectivity with devices.

Figure 4.13 Wi-Fi connectivity in smart cities

4.4.2 Examples of Smart Cities

A smart city supports a technology-based infrastructure that takes environmental initiatives, performs urban planning, has a high-functioning public transportation system and allows humans to live and work within the city and utilize its resources.

New York City

The New York City Department of Transportation's use a **congestion management system** that has improved travel times by 10%. The NYCx Challenges initiative invites entrepreneurs, technologists, and tech professionals to participate in open competitions and propose ideas that solve problems related to urban areas (like pollution, income inequality, and transport).

Automated water meters in New York consist of small devices connected to individual water meters that send daily readings to a computerized billing system.

Amsterdam Smart City

Amsterdam is a smart city that shares **traffic and transportation data** with interested parties such as developers for creating mapping apps that connect to the city's transport systems.

The city has autonomous delivery boats called **roboats** to keep things moving in a timely fashion. It also supports a floating village of houses, solving the city's overcrowding problem with sustainable, energy-efficient technology. In this city, power is generated within communities, and homes receive water from the river after it is filtered within their tanks.

Copenhagen Smart City

Copenhagen is known as one of the smartest cities in the world. The city uses open data in its collaboration with the Massachusetts Institute of Technology (MIT) to develop an **innovative smart bike system**.

The city is embedded with sensors that provide real-time information that is shared to monitor and manage air quality and traffic congestion.

Singapore Smart City

Singapore uses sensors and IoT-enabled cameras to monitor the cleanliness of public spaces, crowd density and the movement of locally registered vehicles. Companies monitor energy use, waste production and water use in real time. Singapore is also working on autonomous vehicles including robotic buses, and an elderly monitoring system to ensure the health and well-being of its senior citizens.

According to Forbes (21 May 2019), top 10 smart cities in the world are London, New York, Amsterdam, Paris, Reykjavik, Tokyo, Singapore, Copenhagen, Berlin and Vienna.

Dubai Smart City

Dubai has smart buildings, smart utilities, smart education, telemedicine, smart healthcare and smart tourism. It also uses smart systems for traffic routing, parking, infrastructure planning and transportation.

Barcelona Smart City

This smart city has smart transportation system and smart bus systems with smart bus stops that provide free Wi-Fi, USB charging stations and bus schedule updates for riders. Barcelona has an app-based bike-sharing and smart parking system that includes online payment options. Sensors are used to monitor temperature, humidity, amount of rainfall, pollution and noise.

4.4.3 Security Objectives in a Smart City

Availability ensures actionable, real-time, and reliable access to data without which the smart city cannot thrive.

Integrity is an important feature as smart cities rely on reliable and accurate data. Stored data should be accessed and modified only by authorized persons.

Confidentiality refers to sensitivity of the data collected, stored, and analyzed. Due care must be taken to prevent unauthorized disclosure of sensitive information.

Accountability makes the users of the data responsible for their actions. In whatever way they access and interact with the system, it is recorded (also known as logged). These logs or records should be difficult to forge.

The above security features call for strong authentication and ID management systems that must be integrated into the ecosystem to ensure that data is shared, accessed and manipulated only by authorized parties (Fig. 4.14).

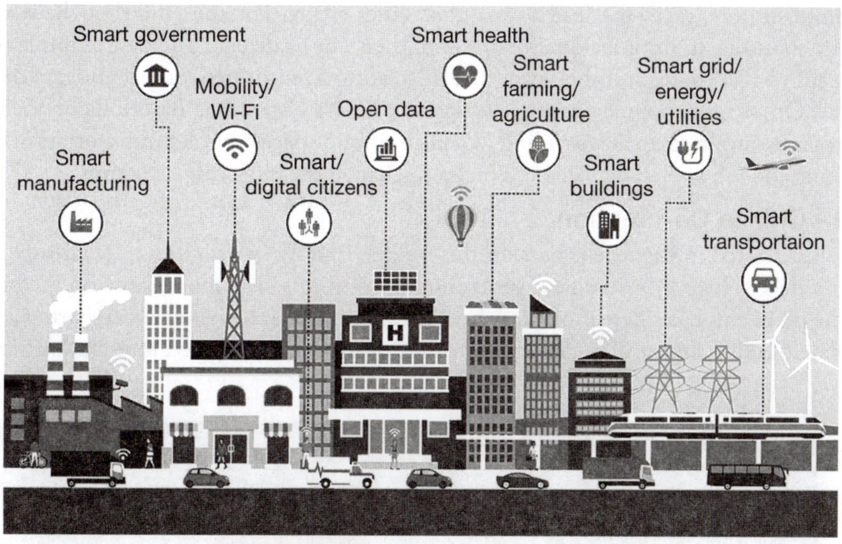

Figure 4.14 Smart city components

4.4.4 How a Smart City Works

Smart cities utilize their web of connected IoT devices and other technologies to achieve their goals of improving the quality of life and achieving economic growth. Successful smart cities follow four steps:

Collection: Smart sensors throughout the city gather data in real time.

Analysis: Data collected by the smart sensors is assessed in order to draw meaningful insights.

Communication: The insights that have been found in the analysis phase are communicated with decision-makers through strong communication networks.

Action: Cities use the insights pulled from the data to create solutions, optimize operations and asset management and improve the quality of life for residents.

4.4.5 Challenges

Data privacy and **security** are top concerns in a smart city. There is always a fear of data being hacked and misused.

Presence of sensors and cameras everywhere may be perceived as an **invasion of privacy** or government surveillance by the citizens.

Another issue is **connectivity**. IoT devices scattered across the city will not work in the absence of a powerful network connection.

> To address privacy issues, data collected should be anonymized and not be personally identifiable information.

4.4.6 Three Generations of Evolving Smart Cities

To understand how cities have embraced technology and development, we can divide the growth of smart cities in three phases: tech-company driven, city government driven, and finally, citizen driven.

Smart Cities 1.0 – Technology Driven

In this phase, tech companies approached cities, encouraging them to adopt smart solutions. However, many of these cities were not actually equipped to properly understand the implications of the technology solutions or how these solutions could enhance the quality of life of its citizens.

So, the main limitation of smart cities 1.0 was that it missed out on relating to how cities interact with their citizens. However, despite this shortcoming the technology-driven model laid the foundation for numerous smart city projects around the globe – from PlanIT in Portugal to Songdo in South Korea.

Smart Cities 2.0 – Technology Enabled, City-led

In this phase, the cities themselves take the initiative for Smart City projects. A municipality, led by forward-thinking mayors and city administrators, takes the lead to make its cities smart. For this, the thought leaders emphasize on deploying technology solutions to improve quality of life of their city's citizens. The best example of smart city 2.0 is Rio, whose mayor went to IBM to exploit their expertise in creating a sensor network to mitigate the role of landslides in the hillside favelas. Other most popular example of leading Smart City 2.0 is Barcelona or Vienna. Barcelona has more than 20 smart cities program areas providing Wi-Fi in public spaces, public transportation system, intelligent lighting and promoting the use of electric vehicle vehicles to change the city's infrastructure.

Smart Cities 3.0 – Citizen Co-creation

The third phase has just started in the recent past. In this model, leading smart cities have already started to embrace citizen co-creation models to help drive the next generation of solutions. The model rests on the pillars of equity and social inclusion as the main emphasis here is on creating viable conditions that allow local sharing activities to emerge. For example, Vienna, a leading Smart City designed on the 2.0 model, has started to include citizens as investors in

Figure 4.15   Barcelona, leading smart city providing a range of opportunities

its local partnerships for clean energy. Its citizens invested in local solar plants as contribution to the city's 2050 renewable energy objectives. The citizens are also actively involved in addressing affordable housing and gender equality.

Similarly, Vancouver, in Canada, engaged 30,000 citizens in the co-creation of its Vancouver Greenest City 2020 Action Plan. Moreover, Medellin in Colombia, has involved citizens from the city's most vulnerable neighborhoods in transformative projects. For example, it initiated the cable car and electric stairs projects and new technology-enabled schools and libraries. It has also developed an impressive innovation district (Ruta N) to attract and retain entrepreneurial talent.

> Medellin received the Urban Land Institute's Innovative City of the Year Award.

Barcelona recently launched an innovation project (called BCN Open Challenge). A platform, Citymart, was used to post six challenges and ideas from local and global citizens and innovators were solicited.

Many projects like Repair Cafes, tool-lending libraries for performing home repairs, and bike-sharing services have the potential to optimize the underutilized resources and raise the quality of life of all citizens. Upcoming smart cities are focusing on sharing activities amongst citizens and fostering shared startups as well.

4.5   SMART SCHOOL

Unlike our traditional schools, a smart school uses advanced equipment and technology to provide an excellent learning experience to the students. These days, especially after the break of the Covid pandemic, teaching is being done online as age-old methods of lectures could no longer be practiced. Teachers, parents as well as the students realized that schools equipped with technology can be very effectively used to deliver content that was otherwise monotonous to read and interpret. Other advantages of a smart school include,

Easy Access to Information: A smart classroom uses internet-enabled gadgets (mobile, laptops, and tabs) to access enormous amount of information on any topic present on the World Wide Web. This helps teachers to teach and students to learn beyond the scope of their prescribed books (Fig. 4.16).

Figure 4.16   A smart classroom

Taking Notes on a Digital Medium: Students can easily write their notes on their digital devices, thereby helping them avoid carrying hefty bags to schools. Taking notes digitally takes less time than that required while writing with pen and paper. Digital notes can be easily edited or enhanced. Moreover, it also helps to save paper and thus our environment. Now, the need of photocopies and printouts has also reduced, which in turn reduces the carbon footprint.

A Better Understanding of Topics Through Digital Tools: It is rightly said that a simple picture can replace a thousand words and the use of such instructional tools in smart classes make learning more effective. With digital tools, students can easily visualize a complex topic through online videos and other audio-visual aids including presentations, text documents, audio sessions, etc. Students can also use quizzing apps (like Jruma) to test their understanding about a particular topic.

Keep Parents in the Loop: With digital technology, teachers can easily keep parents updated with their ward's curriculum and performance. Even parents can easily communicate with teachers using these apps.

Increased Productivity: Productivity means amount of work done in a particular duration of time. When teaching is done through audios, videos, pictures and other digital content, it takes less time for students to understand the concept. The time saved in teaching can then be used to perform other activities that enhance understanding (like quizzing, group discussion, etc.), thereby increasing the productivity of both teachers as well as students.

Great help for Absentees: Lectures in smart classes are recorded. So, even if a student is absent in the class, he/she can go through the video recordings to learn what may otherwise have been missed.

Making Slow Learners to Learn at Their Own Pace: Listening to lectures and taking notes at the same time is difficult for some students. Those students can now listen to recorded lectures and learn and write at their own pace.

Interactive Teaching Environment: In an interactive teaching environment, both teachers and students are actively involved. This active involvement increases the bond between teachers and students and amongst students themselves.

Apart from these benefits, smart classes allow students to learn from the experts of various subjects. They are no longer bound to learn different subjects from the same teacher. Smart classes also make learning a fun-filled activity in which students can learn new technology, collaborate with others and learn, resulting in improved grades.

4.5.1 What Else Makes for a Smart School?

A smart school has smart boards and projectors and automatic fire detection systems in the classrooms, GPS tracking in their school buses, Internet connectivity in the entire campus, and computerized attendance system. Other infrastructure that helps a school become really smart include,

* Personal computers for students in the library
* Futuristic labs like robotics, mathematics, and language to help students learn communication and modern skills
* Automatic security systems to minimize manual errors and provide a safe environment.

4.6   SMART HOME

A smart home means a convenient home setup where appliances and devices can be automatically controlled remotely from anywhere with an Internet connection (wired or wireless) using a mobile device. Devices in a smart home are connected to each other through the Internet. This allows users to control them remotely using a smartphone, tablet, laptop or even a game console (Fig. 4.17).

Door locks, televisions, thermostats, home monitors, cameras, lights, refrigerator and other devices can be controlled through a single home automation system installed on the user's device. The user can even create time schedules for certain changes to take effect. In addition to this, smart home appliances have self-learning capabilities. They automatically learn the user's schedules and make adjustments as and when required. For example, in a smart home, lighting control allows users to optimize the use of electricity for cutting costs. To manage security, home automation systems alert the user when any movement is detected in the home in the absence of user. These systems also call authorities (like the police) in case of imminent situations.

> All smart devices, when connected over the Internet to share information, become a part of IoT (Internet of Things).

Other examples of devices in a smart home include,
A smart sprinkler that automatically sets on to **water the plants**.

A smart air conditioner or a smart heating system can be set to maintain a specific **temperature**.

Smart locks can be used **lock** and **unlock** the door remotely. Users can also check whether or not he/she has locked the door before leaving the house. Apart from this, a record of who has come and gone can also be maintained.

Smart **smoke detectors** automatically alert the user as well as the fire service as soon as smoke is detected.

> The global home automation market was about $24 billion in 2016 and is expected to be about $53.5 billion by the end of 2022.

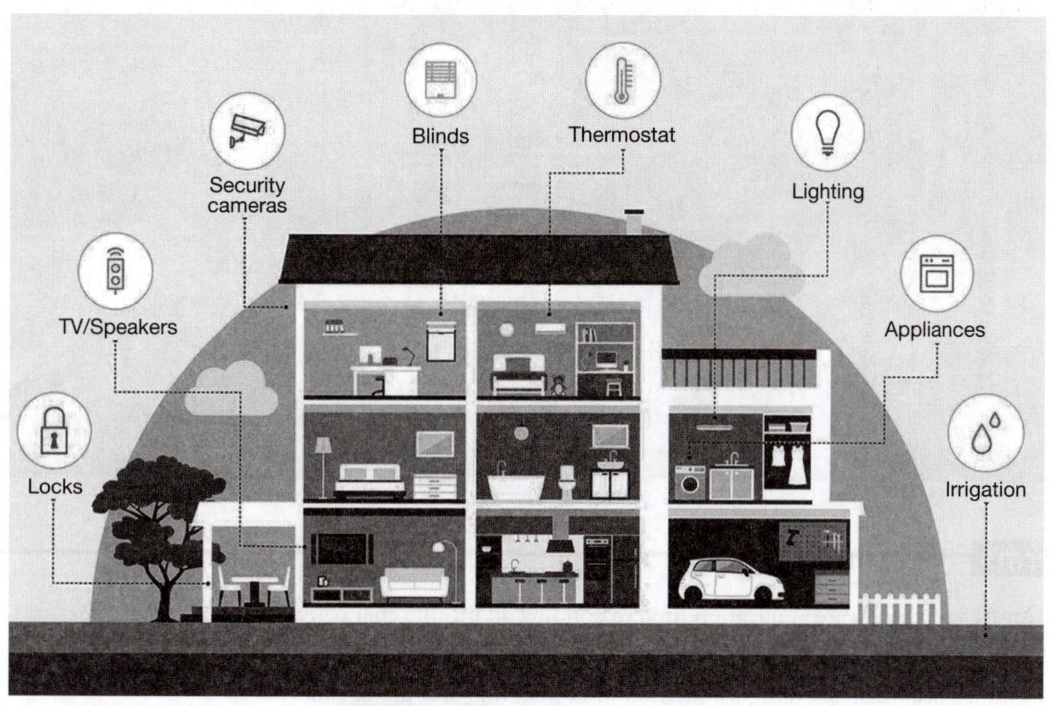

Figure 4.17   Smart home set-up

Virtual assistant like Google Home or Amazon Echo Delegate allows users to delegate tasks by giving simple voice commands. For example, to turn on music, search the Web or control other smart devices.

Smart devices can be used to streamline household chores. For example, smart TVs, dishwashers, refrigerators and dryers can automatically detect when **energy consumption** is the lowest in that particular area and turn on during that time. Another example could be a refrigerator scanning groceries, sending an alert to the user notifying to buy it before coming home.

Besides being controlled remotely, smart **lighting systems** (like Hue from Philips Lighting Holding B.V.) can detect when there is no one in the room. In such a case, it automatically adjusts lighting as needed. Such lights can also adjust brightness based on the availability of daylight.

Smart **pet care** systems can have feeders connected with them

> Video entertainment is expected to be the largest component of smart home technology, followed by home security and monitoring services.

> Smart speaker technology like the Amazon Echo or Google Nest is already being used in many homes in India.

Custom home theater can be used to play any movie of choice, a touch panel to automatically dim the lights, cover the windows, lower the screen, and power the components.

Outdoor living experience can also be made incredible and smart. For example, a backyard oasis with hidden speakers, outdoor TVs, lighting systems, etc. can be used to create fantastic effects.

Key Terms

Chatbot: An AI-based software application used to conduct an on-line chat conversation via text or text-to-speech, in lieu of providing direct contact with a live human agent.

Robotics: The science involving design, construction, operation, and use of robots.

Bitmoji: A personalized cartoon avatar that is created to look just like the user.

Pre-programmed robots: Robots that operate in a controlled environment to perform simple, monotonous tasks.

Autonomous robots operate without human operators. They are designed to perform tasks in open environments that do not require human supervision.

Tele-operated robots: Mechanical bots, controlled by humans, that are often used in extreme geographical conditions, weather circumstances, etc.

Drone: Any unpiloted aircraft that operates using a combination of technologies including computer vision, artificial intelligence, object avoidance tech, and others.

Smart city: A framework that makes extensive use of Information and Communication Technologies (ICT), to develop, deploy, and promote sustainable development practices to cater to growing urbanization issues.

Chapter Highlights

- Artificial Intelligence is widely being used by companies to improve their process efficiencies, automate resource-heavy tasks, and to make business predictions by analyzing data.

- Autopilot technology uses AI in flying commercial and military aircraft.

- AI techniques can optimize search results to reduce the gap between the demand and supply of results.

- Smart computer systems can easily detect forgery as compared to humans.

- In the first phase, tech companies approached cities, encouraging them to adopt smart solutions. In the second phase, the cities themselves took the initiative for Smart City projects. The third phase embraces citizen co-creation models.
- In a smart city, smart sensors throughout the city gather data in real time.
- A smart home means a convenient home setup where appliances and devices can be automatically controlled remotely from anywhere with an Internet connection (wired or wireless) using a mobile device.

Review Questions

1. Explain any three ways in which AI can be used in the healthcare industry.
2. In which fields AI is used as a self-driven system?
3. How does AI help in HRM applications?
4. Write any three tasks that a robot can perform in a manufacturing company.
5. How is a Bitmoji used for criminal identification?
6. How is AI useful in the education industry?
7. Write a short note on robots.
8. Differentiate between autonomous and tele-operated robots.
9. Give any five applications of robots.
10. Give any five applications of drones.
11. Give five ways in which you can make your city a smart city.
12. Write any three advantages of a smart school.
13. List some features of a smart home.
14. Imagine that you are the principal of your school. What points will you consider to implement a smart security system for the students.
15. Give any one feature of the following smart cities:
    a. Singapore   b. Dubai   c. Amsterdam   d. New York
16. State any one way in which the following companies use AI.
    a. Google   b. Netflix   c. Facebook

Fill in the Blanks

1. ______________ is an AI-based software application that conducts chat conversation with the user.
2. ________ recognition is used in computer dictation software, TV voice remotes, voice-enabled text messaging, GPS, and voice-driven phone answering menus.
3. ________ technology uses AI in flying commercial and military aircraft.
4. ________ is a personalized cartoon avatar that is created to look just like the user.
5. The Roomba vacuum cleaner uses ________ to roam freely throughout a home to clean it.
6. Bots that work alongside humans are known as ____________.

State True or False

1. The more data you feed to an AI system, the more accurate they become.
2. Tele-operated robots operate without human operators.
3. Augmenting robot is used to fix underwater pipe leaks during the BP oil spill.

4. Drones are being used to provide Internet access in remote areas and over irregular landforms.

5. Smart city initiatives have an adverse effect on the environment.

6. Data Confidentiality refers to sensitivity of the data collected, stored, and analyzed.

7. Rio and Barcelona are examples of Smart Cities 1.0.

8. Phase 1 of smart cities actively involves citizen's participation.

9. AI-powered surveillance system uses facial recognition techniques.

10. Smart cities use Strong AI applications.

11. Smart buildings do not require maintenance.

12. We can use AI to identify fake news.

Multiple Choice Questions

1. NLP is used to identify _______.
   a. spam emails
   b. fake reviews
   c. virus
   d. All of these.

2. Google's Waymo is an example of AI-based _________.
   a. Self-driven cars
   b. airplanes
   c. healthcare system
   d. speech recognition system.

3. Terminator is an example of a _______.
   a. robot
   b. science fiction movie
   c. drone
   d. AI game

4. _________ tools use AI to identify text that is taken from other websites, books or any other sources.
   a. Translation
   b. Plagiarism checker
   c. Search engine
   d. Recommendation engines

5. Sophia and Atlas are two popular examples of _________ robots.
   a. humanoid
   b. tele-operated
   c. augmenting
   d. pre-programmed

6. They are designed to perform tasks in open environments that do not require human supervision:
   a. Humanoid
   b. Tele-operated robots
   c. Augmenting robots
   d. Autonomous robots

7. _______ is the world's first robot that can recognize human emotions.
   a. REEM
   b. PEPPER
   c. ASIMO
   d. BUDDY

8. _______ is also known as Unmanned Aerial Vehicle.
   a. Robot
   b. Robonaut
   c. Drone
   d. Co-bot

9. Which of the following companies is not developing a robotaxi?
   a. Uber
   b. Boeing
   c. Airbus
   d. BMW

10. Stored data should be accessed and modified only by authorized persons to ensure _______ of data.
    a. Accountability
    b. Integrity
    c. Accessibility
    d. Confidentiality

11. Identify the odd one out in the context of Smart City.
    a. Vienna
    b. Vancouver
    c. Medellin
    d. New Delhi

12. __________ is an example of smart speaker.
   a. Google Nest
   c. Both of these.
   b. Amazon Echo
   d. None of these.

13. Amazon Alexa uses __________ technique to perform its task.
   a. Image Recognition
   c. Neural Networks
   b. Speech Recognition
   d. Robotics

Group Discussion

1. Discuss the ways in which AI can be used by the Indian military to protect its borders from enemies and intruders.

2. Is your school a smart school? If yes, what makes it smart? If no, what changes do you think needs to be incorporated to make your school a smart one?

3. Would you love to live in a simple home or a smart home?

Ice-breaker Activity – Dream Smart Home Idea

Are you ready for the home automation revolution?
We have already seen that IoT devices including home appliances (washers, fridges, etc.), as well as safety and security systems not only bring convenience to homeowners but also reduce cost and energy. Let us think of a smart home system and design the integration of a floor plan. Doing this will help us to:

- Display all functions on a single floor plan view.
- Zoom in and out of different rooms and control the appliances only in that room.
- Set up a home map for the robot to work conveniently (for example, to clean the house or move from one room to another).
- Mark rooms that need to switch devices off with different colors (alarm mode).

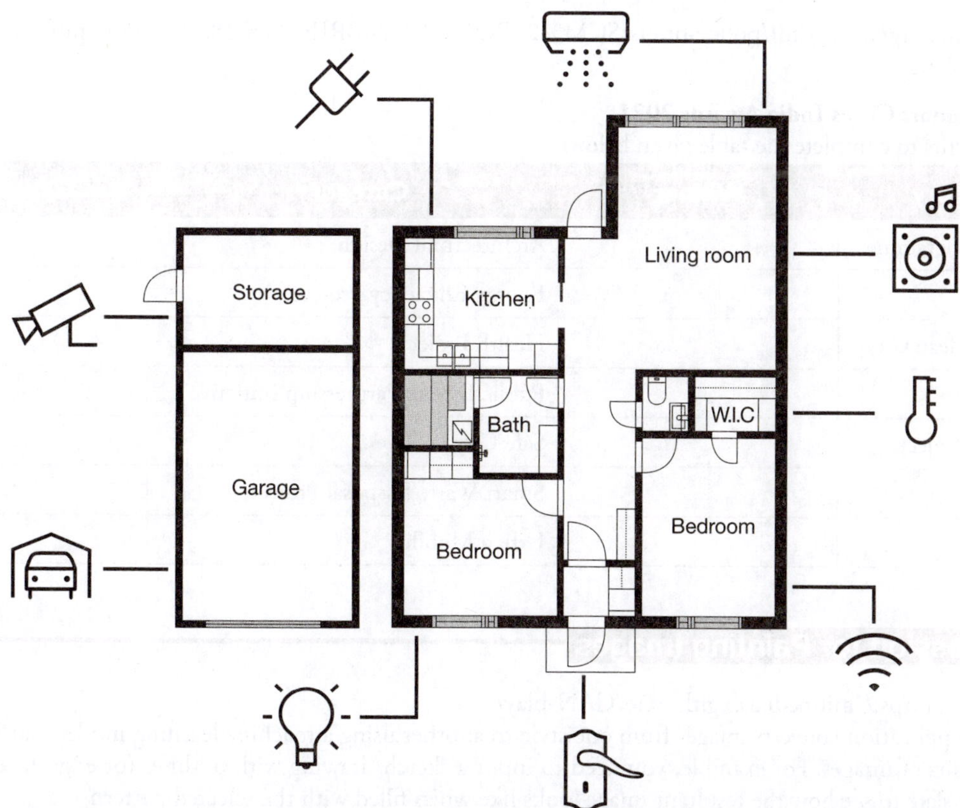

RoomSketcher provides an online floor plan that allow users to create floor plans, furnish and decorate them and visualize the design in impressive 3D. Click on the following to get started:
https://www.roomsketcher.com/features/draw-floor-plans/

Fun Activity – Story Speaking in a Google Device

Use the following link to go to story-speaker page:
https://experiments.withgoogle.com/story-speaker

Story Speaker lets anyone create talking, interactive stories with no coding required. The story can then be played anytime.

Project Work

Make a presentation reflecting the utility of the following devices. Chromecast, Echo Dot, Harmony Elite, Nest Hib and Samsung Smart Things
   Students may collect any five smart initiatives taken in their area/city/town/state.

Activity for Creating Awareness

Teachers can give students an overview of the smart cities mission in India. Details may be fetched from the link given here.
https://cprindia.org/system/tdf/policy-briefs/SCM%20POLICY%20BRIEF%2028th%20Aug.pdf?file=1%26type=node%26id=7162

Winners of Smart Cities India Awards 2021
Ask the students to complete the table given below.

Category	Winner	Category	Winner
Academic Programme		Architectural Design	
Digital City		Energy Efficiency Project	
Green and Clean City		Health Project	
Heritage City		Public Private Partnership Initiative	
Real Estate Project		Safe City	
Smart Village		Smart Waste Disposal Project	
Start up		Urban Mobility	

AI Lab Session for Painting Images

Visit the URL, https://mitmedialab.github.io/GAN-play/.
The pix2pix application converts images from one style to another using a machine learning model that is specifically trained on pairs of images. For example, you need to input a sketch/drawing with outlines (or edges), select a model and then translate to see how the resultant image looks like when filled with the selected pattern.

Fun Time – Test Your AI Vocabulary

The maze given below has 12 terms with which you are now familiar. Can you identify any 10 terms related to Artificial Intelligence?

A	B	C	C	D	A	U	T	O	P	I	L	O	T	E
N	F	G	O	H	S	I	M	J	K	L	G	S	O	S
E	A	M	M	N	U	O	A	P	S	Q	E	R	S	M
U	T	T	P	U	P	V	C	W	E	X	N	V	Z	A
R	A	B	U	C	E	D	H	E	N	F	E	G	S	R
A	M	L	T	R	R	K	I	J	S	I	R	H	E	T
L	N	O	E	P	A	Q	N	R	O	S	A	T	L	S
N	Z	V	R	X	I	L	E	W	R	V	L	U	F	C
E	A	B	V	C	D	E	L	F	G	H	A	I	D	H
T	N	M	I	L	K	W	E	A	K	A	I	J	R	O
W	O	P	S	Q	R	S	A	T	N	U	V	W	I	O
O	F	E	I	D	C	B	R	A	Z	G	V	X	V	L
R	G	H	O	I	J	K	N	O	L	M	U	N	I	O
K	X	W	N	V	U	T	I	S	B	R	Q	A	N	P
V	Z	A	B	D	R	O	N	E	C	O	D	E	G	F
C	H	A	T	B	O	T	G	K	J	I	T	H	G	E

Answers

Fill in the Blanks
1. Chatbot
2. Speech
3. Autopilot
4. Bitmoji
5. sensors
6. cobots

State True or False
1. True
2. False
3. False
4. True
5. False
6. True
7. False
8. False
9. True
10. False
11. False
12. True

Multiple Choice Questions
1. d
2. a
3. b
4. b
5. a
6. d
7. b
8. c
9. d
10. b
11. d
12. c
13. b

AI on Sustainable Development Goals

5

Chapter Objectives

The chapter aims to broaden our vision of AI technology and help us to learn how AI can be used for sustainable development. In this context, important concepts like those given below are discussed.

- Using AI to solve problems and mitigate risks
- Expanding skills and capabilities
- Using AI to protect data
- UN projects for sustainable development

5.1   AI FOR SUSTAINABLE DEVELOPMENT

AI development practitioners are seriously looking to innovate the process of decision-making and solving problems to accelerate progress towards the United Nation's Sustainable Development Goals (SDG) by 2030. Such innovations can be enabled by automating activities that are typically associated with human thinking, such as learning, decision-making, or natural language processing, using algorithms that mimic human learning and cognition to address narrowly specified tasks.

Today, we are less than a decade away from the timeline for achieving the SDGs. However, AI holds great promise in this direction. Ethical use of AI will benefit the entire human kind. For example, AI systems using machine learning algorithms can be used to monitor a child's growth and detect if the child is suffering from malnutrition.

5.1.1 Solving Problems by Making Better Decisions

New forms of impact assessment and prediction using AI techniques can improve impact and identification of optimal interventions. For example, The Red Cross used AI to integrate multiple data sources to predict overspills of the Nangbeto Dam in Togo. Data-driven and knowledge-driven forecasts helped to decrease the impact of torrential rainfall and corresponding floods, thereby saving the lives of vulnerable communities.

AI also paves the way for entirely new ways of smart service provision, sources of income, providing humanitarian and environmental interventions. For example, Apollo Agriculture in Kenya uses satellite data to train machine learning models that automatically build digital processes for tasks including customer acquisition or collecting payments. Using these digital processes, decisions about lending to a customer can be made in a better way.

5.1.2 Expanding an Individual's Capabilities and Skills

AI can be used to enhance individual skills and community capabilities through peer-to-peer knowledge sharing and remote learning. For example, the mobile platform M-Shule delivers lessons based on the national curriculum to each student via SMS. AI systems can also be adapted based on individual student's skills and abilities.

AI systems also improve the agility and efficiency of an individual through automation by allowing humans to perform complex tasks. ML algorithms can easily analyze large amounts of data. This work, when done by a human, would take a long time. For example, poor road conditions not only pose hazards for drivers but also force them to go slow, thereby inhibiting economic growth. Therefore, in Tanzania, an automated road condition survey project used satellite images and deep learning techniques to evaluate the quality of unpaved roads with 73% accuracy.

5.1.3 Mitigating the Risks Associated with Use of Emerging Technologies

Reliability of any AI system depends on the quality of training data. Lack of good quality and diverse training data results in biased and erroneous results that will not be useful in achieving development objectives. Therefore, at times, we need to invest money to acquire sound data collection technologies.

Moreover, deviation from ethical AI also results in negative impacts of development projects. AI technology may also result in reduction of low-skilled labor. So, the development practitioners must take utmost care to ensure that the adoption of AI should occur in an inclusive manner.

5.1.4 Data Privacy, One of the Overarching Challenges of the Digital Era

Data is the lifeblood of AI and data privacy issues play a significant and often limiting role in AI's growth trajectory. The General Data Protection Regulation (GDPR), introduced by the European Union (EU), can restrict the benefits of AI for development if data protection principles are not strictly adhered to. However, the development of AI systems giving prime importance to data privacy entail some additional costs.

To improve data accessibility, data collectors and data generators (whether governments or companies) must grant greater access to NGOs and others seeking to use the data for public service.

Development practitioners, these days, actively engage in communication with data protection authorities, and all stake-holders (investors, employees, customers, suppliers, etc.) to provide high-level solutions that follow data protection principles. Such systems are often successful as they help in generating trust and preventing risks.

Given the fast pace of growth of AI technology, five years from now, models that are currently considered cutting-edge will have become obsolete. Novel (new, better, efficient) AI approaches will unlock currently unimaginable possibilities in technology and hence for development.

5.2   UNITED NATIONS PROJECTS – AI SUSTAINABLE DEVELOPMENT

According to a report by Max Tegmark, Anna Felländer, and eight co-authors, 79% of the SDGs could be enabled with AI (Vinuesa, R, Azizpour, H, Leite, I *et al.*, 2020). Moreover, the UN has listed a global collection of AI projects and proposals that impacts its Sustainable Development Goals, positively or negatively (Fig. 5.1). The key focus here is to promote the use of AI for positive and sustainable development, and also to discover the negative impact of AI on sustainable development. All the projects are evaluated through a rating scheme. Anyone can share his/her project with the world and get it evaluated on the UN AI for SDG website.

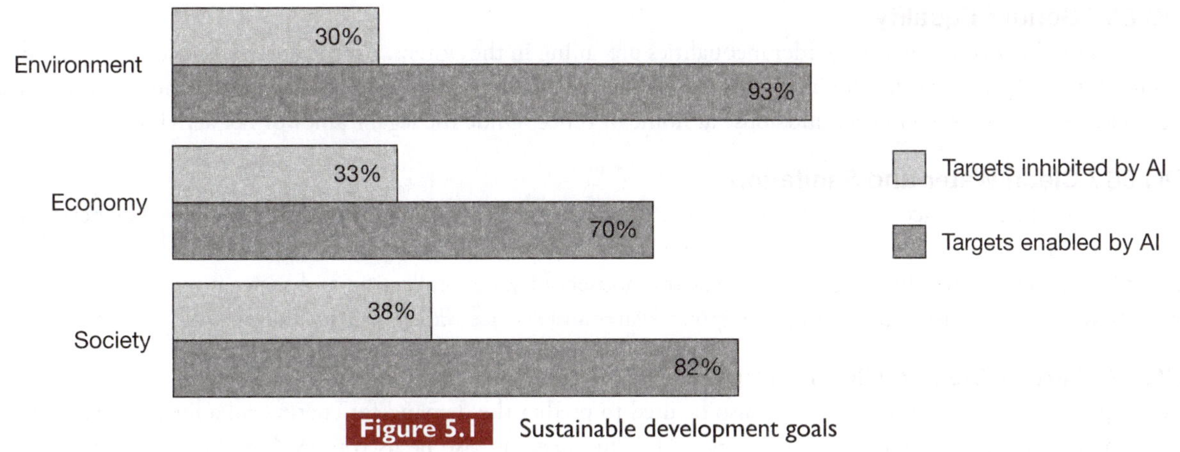

Figure 5.1   Sustainable development goals

Some projects to help humanity reach the UN's 17 Sustainable Development Goals are:

SDG 01 / No Poverty

AI can be used to predict and prevent extreme climate-related events, reduce people's vulnerability and risk of exposure to such events and also reduce poverty. For example, AI can be used to detect as well as predict forest fires. Machine Learning algorithms can be used to assess consumer spending, malnutrition status in children, refugee migration patterns, etc., to make predictions about the status of poverty in a region.

SDG 02 / Zero Hunger

More than 820 million people all over world go to bed hungry. AI can be used to monitor food along the whole chain from production to transportation to distribution, so that food wastage can be reduced and food can reach those who need it the most.

For example, a large amount of data is collected, digitized and analyzed to help growers control and optimize their production systems. AI techniques are also empowering farmers to increase their income through higher crop yield and greater price control.

SDG 03 / Good Health and Well-being

AI is used to predict serious diseases including diabetes and cancer. More methods can be discovered by working closely with radiologists to locate brain tumors using AI techniques. Besides this, AI can be used to discover drugs, study genome sequencing, monitor heart rate, and detect depression in speech at a very early stage.

SDG 04 / Quality Education

AI can be used to make education accessible to all young boys and girls despite their location, caste, creed, religion and other discriminating factors. AI can be used for automatic essay correction, create a chat-like learning process personalized for each student, identify if a student is paying attention or not, personalize curriculums based on the results of assessments in language and mathematics, etc.

> Did you know that an application using AI can generate an alarm to alert the invigilator when a student is about to cheat during an examination?

SDG 05 / Gender Equality

AI systems can be used to identify gender inequalities prevailing in the system. An AI tool can be used to highlight the life stories of women scientists who have won the Noble Prize, and discover deep connections of these women. It can be used to detect domestic violence and abuse at home or office, guide the legal framework of activities, etc.

SDG 06 / Clean Water and Sanitation

AI can be used to ensure access to clean water for a greater number of people by increasing water efficiency by measuring water consumption, predicting water demands and adjusting water supply in a given area. For example, AI is already being used for desalinating seawater, reusing household water, collecting and segregating garbage, detecting irrigation leak to minimize wastage, improve groundwater and surface water quantity and quality.

SDG 07 / Affordable and Clean Energy

AI can optimize energy production. It can also be used to predict the demand for energy and adjust to circumstances depending on the demand and supply of energy. AI techniques can also be used to explore the use and efficiency of renewable energy and eventually promote it as a replacement for non-renewable sources.

AI techniques are being used by oil and gas companies to identify the location and accelerate extraction of fossil fuels at a lesser cost and a faster pace. Electric vehicles are constantly undergoing improvements to reduce emission and recharge at lower costs.

SDG 08 / Decent Work and Economic Growth

Our life is filled with one or more risks. Many tasks performed by humans are not only dangerous but also time-consuming and expensive. AI can help to relieve the stress on workers and restore their work-life balance by initiating predictive maintenance of systems, plants, bridges, machines, etc. AI systems can also be used to fight against forced labor, modern slavery, human trafficking, and child labor.

In addition to this, AI is already being used to help thousands of small- and medium-sized businesses to grow at a rapid pace. This is being done by improving policy impact and social outcomes in real-world economies

SDG 09 / Industry, Innovation and Infrastructure

AI, when applied in the manufacturing of goods, can make the process faster, produce higher quality products, create smarter distribution chains, monitor crops, warn about potential risks (pest and disease detection). make roads safer by sending alerts of crashes and illegal driving, improve traffic management by counting and identifying vehicles and pedestrians, review massive collections of research papers to extract the most precise pieces of knowledge, help in urban planning and crime prevention, extract customer preference from their social media posts and address climate change.

> Did you know that an application using AI can teach you correct pronunciation of words in English language? It can also be used to test your reading skills and help to enhance your command in the language.

SDG 10 / Reduced Inequalities

AI can be used to establish new and equal foundations in the legal system by spotting existing inequalities in legal practices and regulations, and also help realize and uphold child rights.

The financial advisor system can learn from historical data to predict the account balances of individuals for a future time period, and analyze the spending patterns of users to know about their financial health. This information can then be used to help low-income individuals to better plan their financial spending behavior and avoid taking debts.

> According to Arti Zeighami, global head of advanced analytics and AI at H&M, H&M set up its AI department to align demand and supply, to eventually avoid wasting resources and to reduce emissions.

To help people with impaired hearing in public places, AI can be used to recognize a variety of signs (in sign language) and translate them into written text.

SDG 11 / Sustainable Cities and Communities

AI technology is being extensively used to create smart cities. In a smart city, electric and autonomous transportation is developed. The city also exhibits smarter planning of infrastructure using AI techniques to significantly reduce air pollution, better manage industrial and domestic waste, treat waste water, use 3D printing to construct forts and other monuments of historical importance, study street imagery for measuring spatial distributions of income, education, unemployment, housing, living environment, health, and crime (Fig. 5.2).

> Lookout is a Google app that uses AI to detect and report items (like people, text, objects) in the scene to help people with visual disabilities.

Figure 5.2   Sustainable cities and communities

SDG 12 / Responsible Consumption and Production

AI can be used to reduce wastage of produced goods by improving their quality, detecting any deviations from standards to minimize defects in the finished products and finally optimizing the logistics.

For example, AI is already being used to reduce food waste by providing restaurants with automated hardware and software solutions to identify, manage, and monitor the source and quantity of food waste. Avoiding food wastage also helps restaurants to cut operational costs to a great extent.

SDG 13 / Climate action

AI can help in the use of electric transportation thereby enabling sustainable solutions in response to raised energy demands. Climate forecasts can be made using AI models to predict crop-yields in near-future. Similarly, flood forecasting uses AI to provide accurate real-time flood forecasting and alerts. Such forecasts help to know in advance when and where a flood might occur and with what severity.

Moreover, companies like Google are using AI to reduce the power consumption for cooling down its considerable number of data centers. AI is extensively being used by multiple energy-intensive industries to decrease the time and resources required, thereby promoting sustainable growth.

Technologies including artificial intelligence, satellite image processing, machine learning, and remote sensing, when used together, can be used to track human-caused greenhouse gas (GHG) emissions worldwide to assist all projects initiated to control the effects of climate change.

In many countries, AI is already being used to analyze environmental data for restoring freshwater bodies from extreme damage caused by macro-pollutants.

SDG 14 / Life Below Water

AI can help in keeping a track of the status of marine resources. This can be very helpful in preventing as well as reducing pollution (like oil, plastics) in the oceans, preserve biodiversity, protect livelihoods, and prevent slave labor in the seafood industry, identify fish species in the ocean and identify illegal fishing vessels

SDG 15 / Life on Land

AI can be used to detect desertification and help in planning to prevent further damage and even reverse the situation, monitor crops and warn about potential risks (including early pest and disease detection), monitor tree loss in forests, classify the species of individual trees in a forest, help farmers shift to more sustainable farming methods, measure bird biodiversity by their sound, and assess the conditions of threatened species and ecological systems.

SDG 16 / Peace, Justice and Strong Institutions

AI can help to detect and even prevent crime including corruption, bribery, and fraud. It can help to identify suspicious people and objects meant to disrupt large events, determine the model of automobiles used for illegal purposes, and analyze suspicious financial transactions.

SDG 17 / Partnerships

AI can help us to identify potential partners with whom we could work together across institutions, across countries, across academia and industry.

Key Terms

Sustainable development: An organizing principle for meeting human development goals while sustaining the ability of natural systems to provide the natural resources and ecosystem services for future generations.

Sustainable city: Also known as an eco-city or green city, it is a city designed with consideration for social, economic, environmental impact and resilient habitat for existing populations, without compromising on the ability of future generations to experience the same

Data privacy: Protecting personal data from those who should not have access to it and the ability of individuals to determine who can access their personal information.

Chapter Highlights

- AI Development practitioners are seriously looking to innovate the process of decision-making and solving problems to accelerate progress towards the United Nation's Sustainable Development Goals (SDG) by 2030.
- Ethical use of AI will benefit the entire human kind.
- AI can be used to enhance individual skills and community capabilities through peer-to-peer knowledge sharing and remote learning.
- AI technology may also result in reduction of low-skilled labor.
- UN has listed a global collection of AI projects and proposals that impacts its Sustainable Development Goals, positively or negatively.
- AI techniques are also empowering farmers to increase their income through higher crop yield and greater price control.
- AI can be used to discover drugs, study genome sequencing, monitor heart rate, and detect depression in speech at a very early stage.
- AI can be used to establish new and equal foundations in the legal system by spotting existing inequalities in legal practices and regulations, and help realize and uphold child rights.

Review Questions

1. Give three benefits of using AI.

2. What are SDGs? Give at least three examples.

3. How can healthcare projects be benefitted by AI techniques?

4. Suggest any two ways in which you think AI can be used to counter gender equality issues.

5. How can AI help us to protect our environment? Discuss any three ways.

6. How can we manage traffic using AI?

7. Write any two goals for each project:

   a. No poverty   b. Reduced inequalities.

8. With the help of an example, explain how the following ideas can be realized:

   a. Data Privacy   b. Sustainable Development   c. Sustainable City.

Fill in the Blanks

1. SDG stands for __________.

2. _________ use of AI will benefit the entire human kind.

3. AI can be used to enhance individual skills and community capabilities through _________ knowledge sharing and ___________ learning.

4. _________ is a Google app that uses AI to detect and report items in the scene to help people with visual disabilities.

5. AI technology is being extensively used to create _________ cities.

6. AI can be used to improve the ___________ of goods.

7. AI can ___________ defects in the finished products and _______ logistics.

Identify the SDGs that Work in the Given Areas

Environment ___________________   Economy ___________________

Equality ___________________   Smart Cities ___________________

Write any Two Goals of the Following SDG Numbers

2 ___________________ ___________________   5 ___________________ ___________________

9 ___________________ ___________________   13 ___________________ ___________________

State True or False

1. The mobile platform, M-Shule delivers lessons based on the national curriculum to each student via SMS.

2. AI systems cannot improve the agility and efficiency of an individual through automation.

3. USA has listed a global collection of AI projects and proposals that impacts its SDGs.

4. Using AI to predict and prevent extreme climate-related events can in turn reduce poverty.

5. AI can be used to identify if a student is paying attention or not.

6. AI cannot be used to improve groundwater and surface water quantity and quality.

7. Smart cities support SDGs.

Multiple Choice Questions

1. ______________ algorithms can easily analyze large amounts of data.
   a. Machine Learning   b. Image processing   c. Text processing   d. None of these.

2. Reliability of any AI system depends on the quality of ___________ data.
   a. training   b. testing   c. Both of these.   d. None of these.

3. The main challenge of the digital era is ____________.
   a. Data Security   b. Data Privacy
   c. reduction in low-skilled labor   d. None of these.

4. AI is used to predict diseases like ___________
   a. diabetes   b. cancer   c. COVID   d. All of these.

5. AI can be used to ensure access to clean water to a greater number of people by ___________ water demands in area.
   a. measuring   b. predicting   c. evaluating   d. All of these.

6. Identify the incorrect statement about AI.
   a. AI can be used to fight against forced labor, modern slavery, human trafficking, and child labor.
   b. AI is being used by oil and gas companies to identify the location and accelerate extraction of fossil fuels at a greater cost and a slower pace.
   c. AI is already being used for desalinating seawater, reusing household water, collecting garbage.
   d. All of these.

7. AI should be used to prevent ___________.
   a. corruption   b. bribery   c. water scarcity   d. fraud

8. SDG 11 deals with ________
   a. Climate Change   b. Poverty   c. Sustainable Cities   d. Water

Group Discussion

Discuss how AI can bring a revolution in the field of education.

Role-play Activity

Imagine that you are the President of your RWA Society. Brief everyone about your plans to make your society a smart society using AI.

Game Activity – Go Goals Board Game

The **UN Regional Information Centre for Western Europe (UNRIC)** is committed to help people, especially the youngsters, to understand their role in the future of the planet as individuals, team players and responsible global citizens for a brighter future. To achieve this goal, the UNRIC has created the "Go-Goals!" game for creating awareness and motivating them to actively pursue the SDGs.

There are 63 spaces on the board game. Children have to roll a dice and accordingly have to move forward by the number of spaces as shown on the dice. It is like the snakes-and-ladders game, wherein the player climbs to the top if he/she is at the bottom of the ladder. Correspondingly, if the payer is at the top of a waterslide, he/she has to move to the bottom of the slide.

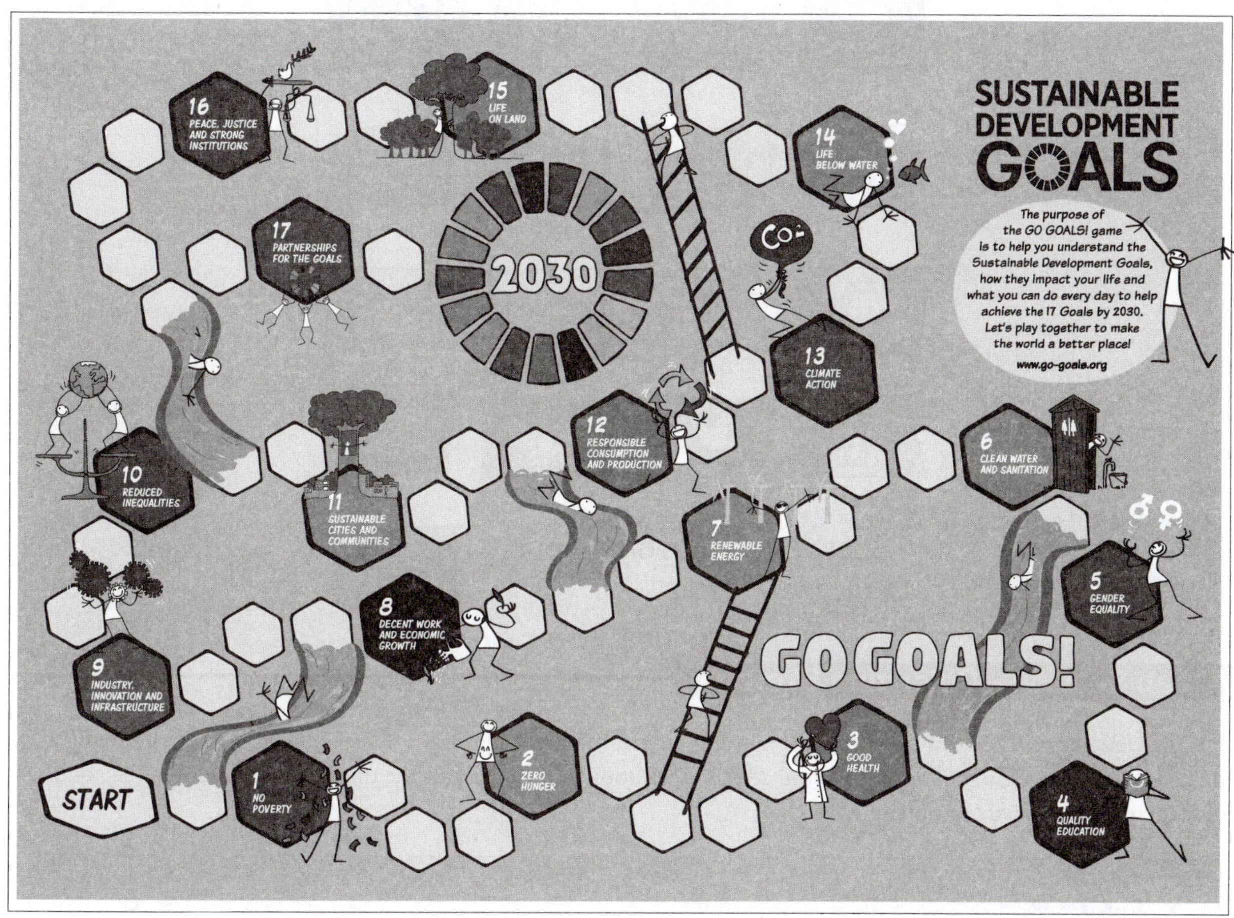

If the player lands on a Sustainable Development Goal field (1–17), he/she can draw a card corresponding to the goal number. Another player should read the card question. A correct answer from the card drawer will allow the player to roll the dice once again. ***The first player to arrive on the field '2030' is the winner!***

Benefits: The "Go-Goals!" SDG board game helps children understand the Sustainable Development Goals. Children are encouraged to develop their own set of questions and to discuss the ways in which they can implement the SDGs at home and at school. The game can be downloaded at https://go-goals.org/downloadable-material/

Arousing Awareness – Ethics in AI

Activity 1: Ask students to brainstorm ideas and think how AI can be used ethically for the benefit of humans.

Activity 2: Divide the entire class in 5–6 groups and ask them to find out how IBM is catering to the concerns raised by experts on the ethical use of artificial intelligence. Students can refer to the document available the given link: https://www.ibm.com/watson/assets/duo/pdf/everydayethics.pdf

Activity 3: Let the students debate the benefits and danger of AI Technology.

Preesentation Activity

Ask the students to identify the projects as shown in the image. Then, they can select any one project and present the utility of that project

Sustainable development goals

AI Lab Session – Colorizing Sketches

Visit the URL, https://petalica-paint.pixiv.dev/index_en.html You will be amazed to see that, with Artificial Intelligence, you can draw within the tool or upload your sketches without worrying about the quality of the original file and then color them automatically in different ways.

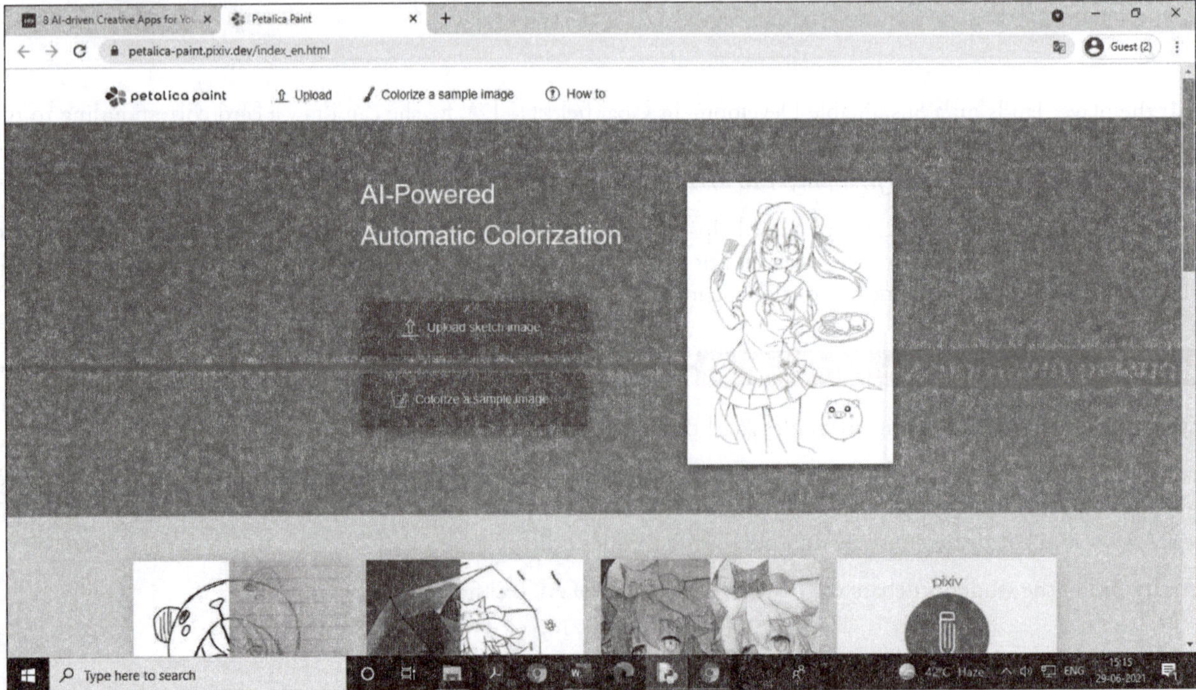

Answers

Fill in the Blanks

1. Sustainable Development Goals

2. Ethical

3. peer-to-peer, remote

4. Lookout

5. Smart

6. quality

7. minimize, optimize

State True or False

1. True

2. False

3. False

4. True

5. True

6. False

7. True

Multiple Choice Questions

1. a

2. c

3. a

4. d

5. d

6. b

7. c

8. c

Skills for AI

6

Chapter Objectives

It is a matter of great pride that India is fast emerging as a technology hub that serves clients across the world. With a great number of unicorns and startups, India is shining bright because of its talented and focused workforce. This chapter talks about the skill set required to have a successful career in the field of Artificial Intelligence to motivate our readers to consider it as a feasible option. It also discusses the different startups that have come up in the AI domain.

6.1 SKILLS REQUIRED FOR AN ARTIFICIAL INTELLIGENCE ENGINEER

Artificial intelligence has not only brought major changes in the industry and every human being but also accelerated the growth of other emerging technologies like big data, robotics and IoT. No doubt, AI will continue leading as a technological innovator for the foreseeable future. Hence, there are immense opportunities for trained people to get into this rewarding career.

There has been a steady increase in AI jobs over the past few years and it will continue growing at a fast pace. It is said that 133 million new Artificial Intelligence jobs will be created by the year 2022. Most Indian companies are looking forward to hiring the right talent to match up the Market Sentiment. Moreover, companies are giving a 60–70% hike in salaries of those employees who are well-versed in this technology. Among Indian cities, most of the AI work is being done in Mumbai followed by Bangalore and Chennai. However, the demand for AI Jobs has increased to an extent that the demand for efficient workforce in this area is not being met.

To start as an AI engineer, one must have good knowledge of the following subjects:

- Mathematics, to understand the concepts of Calculus, Statistics, Probability, Discrete Mathematics
- Programming languages like R, Java, or Python
- Data analytics skills
- Machine learning techniques.

6.2 SPECIFIC JOBS IN AI

AI and machine learning, in themselves, entail a broad category of jobs including:

Big Data Engineer: A big data engineer works to ***create an ecosystem for the business systems to interact efficiently***. This is done by effectively administering huge amount of data of an organization to obtain valuable information from it.

A big data engineer gets the highest salary as compared to other AI roles. For doing his job, he must know Spark, Hadoop, SQL and programming languages like Python, R and Java. The aspirant must also know techniques to visualize data using relevant graphs (plots or charts). A PhD degree in the field of Computer Science or Mathematics is preferred for this role.

Business Intelligence Developer. A business intelligence developer *identifies business trends by assessing complicated data sets.* They help in increasing the company's profits manifold through business intelligence solutions. Such solutions optimize different processes and workflow across the organization.

Any person having the knowledge of computer programming and data sets can work on this role. Besides a bachelor's degree in the field of computers, mathematics or engineering, the person must have problem-solving and analytical skills.

Data Scientist: A data scientist helps to *collect relevant data from multiple sources for analyzing it to derive useful information*. The information obtained is then used to take complex business decisions. For this, the data scientist is supposed to gather a variety of data – current data as well as historical data to make predictions about trends in the future.

An aspirant looking for a data scientist job must know modern tools like Spark, Hadoop, Pig or Hive and be comfortable using programming languages like Python, Scala or SQL.

Machine Learning (ML) Engineer: ML engineers *develop and maintain self-running software that facilitates machine learning initiatives*. They make extensive use of ML techniques for image and speech recognition, prevention of frauds, customer insights, and management of risks. A machine learning engineer must know how to apply predictive models dealing with huge sets of data. For this, he must also possess sound programming (Python, R, Scala, and Java), computing (including deep learning, neural networks), and mathematical skills. A master's degree in mathematics or computer science is preferred for this job.

Research Scientist: Research scientists carry out *extensive research dealing with applications of machine learning and machine intelligence.* For this, they must have expertise in the field of applied mathematics, statistics, deep learning, and machine learning. A PhD degree or advanced master's degree in mathematics or computer science is always preferred for this role.

AI Data Analyst: The AI data *analyst performs data mining, data cleaning, and data interpretation tasks. While cleaning the data, all irrelevant data is discarded.* Statistical tools and methods are then applied on cleaned data to draw inferences (Fig. 6.1). An AI data analyst aspirant must have a bachelor's degree in mathematics or computer science.

Figure 6.1   Analytics dashboard

Source: https://online.hbs.edu/blog/post/data-analytics-vs-data-science

Product Manager: The job of a product manager is *to overcome challenges by strategically collecting and analyzing data*. The implications of this study are then used to estimate business impacts from the outcomes of data interpretation.

AI Engineer: AI engineers are the actual problem-solvers who *develop, test and apply different AI models*. They know how to optimize the use of AI infrastructure. They are also well-versed in developing and deploying ML algorithms to make effective business decisions. For this role, an undergraduate or postgraduate degree in the field of data science, computer science or statistics is mandatory. Proficiency in programming languages (like Python, R or C++), Machine Learning algorithms, applied mathematics, and data analytics is preferred.

Robotics Scientist: As the name suggests, a robotics scientist is used to *program robots*. The aspirant must have a master's degree in robotics, computer science or engineering.

Top 10 companies using AI are Amazon, Apple, Google, Facebook, DJI, Anki, Clarifai, Deepmind, Casetext and DataVisor.

6.2.1   Startups in AI

India has now emerged as a land of startups. Cities like Bengaluru, Chennai, Pune, Mumbai, Delhi lead innovation. Every year more than a thousand AI-based companies worth multiple billion dollars are started up in the country. We will discuss only a few of these startups here.

> Delhi-NCR is poised to be one of the top five startup hubs in the world. Mumbai, having big entrepreneurs' support, has more than 250 AI startups.

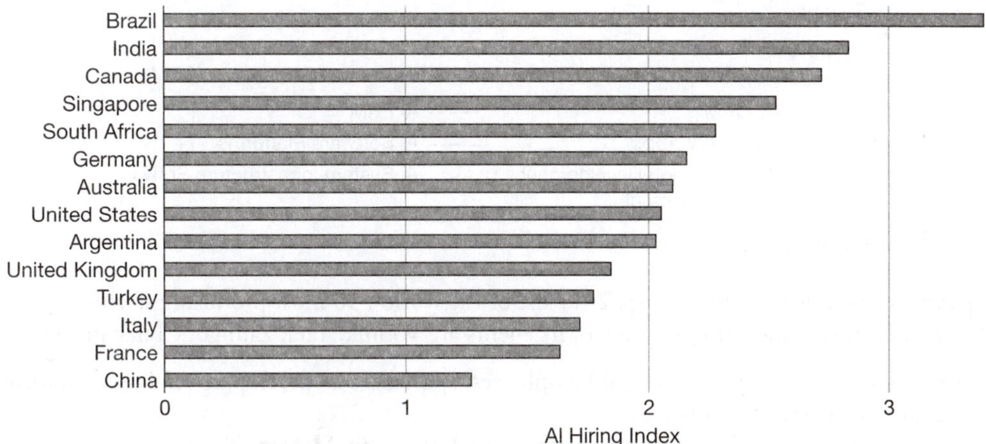

Figure 6.2   AI hiring index by country, 2020

Source: LinkenIn, 2020 | Chart: 2020 AI index report

Manthan, a Bengaluru-based AI company was founded in 2003 with an initial investment of $98 million. Today, it has 501 employees and 170 customers across 21 countries. Its NLP engine Maya, acts as a business assistant and can answer questions such as sales trends, last month's profits, etc. And the company provides AI solutions for **marketing, customer targeting, inventory, pricing, and promotions** to its clients.

SigTuple, a Bengluru-based company with 51–200 employees was started in 2015. The company uses AI and machine learning algorithms to develop medical diagnostic solutions that perform **screening and advanced diagnosis of urine, blood, semen samples, along with retinal scans and X-rays.** Results of the diagnosis are then sent to a pathologist for review and, if required, to the point-of-care in 5 minutes.

Just imagine, if the initial diagnosis is done on time, then ambulances can be dispatched to carry emergency medicines to patients, thereby reducing risk of life. SigTuple also creates automated microscope to make up for the lack of pathologists.

Mad Street Den, a Chennai-based company having 51–200 employees, aims to bring AI straight to customers through IoT, connected cars, user engagement, data analytics, online fashion, mobile gaming, social media, etc. The company

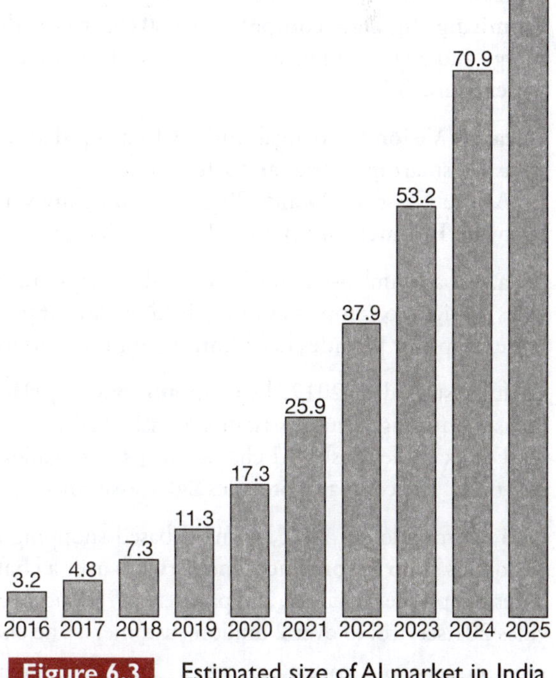

Figure 6.3   Estimated size of AI market in India

Source: Statista | value in $ billion

enhances shopping experience of customers by **displaying products that are most relevant to them across sites, apps, and stores**.

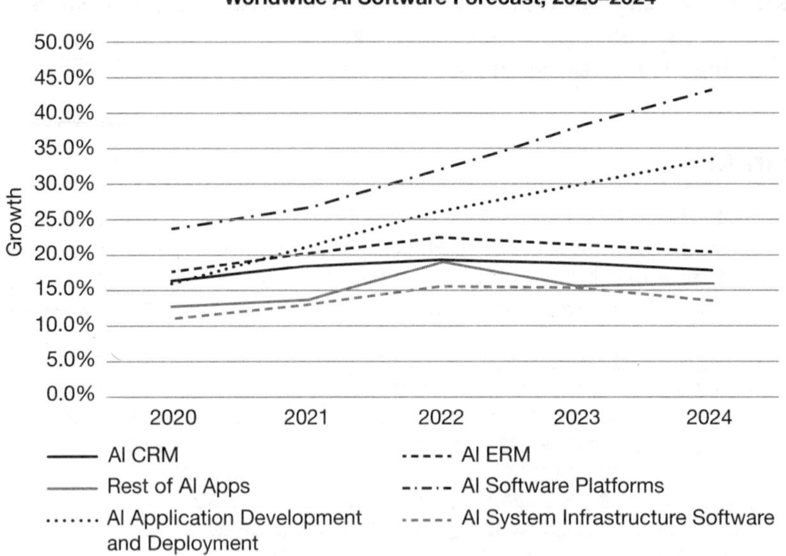

Source: IDC 2021

The company was included in Bloomberg's 2017 list of the world's 50 most promising startups catering to clients across Asia, Middle East, US, and Europe. Some of its clients are Voonik, Tata, Zilingo, Craftsvilla, etc.

Haptik, a Mumbai-based company with 51–200 employees, specializes in developing **AI-based chatbots for enterprises, service companies, and consumers.**

Haptik provides customers with a **hybrid interface for human-to-AI transitions.** In 2018, the company did a partnership with Amazon AWS to incorporate AWS's cloud offering, AI tools, and advanced database framework. **Coca Cola, Amazon Pay, and Samsung** are well-known clients of Haptik.

Flutura, a Bengaluru based **IoT company**, was recognized by CIO Review magazine as one of the **Top 20 Most Promising Big Data companies in 2015**. It provides big data analytics solutions to **unlock new business value** for energy and engineering customers across the world. Its **clientele** includes prominent companies like **Hitachi, Henkel, Sodexo and GTT.**

Uncanny Vision is a Bengaluru-based startup that uses deep learning vision algorithms **to develop surveillance solutions** for smart industries and safe cities.

At the Nasscom Awards 2017, the company was selected as one of **India's Most Innovative Top 50 Emerging Software Product Companies**. Uncanny Vision is also in the YourStory's search for **Top 30 Tech Startups for 2018.**

Arya.ai is a Mumbai-based AI startup that helps other AI startups solve complex problems at a much faster pace. It provides services to companies in the field of **Banking, Insurance, Medicine and Healthcare, Retail, and Oil and Gas.** For example, it provides deep learning solutions to insurance firms to help them process insurance claims in minutes.

Bash.ai, started in 2017, helps in **automating HR systems** by using AI and big data technologies. The company focuses on using virtual assistants to assist HR for businesses by mimicking cognitive functions related to HR.

For example, Bash's AI chatbot helps companies to automate conversation with employees with full accuracy in real-time. The company provides 24×7 assistance to enhance productivity.

Niki.Ai, founded in 2015, is an AI-based shopping assistant and chatbot that uses NLP and ML algorithms to help customers **shop for products and services over a chat interface**. The assistant also helps in automating tasks like online ordering, phone recharges, and payments. The success of this company can be easily understood from the fact that it provides 20+ services to over 2 million customers. The chatbot is now available on Android, iOS, and Facebook Messenger.

DailyHunt, a Bengaluru-based AI company founded in 2007, is an India-exclusive news-based company that collects news headlines and updates from different regions in the country to provide content in 14 Indian languages.

The company, having 500–1000 employees, uses machine-learning techniques to **prepare content and display them as per reader preferences.**

MFine, founded in Bangalore in 2017, is a health-tech startup that developed an AI-powered telemedicine mobile app. The app allows its users to **find the best specialist doctors, references to medical stores, pathology services and other related services via chat, audio or video call.**

Users can get prescriptions and/or routine care, thereby making access to healthcare simple, fast, and effective.

NetraDyne, a startup in Bangalore, provides AI- and ML-based solutions to transform road safety. The company attempts to decrease road mishaps by creating greater awareness among commercial drivers about risky driving behavior. Netradyne aims to provide a holistic view of the driving experience, highlighting drivers' driving skills and allowing them visibility into everything they experience while on the road.

Vymo, founded in 2013, creates solutions for automating sales activities and making the whole sales process less complex. The Vymo personal assistant app **assists enterprise sales/service teams**. The app analyzes rich, contextual data to predict the sequence of steps that should be followed, detects whether similar events have taken place in the past, and further links them to drive better predictions.

Credit Vidya is an AI startup having 150–200 employees. The AI solution created by Credit Vidya accesses only **transactional SMSes with filters to omit messages containing OTPs, passwords or any similar identifiers.**

Joveo is an AI startup that has created a programmatic job advertising platform using machine learning and AI techniques to assist **efficient job ad placements and bids**. The platform effectively executes data-driven recruitment media campaigns, resulting in more relevant applicants.

Altizon, founded in 2013, provides an industrial platform for **manufacturing applications**. The platform uses huge amount of data to make astute business decisions.

NLPBots develops chatbots for integration across websites, applications and messaging platforms to make **man–machine conversations intuitive and meaningful**. It also helps organizations to understand unstructured text. The chatbot has helped large enterprises from automobile majors to pharmaceutical giants, from legend enterprises to new-age unicorns.

> Gurugram has the third-highest per-capita income in India.

Perfint Healthcare specializes in medical device technology and develops diagnostic equipment to help in the research of cancer. The company aims to **improve the quality of life of those fighting cancer and struggling with pain.**

Qure.ai is an AI-based company founded in 2016 with an aim to make healthcare more cost-effective and easier to access. The company provides a clinical decision support tool that aids in the analysis of diagnostic images by **combining clinical, scientific and regulatory knowledge with deep learning expertise.**

GreyOrange, founded in 2011, automates warehouse fulfillment using a combination of AI software and autonomous **mobile robots** to deliver high-yield fulfillment.

INDWealth, founded in2018, is an artificial intelligence and machine learning-based wealth management platform for high-net-worth families. The platform enables clients to **track and organize their financial investments** across different avenues, expenses, loans, and associated taxes.

Farmagain, founded in 2013, focuses on solving farming-related challenges and making the farmer more productive and profitable. The company is using advanced technologies like Artificial Intelligence and IoT in the field of agriculture.

THIRAI, founded in 2019, offers AI-enabled technology for **thermal screening, contact tracing solutions, vision technology along with face recognition** based on demographics and behavioral data.

Intello Labs, founded in 2016, is an AI-based agritech startup that provides solutions such as **image detection, analysis, grading and testing of the commodities**. They also offer testing and grading of corn, tomato, wheat, potato, onions, and soybean. For this, the farmers just have to click pictures of the commodity, upload it on the app and get a detailed quality report of that commodity.

Leverage Edu is an AI based company that help students make decisions while selecting a particular course, college or university.

The startup has created an app that uses AI to match students' profile with courses offered at different colleges that best suit their requirements and aptitude. They also arrange for experts to guide the student throughout the admission process.

Key Terms

Data Scientist: A data scientist helps to collect relevant data from multiple sources for analyzing it to derive useful information.

Machine Learning Engineer: A person who develops and maintains self-running software that facilitates machine learning initiatives.

Research Scientist: Scientists carrying out extensive research dealing with applications of machine learning and machine intelligence

AI Data Analyst: A person who performs data mining, data cleaning, and data interpretation tasks. While cleaning the data, all irrelevant data is discarded

Product Manager: A person who overcomes challenges by strategically collecting and analyzing data.

AI Engineer: Actual problem-solvers who develop, test and apply different AI models.

Robotics Scientist: A scientist who program robots.

Chapter Highlights

- There has been a steady increase in AI jobs over the past few years and they will continue growing at a fast pace. It is said that 133 million new Artificial Intelligence jobs will be created by the year 2022.
- A Big Data Engineer works to create an ecosystem for the business systems to interact efficiently. This is done by effectively administering huge amount of data of an organization to obtain valuable information from it.
- An aspirant looking for a data scientist job must know to work with modern tools like Spark, Hadoop, Pig or Hive and be comfortable using programming languages like Python, Scala or SQL.
- ML engineers develop and maintain self-running software that facilitates machine learning initiatives.
- While cleaning the data, all irrelevant data is discarded. Statistical tools and methods are then applied on the cleaned data to draw inferences.
- India has now emerged as a land of startups. Cities like Bengaluru, Chennai, Pune, Mumbai, Delhi lead innovation

Review Questions

1. Discuss the different roles in an AI-based company.
2. Name some programming tools used for big data analysis.
3. Name some programming languages used for big data analysis.
4. Write a short note on any two AI startups, which impressed you the most.
5. How can an AI-based startup help mankind in times of a big crisis, especially during a pandemic?

Fill in the Blanks

1. ___________ helps to collect relevant data from multiple sources for analyzing it to derive useful information.
2. _________ algorithms are used for image and speech recognition, prevention of frauds, customer insights, and management of risks.
3. While __________ the data, all irrelevant data is discarded.
4. A _________ scientist programs robots.
5. _______ develops and maintains self-running software that facilitates machine learning initiatives.

State True or False

1. Machine-learning techniques are a necessary skill for AI.
2. BI Developer may not have the knowledge of computer programming and data sets.
3. Spark, Hadoop, Pig or Hive are programming languages used for data analysis.
4. Scala is a programming language used for data analysis.
5. A research scientist must know subjects like mathematics and statistics.
6. After applying statistical tools, irrelevant data must be removed.
7. Delhi-NCR is poised to be one of the top five startup hubs in the world.
8. An ML Engineer performs extensive research dealing with applications of machine learning and machine intelligence.
9. AI Data Analysts develop, test and apply different AI models.

Multiple Choice Questions

1. In India, most of the AI is done in which city?
   a. Indore   b. Tiruchirappalli   c. Mumbai   d. Kolkata
2. Which of the following languages is generally not used for AI?
   a. R   b. Python   c. Julia   d. C++
3. __________ skill is not necessary for a Business Intelligence Developer.
   a. Analytical   b. Programming   c. Problem-solving   d. Managerial
4. __________ data is used to make predictions about trends in the future.
   a. Current   b. Historical   c. Both of these.   d. None of these.
5. Identify the odd one out:
   a. Spark   b. Hadoop   c. Pig   d. Python
6. __________ estimates business impacts from the outcomes of data interpretation.
   a. AI Engineer   b. Product Manager   c. Research Scientist   d. ML Engineer
7. ________ helps to collect relevant data from multiple sources for analyzing it to drive useful information.
   a. AI Engineer   b. Data Engineer   c. Research Scientist   d. ML Engineer
8. An AI Data Analyst does not perform data ________ tasks.
   a. mining   b. cleaning   c. interpretation   d. collection
9. A PhD degree in Computer Science is not required for which job profile?
   a. Big Data Engineer   b. Business Intelligence Developer
   c. Research Scientist   d. None of these.

Identify the Profile

1. Helps to collect relevant data from multiple sources for analyzing it to derive useful information. ____________
2. A person who develops and maintains self-running software that facilitates machine learning initiatives. ____________
3. Scientists carrying out extensive research dealing with applications of machine learning and machine intelligence. ____________
4. A person who performs data mining, data cleaning, and data interpretation tasks. ____________
5. A person who overcome challenges by strategically collecting and analyzing data. ____________
6. Actual problem-solvers who develop, test and apply different AI models. ____________
7. Scientist who programs robots. ____________

Group Discussion

Are you interested to take up Artificial Intelligence as a career?
Would you like to have a startup delivering smart solutions? If yes, what problem would you like to solve?

Role-playing Activity

Imagine that you are a Robotics Engineer and you have visited a school to inspire students to take up career in artificial intelligence. Give a 5-minute speech highlighting what you would say.

AI Lab Session – Generate New Images

Visit the URL, https://www.artbreeder.com/ The AI application allows users to keep selecting interesting images to discover totally new images. Artbreeder turns the simple act of exploration into creativity by helping users make images by mixing any Artbreeder images together. Users can use any shared image for editing and mixing.

 +  = 

Arousing Awareness Activity

Collect information about any five more AI startups in India and present a brief report on your findings.

Answers

Fill in the Blanks

1. Data scientist	**2.** Machine Learning	**3.** cleaning	**4.** robotics	**5.** ML Engineer

State True or False

1. True   **3.** False   **5.** True   **7.** True   **9.** False
2. False   **4.** True   **6.** False   **8.** False

Multiple Choice Questions

1. c   **3.** d   **5.** d   **7.** b   **9.** b
2. d   **4.** c   **6.** b   **8.** d

Identify the Profile

1. Data Scientist
2. Machine Learning Engineer
3. Research Scientist
4. AI Data Analyst
5. Product Manager
6. AI Engineer
7. Robotics Scientist

Ethical Issues Around AI

7

Just building computer programs that can think will not solve human problems. Instead, they may further introduce a new set of problems. In this chapter therefore, the focus is on identifying such issues and designing ethical AI systems, rather than simple AI systems.

7.1   IS AI DANGEROUS? WILL ROBOTS TAKE OVER THE WORLD?

Rapid growth and increase in capabilities of AI systems have made us wonder about the risks involved in using AI. Some of us think that AI will quickly takeover tasks performed by humans. But most researchers believe that super-intelligent AI is unlikely to exhibit human emotions, so there is no point thinking that AI will become malevolent. AI can become a risk only in two conditions.

AI system could be programmed specifically to do something devastating. For example, autonomous weapons are AI systems that are programmed to kill. If acquired by unscrupulous people having ill intentions, such weapons could inadvertently lead to an AI war, and mass casualties, potentially even the end of humanity.

Autonomous weapons are designed to be extremely difficult to "turn off", and once they become operational, humans could themselves rapidly lose control over them. This risk is also present with narrow AI, when given autonomy.

Just imagine what would happen if an autonomous drone with facial recognition as well as a 3D-printed rifle, pistol or any other type of gun becomes available. Or if a self-driving car connected to the Internet is hacked to get into some serious accident.

Even in the hospitals, more and more equipment are now connected to the Internet. If any or all of these are hacked, then can you imagine what the hacker can do with the patient's body?

AI could be programmed to do something beneficial, but the method used to achieve its goal can be highly destructive. This is especially true when the AI programmer asks the machine to complete a task, but does not clearly outline the goals. For example, you can instruct a self-driven car to take you to a particular destination as soon as possible. However, the instruction "as soon as possible" fails to address safety, road rules, etc. The smart car may successfully complete its task, but after creating a great havoc. So, there must be some provision to continuously monitor and control the machine; its process must be designed to achieve that goal.

> Of the 9 million low-skilled services and BPO roles, 30 percent or around 3 million will be lost by 2022, principally driven by the impact of robot process automation or RPA.

As of now, there is no liability for actions on machines. There is no clarity on what legal aspects bind machines when they become increasingly smart. Questions like,

- Do we judge AI systems the same way as we judge a human?
- Who is responsible if the AI system becomes self-learning and autonomous to a greater extent?
- Is there any error margin for AI machines, even if it has fatal consequences?

Apart from these serious concerns, AI also poses some additional threats/risks that calls for attention.

The immediate risk posed by job automation As AI robots become smarter and more dexterous, they will quickly replace humans. For example, you must have heard of restaurants having robots as waiters. Just imagine, where will the less-educated people go if machines start taking their jobs? Figure 7.1 illustrates the scenario.

It is rightly feared that deployment of AI systems for job automation will eventually replace certain types of jobs, especially those that are predictable and repetitive. According to a 2019 Brookings Institution study, 36 million people work in jobs that they may soon lose owing to automation as at least 70 percent of their tasks (varying from retail sales, market analysis to hospitality and warehouse labor) will be done using AI. In fact, a newer Brookings report even states that white collar jobs may be worst affected. As per McKinsey & Company report (2018), the African American workforce will be hit hardest by automation.

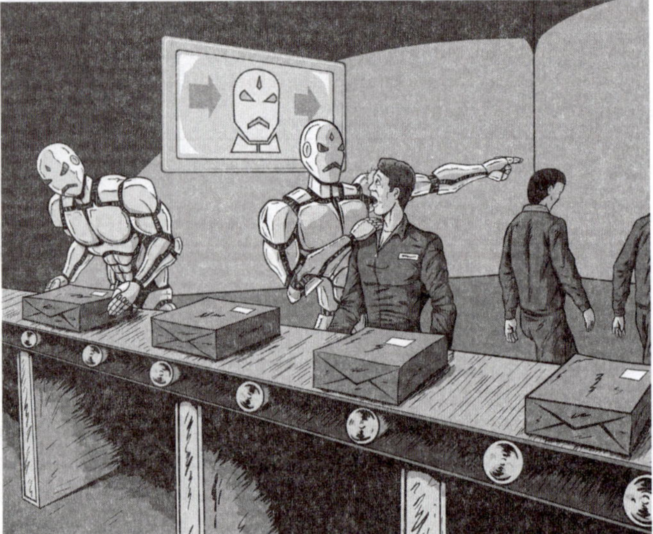

Figure 7.1   Risk posed by job automation

Biased algorithms We know that computers work on GIGO concept, which says Garbage-In-Garbage-Out. This is a very serious limitation in AI applications. If we feed our algorithms data sets that contain biased data, then the output generated from such systems will only produce biased results. This biased result, if applied to solve a real-world problem, may lead to an even bigger problem.

A dynamic advertising billboard in Utrecht was switched off because the spy software installed on these billboards aroused public outrage.

Too little privacy With using IoT or AI systems, a lot of data is generated. It is said that approximately 2.5 quintillion bytes (or 2.5 million terabytes) of data is added each day. It is interesting to note that 90% of the digital data has been created in the last two years. A lot of data is required for proper functioning of the smart systems. As a result, much data about us is collected thereby eroding our privacy. Once the systems collect our data, we have no means to know what data about us is used by whom and for what purpose.

These days, cameras can easily be fitted with facial recognition software to capture details about us (including our gender, age, ethnicity, gesture and state of mind). Do you know that in China, some police officers wear glasses with facial recognition technology having a database with facial pictures of thousands of 'suspects' (judged on the basis of certain behavior)?

Everything becomes unreliable These days, fake news and filter bubbles are not uncommon. Smart systems can create faces, compose texts, produce tweets, manipulate images, clone voices and engage in smart advertising.

An AI system can be used to depict day into night or create highly realistic faces of people who have never existed.

For example, open-source software Deepfake can easily stick pictures of faces on moving video footage. Because of such fake videos, celebrities are worst affected. People with malicious intentions are easily creating pornographic videos starring them. Even normal citizens are blackmailed with morphed images and/or videos. This is often known as **Faceswap video blackmailing.** See Fig. 7.2 to understand the concept.

Even in politics, fake or manipulated videos are produced at a high speed to influence the opinions of the masses.

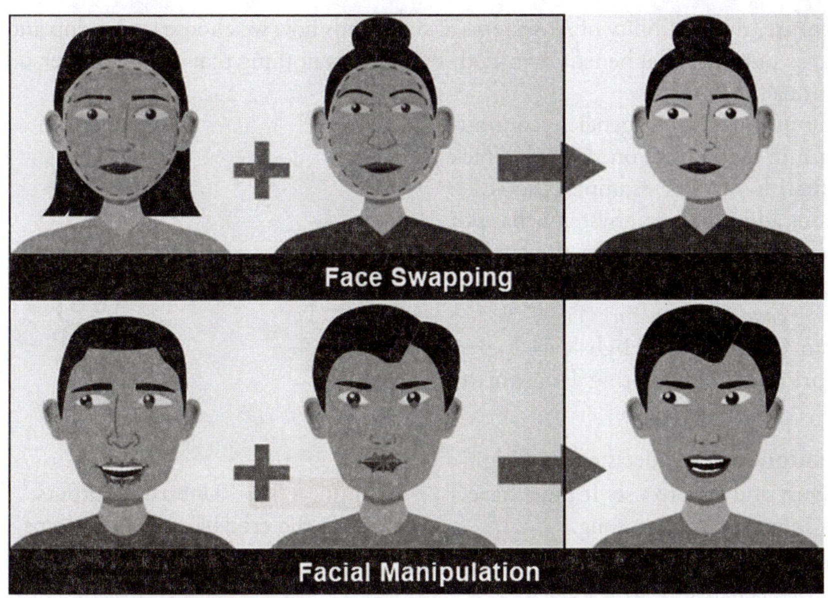

Figure 7.2   Face swapping and facial manipulation

Did you know that the company Cambridge Analytica, was found to manage access to data from 87 million Facebook profiles of Americans to campaign for President Trump so that he could come to power?

7.2   ETHICS IN AI

The current world is quickly getting transformed by artificial intelligence and those who use this technology are living a richer and easy-going life. But this is possible only when we talk about ethical AI, not just AI.

The term, Ethical AI, is composed of two words, ethical and AI. We are now already familiar with the term AI. Ethical means one that is according to ethics. And ethics relates to moral principles that govern the behavior and actions of a group or individual. So, ethical AI is the theory behind developing computer systems that can perform tasks that require human intelligence. It focusses on how right, how fair and how just is the AI's output, outcome and impact.

An Example: We know that AI can produce biased results if it is trained with biased data or if it does not do anything to avoid bias. So, any AI system that works on biased data is actually not ethical (or unethical). For example, Microsoft released a chatbot called Tay on Twitter in 2016, to learn by engaging people in a dialogue through tweets or direct messages. However, trolls made Tay learn all negative words that spread hatred for women, a particular race and all sorts of biased data within hours. Tay was also taught to give repulsive and toxic responses. This aroused anger of Twitter users and finally Microsoft had to silence Tay forever in even less than 24 hours.

An ethical AI system, designed to solve a particular problem, uses unbiased data. It is trained using the right learning model for the problem and is monitored to evaluate if the results produced by it is right and fair.

Why ethical AI is important

Since AI is used in areas like medicine, law enforcement, recruiting, data privacy, military defense and self-driving vehicles, it is mandatory that the AI systems must produce accurate, transparent and understandable results that are in synchronization with the ethical standards and norms of our society. To understand the need of ethical AI systems, we must first understand that biased or incorrect output from an AI system that assist in law enforcement, job recruitment, defense work, or self-driving vehicles can result in eroding people's privacy (by misusing data in unintended ways), and taking decisions that are impossible for people to understand or to accept liability for damages when harm is caused.

In October 2019, researchers found that an algorithm used in US hospitals to predict which patients may require extra medical care heavily favored white patients over blacks. This bias creeped in because of the fact that white patients paid more bills and availed extra medical facilities for the same medical problem as compared to black patients.

Amazon's hiring algorithm also suffered from bias-related issues. The algorithm was found to be biased against women. This was probably due to the fact that the system saw a greater number of men applicants than women.

Apart from being **unbiased and accurate**, the credibility of AI systems also depends how we choose to develop and use it. We can hope that AI will be used for purposes that benefit mankind. But there is nothing that can stop a person from creating systems that can be disastrous for humanity.

Nonetheless, efforts are being made by numerous agencies, committees, coalitions, and expert groups to ensure that we are on the right track to make AI systems do more to heal than harm. For example, the IEEE Global Initiative on Ethics of Autonomous and Intelligent Systems that put out *Ethically Aligned Design*, a publication from 2016, outlines the guiding standards for developing and administering ethical AI solutions. Therefore, ethical AI aims to *ensure is that AI is doing good for the planet* (Fig. 7.3).

Going further on this, the European Commission High-level Expert Group on AI identified seven guiding principles for creating Trustworthy AI. These guidelines are:

- AI systems should support **human autonomy** and decision-making.
- AI systems should be technically robust and **safe** to use. It must have a fallback plan that can be used when something goes wrong.
- AI systems should ensure data privacy by protecting user's data, and providing adequate mechanisms to maintain the **quality and integrity** of the data.
- AI system should not work on biased data. The system should be **clear, explicable and transparent** about its underlying data and the models.
- AI system should be trained with diverse, non-discriminatory and **fair data** and models to avoid unfair bias.
- AI systems should be designed to **benefit** everyone, now and in future. They must focus on societal and environmental wellbeing to be sustainable and environmentally friendly.
- An AI system should have the **accountability** to ensure accurate, unbiased outcomes with utmost responsibility.

Figure 7.3   Unbiased outputs increase the credibility of AI systems

Have you ever wondered how much information Google has about you? In an Android Phone, Google has your entire Contact List. Google knows names and numbers of people you talk to. Google knows your location. It knows where you go everyday and on holiday. Google knows what email you write and to whom. Google has your photographs (Google Photos), knows details about your friends (Google Hangouts). All this is done in lieu of the free services it provides. But imagine what big risk it poses to our privacy.

Key Terms

AI war: Use of autonomous AI weapons that can be used for mass killing, devastation and may be, ending humanity.

Faceswap video blackmailing: People with malicious intentions use morphed images and/or videos to create pornographic videos starring celebrities and normal citizens to blackmail them.

Ethics: Moral principles that govern the behavior and actions of a group or individual.

Ethical AI: Theory behind developing computer systems that can perform tasks that require human intelligence.

Chapter Highlights

- Super-intelligent AI is unlikely to exhibit human emotions.
- AI could be programmed to do something beneficial, but the method used to achieve its goal can be highly destructive
- There is no liability for actions on machines.
- The immediate risk posed by AI is loss of livelihood for the less-educated due to job automation.

Review Questions

1. Super-intelligent AI is unlikely to exhibit human emotions. How can AI lead to devastation?

2. AI could be programmed to do something beneficial, but the method used to achieve its goal can be highly destructive. Comment.

3. What do you think, is it justifiable for not having any liability on machines?

4. List any two risks posed by AI.

5. With the help of an example, explain the meaning of the term 'Ethical AI'.

6. What are biased algorithms?

7. What is Faceswap video blackmailing?

8. Self-driving cars and AI powered surgeries can actually pose more danger to a person's life. Justify this statement.

9. Why should we focus on creating ethical AI systems and not just AI systems?

10. Imagine that your neighbor has installed a CCTV camera that collects a video footage of all visitors coming to his house as well as yours. Is such a behavior justified? Give reasons to support your answer.

Fill in the Blanks

1. Autonomous ___________ are AI systems that are programmed to kill.

2. A self-driving car connected to the Internet can be ________ to get into some serious accident.

3. There is no liability for actions of __________.

4. ________ means moral principles that govern the behavior and actions of a group or individual.

5. _________ is the theory behind developing computer systems that can perform tasks that require human intelligence.

State True or False

1. Super-intelligent AI is unlikely to exhibit human emotions.

2. Autonomous weapons are designed to be extremely difficult to "turn off".

3. An autonomous drone with facial recognition as well as a 3D-printed rifle is a fiction that can never be realized.

4. An AI system that completes its task in a destructive way should be avoided.

5. There is no liability for actions on machines.

6. There is no need to fear about job loss due to AI.

7. Approximately 2.5 quintillion bytes (or 2.5 million terabytes) of data is added each day.

8. Faceswap video blackmailing has affected only big celebrities.

9. Widespread use of AI will result in job loss.

10. Shortage of skilled manpower is holding back the growth of AI.

11. Adoption of AI systems will always be beneficial to the society.

12. AI can be used to reduce inequalities in society.

13. Ethical AI is concerned with the benefit of individuals but not of society.

Multiple Choice Questions

1. An AI system with ___________ instructions can be dangerous.
   a. unclear   b. incomplete   c. Both of these.   d. None of these.

2. Employees doing which type of tasks suffer the most due to job automation?
   a. Low-skilled   b. predictable   c. repetitive   d. All of these.

3. We must use _________ data for accurate results from an AI system.
   a. biased   b. unbiased   c. Both of these.   d. None of these.

4. More data collected about us means ___________ privacy of our data.
   a. more   b. less   c. moderate   d. None of these.

5. The most important feature of results generated from an ethical AI system is that it is __________.
   a. accurate   b. transparent
   c. synchronized with the norms of our society   d. understandable

6. Identify the incorrect statement:
   a. AI system must be transparent.
   b. Users should be able to see what data is shared about them.
   c. The system can collect any data about users.
   d. Users should have the option to leave the system anytime.

Group Discussion

1. Assume that you are a research engineer. How would you use AI for a good cause and a bad cause?

2. Imagine that your RWA President has decided to install smart security cameras at multiple locations in the society. This is indeed a very good step to ensure security. But there are always two sides of a coin. Discuss the ethical concerns that must be addressed before installation.

Debate

AI has done mankind more harm than help.

Role-play Activity

Imagine that you are a project manager and your team has developed an AI-powered software for conducting online examination. Present a report highlighting the pros and cons of this system. Students can take up any other project also for presentation.

Job AD Creating Activity

1. Create an advertisement for a job with a given skill-set and requirement. Frame it in a way that it describes the job 10 years down the line. Consider how AI will transform the nature of jobs while creating the ad.

2. Read this sample ad and design one for the opening of a housekeeper.

   Education: Minimum XII Pass with Computer Applications

   Credentials: X and XII marksheet and passing certificate; Letter of recommendation

   Experience: At least 2 years of experience in a smart home is mandatory.

Languages: Speak English/Hindi, Read English/Hindi, Write English/Hindi

Specific Skills: Cleaning and maintaining the house.

Operate robots for sweeping, mopping and washing floors, making beds

Work with IoT devices to vacuum carpets; Clean and disinfect bathrooms and fixtures; Use smart gadgets for cooking, cleaning utensils.

Must have technical know-how to maintain terrace gardening and water harvesting.

Work Location Information: Work in employer's home, Smart City

Work Conditions and Physical Capabilities: Fast-paced environment, high-pressure work, tight deadlines, repetitive tasks, mentally and physically demanding; Attention to detail required, reflecting new and efficient ways of doing traditional tasks; Should have basic knowledge for troubleshooting defective machines, interpreting information collected from security cameras and other devices.

Essential Skills: Reading text, understanding written and oral communication, working with others, decision-making

Other Information: Team-oriented, Leadership skills, Monday–Friday, no nights/weekends, competitive salary, paid training/holidays. Driver's license an asset.

How to Apply: Please fax or email your résumé.

Contact Name: Chinmay; Fax: Between 9:00 and 5 PM. (555) 287-28974. Email: chinmay@linkednet.in

AI Lab Session – Creating Comics from Video

Visit the URL https://comixify.ai/?last=month&sortBy=trend. Upload a video and convert it into a comic. You can use this website to tell your story by making a video (less than 25 minutes) and then converting it into an interesting story using comics text.

Answers

Fill in the Blanks

1. weapons
2. hacked
3. machines
4. Ethics
5. Ethical AI

State True or False

1. True
2. True
3. False
4. True
5. True
6. True
7. True
8. False
9. True
10. True
11. False
12. True
13. False

Multiple Choice Questions

1. c
2. d
3. b
4. b
5. c
6. c

AI Project Cycle

8

Chapter Objectives

Going into the details of Artificial Intelligence, this chapter focusses on:

- Relationship between AI and machine learning
- Project cycle that is followed in any AI project
- Types of machine learning algorithm
- Problem scoping in AI
- Data acquisition
- Data modeling
- Evaluation and deployment of AI project

We all know that human beings are the most intelligent species on this planet. Humans can think, evaluate and solve complex problems. Therefore, humans now want to impart this intelligence in machines so that even they can think, analyze and deduce solutions to otherwise complex problems.

To this end, AI aims at making the machines take decisions based on data, with efficiency and scale, particularly to automate the data-driven decision-making process. Some factors which have escalated the growth and application of machine learning techniques are discussed below:

1. Lack of availability of human expertise in situations where it is not safe or practically feasible for humans to work. For example, navigation in unknown territories or spatial planets.
2. Dynamic scenarios where conditions keep changing fast and humans are quite slow to respond. Apart from other reasons, it may also be due to limited network connectivity or inadequate availability of infrastructure in the organization.
3. Difficulty faced by humans to provide 100% accurate results, especially for computational tasks. For example, in applications like handwriting recognition, voice recognition, face recognition, and so on.

8.1 MACHINE LEARNING AND AI

AI-based systems make extensive use of ML algorithms. We can better understand the role of machine learning techniques through a very simple definition given by professor Mitchell –

"A computer program is said to learn from experience E with respect to some class of tasks T and performance measure P, if its performance at tasks in T, as measured by P, improves with experience E." Based on this definition, the Machine Learning Model can be given as shown in Fig.8.1. Here,

Task(T), is the real-world problem to be solved. For example, predicting the sales of a product, classifying an email as spam or not a spam, etc. Technically, examples of ML-based tasks are Classification, Regression, Clustering, Recognition, etc.

Experience (E) is the knowledge gained from data provided to the algorithm or model. Once data is provided, the model runs iteratively to learn some inherent patterns. Therefore, like humans, machines now learn from experience by analyzing the situation, relationships etc. Supervised, unsupervised and reinforcement learning are some ways to learn or gain experience. Experience acquired through ML model or algorithm is used to solve task T.

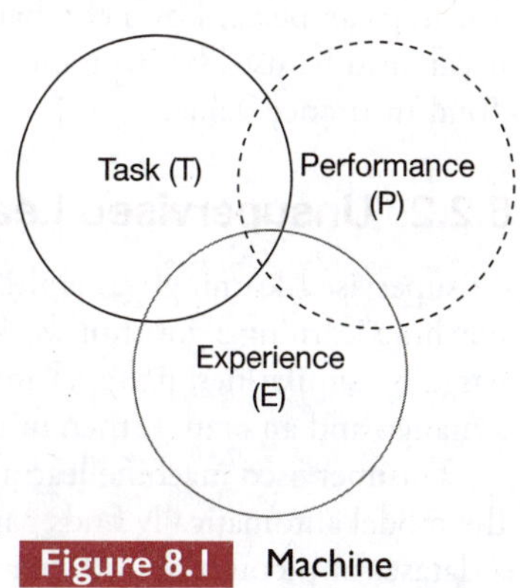

Figure 8.1 Machine learning model

Performance (P) is a measure that indicates how well a particular ML algorithm has performed the given task T using experience E. Performance is analyzed based on well-defined metrics including accuracy, F1, confusion matrix, precision, recall, sensitivity etc.

8.2   TYPES OF MACHINE LEARNING ALGORITHMS

Machine learning algorithms can be categorized as supervised or unsupervised. In addition, there is also the reinforced learning approach.

8.2.1 Supervised Learning

Supervised machine learning algorithms, as the name indicates, has a supervisor as teacher. These algorithms apply learning from past data (or experiences) to new data using labeled examples.

Technically, supervised learning algorithms learn an association between input data and output. For example, if we have input variable(s) X and output variable (Y), then the mapping function from input to output can be given as, $Y = f(X)$. This mapping function can be used to predict the output value for any new input after learning from the existing data.

For example, if you have a basket filled with different variety of fruits then the first step is to train the machine to identify a fruit. Now, our machine can easily identify an apple and a banana. Supervised learning algorithms can be further classified into two categories:

> Supervised learning should be used when output of data in the training set is known.

Classification algorithm A classification algorithm classifies data into a particular group. Classification techniques predict discrete categories. The output will be based on what the model has learned in training phase.

For example, a fruit as either an apple or a banana. In real-world applications, classification can be used in medical imaging, speech recognition, hand-writing recognition, credit scoring, predicting if an incoming email is authentic or spam, or whether a tumor is cancerous or benign.

Classification algorithms are best used if data can be tagged, categorized, or separated into specific groups or classes.

Regression A regression algorithm predicts a real value. The output value is based on what the model has learned in its training phase. In contrast to classification algorithms, regression predicts continuous values. For example, the cost of a product, the value of a stock, changes in temperature or fluctuations in power demand.

> In supervised learning, clear instructions are given specifying what needs to be learnt and how it needs to be learnt.

Thus, in supervised machine learning algorithm, data input and desired output, along with a feedback about the accuracy of predictions during algorithm training are provided. Data scientists can select variables or features that can be used by the model to analyze data and make predictions. For example, supervised learning can be used by a company to identify customers who are likely to churn (stop using the company's service). It can also be used by insurance companies to predict the likelihood of occurrence of a mishap and determine the Total Insurance Value.

8.2.2 Unsupervised Learning

Unsupervised learning trains the machine using information that is neither classified nor labelled. In this case, the machine learning algorithm works on that information without any guidance. The unsorted information is grouped based on similarities, patterns and differences without any prior training of data. For example, if we give an image of a mango and an orange, then initially the machine has no idea about how a mango looks and how an orange looks.

Unsupervised machine learning algorithm learns through observation and finding structures in the data. That is, the model automatically finds patterns and relationships in the dataset by creating clusters in it. For example, if given a dataset of pictures of both mangoes and oranges, the algorithm can make two clusters – one containing only pictures of oranges and the other of mangoes (Fig. 8.2). What an unsupervised machine learning cannot do is specifying labels to the clusters. That is, it can only segregate the pictures but cannot tell that this is a real-world orange or that is a mango.

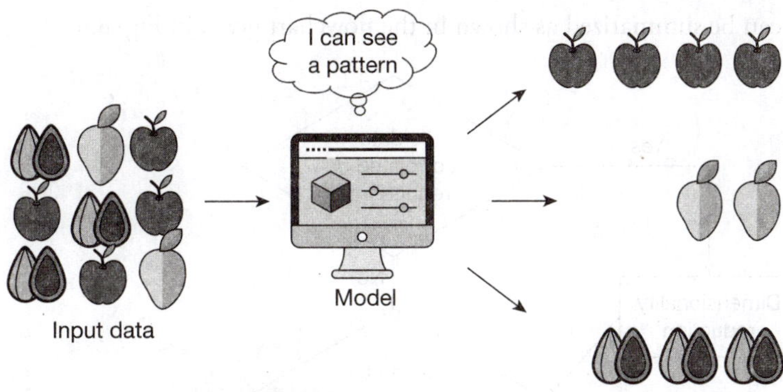

Figure 8.2   Unsupervised learning

Unsupervised learning can be categorized into the following sets of algorithms:

Clustering In clustering, the aim is to discover inherent groupings in the data or discover hidden patterns. It is one of the most useful unsupervised machine learning technique as it finds similarity as well as relationship in the underlying data. For example, a company may like to group its customers by their purchasing behavior, a cell phone company can use clustering to optimally decide the locations where they can build cell phone towers (these clusters can depict the number of people relying on their towers). Other applications include gene sequence analysis, market research, and object recognition.

Association analysis In association mining (or analysis), the aim is to discover rules that describe large portions of data. For example, a company can use association analysis to conclude that a customer who buys product X also buys product Y.

Dimensionality reduction It is used to reduce the number of feature variables for the data set. It is done by selecting a set of principal or representative features. Dimensionality reduction is a very important technique, especially when the data set has a large number (millions).

Outlier analysis This technique is used to find out the occurrences of rare events or observations that generally do not occur. Application of learned knowledge helps to differentiate between outliers or a normal data point.

Thus, unsupervised machine learning algorithms (also called neural networks) are used when the information used to train is neither classified nor labelled. These algorithms use an iterative approach called deep learning to review data and arrive at conclusions (Fig. 8.3). Unsupervised learning algorithms are used for more complex tasks than supervised learning systems. For example, these algorithms are used in image recognition, speech-to-text and natural language processing applications, and to predict the probability of presence of a particular disease. A retailer can use unsupervised learning technique to find out products that are frequently bought by customers or tend to be bought more frequently.

Figure 8.3   Supervised and unsupervised learning

8.2.3 Semi-supervised Learning

Semi-supervised machine learning algorithms fall somewhere between supervised and unsupervised algorithms since they use both labelled and unlabeled data for training. These algorithms improve accuracy.

Semi-supervised learning algorithms use a small amount of pre-labelled data and a large number of unlabeled data for training. Semi-supervised learning techniques can be applied using any of the two approaches given below.

We can build the supervised model based on a small amount of labelled data followed by building an unsupervised model by applying the same to large amounts of unlabeled data. The experience gained by generating more labelled data is used to train the model. This process is repeated multiple times.

In the second approach, unsupervised methods are used to cluster similar data samples, annotate these groups and then use this information to train the model.

The two approaches can be summarized as shown in the flowchart given in Fig. 8.4.

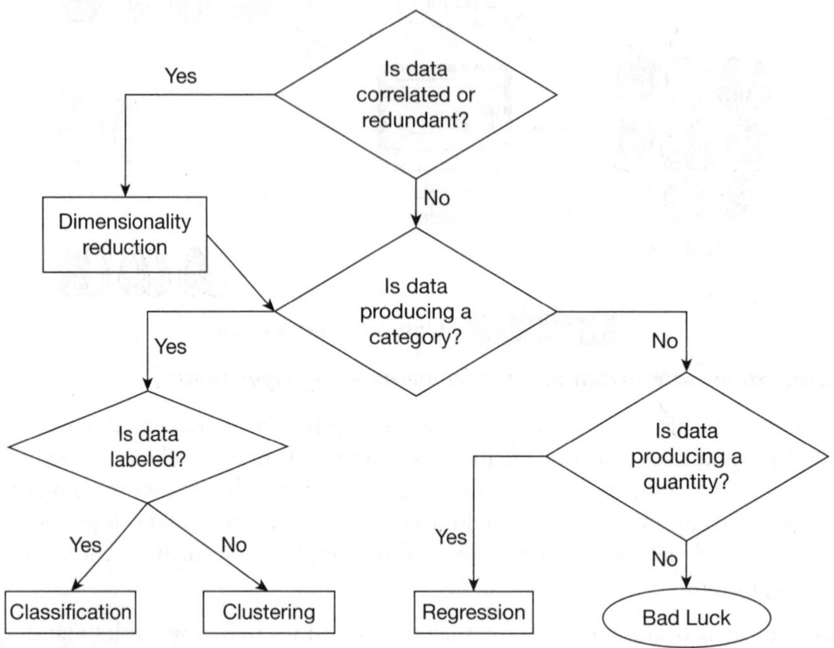

Figure 8.4 Classification of data using machine learning approach

8.2.4 Reinforcement Learning (RL)

These techniques are different from the previously discussed techniques and are rarely used. In a reinforcement learning algorithm, an agent is trained over a period of time so that it can interact with a specific environment.

Reinforcement learning is a type of dynamic programming that trains algorithms using a system of reward and punishment. The agent receives rewards for performing correctly and penalties for performing incorrectly. In this way, the agent learns without any human intervention to maximize its reward and minimize its penalty.

Since RL requires a lot of data, it is mostly used in areas where simulated data is readily available like in gameplay or robotics. In these areas, RL is used to find the best possible behavior or path that can be taken in a particular situation.

Reinforcement learning is different from supervised learning. In supervised learning, the training data has labels and the model is trained with the correct answer, but in case of RL, the reinforcement agent decides what to do to perform the given task. In the absence of a training dataset, it is bound to learn from its own experience.

Example: In the game shown in Fig. 8.5, there is an agent (robot) and a reward (diamond), with many hurdles (fire) in between. The robot has to learn by trying all the possible paths and then choose the path that gives him the reward with the least hurdles. Each right step earns a reward and every wrong step will subtract the reward of the robot. The total reward is calculated when it reaches the final reward that is the diamond.

To summarize technically, in an RL algorithm,

Figure 8.5 Reinforcement learning: Reward and punishment

- Input is an initial state from which the model will start
- Output is a list of possible outputs for a particular problem
- Training is based on the input. The model returns a state and the user will decide to reward or punish the model based on its output. The model keeps learning this way until it finds the best solution (or the solution with maximum reward).

8.2.5 Types of Reinforcement

There are two types of reinforcement:

Positive reinforcement has a positive effect on behavior. It occurs when a particular behavior increases the strength and the frequency of the behavior. Such a reinforcement maximizes performance and sustains changes for a long period of time.

Negative reinforcement is defined as strengthening a behavior by stopping or avoiding a negative condition.

> An RL agent perceives and interprets its environment, takes actions and learns through trial and error.

Applications of Reinforcement Learning RL is used in large environments when a model of the environment is known, but an analytic solution is not available.

- RL can be used in robotics for industrial automation.
- It is used to make machines learn.
- RL is used in data processing applications.
- RL can be used to create training systems that provide custom instruction and materials according to the requirement of students.
- RL is used for creating game playing software (playing chess).
- RL is used in a self-driving car where the car (agent) interacts with its environment, receives a reward depending on how it performs, such as driving to the destination safely. Similarly, the agent receives a penalty for performing incorrectly, such as going off the road or hitting a hurdle.

8.3 PROBLEM SOLVING IN AI

Most organizations that take up AI projects solve their problems by following a Project Cycle. Problem solving, here, refers to AI techniques such as forming efficient algorithms, heuristics and performing root-cause analysis to find desirable solutions for the given situation. Any AI project cycle can be divided into various stages including,

1. Problem scoping
2. Data acquisition
3. Data modelling
4. Evaluation and development

We will discuss each of these stages in detail in the following sections.

8.4 PROBLEM SCOPING

The first stage of an AI project cycle is Problem Scoping, in which problems are identified. Once the problem is identified, designing, developing and finally testing is performed.

This stage forms the backbone of the entire AI project as incorrect problem scoping will result in failure of the project.

The 4Ws of Problem Scoping

For identifying problems accurately, we must focus on 4Ws. These Ws are very helpful in problem scoping. They are:

Who? It helps us to identify who is facing the problem and who are the stakeholders of the problem.

What? Refers to what the problem is and how it was noticed.

Where? Specifies the context/ situation/ location of the problem

Why? Helps to know why a solution is required and how the stakeholders will benefit from the solution.

8.4.1 The Problem Statement Template

The outcome of Problem Scoping stage is the problem statement template that contains a summary of the 4Ws. This template is a very useful document as it acts as a guideline for the current as well as all future projects experiencing similar problems.

Activity – Brainstorm Around the Theme and Set a Goal for the AI Project

Given below is a list of themes, select any one for problem scoping.

Select the Theme

The first question then to be answered is,

Why you have selected the theme?

For example, if your theme is

- **Environment**, then enumerate problems such as polluted air, water, and land, etc.
- **Agriculture**, then problems could be excess use of pesticides to increase the productions, knowing the appropriate time for sowing and harvesting
- **Traffic**, then think about traffic issues and ways to reduce accidents or any other related problem.

You can take any theme and jot down issues that exist in the context of that theme. The next step is to place the problems into a problem statement template.

Set up the goal

Once the problem statement is created, set goals that will be fulfilled by the AI project.

For example, if the selected theme is Agriculture, then possible goals can be to identify,

Goal 1: Ideal time for seeding
Goal 2: Ideal time for harvesting
Goal 3: Ideal amount of fertilizer required for the selected crop

Note that the list of goals can be even more. However, before finalizing the goals, let us note two important points.

Do not set the goals with too much enthusiasm as in that case we may set goals that are difficult to achieve and require a lot of time and other resources. This may de-focus the development team (responsible for designing AI-based solution), thereby resulting in delayed projects with a higher budget.

Do not be too skeptical and set goals that are too small to achieve the desired outcome. In such a case, even AI-based solution will be unable to make any effective impact. All the efforts and resources invested in developing a solution would become irrelevant.

To avoid such problems, we must have an expert team that can analyze the problem well, consider the existing measures, talk to customer representatives to elicit more information and then finally set a goal that addresses all ethical concerns as well.

Identify the 4Ws

Your final problem statement will look like the following table:

Who	Stakeholders
	Farmers, Fertilizer Producers, Laborers, Tractor Companies, Consumers
What	The problem, Issue, Need
	Identify the ideal time for seeding or crop harvesting.
When	Context/Situation
	Determine when the crop is mature enough to be harvested.
Why	Benefits
	Farmers will be able to grow and harvest the crop at the most appropriate time and supply it to the consumers on time.

8.5   DATA ACQUISITION

The term 'data acquisition' consists of two words – data and acquisition, where,

Data refers to the raw facts, figures, collected for reference or analysis.

Acquisition means acquiring data for the project from relevant sources. For example, if our theme is Travel Tourism, then we need to collect data from websites, user's reviews, magazines, news reports, etc.

(Some sources of data sets from where crucial data can be freely downloaded for analysis are included in the annexure to this chapter.)

8.5.1 Classification of Data

Data can be broadly classified into three broad categories – Basic, Structured and Other (Fig. 8.6). In this section, we will look into all of them in detail.

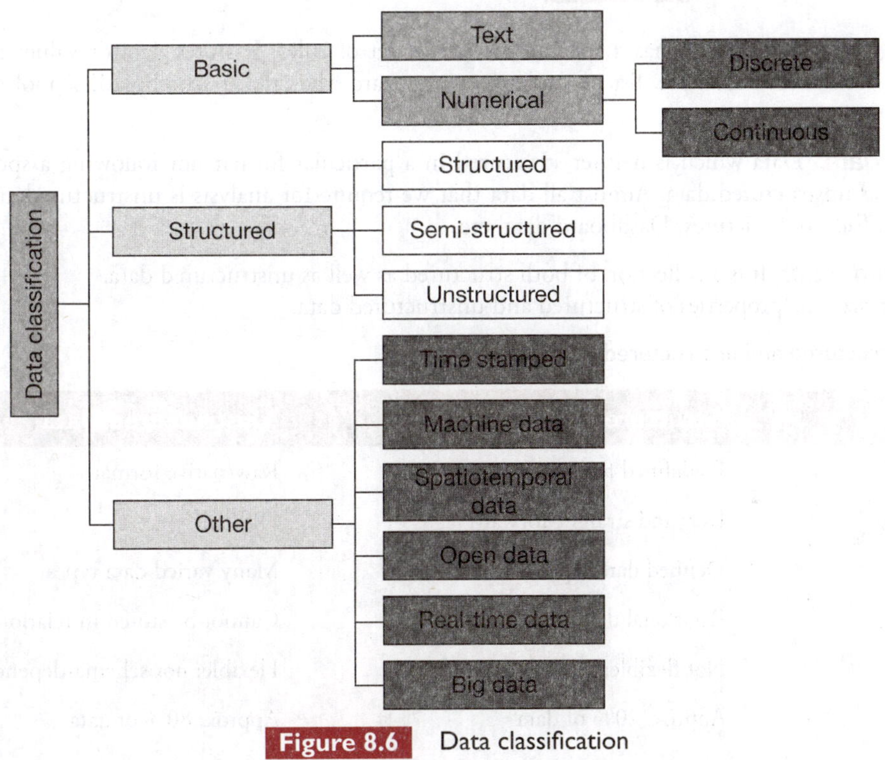

Figure 8.6   Data classification

Basic Data Basic data can be classified as:

Numeric data that is mainly used in computations and can be either discrete or continuous.

Discrete data contains integral numeric data that does not have any decimal or fractional value. For example, number of students in a class is 50. In the inter-school quiz competition, 200 students have registered.

Continuous data that is uncountable represents data in this category. For example, the average weight of class IX boys is 48.5 kgs.

Textual data is a collection of words that may consist of alphabets, digits and/or special characters. For example, we use textual data to represent names, address, subjects, etc.

Structural Classification Data required to train the ML model must follow a specific set of constraints or rules or unique pattern to form the underlying structure of the data. Based on this structure of data, it can be classified into three categories as given below (Fig. 8.7).

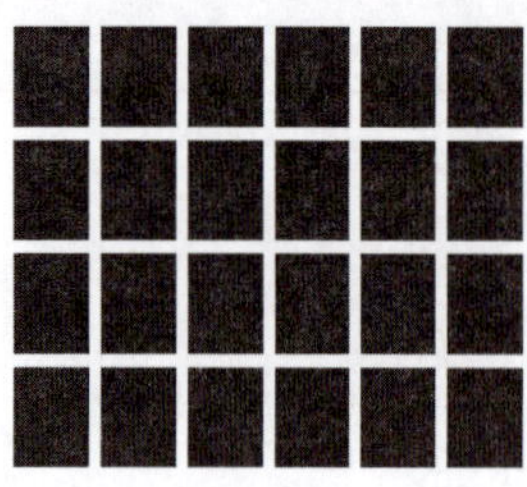

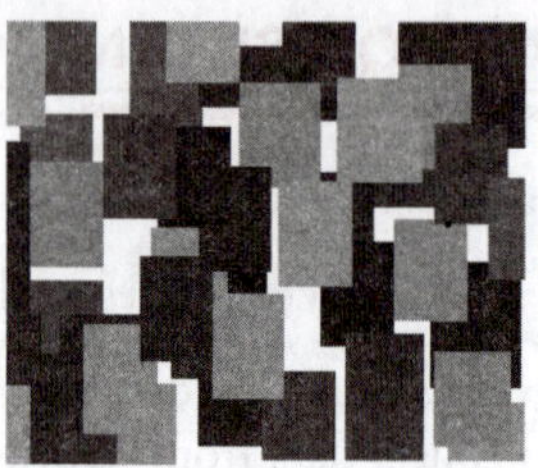

Figure 8.7   Structural classification of data

Structured data Structured data has a specific pattern or set of rules. It stores data or values in specific forms like in a tabular format. For example, list of students, report card, the cricket scoreboard, school time-table, exam datasheet, etc.

Unstructured data: Data which is neither structured in a particular format nor following a specific set of rules can be recorded as unstructured data. Almost all data that we require for analysis is unstructured and is available as YouTube Videos, Facebook Pictures, Dashboard data, etc.

Semi-structured data: It is a collection of both structured as well as unstructured data.
Table 8.1 summarizes the properties of structured and unstructured data.

Table 8.1   Structured and unstructured data – Properties

Properties	Structured Data	Unstructured Data
Characteristics	Predefined format	Raw/native format
Ease of searching	Easy and straight-forward	Difficult
Data types	Defined data types	Many varied data types
Storage	Relational databases	Cannot be stored in relational databases
Flexibility	Not flexible; schema-dependent	Flexible; not schema-dependent
Availability	Approx. 20% of data	Approx. 80% of data
Examples	Excel, Google Sheets, SQL, customer data, phone records, transaction history	Text data, social media comments, phone calls transcriptions, various logs files, Images, audio, video

Other Classification Data can be further classified as,

Time-stamped data follows a specific time-order to define the sequence of events. For example, a student's performance reported every 3 months.

Machine data is obtained as a result or output generated from a specific ML program. Machine data may also be obtained from user search records, comments, likes, data shared by users, and log records of their interaction with the system.

Spatiotemporal data, as the name suggests, contains information related to geographical location and time. For example, data collected through GPS systems is spatiotemporal data.

Open data is the one that is freely available for anybody to use. For example, various statistics posted by government for analysis by anyone.

Real-time data available with an event is considered as real-time data.

Big data means huge amounts of data that cannot be stored by any system or analyzed by traditional data management software.

Data Features Data features refer to the type of data used for a specific purpose.

Training data is the data collected to train the machine learning model. In other words, this data makes the machine learn.

Testing data is used to check the validity of the results generated by the machine learning model.

For example, if we have 1000 records then, 700 records can be used to train the model and 300 records can be used for testing the model. While testing, we can use our trained ML model to predict values of a particular variable and then compare the predicted values with actual values to see how accurate the results were.

When creating the ML model, we have values for all the records and we use them to train and test the model. This helps us to use the ML model to predict values for a new record. For example, we can use this model to predict the performance of a new student or the results of the next final exam when the marks in the final exam is not yet known (Table 8.2)

Table 8.2   Training and testing data for ML model

Marks in Test 1	Marks in Test 2	Marks in Project	Marks in Final Exams
49	48	49	Use 70 % values to train ML model to predict final marks
48	46	49	
39	45	44	Use 30 % values to test ML model by comparing predicted with actual values for final marks
44	31	36	
40	35	42	

8.6   DATA EXPLORATION

Data Exploration refers to the tools and techniques used to easily visualize data that is otherwise difficult to interpret. Acquired data is usually too complex to understand and analyze. Data visualization helps us to,

- get a better understanding of data
- get deep insights into data
- facilitate user interaction
- allow real-time analysis
- assist in making business decisions
- lower data complexity
- reveal underlying relationships, patterns and trends within data
- define a strategy for the data model
- provide an effective way of communication among users.

8.6.1 Data Visualization

Select a proper graph for data visualization.

There are different types of graphs that can be used to visualize data. However, we need to choose the most appropriate chart for analyzing data in the current context. For example, users can plot the following graphs for a given purpose.

Bar graph for comparing values.

Line chart for comparing trends and visualizing changes over a period of time.

Histogram to visualize distribution of data into different categories.

Pie chart clearly reveals contribution of one particular value in the whole.

Remember that we can create multiple charts also to understand the relationship between data.

8.7   MODELLING

In the last section, we have learnt that graphical representation of data not only makes it easy for us to understand it but also assists us in decision-making. However, when data has to be accessed and analyzed by machines, machine learning models are used to represent data. The process of creating a model is known as modelling, data modelling or AI modelling.

Three main approaches used for AI modelling are:

1. Rule-based approach
2. Learning-based approach
3. Decision tree (discussed in the next chapter)
4. Neural networks (discussed in the next chapter)

8.7.1   Rule-based Approach

This approach centers around data and rules fed to the machine. The machine processes data based on the specified rules to produce the desired output. Therefore, rule-based learning model helps machines to learn the relationship or patterns in data according to the rules laid by the developer. Consider the set of rules specified to compute a category of students.

```
IF MARKS < 50, "FAIL"
IF MARKS >= 50 AND MARKS < 60, "AVERAGE"
IF MARKS >= 60 AND MARKS < 70, "GOOD"
IF MARKS >= 70 AND MARKS < 80, "VERY GOOD"
IF MARKS >= 80 AND MARKS < 90, "EXCELLENT"
IF MARKS >= 90 AND MARKS <= 100, "OUTSTANDING"
```

Consider another example. You have a dataset containing 100 images of apples, 100 images of pear and 100 images of bananas. We make a machine learning model to feed this data into the machine so that the machine can accurately label each image as either apple, pear or banana.

Once the model is created, we can test the model by giving it an image of apple. The trained model will compare the image with the trained data and identify the test image as an apple. This is known as rule-based approach. In this approach, rules given to the machine specify the labels for each image in the training dataset (Fig. 8.8).

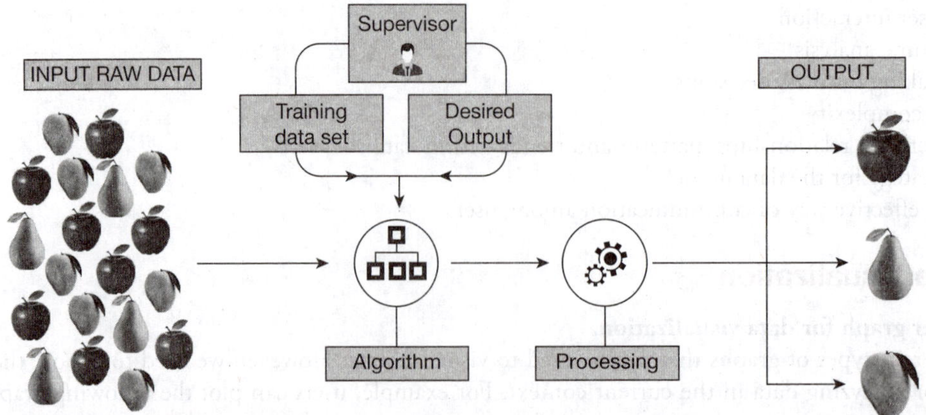

Figure 8.8   Rule-based approach for training dataset

8.7.2 Learning-based Approach

In the learning-based approach, the machine is fed with data and the desired output. The machine then automatically designs its own algorithm (or set of rules) to match the input to the desired output.

Therefore, in the learning-based approach, the relationship or pattern in the data is not defined by the developer. Rather, it is left to the machine to identify patterns or required trends.

Generally, this approach is used when the data has no existing labels. In this scenario, the machine looks into the data, extracts similar features out of it and forms clusters of similar datasets. Finally, the machine reveals trends existing in the input (training) data. Therefore, this approach is used to train the data which is either unpredictable or for which the users have no idea.

Example: In a dataset of 1000 images of random stray dogs, you may not have any idea about their breed, color or any other feature. We can feed this into a learning-approach based AI machine that will extract patterns and form clusters of data on the basis of color, size, fur style, etc. Figure 8.9 shows that input data containing a mix of certain shapes, when fixed to ML model, will produce clusters of similar shapes.

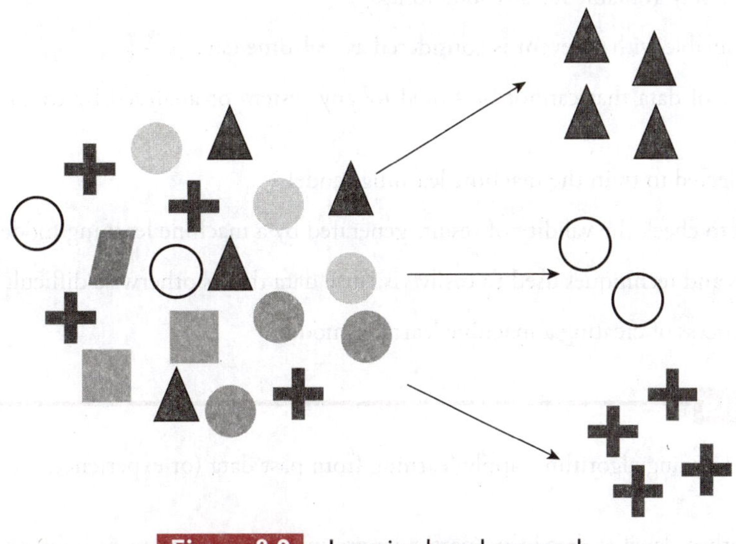

Figure 8.9   Learning-based approach

8.8   EVALUATION AND DEPLOYMENT

Every AI system must be evaluated. In the evaluation phase, the system is tested to make sure that it processes the data accurately without any error(s). The system is verified as well as validated to check that it meets the stated goals. Any deviation(s) from accuracy or goals may result in modification(s) in the system.

Once the system is thoroughly tested to meet its design goal with efficiency and accuracy, it is deployed (or installed) to allow users reap its benefits. An undeployed system is hardly of any use.

However, the AI project cycle does not end with deployment. Maintenance or System Tuning is a never-ending task that is done at regular intervals for improving the system's effectiveness.

Key Terms

Experience (E): Knowledge gained from data provided to the algorithm or model.

Task (T): Real-world problem to be solved.

Unsupervised learning: ML algorithm that trains the machine using information that is neither classified nor labelled.

Outlier analysis: Unsupervised learning technique used to find out the occurrences of rare events or observations that generally do not occur.

Data: Raw facts and figures, collected for reference or analysis.

Acquisition: The process of acquiring data for the project from relevant sources.

Structured data: Data that has a specific pattern or set of rules.

Unstructured data: Data which is neither structured in a particular format nor following a specific set of rules can be recorded as unstructured data.

Semi-structured data: It is a collection of both structured as well as unstructured data.

Time-stamped data: Data which follows a specific time-order to define the sequence of events.

Machine data: Data obtained as a result of output generated from a specific ML program.

Spatiotemporal data: Data containing information related to geographical location and time.

Open data: Data that is freely available for anybody to use.

Real-time data: Data available with an event is considered as real-time data.

Big data: Huge amounts of data that cannot be stored by any system or analyzed by traditional data management software.

Training data: Data collected to train the machine learning model.

Testing data: Data used to check the validity of results generated by a machine learning model.

Data exploration: Tools and techniques used to easily visualize data that is otherwise difficult to interpret.

Data modelling: The process of creating a machine learning model.

Chapter Highlights

- Supervised machine learning algorithms apply learning from past data (or experiences) to new data using labeled examples.

- A classification algorithm classifies data into a particular group. Classification techniques predict discrete categories.

- A regression algorithm predicts a real value.

- In association mining (or analysis), the aim is to discover rules that describe large portions of data. For example, a company can use association analysis to conclude that a customer who buys product X also buys product Y.

- Semi-supervised learning algorithms use small amount of pre-labelled data and a large number of unlabeled data for training.

- In a reinforcement learning algorithm, an agent is trained over a period of time so that it can interact with a specific environment.

- In Problem Scoping stage, problems are identified. Once the problem is identified, designing, developing and finally testing is performed.

- The outcome of Problem Scoping stage is the problem statement template that contains a summary of the 4Ws.

- Data can be broadly classified into three broad categories – basic, structured and other.

- In the learning-based approach, the machine is fed with data and the desired output. The machine then automatically designs its own algorithm to match the input to the desired output.

Review Questions

1. Discuss the scenarios in which an AI-based system is preferred over human beings.

2. Differentiate between classification and regression.

3. How is supervised learning different from unsupervised learning?

4. Explain the AI project cycle.

5. What are the 4Ws in Problem Scoping phase?

6. What do you understand by the term 'data acquisition'?

7. Give any three points of difference between structured and unstructured data.

8. Define data exploration. Why is visualization an important part of exploring data?

9. Explain the different approaches for creating a data model.

Fill in the Blanks

1. ___________ acquired through ML model or algorithm is used to solve task T.

2. ___________ learning should be used when output of data in the training set is known.

3. ___________ learning trains the machine using information that is neither classified nor labelled.

4. ___________ discovers rules that describe large portions of data.

5. Deep learning is an _________ learning technique.

6. In a ___________ learning algorithm, an agent is trained over a period of time so that it can interact with a specific environment.

7. Reinforcement learning is used in ___________.

8. Problem is identified in the _________ stage.

9. Once the problem statement is created, we can set _________ that will be fulfilled by the AI project.

10. A student's performance reported every 3 months is an example of _____________ data.

11. _________ data means very large amount of data.

12. Data Exploration includes tools and techniques to _________ data that is otherwise difficult to interpret.

13. _______ Chart clearly reveals contribution of one particular value in the whole.

State True or False

1. Supervised machine learning algorithms learn from past data (or experiences) to interpret new data using unlabeled examples.

2. Unsupervised learning algorithms are used for more complex tasks than supervised learning systems.

3. The outcome of data modeling stage is the problem statement template that contains a summary of the 4Ws.

4. Goals must be difficult to achieve and require a lot more time and other resources.

5. Textual data can be either discrete or continuous.

6. Structured data has a specific pattern or set of rules.

7. YouTube Videos and Facebook Pictures are examples of structured data.

8. Various statistics posted by government for analysis by anyone is an example of open data.

9. Big data cannot be analyzed by traditional data management software.

10. Machine data is used to train the machine learning model.

11. Learning based AI model processes data according to the specified rules to produce the desired output.

12. Goal setting involves identification of reasons for problems.

13. Modelling is the last stage of an AI project cycle.

14. AI applications work well with large amounts of data.

15. Machine data is generated by AI systems.

16. Problem Scoping is an important phase in any AI project.

Multiple Choice Questions

1. ML tasks does not include ____________.
   a. Classification
   b. Regression
   c. Clustering
   d. None of these.

2. ML models gain experience using ____________ learning.
   a. supervised
   b. unsupervised
   c. reinforcement
   d. All of these.

3. ____________ algorithm categorizes data into discrete categories.
   a. Classification
   b. Regression
   c. Clustering
   d. None of these.

4. ____________ predicts continuous values.
   a. Classification
   b. Regression
   c. Clustering
   d. None of these.

5. ____________ learning finds patterns and relationships in the dataset by creating clusters in it.
   a. Supervised
   b. Unsupervised
   c. Reinforcement
   d. All of these

6. ____________ technique finds occurrences of rare events or observations that generally do not occur.
   a. Classification
   b. Regression
   c. Clustering
   d. Outlier Analysis

7. Semi-supervised learning algorithms use ________ amount of pre-labelled data and a ________ number of unlabeled data for training.
   a. small, large
   b. large, large
   c. large, small
   d. small, small

8. In ________ learning algorithm, the agent receives rewards by performing correctly and penalties for performing incorrectly.
   a. supervised
   b. unsupervised
   c. reinforcement
   d. All of these.

9. Which of the following is used in robotics, game playing and self-driving cars?
   a. Supervised
   b. Unsupervised
   c. Reinforcement
   d. All of these.

10. Data collected through GPS systems is an example of _____________ data.
    a. time-stamped   b. spatial
    c. machine   d. spatiotemporal

11. _________ is used to check the validity of results generated by the machine learning model.
    a. Big Data   b. Training Data
    c. Real-time Data   d. Testing Data

12. Data visualization help users to identify ____________.
    a. underlying relationships   b. patterns
    c. trends within data   d. All of these.

13. ____________ is used for comparing trends and visualizing changes over a period of time.
    a. Bar Graph   b. Line Chart
    c. Pie Chart   d. Histogram

14. Data _________ is an ongoing phase in the development of an AI system.
    a. Collection   b. Modelling
    c. Evaluation   d. Maintenance

15. Every AI system must be __________ to ensure that the system meets its goal accurately.
    a. validated   b. verified
    c. Both of these.   d. None of these.

16. Which of the following activities are not done as a part of AI system deployment?
    a. Review   b. Maintenance
    c. Testing   d. Modelling

17. Errors in the results are identified and the AI system is rectified in the __________ phase.
    a. Data Visualization   b. Modelling
    c. Evaluation and Deployment   d. Problem Scoping

18. A flight's arrival and departure schedule is an example of _________ data.
    a. Structured   b. Unstructured
    c. Semi-structured   d. All of these.

19. Which of the following data is available as the event takes place?
    a. Big Data   b. Real-time Data
    c. Spatiotemporal Data   d. Time-stamped Data

Group Discussion

1. Select any graph from a daily newspaper and ask students to discuss what information they are able to interpret from it.

2. Ask the students to list the issues faced by them. Identify the ways in which an AI system can resolve their problems. Also discuss the ethical concerns involved.

Brainstorming Activities

Make groups of 3 students and allot the following projects to each group. Ask the students to set goals for the project assigned to them. Also ask them to identify sources from which data will be collected.

1. Smart Online Examination System
2. Smart Grievance System
3. Smart Library
4. Smart Waste Disposal System
5. Smart Car Parking System
6. Smart Online Attendance System
7. Smart Security System
8. Smart Game Playing System (Any game)
9. Smart Healthcare System

Data Plotting Activities

1. Using the following set of data, plot a line chart for each column in MS Excel.

Date	Revenue collected from Delhi	Revenue collected from Mumbai	Revenue collected from Chennai	Revenue collected from Kolkata	Revenue collected from Exports
2018-01-05	4492978	3450315.0	2408365.0	2685857.0	2869783.0
2018-01-06	4416476	3394284.0	2188035.0	2559044.0	2743748.0
2018-01-07	4009104	3020789.0	1908129.0	2350985.0	2441045.0
2018-01-08	4135505	2755266.0	2023251.0	2523265.0	2622693.0
2018-01-09	4168506	2791601.0	2058016.0	2727678.0	2627334.0

2. Consider the data given below, select any ten rows and create a bar graph representing the figures.

Province	Country	Confirmed Covid cases	Deaths	Recovered
Uttar Pradesh	India	1688152	20208	1621743
Uttarakhand	India	327112	6360	289642
Vermont	US	24200	255	0
Vichada	Colombia	1772	25	1727
Victoria	Australia	20593	820	19725
Vinnytsia Oblast	Ukraine	70474	1661	65696
Virgin Islands	US	3442	27	0
Virginia	US	675165	11160	0
Vladimir Oblast	Russia	33442	1192	31122
Volgograd Oblast	Russia	59618	1296	56864
Vologda Oblast	Russia	46023	1092	42907
Volyn Oblast	Ukraine	61187	1148	57004
Voronezh Oblast	Russia	84672	2910	80119
Wakayama	Japan	2612	41	2410
Wales	UK	212672	5569	0
Wallis and Futuna	France	445	7	438
Walloon Brabant	Belgium	40604	0	0
Washington	US	435849	5765	0
West Bengal	India	1354956	15268	1237290
West Flanders	Belgium	95724	0	0
West Virginia	US	161287	2792	0
Western Australia	Australia	1017	9	1006
Yamagata	Japan	1963	42	1692
Yamaguchi	Japan	2903	60	2330

Province	Country	Confirmed Covid cases	Deaths	Recovered
Yamalo-Nenets Autonomous Okrug	Russia	39063	419	37848
Yamanashi	Japan	1541	19	1390
Yaroslavl Oblast	Russia	40903	605	38968
Yucatan	Mexico	39748	3917	0
Yukon	Canada	84	2	82
Zabaykalsky Krai	Russia	43126	669	41650
Zaporizhia Oblast	Ukraine	102641	2335	95289
Zeeland	Netherlands	29147	245	0

3. Download the data set from https://www.kaggle.com/spscientist/students-performance-in-exams and create illustrative charts in Excel to derive meaningful information it.

Identify the Chart and Write what Information it Conveys

1. Favorite Color

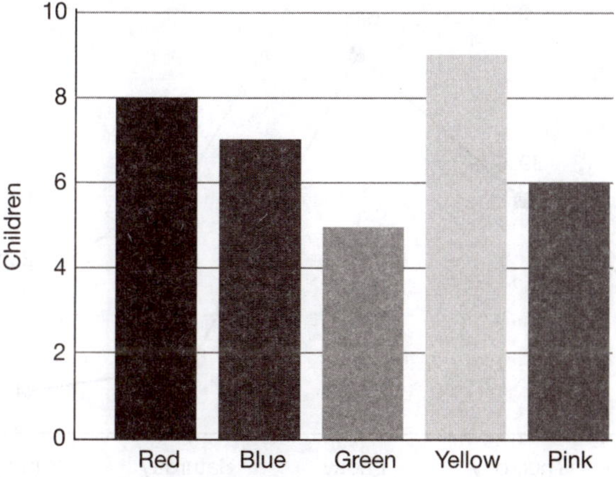

2. How Much Water Do We Use?

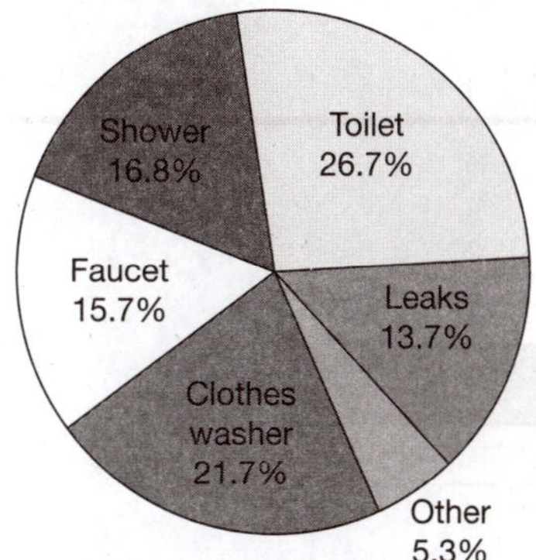

Source: American water works association research foundation, "Residential end uses of water." 1999

3. Experiment History

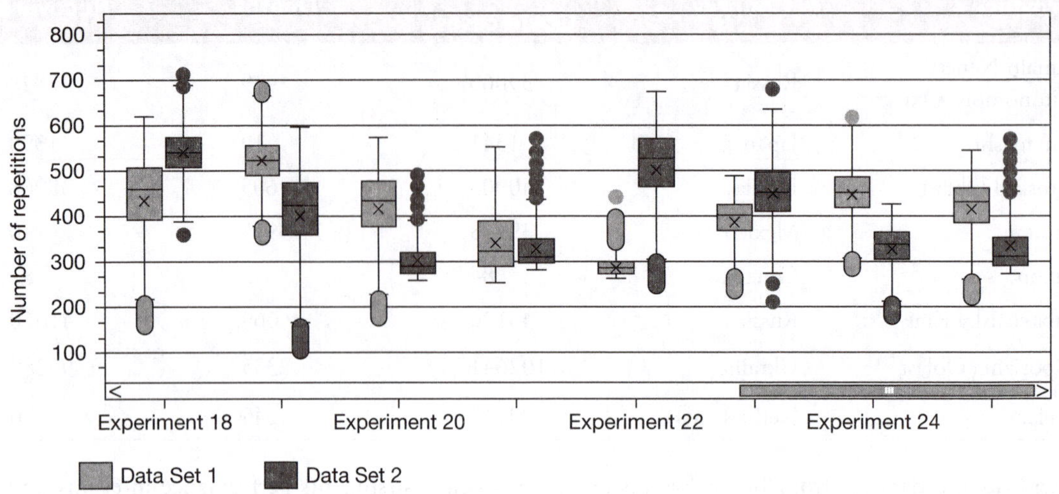

4. Server CPU Load by Days

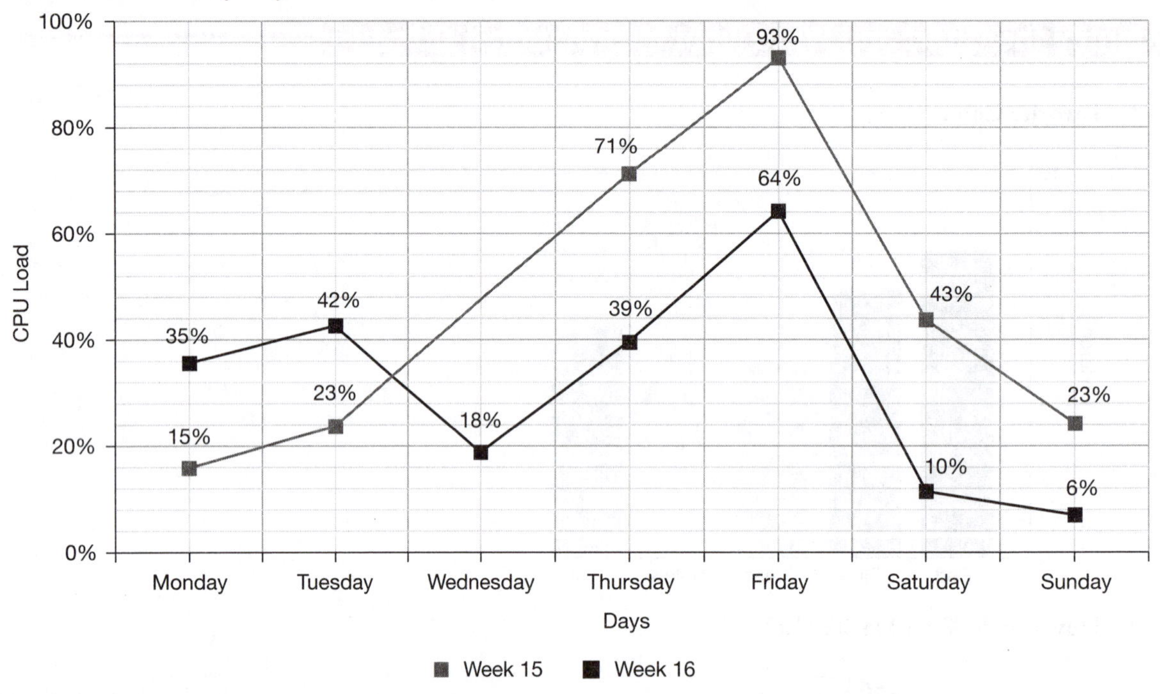

Plot Charts Using the Information Given

1. Consider the data given below and draw a pie chart.
   Table: Favorite Type of Movie

Comedy	Action	Romance	Drama	SciFi
4	5	6	1	4

2. Draw a histogram to represent the following data.
   Each month you measure how much weight your pup has gained and get these results:
   0.5, 0.5, 0.3, –0.2, 1.6, 0, 0.1, 0.1, 0.6, 0.4

AI Lab Session – Train a Machine Learning Model

Visit the link https://machinelearningforkids.co.uk/ and create a project that can classify text, images and numbers. You can train the model and test how accurate the results are.

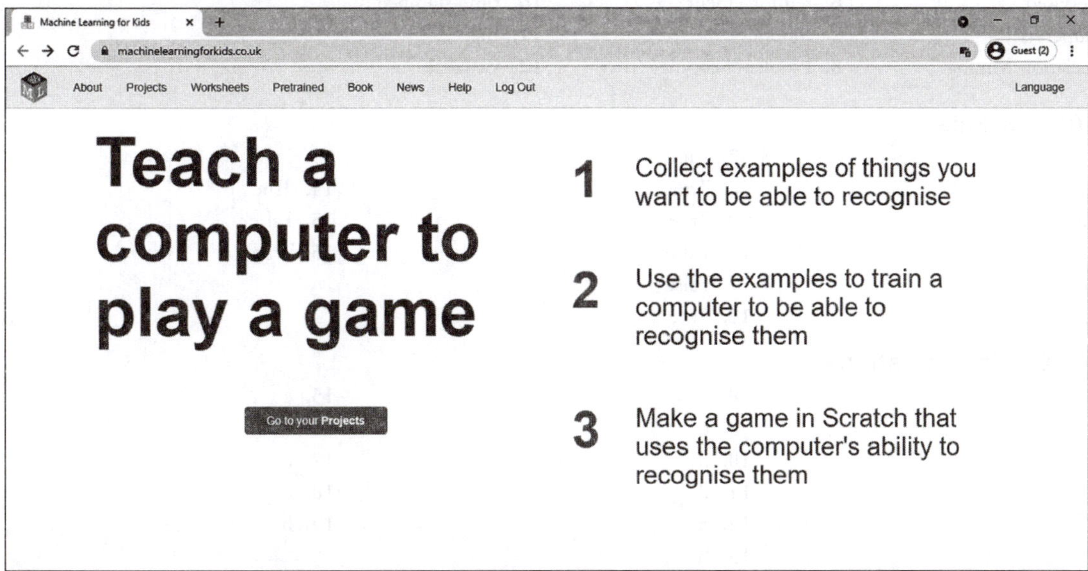

Annexure – Acquiring Free Data for Analysis

Open datasets are extensively being used these days by researchers, analysts, professionals and students to conduct their projects and research. Some of these vital data sets are listed below.

- **RBI Database of Indian Economy** (https://dbie.rbi.org.in/DBIE/dbie.rbi?site=home) is a website launched by Reserve Bank of India for publishing data on macroeconomic indicators of the Indian economy including money and banking, financial markets, national income, saving, employment, and others.

- **Ministry of Statistics and Programme Implementation Dataset** (http://mospi.nic.in/data) presents data sets collected by conducting large-scale sample surveys across India for various parameters.

- **Gateway to Indian Earth Observation** (http://bhuvan.nrsc.gov.in/data) is an initiative by ISRO that releases free satellite data and other government data.

- **Survey of India** (http://www.surveyofindia.gov.in/) responsible for conducting surveys under the Department of Science and Technology, and having its data centers spread across India, provides quality geospatial data for analysis.

- **India Weather Data** (https://www.meteoblue.com/en/weather/archive/export/india_el-salvador_3585481) posts datasets for various meteoroid indicators, water resource planning, rainfall, temperature, pressure, relative humidity, precipitation amount, wind speed, solar radiation, etc.

- **Aadhaar Metadata** (https://data.uidai.gov.in/) provides a very large number of records generated by the daily count of total registrations, enrolment applications accepted and rejected by state and district. It also contains other Aadhaar-generated details such as age, gender, etc.

- **Import Exports Datasets** (https://www.icegate.gov.in/jsp/DailyReport.jsp) provides information such as documents, messages, and other processes by the Indian Customs EDI System (ICES).

- **Open Government Data (OGD)** Platform India (https://data.gov.in/) gives access to government-owned shareable data as a part of the Digital India initiative. It publishes datasets, documents, tools and applications collected by the government for public use.

- **Wildlife Institute of India Dataset** (https://data.gov.in/) offers datasets on different wildlife species in India.

Answers

Fill in the Blanks

1. Experience
2. Supervised
3. Unsupervised
4. Association Mining
5. unsupervised
6. reinforcement
7. robotics
8. Problem Scoping
9. goals
10. time-stamped
11. Big
12. visualize
13. Pie

State True or False

1. False
2. True
3. False
4. False
5. False
6. True
7. False
8. True
9. True
10. False
11. False
12. True
13. False
14. True
15. False
16. True

Multiple Choice Questions

1. d
2. d
3. a
4. b
5. b
6. c
7. a
8. c
9. c
10. d
11. d
12. d
13. b
14. d
15. c
16. d
17. c
18. a
19. b

Data Modelling

9

We have already seen different steps that are applicable in any AI project. In this chapter, our focus will revolve around data modelling. In this context, we will learn about:

- Big data and its challenges
- Decision trees
- Neural networks

9.1 WHAT IS BIG DATA?

Data is everywhere. Our phones, credit/debit cards, software applications, vehicles, records, websites, etc. generate, store, transmit and process massive amounts of data that provide incredibly valuable information. This data, also known as Big Data, therefore, refers to huge amounts of complex data that may be structured or unstructured. This data is rapidly and continuously generated from a wide variety of sources.

Analytical systems, capable of handling complex data for analysis, integrate Big Data into existing processes to output insights into data for making vital business decisions. Big Data is used in nearly every industry to identify patterns, trends, gain insights into customers, make complex decisions to grow business, enhance research, make predictions and target key audiences for advertising.

> One gigabyte is equivalent to a seven-minute video in HD and One zettabyte is equal to 250 billion DVDs.

For example, companies can collect and analyze customer's reviews and shopping behavior for recommending other products/brands and enhance sales. Remember the $3V$'s of Big Data, which may be explained as follows:

- **Volume** means enormous amounts of data being stored. While the size of traditional data is measured in units like megabytes, gigabytes and terabytes, Big Data's size varies from petabytes to zettabytes.
- **Velocity** refers to the speed at which large amounts of data is processed and analyzed. Organizations must harness data and derive useful information from it in real time to reap its true benefits. While some data can be collected and then processed at a later point of time, others require immediate action for the best outcomes. For example, data collected from sensors fitted in health devices can collect and process health data to provide physicians with potentially life-saving information.
- **Variety** indicates different sources and forms from which data is collected. This data can be numbers, text, video, images, audio and text.

The $3V$'s of Big Data can be visualized as shown in Fig. 9.1. These days, data is continuously generated whenever we use an app, search on Google or open GPS to track our location in real time. This data needs to managed, stored, visualized and analyzed.

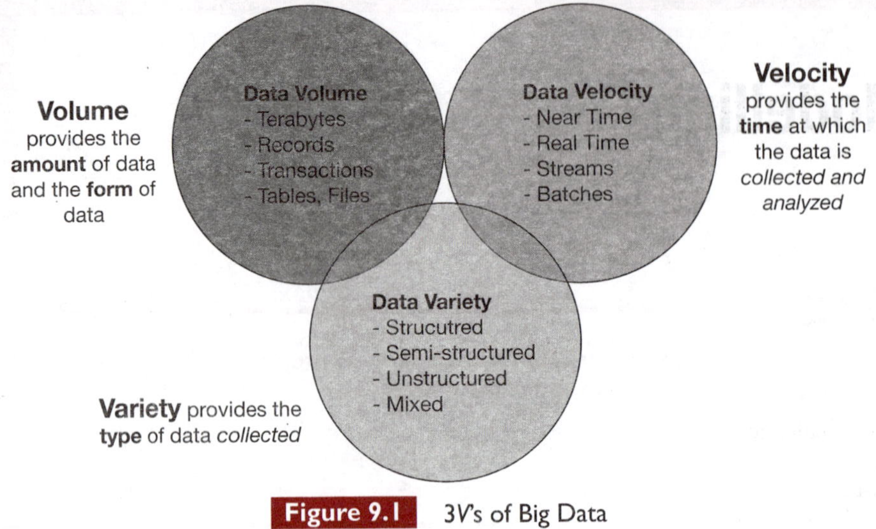

Figure 9.1   3V's of Big Data

9.1.1 How Big Data works

Big Data provide users an opportunity to extract important pieces of information to discover new opportunities and business models. To work with Big Data, we need to perform the following key actions:

10^{21} bytes equal to 1 zettabyte or one billion terabytes forms a zettabyte.

- **Integrate:** Big Data is a collection of data from several varieties of sources and applications.
- **Manage:** Big Data requires huge storage. These days, data is usually stored on the Cloud.
- **Analyze:** Data is visualized and explored in detail using machine learning models and artificial intelligence. Results of data analysis are then put into action.

9.1.2 Challenges of Big Data

We have seen that enormous amount of data is being generated every second from business transactions, sales figures, customer logs, and stakeholders. Though this huge data is the fuel that drives companies, there are certain challenges that need to be tackled wisely. Many companies get stuck at the initial stage of their Big Data projects.

Statistics shows that 500+ terabytes of new data is added to the databases of social media site Facebook every day, in the form of photo and video uploads, message exchanges, putting comments, etc.

Let us take a closer look at these challenges and the ways to overcome them.

Lack of Proper Understanding of Big Data Companies often are not able to fully utilize Big Data technologies as the employees themselves do not understand what data is, its storage, processing, importance, and sources. For example, if employees are not aware about the importance of data storage, then they may not know the techniques to properly store and retrieve data efficiently.

Solution Big Data workshops, seminars and training programs must be arranged for all the employees who are involved in Big Data projects.

Data Growth Issues Data grows exponentially with time and becomes so huge that it becomes difficult to handle.

Solution Employees must be trained to compress data for reducing the number of bits in the data, thus reducing its overall size, remove redundant or unwanted data from a dataset. Moreover, with data tiering, companies can store data in different storage tiers to ensure that the data is residing in the most appropriate storage space. For example, depending on the data size and importance, data tiers can be public cloud, private cloud, and flash storage.

Lack of Data Professionals There is a scarcity of talent in the new technologies. Skilled data professionals including data scientists, data analysts and data engineers having sufficient experience in working with the techniques are difficult to find.

Solution Companies are investing more money in the recruitment and regular training of skilled professionals. They are also using AI tools that can be run by professionals who are not experts in this area.

Securing Data Companies get so engrossed in collecting, transforming, visualizing, analyzing and interpreting data that maintaining security of this data is a real big challenge. Unprotected data acts as breeding grounds for malicious hackers. According to a study, companies can lose up to $3.7 million for a stolen record.

Solution Companies are recruiting more cyber-security professionals to protect their data. They are also using techniques like data encryption, access control, end-to-end security, real-time security monitoring and Big Data security tools (like IBM Guardian) to maintain security of data.

Integrating Data from a Variety of Sources Data in an organization comes from a variety of sources. Combining all this data is a challenging task.

Solution Companies are solving their data integration problems by deploying appropriate tools for data integration like Talend Data Integration, Centerprise Data Integrator, ArcESB, IBM InfoSphere, Xplenty, Informatica PowerCenter, CloverDX, Microsoft SQL, QlikView, Oracle Data Service Integrator.

> A single jet engine can generate 10+ terabytes of data in 30 minutes of flight time. With many thousand flights per day, generation of data reaches up to many petabytes.

Poor Quality Data Analyzing wrong, incorrect, incomplete data is more harmful than not performing any data analytics. In the absence of good-quality input, output will be unreliable. The main reason for having inaccurate data is manual errors made during data entry. Another reason for presence of incorrect data is updating data in one system but not using the updated data when working on another system, which may have the previous version of the data. This makes the final output outdated and inconsistent.

Solution Companies are using a centralized data storage to eliminate using inconsistent data. There is only one copy of data in such systems. So, whenever a piece of information is updated, the change(s) will be reflected everywhere at all times. Moreover, data is now input automatically with mandatory or drop-down fields, leaving little room for human error.

9.2   DECISION TREES – DATA MODELLING TECHNIQUE

Do you remember the 'Guess What' game that we used to play in our childhood? One of us will think of something, and the others had to guess what it is. Players can ask close-ended questions, answers to which will be either "Yes" or "No". Based on these clues, the answer is given. For example, consider the tree given in Fig. 9.2. (Note, it is just a sample tree, not a general tree). According to the rules specified, if you are thinking of an animal that is herbivorous and does not live in a forest, then it is a rabbit. The same concept is used to create a **Decision Tree**.

Therefore, a decision tree algorithm forms a tree-like structure to represent decisions. It is similar to a rule-based approach. A decision tree consists of various nodes and follows a top-to-bottom approach. The top-most node of the

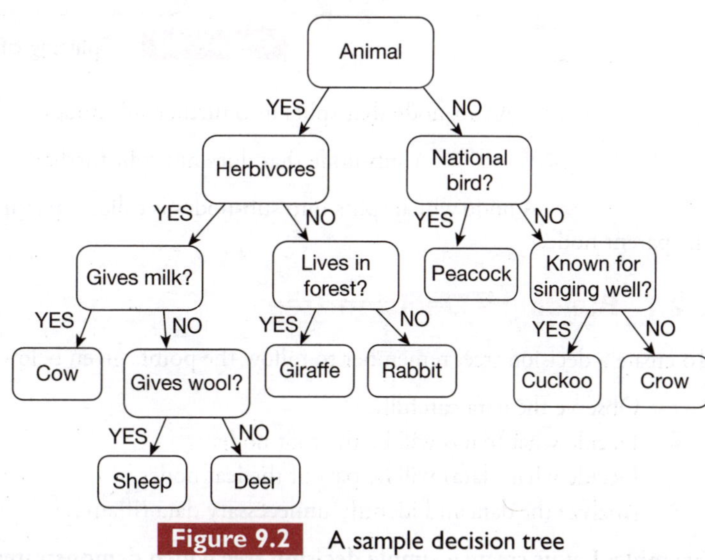

Figure 9.2   A sample decision tree

decision tree is known as **root**. The formation of the tree continues at all levels below the root node by breaking a node to two or more nodes. Nodes in the last level of the decision tree are known as the terminal nodes or leaf nodes. All these nodes are connected with each other by arrow lines.

In a decision tree, nodes represent an event or choice and the edges of the graph represent the decision rules or conditions.

Key Terminology Some important terms that are frequently used in decision trees include:

Root node: This is the node that performs the first split.

Terminal nodes/Leaves: These nodes predict the outcome.

Branches: They are depicted by arrows that connect nodes and show the flow from question to answer. Technically, a branch is a sub-section of the entire tree.

Splitting: The process of dividing a node into two or more sub-nodes (Fig. 9.3). In a decision tree, splitting is done until a user-defined stopping criteria is reached. For example, the programmer may specify that the algorithm should stop once the number of items per node becomes less than 30.

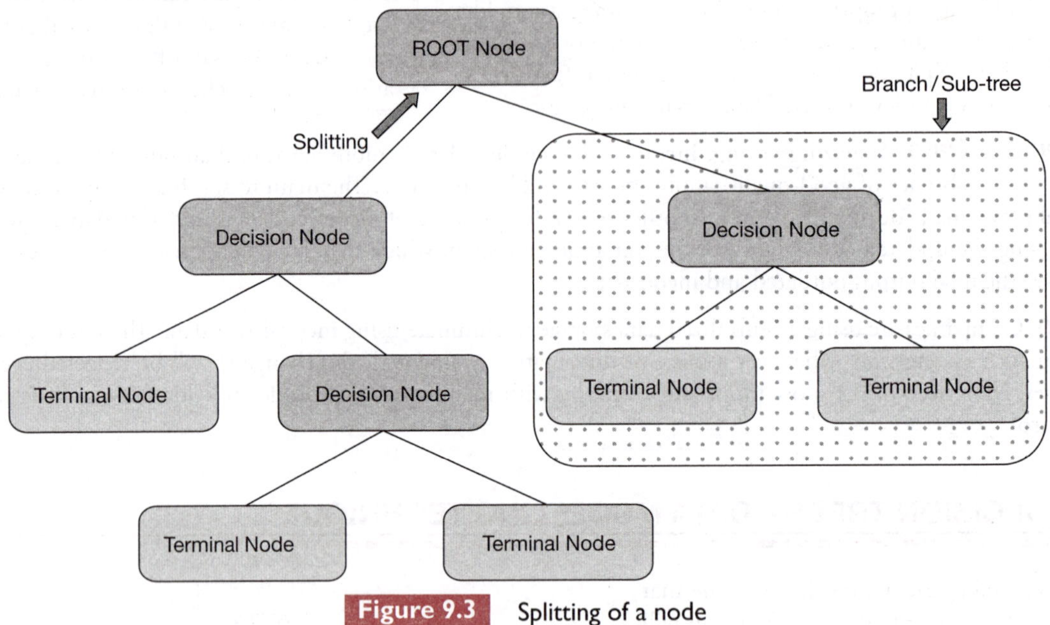

Figure 9.3   Splitting of a node

Decision node: A sub-node that splits into further sub-nodes

Terminal or leaf node: A sub-node that does not split further.

Parent node: A node which splits into sub-nodes is called a parent node of the sub-nodes. (A sub-node is a child of the parent node.)

9.2.1 Building a Decision Tree

To create a decision tree, remember to follow the points given below.

1. Observe the data carefully.
2. Decide what (data) will be the root node.
3. Decide what (data) will be part of the leaf nodes.
4. Analyze the data and identify unnecessary data (if any).

Example: Let us create a simple decision tree which demonstrates your decision whether you should eat Maggi or not (Fig. 9.4).

In the above decision tree, the first decision that has to be taken is whether you are hungry or not. In case the decision is YES, another decision is made – whether Maggi is available at home or not. If it is available, the final decision is to cook it and eat.

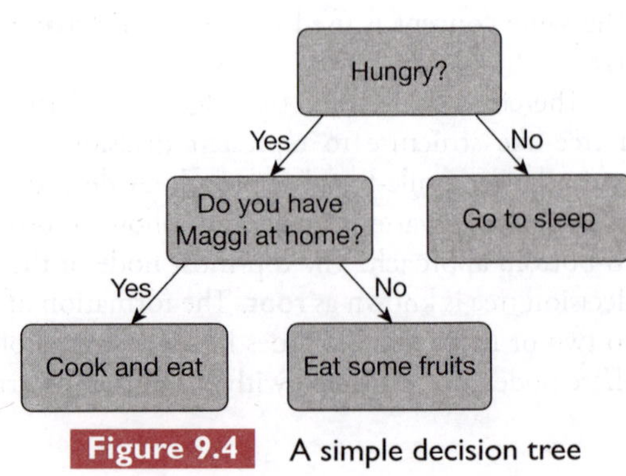

Figure 9.4   A simple decision tree

However, if you are not hungry then you can go and sleep. But if Maggi is not available at home and you are hungry, then you may take some fruits that are available at home.

Therefore, looking at the above decision tree, we see that there are 3 leaf nodes, thus three decisions – Go to sleep, Cook and eat or Eat some fruits and every decision node has two branches – YES or NO.

9.3   NEURAL NETWORKS

Neural Network (NN) or Artificial Neural Network (ANN) is a machine learning algorithm that is inspired by the biological neuron system and learns by examples. Table 9.1 highlights the differences between a human brain and a computer neural network that mimics a human brain. Note that a neural network consists of a large number of highly interconnected processing elements called neurons to solve problems. The algorithm follows a non-linear path and information is processed in parallel throughout the nodes.

Human Brain	Computer
Takes more time to execute instructions	Executes instructions in nanoseconds.
Human brain has 10^{11} neurons and is more complex than a computer.	Number of neurons (or nodes) depends on the programmer.
In humans, new information does not delete the one that is previously stored	In a computer, newly added information may overwrite the one that was previously stored.
May fail to recollect some information	Never fails to access any information
Consumes 6–10 Joules energy per operation	Consumes 10–16 Joules energy per operation

Neural network algorithm works using a set of connected input/output units. In this structure, (Fig. 9.5) each connection has a weight associated with it. In the learning phase, the network learns by adjusting the weights to predict the correct class label of the given inputs.

The learning phase is used along with back-propagation error method. Therefore, when error is calculated at the output unit, it is back-propagated to all the units because an error at each unit contributes to the total error at the output unit. The errors at each unit are then used to optimize the weight at each connection.

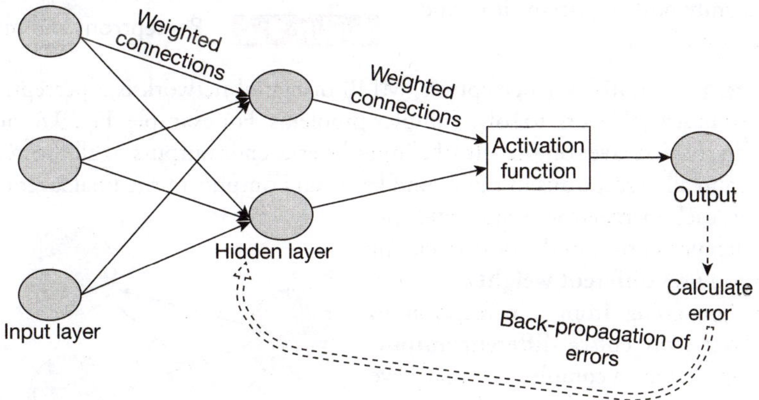

Figure 9.5   A simple neural network model

In Fig. 9.5, we can see that it is a feedback neural network in which information is passed in both directions (forward as well as backward). The structure of the neural network can change over time based on the inputs. Though the figure shows that there is one input layer, one hidden layer and one output layer, we can have multiple hidden layers as shown below (Fig. 9.6).

The output of a neuron is in the range – inf to + inf. So, we need a mapping function also known as the Activation Function that maps inputs to the outputs.

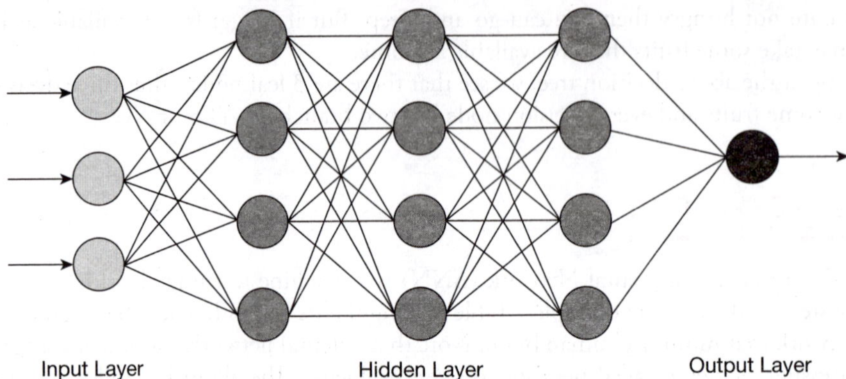

Input Layer   Hidden Layer   Output Layer

Figure 9.6 Hidden layers of a neural network

Here, the input layer is the first layer of the neural network and receives the raw input. It processes the input and passes the processed information to the hidden layers. The hidden layer passes the information to the last layer, which gives the final output.

The output of a neuron can range from –inf to +inf. The neuron does not know the boundary. So, we need a mapping mechanism between the input and output values of the neuron. This mechanism of mapping inputs to output is known as Activation Function. Activation functions decide whether a neuron should be activated or not by calculating the weighted sum and adding bias to it.

9.3.1 Perceptron

Perceptron or the artificial neuron, when used with other perceptrons, can be used to solve complex, undefined problems much like humans do (Fig. 9.7). Understanding how multi-layer perceptrons work together, lays the foundation of neural networks.

A perceptron helps us to divide a set of input signals into two parts – 'yes' and 'no' as shown in Fig. 9.7.

Here, we can think of the perceptron as a very simple learning machine that accepts a few inputs, each of which has a weight to signify how important it is, and generate an output decision of '0' or '1'.

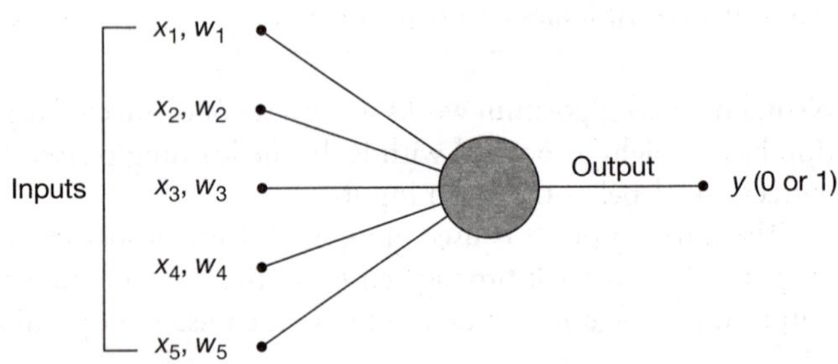

Figure 9.7 Perceptrons and multi-layer perceptrons

Multi-layer Perceptron A multi-layer perceptron (MLP) or neural network is a perceptron that combines with other perceptrons stacked in several layers, to solve complex problems. For example, Fig. 9.8 shows an MLP with three layers. Each perceptron in the first layer on the left (the input layer), sends outputs to all the perceptrons in the second layer (the hidden layer), and all perceptrons in the second layer send outputs to the final layer on the right (the output layer). This means that each perceptron sends multiple signals – one signal to each perceptron in the next layer. For each signal, the perceptron uses **different weights.**

In Fig. 9.8, every line going from a perceptron in one layer to the next layer represents a **different output.** Though this is a very simple figure, a complex one may have a large number of perceptrons in each layer and there can be multiple layers. A three-layer MLP (as shown in figure) is called a **Non-deep** or **Shallow Neural Network**. But, an MLP with four or more layers is called a **Deep Neural Network**.

An interesting point to note here is that neural networks evolved from MLPs. While in the classic perceptron, the decision function is a step function and the output is binary, neural networks on the other hand use activation

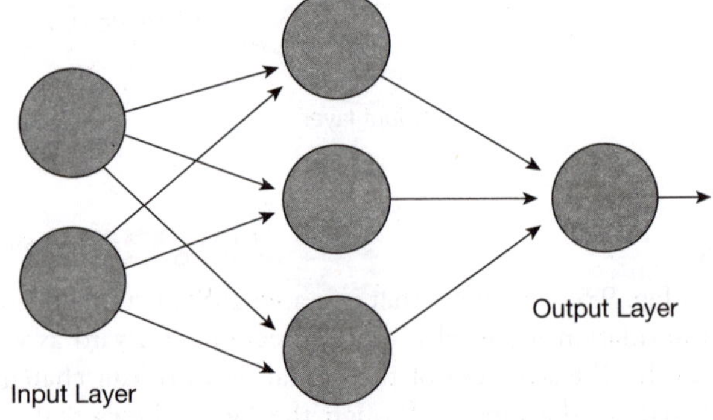

Figure 9.8 Perceptron input and output

functions **to generate** outputs of real values, usually between 0 and 1 or between −1 and 1. This helps users to make probability-based predictions or classification of items into different labels.

The Perceptron Learning Process A perceptron follows these steps:

Step 1: Perceptrons in a layer take input, multiply it by their weight, and then a weighted sum is computed. The weights are assigned depending on the relative importance of each perceptron in calculating the output of that layer. Neural network algorithms learn by finding out better values for these weights to enhance accuracy in the predicted output. Several algorithms including back-propagation is used to fine-tune the weights.

Step 2: A bias factor is added to fine-tune the numeric output of the perceptron.

Step 3: The sum is fed through the activation function to map the input values to the required output values. For example, input values in the range 1 to 100 may generate outputs as 0 or 1. In a multilayer perceptron, the activation function also helps the perceptron to learn.

Step 4: The perceptron output which is usually a classification decision, is produced. Output of the perceptrons, in the 'output layer', is the final prediction of the perceptron learning model.

Pros and Cons

Pros

- Neural networks are flexible algorithms that can be used to solve both regression and classification problems.
- Neural networks perform well on nonlinear dataset with a large number of inputs such as images.
- Neural networks can work with any number of hidden layers.
- Neural networks work very fast as compared to other classification algorithms since they perform calculations in parallel.

Cons

Algorithms like Decision Tree and Regression that are simple, fast, easy to train, and provide better performance are seen as a preferred choice for classification and regression problems because

- Neural networks require more time for development and needs more computation power.
- Neural networks need more data than any other Machine Learning algorithm.
- Neural networks can be performed only on numerical inputs and non-missing value datasets.

Applications of Neural Networks Neural network algorithms are extensively used in the following fields.

Pattern Recognition applications like facial recognition, object detection, fingerprint recognition, etc. use neural network algorithms.

Anomaly Detection or Outlier Analysis applications that are specifically designed to detect unusual patterns that don't fit in the general patterns use neural networks because of their ability to perform well in pattern recognition tasks.

Time Series Prediction applications like predicting stock prices and forecasting weather prefer to use neural networks.

Natural Language Processing applications including text classification, Named Entity Recognition (NER), Part-of-speech Tagging, Speech Recognition, and Spell Checking. These are used in a wide range of applications and make use of neural network algorithms.

How Neural Networks Work We have seen that neural networks take several inputs, process it through multiple neurons from multiple hidden layers, and return the final result using an output layer. This process is known as **Forward Propagation**.

To make a perfect model, we need to minimize the value or weight of neurons that are contributing more to the error. For this, we need to travel back to the neurons of the neural network and find where the error lies. This process is known as **Backward Propagation**. We can reduce the number of iterations to minimize the error by using the 'Gradient Descent' algorithm.

> Neuron applies non-linear transformations (activation function) to the inputs and biases.

A simple strategy of creating input–output relationships is discussed below.

1. **Use a subset of inputs to calculate the output.** Take only those inputs that satisfy a given threshold value. For example, if the threshold value is 0, then if x1 + x2 + x3 > 0, the output is 1 and 0, otherwise.

2. **Add weights to the inputs.** Weights give importance to an input. For example, if w1 = 4, w2 = 5, and w3 = 6, then on assigning these weights to x1, x2 and x3, we will multiply the inputs with their weights and compare the result with a threshold value. That is, w1 * x1 + w2 * x2 + w3 * x3 > Threshold. As per the details provided, more importance has been given to x3 in comparison to x1 and x2.

3. **Add bias.** Each perceptron has a bias that indicates how flexible the perceptron is. Therefore, linear representation of input will now be, w1 * x1 + w2 * x2 + w3 * x3 + 1 * bias.

Now, back-propagation (BP) algorithms determine the loss (or error) at the output and then propagate it back into the network. The weights are updated to minimize the error resulting from each neuron. In this process, the first step is to determine the gradient (derivatives) of each node with respect to the final output.

Note that one round of forward and back propagation iteration is known as one training iteration or **Epoch**.

Key Terms

Unsupervised learning: ML algorithm that trains the machine to use information that is neither classified nor labelled.

Outlier analysis: Unsupervised learning technique used to find out the occurrences of rare events or observations that generally do not occur.

Data: Raw facts and figures, collected for reference or analysis.

Structured data: Data that has a specific pattern or set of rules.

Unstructured data: Data which is neither structured in a particular format nor adhering to a specific set of rules can be recorded as unstructured data.

Semi-structured data: It is a collection of both structured as well as unstructured data.

Big data: Huge amounts of complex data that may be structured or unstructured and is difficult to be analyzed by traditional data management software.

Training data: Data collected to train the machine learning model.

Testing data: Data used to check the validity of the results generated by machine learning model.

Data exploration: Tools and techniques used to easily visualize data that is otherwise difficult to interpret.

Data modelling: The process of creating a machine learning model.

Splitting: The process of dividing a node into two or more sub-nodes.

Decision node: A sub-node that splits into further sub-nodes.

Terminal or leaf node: A sub-node that does not split further.

Parent node: A node which splits into sub-nodes is called a parent node of the sub-nodes (or child of the parent node).

Deep Neural Network: An MLP with four or more layers is called a Deep Neural Network**.**

Epoch: One round of forwarding and back propagation iteration is known as one training iteration or **Epoch**.

Chapter Highlights

- **Volume means enormous** amounts of data being stored. **Velocity** refers to the speed at which large amounts of data is processed and analyzed. **Variety** indicates different sources and forms from which data is collected.

- Analyzing wrong, incorrect, incomplete data is more harmful than not performing any data analytics.

- A decision tree consists of various nodes and follows a top-to-bottom approach.

- In a decision tree, the root node performs the first split and terminal nodes predict the outcome.

- Neural network algorithm works using a set of connected input/output units. In the learning phase, the network learns by adjusting the weights to predict the correct class label of the given inputs.

- A multi-layer perceptron (MLP) or neural network is a perceptron that combines with other perceptrons stacked in several layers, to solve complex problems.

Review Questions

1. Super-intelligent AI is unlikely to exhibit human emotions Data is everywhere. Justify this statement with examples.
2. What do you understand by the term Big Data?
3. What are the three Vs of Big Data?
4. What tasks must be performed to work with Big Data?
5. Discuss any three challenges in working with Big Data.
6. Explain how a decision tree is created.
7. Write a short note on neural networks.
8. Differentiate between the following:
   a. Root node and terminal node of a decision tree
   b. Input and output layers of a neural network.

Fill in the Blanks

1. The 3Vs of big data are __________, __________ and __________.
2. These days, data is stored and managed on __________.
3. __________ algorithm forms a tree-like structure to represent decisions.
4. The top-most node of the decision tree is known as __________.
5. The process of dividing a node into two or more sub-nodes is known as __________.
6. In the __________ phase, the neural network learns by adjusting the weights to predict the correct class label of the given inputs.
7. The __________ layer is the first layer of the neural network.
8. In a neural network, __________ help us to divide a set of input signals into two parts – Yes and No.
9. An MLP with four or more layers is called a __________.
10. A __________ value is added to the output of a perceptron.
11. In a neural network, the __________ function is used to map the input values to the required output values.
12. Nodes of a neural network layer are arranged in __________.
13. The process of travelling back to the neurons of the neural network and finding where the error lies is known as __________.

State True or False

1. Volume refers to the speed at which large amounts of data is processed and analyzed.
2. Size of Big Data is measured in units like megabytes, gigabytes and terabytes.
3. Data grows exponentially with time.
4. A centralized data storage helps to eliminate data inconsistency issues.
5. Root node predicts the outcome.

6. Decision trees and neural networks follow a linear path to solve a problem.

7. In a neural network, the input layer passes the processed information to the output layers.

8. Neural network is a perceptron that combines with other perceptrons stacked in several layers, to solve complex problems.

9. Decision Tree algorithm is also known as a Multi-layer Perceptron.

10. In an MLP, each perceptron in the hidden layer may have a different weight.

11. To make a perfect neural network model, we need to maximize the value or weight of neurons that are contributing more to the error.

12. All cells in the human brain are connected to each other.

13. Neural networks are the only way of data modelling for AI projects.

14. Edges in the human brain as well as in a neural network can carry data only in one direction.

15. A neural network must have at least three layers.

16. A node in the neural network can accept input from only one node in the previous layer.

17. To check the accuracy of prediction, actual output is compared with the predicted output.

Multiple Choice Questions

1. Which of the following is not included in one of the Vs of big data?
   a. Volume　　　　　　b. Validity　　　　　　c. Variety　　　　　　d. Velocity

2. To work with Big Data, we need to __________ it.
   a. integrate　　　　　b. manage　　　　　　c. explore　　　　　　d. All of these.

3. Big Data is a collection of data from several varieties of sources and applications. For this, we need to __________ the data.
   a. integrate　　　　　b. manage　　　　　　c. explore　　　　　　d. analyze

4. Which of the following is not correct about a decision tree?
   a. It follows top-to-bottom approach.　　　b. It is based on a set of rules.
   c. Nodes represent an event or choice.　　　d. Nodes of the graph represent the decision rules or conditions.

5. In a decision tree, a __________ is a sub-node that does not split further.
   a. Decision　　　　　b. Terminal　　　　　c. Root　　　　　　d. Parent

6. In a neural network, there can be any number of __________ layers.
   a. input　　　　　　b. output　　　　　　c. hidden　　　　　　d. All of these.

7. Neural networks can be used to solve __________ problems.
   a. regression　　　　b. classification　　　c. Both of these.　　　d. None of these.

8. Neural networks can be performed only on __________ inputs.
   a. textual　　　　　　b. numerical　　　　　c. image　　　　　　d. video

9. Predicting stock prices is an example of __________.
   a. Outlier Analysis　　　　　　　　　　　b. Time Series Prediction
   c. NLP　　　　　　　　　　　　　　　　d. Pattern Recognition

10. Speech Recognition and Spell-checking use __________ technique.
    a. Outlier Analysis　　　　　　　　　　b. Time Series Prediction
    c. NLP　　　　　　　　　　　　　　　　d. Pattern Recognition

11. One round of forwarding and back propagation iteration is known as __________.
    a. Forward Propagation　　　　　　　　b. Backward Propagation
    c. Epoch　　　　　　　　　　　　　　　d. Activation Function

Arousing Awareness Activity

Discuss some sources from where you can collect Big Data for analysis.

Data Analysis Activity

1. Consider the data table given below, which predicts whether we can spot an elephant or not. The prediction depends on 4 parameters – Outlook, Temperature, Humidity and Wind. Write a paragraph giving your interpretation about the dataset. Also draw a decision tree for this dataset.

Outlook	Temperature	Humidity	Wind	Elephant Spotted?
Sunny	Hot	High	Weak	No
Sunny	Hot	High	Strong	No
Overcast	Hot	High	Weak	Yes
Rain	Mild	High	Weak	Yes
Rain	Cool	Normal	Weak	Yes
Rain	Cool	Normal	Strong	No
Overcast	Cool	Normal	Strong	Yes
Sunny	Mild	High	Weak	No
Sunny	Cool	Normal	Weak	Yes
Rain	Mild	Normal	Weak	Yes
Sunny	Mild	Normal	Strong	Yes
Overcast	Mild	High	Strong	Yes
Overcast	Hot	Normal	Weak	Yes
Rain	Mild	High	Strong	No

Students can also use a website to draw decision trees. Some of these websites are Creately, Smart Draw and Lucid Chart

2. Look at the decision trees given below and write the information you can infer from it.

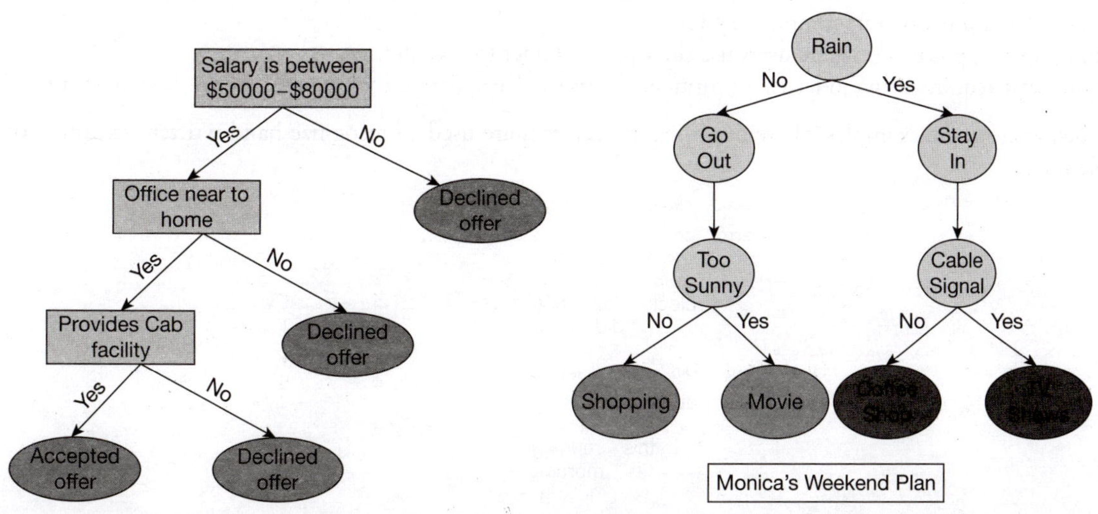

3. Draw a decision tree representing the information given below.

   Rule 1: A hawk has feathers and can fly.

   Rule 2: A penguin has feathers but cannot fly.

   Rule 3: A dolphin does not have feathers but has fins.

   Rule 4: A bear has neither feathers nor fins.

4. Draw a decision tree to make a decision of going to the market or not, based on the following circumstance. *If the shampoo is over then go to the market if it is not raining*

5. Draw a decision tree to represent decisions made in the following circumstances.

   C1: If you have some work or if it rainy outside or if your friends are busy, then stay at home.

   C2: If you do not have any work to do and it is Sunny outside, then go to a beach.

   C3: If you do not have any work to do and it is overcast outside, then go for running.

   C4: If you do not have any work to do and it is rainy outside, then if friends are not busy then go for a movie with them.

Project Work

Ask students to make a project report on Covid Detection. Identify the 4 Ws and goals of the project. Highlight sources from where data can be collected. Which modelling technique would be used to explore the data and why?

Fun Activity – Quick Draw

Can a neural network learn to recognize doodling?
Use the link below to go to the following website and ask students to draw something:
https://quickdraw.withgoogle.com/
   The application will guess what the drawing is about. Just count the number of times the machine guessed it right.

Fun Activity – Handwriting Recognition

Handwriting recognition is a task that categorizes given handwriting patterns into discrete groups (or categories). Though several techniques exist to do this job, the one that uses deep learning such as a convolutional neural network (CNN) supersedes them all.

   Handwriting recognition is especially important in,

- Note-taking applications where users prefer to capture handwritten notes and get them translated into text that can be stored and processed in computer systems.
- Filling form applications where users use their pen or finger to give input.
- Games that require filling in letters or numbers by users. These games include crosswords, hangman, or sudoku

Given below are some examples where deep neural networks are used to recognize hand-written text into computer editable text.

my	alarm	code	soil	rout
		circle	raid	hot
		shute	risk	riot
		clock	visit	not
			did	must

wake	me	up	thai	moving
			taxis	having
			this	running
			tier	morning
				loving

4 → 4
7 → 7
5 → 5

Note that in the figure given below, the character 'C' is converted into pixels (small points on computer screen). The presence of a point on the character is first marked as dark points on the grid-like structure. Now, all dark points are marked as 1 and others as 0 in the matrix.

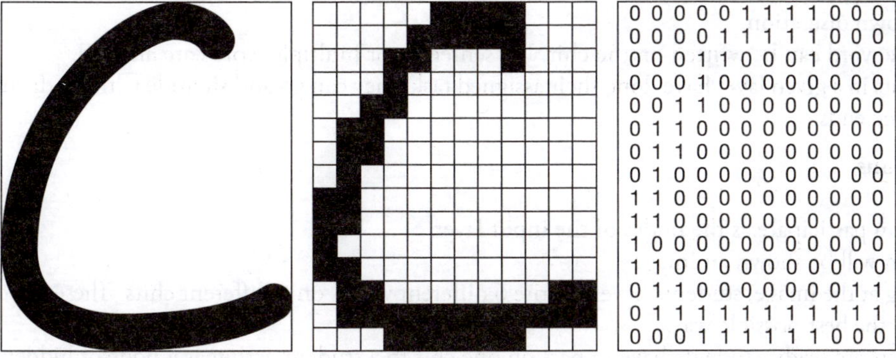

You can convert a handwritten document into computer editable text online for free by visiting the following link: https://www.sodapdf.com/ocr-pdf/.

Game Playing Activity – Human Neural Network

Play a game to help students understand and appreciate the concept of the Neural Network through gamification.
In this activity, each student will be considered as a node. These nodes may belong to any one of the given layers.

Input Layer
Hidden Layer – 1
Hidden Layer – 2
Output Layer

Number of nodes and layers will vary according to number of students in the class. Assuming there are 40 students in the class, the game structure or arrangements can be given as shown in the table. With this structure, the human neural network will look something like,

Layers	No. of students	Chits
Input Layer	7	6
Hidden Layer 1	6	4
Hidden Layer 2	6	2
Output layer	1	–
Total	20	–

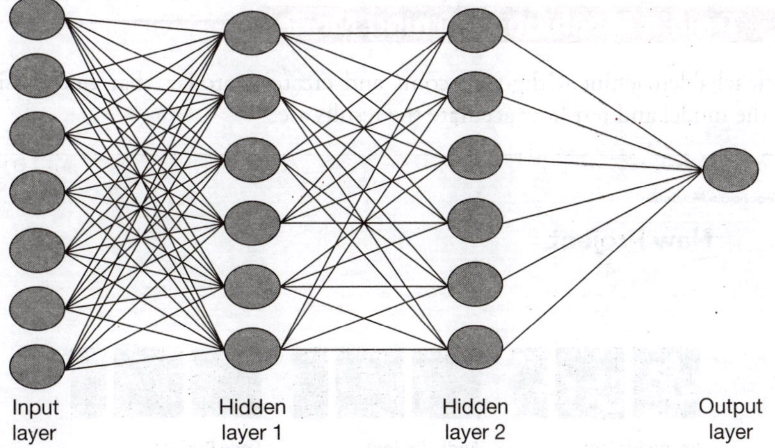

Game Rules
- No student is allowed to talk or discuss while playing.
- Students should play it honestly and maintain proper distance between each other.
- Image chits should be shown to students in the Input layer only and nowhere else.

- Students must silently write a word on the chit and pass the chit to the other student without speaking out aloud.
- Students must process the data as fast as possible. After processing, they must quickly write a word and then pass it on to the next student. Everything should be done in a time-bound manner.
- Students participating as Input Layer nodes must also not discuss the image shown, with each other. Everyone has to use their own discretion.
- Only a single word can be written on the chit. No sentences or multiple words are allowed.
- Once students in a given layer have done their assigned task, they can go and sit aside without disturbing the others until the game ends.

Game Instructions

Input Layer
- 7 students can participate as the nodes of the input layer.
- All 7 of them will be shown an image.
- After looking at the image, students have to write 6 different words on 6 different chits. These words must describe the image in the best possible way.
- Once the chits are ready, students have to pass on one chit to a student acting as a node of hidden layer 1.

Hidden Layer 1
- 6 students will participate as the nodes of hidden layer 1.
- Each of them will receive 6 chits from 7 different input nodes.
- All these 6 students will now write 4 different words on 4 different chits. They may use the same words as received from the input layer or write any other word relevant to the context.
- These 4 chits are then randomly given to any 4 nodes of Hidden Layer 2.

Hidden Layer 2
- 6 students will be standing as the nodes of Hidden Layer 2.
- Each of the students will receive chit(s) from Hidden Layer 1.
- Each student will write two different words on 2 different chits and pass it on to the output layer.

Output Layer
- Students in the output layer receive a total of 12 chits. These chits are used to understand all the words and guess which image was initially shown to the input layer.
- Students in the output layer have to write a summary (not more than 5 lines) using all the words received to justify the deduction.
- Students will then present their summary in front of the entire class and the image is revealed to all.
- If the summary is accurate enough, the whole network wins, else they lose.

AI Lab Session – Train a Machine Learning Model

Visit the link https://teachablemachine.withgoogle.com/ and create a project that can classify images, poses and sounds. You can train the model and test how accurate the results are.

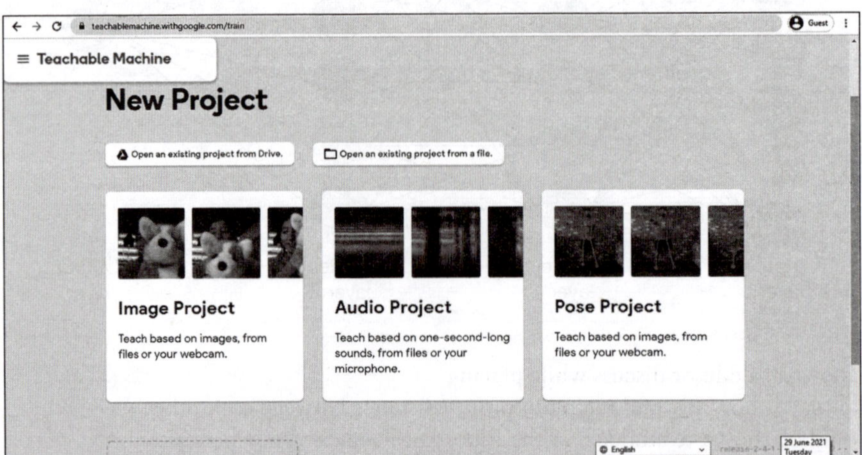

The experiment predicts the drawing which the user wants to create based on a partial drawing made by the user. The user draws a sketch on the left side of the screen. On the right side, AI is used to predict the complete drawing based on the user's inputs.

https://magenta.tensorflow.org/assets/sketch_rnn_demo/multi_predict.html

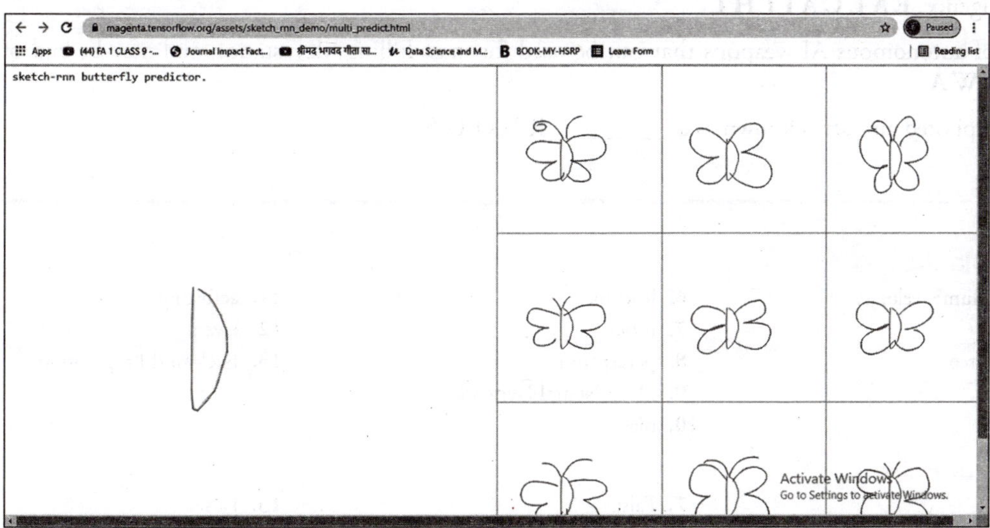

The experiment takes the drawing made by the user as input and uses this input to make similar drawings. Visit the link https://magenta.tensorflow.org/assets/sketch_rnn_demo/index.html to draw interesting sketches. For convenience, users can select a category of the sketch before drawing. However, do not forget to select a category and then draw an entirely different sketch. For example, select cat in the category and draw a butterfly to see how the AI system behaves.

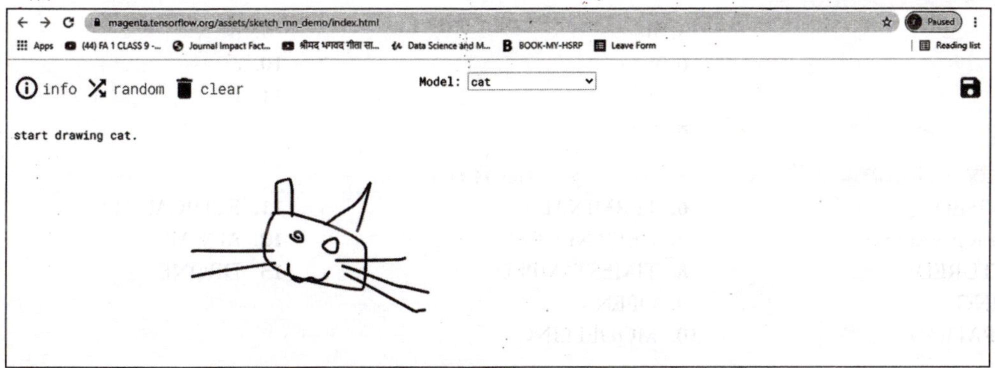

Fun Activity – Unjumble the Words to Guess the Term

1. In _________ learning, ML model is trained with known labels. **R V I S U S E D P E**

2. _________ is an unsupervised learning technique that identifies unusual data. **E U O T L I R A Y S I N A L S**

3. _________ Data has a specific pattern or set of rules. **S R E D U C T T R U**

4. _________ Data helps to make the machine learning model learn. **T N G A I N R I**

5. Data _________ includes tools and techniques used to easily visualize data that is otherwise difficult to interpret. **E R A T P L O I O X N**

6. _________ node cannot be further divided. **T N A L M E R I**

7. An MLP with four or more layers is called a _________ Network. **E E D P N U R A E L**

8. _________ data has a time component associated to define the sequence of events. **M E T I S D M P T A E**

9. _______ Data can be downloaded b anybody for analysis. **O P N E**

10. ML model is created in the Data ___________ phase. **I N G E L M O D L**

11. ___________ is the theory behind developing computer systems, which can perform tasks that require human intelligence. **E A L C A I T H I**

12. Use of autonomous AI weapons that can be used for mass killing, devastation and may be end of humanity. **A R I W A**

13. An unpiloted aircraft is known as a _________. **R N O D E**

Answers

Fill in the Blanks

1. variety, volume, velocity
2. Cloud
3. Decision tree
4. Root
5. Splitting
6. learning
7. input
8. perceptron
9. Deep Neural Network
10. bias
11. activation
12. layers
13. Backward Propagation

State True or False

1. False
2. False
3. True
4. True
5. False
6. False
7. False
8. True
9. False
10. True
11. False
12. True
13. False
14. False
15. True
16. False
17. True

Multiple Choice Questions

1. b
2. d
3. a
4. d
5. b
6. c
7. c
8. b
9. b
10. c
11. c

Fun Activity – Unjumble the Words to Guess the Term

1. SUPERVISED
2. OUTLIER ANALYSIS
3. STRUCTURED
4. TRAINING
5. EXPLORATION
6. TERMINAL
7. DEEP NEURAL
8. TIMESTAMPED
9. OPEN
10. MODELLING
11. ETHICAL AI
12. AI WAR
13. DRONE

Introduction to Programming Language Python

10

The chapter aims to introduce Python as a programming language. To arouse interest in the language and enhance the reader's computational skills, the following topics will be discussed:

- Basic features, historical background, future scope, advantages, applications and limitations of Python
- Working with Python in interactive mode
- Writing Python scripts in IDLE
- Executing programs or rather scripts
- Introduction to Python character set, tokens, literals, numbers, strings, escape sequences
- Formatting numbers and understand basic errors that may pop up while working with floating-point values
- Strings, escape sequences and string operations
- Type conversion

Python is a powerful programming language with the right combination of performance and features that makes programming fun and easy. It is a high-level, interpreted, interactive, object-oriented and a reliable language that uses English-like words. It has a vast library of modules to support integration of complex solutions from pre-built components. In this chapter, we will start with a basic introduction of Python.

10.1 FEATURES OF PYTHON

Python is an open-source project, supported by many individuals. It can be used on any operating system. Some of the features that make Python a complete programming language are given below.

Simple: Python is a simple and a small language. Reading a program written in Python feels almost like reading English.

Easy to Learn: A Python program is easy to read and understand. It uses only a few keywords and a clearly defined syntax. This makes it easy for just anyone to pick up the language quickly.

Versatile: Python supports development of a wide range of applications ranging from simple text processing to games.

Free and Open Source: Python is an example of an open-source software. Therefore, anyone can freely distribute it, read the source code, edit it and even use the code to write new (free) programs.

High-level Language: When writing programs in Python, the programmers don't have to worry about the hardware-related details. They just need to concentrate on writing solutions for the current problem at hand.

Interactive: Programs in Python work in interactive mode. Users can give input and get the results accordingly. In this way, users feel as if they are directly communicating with the program.

> Python has been constantly improved upon by a community of users who have always strived hard to take it to the next level.

Portable: Python is a portable language. Hence, the programs behave the same on a wide variety of hardware platforms. The programs work on any of the operating systems without requiring any change.

Object-oriented: Python supports object-oriented as well as procedure-oriented style of programming. While *object-oriented* technique uses classes and objects to bind data and functions that can manipulate that data, *procedure-oriented* technique, on the other hand, builds program by making extensive use of functions (functions are reusable parts of a program).

Interpreted: Python program is processed at runtime (while it is being executed) by the interpreter. The interpreter checks each statement to ensure that there are no syntactical errors. If a statement has one or more errors, then it is reported to the user. After the error is removed or if there is no error in a particular line, the interpreter converts that statement into machine language (comprising of only 0s and 1s) and then processes the next line.

Dynamic: Python program executes dynamically. They can be copied and used for flexible development of applications.

Extensible: Since Python is an open-source software, anyone can add modules to the Python interpreter. These modules enable programmers to add to or customize their tools to work more efficiently.

Embeddable: Programmers can embed Python programs within their C, C++, COM, ActiveX, CORBA, and Java programs for added functionality.

Extensive Libraries: Python has a huge library that allows programmers to perform a wide range of applications varying from text processing, maintaining databases to GUI programming.

Besides the above-stated features, Python has a big list of good features, such as

Easy maintenance: Codes written in Python are easy to maintain.

Secure: The Python language environment is secure from tampering.

Robust: Python programmers cannot manipulate memory directly. Moreover, errors can be easily handled through exception handling procedures. For every syntactical mistake, a simple and easy-to-interpret message is displayed. All these things make the language robust.

Multi-threaded: Python supports multi-threading, that is, executing more than one process of a program simultaneously.

Garbage Collection: Python performs garbage collection of all objects that are no longer used.

10.2   LIMITATIONS OF PYTHON

- *Parallel processing* can be done in Python but not as elegantly as done in some other languages (like JavaScript and Go Lang).
- Being an interpreted language, Python is *slow* as compared to C/C++.
- Python is not a very good choice for those developing a high-graphic 3D games that take up a lot of CPU.
- As compared to other languages, Python is evolving continuously and there is little substantial *documentation* available for the language.
- As of now, there are fewer *users* of Python as compared to those using C, C++ or Java.
- It lacks true *multiprocessor support*.
- It has very limited *commercial support* points.
- Python is slower than C or C++ when it comes to computation for heavy tasks and desktop applications.
- It is difficult to pack a big Python application into a single executable file. This makes it difficult to distribute Python to *non-technical users*.

> BitTorrent, YouTube, Dropbox, Deluge, Cinema 4D and Bazaar are a few globally used applications based on Python.

10.3 HISTORY OF PYTHON

Python was developed by Guido van Rossum in the late 80's and early 90's at the National Research Institute for Mathematics and Computer Science in the Netherlands. It has been derived from many languages like ABC, Modula-3, C, C++, Algol-68, SmallTalk, Unix shell and other scripting languages. Since early 90's, Python has been improved tremendously. Version 1.0 was released in 1991, which introduced several new functional programming tools and Version 2.0 brought list comprehensions. It was released in 2000 by the BeOpen Python Labs team. Python 2.7, which is still used today was supported until 2020. But there is no 2.8; instead, the support team will continue to support version 2.7 and concentrate on further development of Python 3.

Currently, Python 3.8.x is already available. The newer versions have better features. These days, from data to web development, Python has emerged as a very powerful and popular language.

10.4 APPLICATIONS OF PYTHON

Since its origin in 1989, Python has grown to become part of a plethora of web-based, desktop-based, graphic design, scientific, and computational applications. Some of the key applications of Python include:

- Python is used to develop a wide range of applications including *image processing, text processing, web*, and enterprise levels using scientific, numeric and data from network.

- 3D software like Maya include Python, which can be used for *automating* small user tasks.

- Python is a popular language for *web development*. For example, websites like Quora, Odoo and Google App engine have their codes written in Python. For web development Python has frameworks such as Django, Pyramid, Flask and Bottle.

- *GUI-based Desktop Applications* can be easily developed in Python.

- Python is used to make *2D imaging software* such as Inkscape, GIMP, Paint Shop Pro and Scribus. It is also used to make *3D animation* packages, like Blender, 3ds Max, Cinema 4D, Houdini, Lightwave and Maya.

- Features like high speed, productivity and availability of tools (like Scientific Python and Numeric Python) have made Python a preferred language to perform *computation and processing of scientific data*.

- Python has various modules, libraries and platforms that support development of *games*. Games like Civilization-IV, Disney's Toontown Online, Vega Strike, etc., are coded using Python.

- Python is a suitable coding language for *customizing business applications*. For example, Reddit which was originally written in Common Lips, was rewritten in Python in 2005. A large part of YouTube code is also written in Python.

- Python is also used for *writing codes for operating system*. For example, Ubuntu's Ubiquity Installer, and Fedora's and Red Hat Enterprise Linux's Anaconda Installer are written in Python. Gentoo Linux uses Python for Portage – its package management system.

- Python is used to develop other *languages*. For example, Boo, Apple's Swift, CoffeeScript, Cobra, and OCaml all have syntax similar to Python.

- Since Python is very easy to learn and an open-source language, it is widely used for *prototype development* (that means, for developing user interfaces or screens).

- Python is used for *network programming* to help users write functions for email processing and support for FTP, IMAP and other Internet protocols.

- Python is a perfect language for teaching programming skills at the introductory as well as advanced level.

10.5   THE FUTURE OF PYTHON

Python has a huge user base that is constantly growing. It is a stable language that is going to stay for long. The strength of Python can be understood from the fact that this programming language is the most preferred language of companies such as Nokia, Google, and YouTube, as well as NASA for its easy syntax. Python has a bright future ahead of it supported by a huge community of OS developers. The support for multiple programming paradigms including object-oriented Python programming, functional Python programming, and parallel programming models make it an ideal choice for the programmers. Based on the data from Google Trends (Fig. 10.1), Python is amongst the top five most preferred languages in academics as well industry.

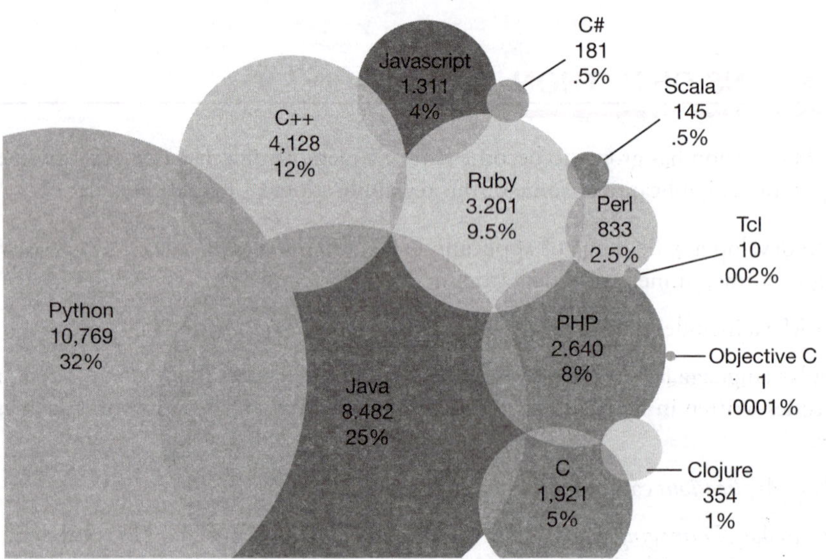

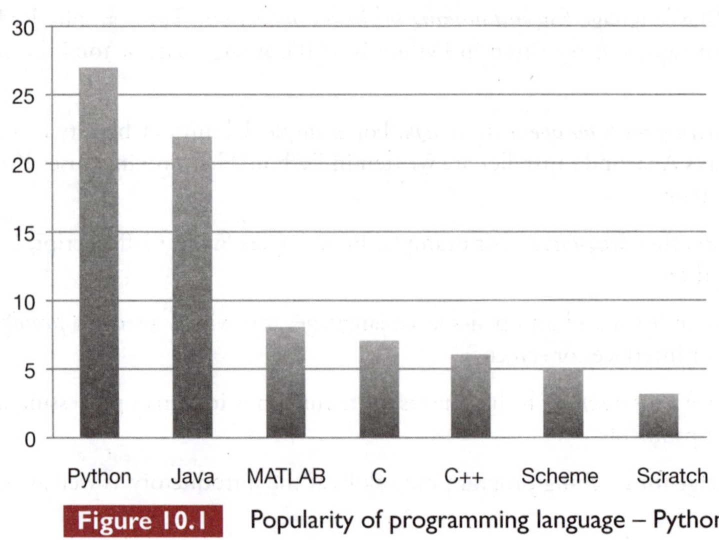

Figure 10.1   Popularity of programming language – Python

Python is a high-speed dynamic language. Therefore, it works well in applications like photo development and has been embedded programs such as GIMP and Paint Shop Pro. In fact, the YouTube architect, Cuong Do, has appreciated this language for the record speed with which the language allows them to work. The best part is that more and more companies have started using Python for a broader range of applications ranging from social networks, through automation to science calculations.

10.6   WRITING AND EXECUTING THE FIRST PYTHON PROGRAM

Here onwards, we will be using Python, via the Python console. For this, you need to first download Python from www.Python.org. The codes in this book have been developed on Python 3.8.3.

Once installed, the Python console can be accessed in several ways. We will discuss only two of them here. First, using the command line and running the Python interpreter directly. Second, using a GUI software that comes installed with Python called IDLE (as shown in Fig. 10.2).

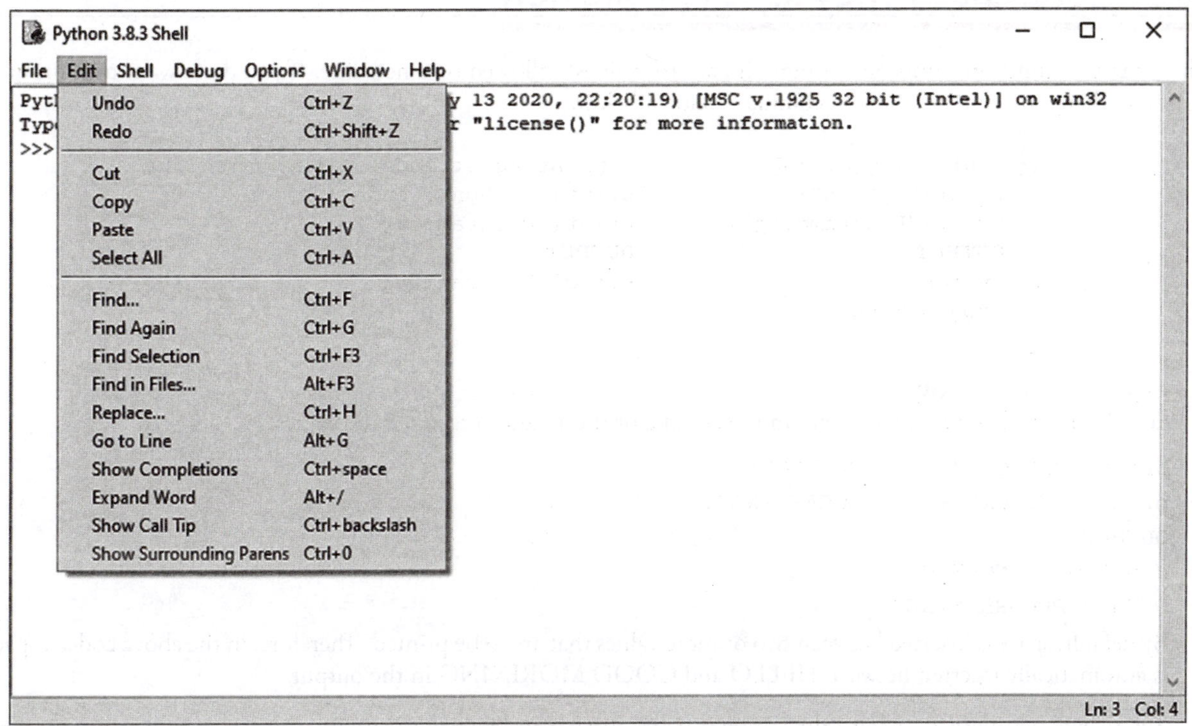

Figure 10.2   Python IDLE

10.7   INTERACTIVE PYTHON

The Python interactive console, also known as the Python interpreter or Python shell, provides programmers a quick way to execute commands without creating a Python file (with a .py extension). For the convenience of users, it provides support for everything including,

- all of Python's built-in functions
- pre-installed modules
- command history
- auto-completion feature.

The interactive console also enables programmers to paste code into programming files as and when required. It is a good alternative to execute commands when programmers want to quickly test some basic functionality of the Python language and don't want to write a whole script. To get the interactive interpreter, follow the steps given below.

Step 1: Click on Start button.

Step 2: Type Idle.

Step 3: Click on IDLE (Python GUI).

The IDLE starts. You get a prompt of three right arrows. Type in your instructions at the prompt and press the enter key. **Let us print Hello World!!!** on the screen. For this, simply type the following line on the IDLE.

> The >>> symbol denotes the Python prompt.

Example: To print a message on the screen

```
>>> print("Hello World!!!")
Hello World!!!
```

10.8   MORE ABOUT THE PRINT() FUNCTION

The `print()` function prints one or more literals (or values) followed by a new line. If you don't want to print on a new line, then write end = ' ' after a comma as shown below.

```
# printing strings              # printing strings on the same line
print("Python")                 print("Python", end= ' ')
print("Programming")            print("Programming")
OUTPUT                          OUTPUT
Python                          Python Programming
Programming
```

Key Points to Remember

- To print more than one value, you can use comma or the + sign to separate the values.

```
print("HELLO","GOOD MORNING")
print("PYTHON" + " PROGRAMMING")
OUTPUT
HELLO GOOD MORNING
PYTHON PROGRAMMING
```

- By default, space is inserted between two or more values that are to be printed. Therefore, in the above code, a space is automatically inserted between HELLO and GOOD MORINING in the output.

- The default separator between values, which is the space, can be changed to any other character using the `sep` argument in the `print()` function as shown below. We shall discuss argument in a later chapter.

```
print("HELLO","GOOD MORNING","INDIA", sep = '#')
OUTPUT
HELLO#GOOD MORNING#INDIA
```

- The `print()` function prints a string (i.e., a group of characters). If any non-string value is specified in the `print()` function, it automatically converts it to a string before printing.

```
print("Neha's Total Marks = ",98)
OUTPUT
Neha's Total Marks =  98
```

- The `print()` function automatically inserts a new line. So, in case we have multiple `print()` functions in the same program, then the output of each `print()` function will be displayed on the next line or the new line.

```
print("HELLO")
print("GOOD MORNING")
OUTPUT
HELLO
GOOD MORNING
```

10.9   WRITING PYTHON PROGRAMS USING THE IDLE EDITOR

In general, the standard way to save and run a Python program is as follows:

Step 1: Open an editor.

Step 2: Write the instructions

Step 3: Save it as a file with the file name having the extension .py.

Step 4: Run the interpreter with the command python program_name.py or use IDLE to run the programs.

To execute the program at the *command prompt*, simply change your working directory to C:\Python37 (or move to the directory where you have saved Python) and then type python program_name.py.

If you want to execute the program in Python shell, then press **F5** key (Fig. 10.3) or click on Run Menu and then select **Run Module**.

> To exit from the IDLE, click on File → Exit, or, press Ctrl + Q keys or type quit() at the command prompt.

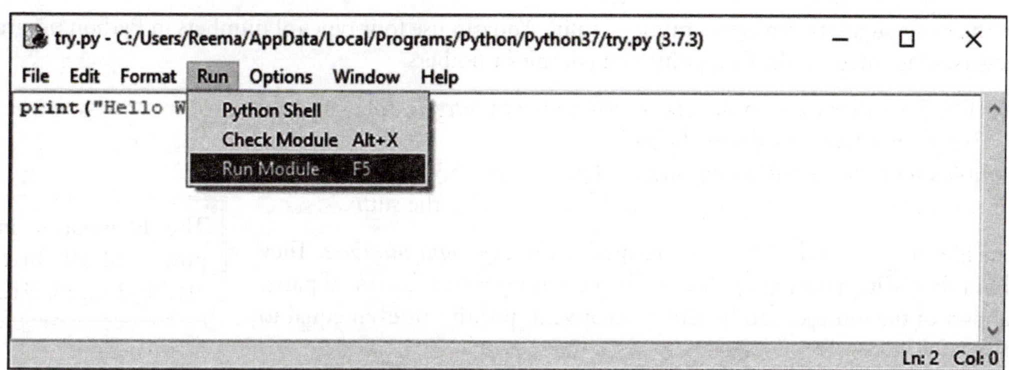

Figure 10.3   Executing Python code in IDLE

10.10 PYTHON CHARACTER SET

The character set of a language is a set of valid characters that the language can recognize. Such characters may be digits, alphabets, or any other symbol. Python supports Unicode encoding. The character set of Python includes:

- Lowercase English letters *a* through *z*.
- Uppercase English letters *A* through *Z*.
- Punctuation symbols like $, !, _ , etc.
- Whitespace characters, which includes a space (" "), tab, newline, etc.
- Non-printable characters like backspace ("\b") that cannot be printed but has a specific meaning.

10.11 PYTHON TOKENS

Tokens are the small units of the programming language (Fig. 10.4). Python supports the following types of tokens. In this chapter, we will read about literals in detail.

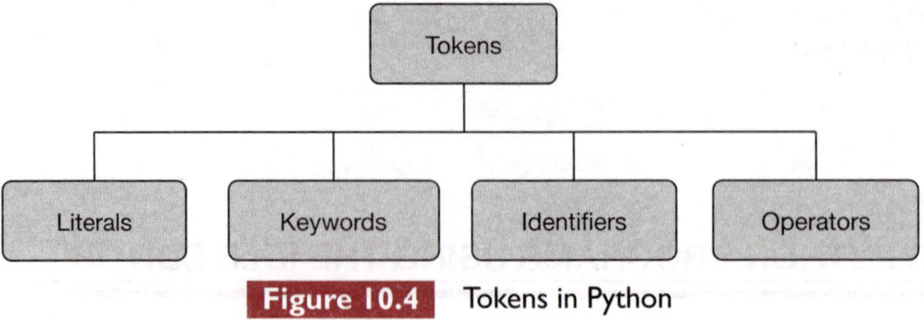

Figure 10.4   Tokens in Python

10.12 LITERAL CONSTANTS

The word 'literal' is derived from 'literally'. The value of a literal constant can be used directly in programs. For example, 7, 3.9, 'A', and 'Hello' are examples of literal constants. The number 7 always represents itself and nothing else. Moreover, it is a constant because its value cannot be changed. Hence, it is known as *literal constant*. In this section, we will read about number and string constants in Python.

> You can specify integers in octal as well as hexadecimal number system.

10.12.1 Numbers

Number, as the name suggests, refers to a numeric value. You can use four types of numbers in Python programs. These include integers, long integers, floating-point and complex numbers.

- Numbers like 5 or other whole numbers are referred to as *integers*. Integers can be positive or negative or even equal to zero. They do not have any decimal point.
  Bigger whole numbers are called *long integers*. For example, 535633629843L is a long integer. Note that a long integer must have 'l' or 'L' as the suffix.

- Numbers like are 3.23 and 91.5E-2 are termed as *floating-point numbers*. They are real numbers with a decimal point dividing the integer and fractional parts. The real part of the number can be either negative or positive or even equal to zero.

> The 'E' notation indicates powers of 10. In this case, 91.5E-2 means $91.5 * 10^{-2}$.

Remember that commas are never used in numeric literals or numeric values. Therefore, numbers like 3,567 1,23.89 −8,904 are not allowed in Python.

Large Floating-point Numbers   Large floating-point numbers are efficiently represented in scientific notation. For example, $5.0012304*10^6$ (6 digits of precision) can be written as 5.0012304e+6 in scientific notation.

Do you remember that in a scientific notation, we have two parts – exponent and the mantissa? The mantissa appears before the e and the exponent part follows the e. While mantissa can be an integer or a floating-point number, the exponent is always an integer. Both mantissa and exponent can be either negative or positive.

Errors when Dealing with Floating-point Values   Although floating-point numbers are very efficient at handling large numbers, there are some issues while dealing with them as they may produce the following errors.

The Arithmetic Overflow Problem: When two very large floating-point numbers are multiplied, it may result in an *arithmetic overflow*. Arithmetic overflow is a condition that occurs when a calculated result is too large. For example, try to multiply 2.7e200 * 4.3e200. You will get result as inf, which means infinity. Infinity denotes that an arithmetic overflow has occurred.

The Arithmetic Underflow Problem: Arithmetic underflow occurs when we divide one floating-point number with another. It is a condition that occurs when a calculated result is too small in magnitude to be represented. For example, try to divide 3.0e-400/5.0e200. You will get the result as 0.0. The value 0.0 indicates that an arithmetic underflow has occurred.

Loss of Precision Problem: When you divide 1/3 you know that the results is 0.33333333…, where 3 is repeated infinitely. Since any floating-point number has a limited precision and range, the result is just an *approximation* of the true value. Python automatically displays a rounded result to keep the number of digits displayed manageable. For most applications, this slight loss in accuracy is of no practical concern but in scientific computing and other applications in which precise calculations are required, it may be a big issue.

Built-in `format()` Function Any floating-point value may contain an arbitrary number of decimal places, so it is always recommended to use the built-in `format()` function to produce a string version of a number with specific number of decimal places. Observe the difference between the following outputs.

```
# Without using format()               # Using format()
>>> float(16/(float(3)))               >>> format(float(16/(float(3))), '.2f')
5.333333333333333                      '5.33'
```

Here, .2f in the `format()` function rounds the result to two decimal places of accuracy in the string produced. For very large (or very small) values, 'e' can be used as a *format specifier*. The `format()` function can also be used to format floating-point numbers in scientific notation. Look at the result of the expression given below.

```
>>> format(3**50,'.5e')
'7.17898e+23'
```

The result is formatted in scientific notation with five decimal places of precision. This feature is especially useful when displaying results in which only a certain number of decimal places is needed. Finally, the `format()` function can also be used to insert a comma in the number as shown below.

```
>>> format(123456.8901,',.2f')
'123,456.89'
```

Simple Operations on Numbers Python can carry out simple operations on numbers. To perform a calculation, simply enter the numbers and the type of operations that need to be performed on them directly into the Python console, and it will print the answer, as shown below.

```
>>> 17 + 56      >>> 90 + 50 - 40      >>> 35 * 15      >>> 108 / 12      >>> -10 * 14
73               100                   525              9.0               -140
```

Dividing a number by zero in Python generates an error, and no output is produced, as shown below.

```
>>> 117 / 0
Traceback (most recent call last):
  File "<pyshell#7>", line 1, in <module>
    117 / 0
ZeroDivisionError: division by zero
```

> The spaces around the plus and minus signs here are optional. They are just added to make the statement more readable. The code will execute even if you remove the spaces.

When one number is divided by another, always a floating-point number is produced.

```
>>> 15 / 5        >>> 75 / 15.0        >>> 39.0 / 3        >>> 24.0 / 2.0
3.0               5.0                  13.0               12.0
```

You can easily work with a floating-point number and an integer because Python automatically converts the integer to a float.

Quotient and Remainder When a number is divided by another, if you want to know the quotient and remainder, use the floor division (//) and modulo operator (%), respectively. These operators can be used with both floats and integers. Observe the following statements and their output. When we divide 78 by 5, we get a quotient of 15 and a remainder of 3.

```
>>> 18 // 4       >>> 18 % 4       >>> 324.0 // 6.0       >>> 234.567 % 6.5
4                 2                54.0                  0.5670000000000073
```

Exponentiation Besides, +, – , *, / Python also supports ** operator. The ** operator is used for exponentiation, i.e., raising of one number to the power of another. Consider the statements given in the example and observe the output.

>>> **11 ** 3**	>>> **5.25 ** 4**
1331	759.69140625

10.12.2 Strings

A *string* is a group of characters. We have already printed a string in our first program in which we had printed 'HELLO WORLD !!!'. In Python, there are three ways in which a string can be used.

- **Using Single Quotes (' '):** For example, a string can be written as 'HELLO'.

- **Using Double Quotes (" "):** Strings in double quotes are exactly same as those in single quotes. Therefore, 'HELLO' is same as "HELLO".

- **Using Triple Quotes (" "):** A multi-line string is specified using triple quotes. We can use as many single quotes and double quotes as required in a string within triple quotes. An example of a multi-line string can be given as,

> All spaces and tabs within a string are preserved in quotes (single quote as well as double).

```
>>> ''' HELLO WORLD !!!
'GOOD MORNING'
"WELCOME TO THE WORLD OF 'PYTHON PROGRAMMING' "
HAPPY LEARNING....'''
' HELLO WORLD !!!\n\'GOOD MORNING\'\n"WELCOME TO THE WORLD OF \'PYTHON
PROGRAMMING\' "\nHAPPY LEARNING....'
```

Note that all the characters, spaces, tabs, new lines, and quotes (single as well as double) are preserved within the triple quotes.

>>> **'Hello'**	>>> **"HELLO"**	>>> **'''HELLO'''**
'Hello'	'HELLO'	'HELLO'

Irrespective of the way in which a string is specified, all strings are **immutable***. This means that once you have created a string, you cannot change it.*

String literal concatenation Python concatenates two string literals that are placed side by side. Consider the code below wherein Python has automatically concatenated three string literals.

```
>>> 'HELLO' 'WORLD'
'HELLOWORLD'
```

Unicode Strings Unicode is a standard way of writing international text. That is, if you want to write some text in your native language like Hindi, then you need to have a Unicode-enabled text editor. Python allows you to specify Unicode text by prefixing the string with a u or U. For example,

```
>>> u"Shubh Prabhat"
'Shubh Prabhat'
```

> The 'U' prefix specifies that the file contains text written in a language other than English.

Escape Sequences Some characters like comma (,), double quotes ("), and backslash (\) cannot be directly included in a string. Such characters must be escaped by placing a backslash before them as given below.

```
>>> print('How's life?')
    SyntaxError: invalid syntax
>>> print('How\'s life?')
How's life?
```

The reason for the error was that Python got confused as to where the string starts and ends. So, we need to clearly specify that this single quote does not indicate the end of the string. This indication can be given with the help of an ***escape sequence*** as specified in the second string – *a single quote preceded by a backslash.*

Similarly, to print double quotes in a string enclosed within double quotes, we must precede the double quotes with a backslash as given below.

```
>>> print("Sheena asked, "Will you come with me?"")
SyntaxError: invalid syntax
>>> print("Sheena asked,\"Will you come with me?\"")
Sheena asked, "Will you come with me?"
```

Other useful escape sequences are given in Table 10.1.

> When a string is printed, the quotes around it are not displayed.

> An escape sequence is treated as a single character.

Table 10.1   Some of the escape sequences used in Python

Escape Sequence	Purpose	Example	Output
\\	Prints Backslash	print("\\")	\
\'	Prints single-quote	print("\'")	'
\"	Prints double-quote	print("\"")	"
\a	Rings bell	print("\a")	Bell rings
\f	Prints form feed character	print("Hello\fWorld")	Hello World
\n	Prints newline character	print("Hello\nWorld")	Hello World
\t	Prints a tab	print("Hello\tWorld")	Hello World
\o	Prints octal value	print("\o56")	.
\x	Prints hex value	print("\x65")	e

Multi-line Strings When specifying a string, if a single backslash (\) is added at the end of the line then it indicates that the string is continued in the next line, but no new line is added otherwise. For example,

```
>>> print("Hello World,\
Good Morning !!!")
Hello World,Good Morning !!!
```

Raw Strings If you want to specify that a string should not handle any escape sequences and want it to be displayed exactly as specified, then you need to specify that string as a ***raw string***. A raw string is specified by prefixing r or R to the string.

```
>>> R"How\'s life at your end?"
"How\\'s life at your end?"
```

> Raw strings are not processed in any special way, not even the escape sequences.

String Formatting We have already used the built-in `format()` function to format floating-point numbers. The same function can also be used to control the display of strings. The syntax of `format()` function is given as,

```
format(value, format_specifier)
```

where, `value` is the value or the string to be displayed, and `format_specifier` can contain a combination of formatting options.

Example: Commands to display 'PYTHON' left-justified, right-justified and centre-aligned in a field width of 30 characters.

`>>> format('PYTHON','<30')` `'PYTHON `	`>>> format('PYTHON','>30')` `'            PYTHON'`	`>>> format('PYTHON','^30')` `'         PYTHON         '`

Here, the `'<'` symbol means to left justify. Similarly to right justify the string, use the `'>'` symbol and the `'^'` symbol to centrally align the string.

We have seen above that `format()` function uses blank spaces to fill the specified width. But you can also use the `format()` function to fill the width in the formatted string using any other character as shown below.

```
>>> print('PYTHON', format('-','-<10')'PROGRAMMING')
PYTHON----------PROGRAMMING
```

String Concatenation Like numbers, we can also add two strings in Python. The process of combining two strings is called ***concatenation***. Two strings, whether created using single or double quotes, are concatenated in the same way.

`>>>'HI... and ....'+'BYE'`
`HI... and .... BYE`
	`>>>'''PYTHON'''+'''`
	`PROGRAMMING''')`
	`'PYTHONPROGRAMMING'`
		`>>>'''PYTHON'''`
		`+'''  PROGRAMMING''')`
		`'PYTHON PROGRAMMING'`

Slice a String A substring of a string is called a **slice**. You can extract subsets (or small parts) of strings by using the slice operator (`[ ]` and `[:]`). You need to specify index or the range of index of characters to be extracted. The index of the first character is 0 and the index of the last character is $n - 1$, where n is the number of characters in the string.

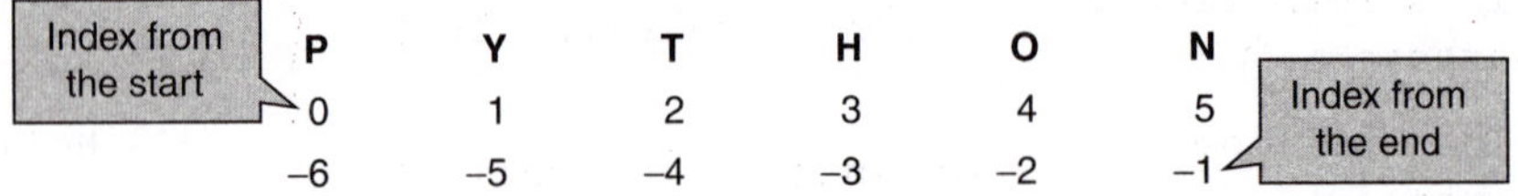

The syntax of slice operation is s[start:end:stride], where start specifies the beginning index of the substring and end is the index of the last character of the string s. *Omitting either start or end index, by default, takes start or end of the string. Omitting both means the entire string.*

If you want *to extract characters starting from the end of the string, then you must specify the index as a negative number.* For example, the index of the last character is –1.

Specifying Stride while Slicing Strings: In the slice operation, you can specify a third argument as the ***stride.*** The stride specifies the number of characters to move forward after the first character is retrieved from the string. By default, the value of stride is 1, which means that every character between two index numbers is retrieved. If stride is 2, then every second character is accessed, if stride is 3 then every third character is accessed, and so on.

```
#Slice operation on string
>>> str = "Python Programming is Fun"
>>> str[0]                 #prints the first character
p
>>> str[4:10]              #prints characters from 4 to 9
on Pro
>>> str[5:]               #prints all characters staring from fifth character
n Programming is Fun
>>> str[-1]                #prints the last character
n
>>> str[:-1]               #prints all except the last character
Python Programming is Fu
>>> str[-7:]               #prints last seven character
is Fun
>>> str[3:15:2]            #prints every 2nd character from 3rd - 15th character
'hnPorm'
```

Did you notice that when we use the slice operator, elements are accessed from left towards right? For any index n (positive or negative), s[:n] + s[n:] = s. This means that the slice operation always partitions the string into two parts in such a way that all characters are conserved.

Even the whitespace characters are skipped as they are also a part of the string. ***If you omit the first two arguments and only specify the third one, then the entire string is used in steps.*** We can even have a negative value in the stride. For example, if the value of stride is –1 then the string is printed in reverse order.

#print every third character	#print string in reverse	#print every second character in the #reversed string
`str="Python programming is fun"`	`str="Python programming is fun"`	`str="Python programming is fun"`
`print(str[::3])`	`print(str[::-1])`	`print(str[::-2])`
OUTPUT	**OUTPUT**	**OUTPUT**
`Ph oai n`	`nuf si gnimmargorp nohtyP`	`nfs nmagr otP`

10.13 TYPE CONVERSION

In Python, it is just not possible to complete certain operations that involve different types of data. For example, it is not possible to perform "4" + 7 since one operand is an integer and the other is of string type.

Another situation in which type conversion is a must is when you want to accept a non-string value (integer or float) as an input. The `input()` function which accepts input(s) from the user takes it as a string. In case the user has to enter a numeric value then the string value must be explicitly typecasted to numbers (integers or floats) so that calculations can be performed on them. In such situations, you must perform conversions between data types.

```
>>>"7"+"4"        >>>int("7")+int("3")
'74'              10
```

```
x =input("Enter the first number:")      x = int(input("Enter the first number: "))
y =input("Enter the second number : ")   y = int(input("Enterthe second number : "))
print(x + y)                             print(x + y)
OUTPUT                                   OUTPUT
Enter the first number: 7                Enter the first number: 7
Enter the second number: 4               Enter the second number : 4
74                                       11
```

Python provides several built-in functions to convert a value from one data type to another. These functions return a new object representing the converted value. Some of them are given in Table 10.2.

Table 10.2   Some commonly used built-in functions in Python for type conversions

Function	Description	Example
`int(x)`	Converts x to an integer	int(3.5) gives 3
`float(x)`	Converts x to a floating-point number	float('123') gives 123.0
`str(x)`	Converts x to a string	str(123.45) gives '123.45'
`tuple(x)`	Converts list x to a tuple	tuple([1,2,3]) gives (1, 2, 3)
`list(x)`	Converts tuple x to a list	list((1,2,3)) gives [1, 2, 3]
`set (x)`	Converts x to a set	set([1,2,3]) gives {1, 2, 3}
`ord(x)`	Converts a single character to its integer value	ord('D') gives 68
`oct(x)`	Converts an integer to an octal string	oct(9} gives '0oll'
`hex(x)`	Converts an integer to a hexadecimal string	hex(1234} gives '0x4d2'
`chr(x)`	Converts an integer to a character	chr(70) gives 'F'
`complex(x)`	Converts to a complex number	complex(3,-8) gives (3-8j)

However, before using type conversions to convert a floating-point number into an integer number, remember that `int()` converts a float to an int by truncation (discarding the fractional part) and not by rounding to the nearest whole number. The `round()` works more appropriately by rounding a floating-point number to the nearest integer as shown below. The `round()` can even take a second, optional argument which is usually a number that indicates the number of places of precision to which the first argument should be rounded.

```
>>> int(3. 7)          >>> round(3.7)          >>> round(1234.56789012,2)
3                       4                       1234.57
```

Note that each argument passed to a function has a specific data type. If you pass an argument of the wrong data type to a function, it will generate an error. For example, you cannot find the square root of a string. If you don't know what type of arguments a function accepts, you should use the `help()` before using the function.

Key Terms

Statement: A statement in Python is an instruction given to the computer to perform any kind of action.

String: A string is a group of characters.

String concatenation: The process of combining two strings.

Slice: A substring of a string is called a slice.

Chapter Highlights

- Python is a high-level, interpreted, interactive, object-oriented and reliable language.

- Once installed, the Python console can be accessed in several ways. First, using the command line and running the Python interpreter directly. Second, using a GUI software that comes installed with Python called IDLE.

- If you want to execute a program in Python shell, then press **F5** key or click on Run Menu and then select **Run Module**.

- The character set of a language is a set of valid characters that the language can recognize. Such characters may be digits, alphabets, or any other symbol.

- Tokens are the small units of the programming language. Python supports literals, keywords, identifiers and operators as tokens.

- Number, as the name suggests, refers to a numeric value. You can use four types of numbers in Python programs. These include integers, long integers, floating-point and complex numbers.

- When two very large floating-point numbers are multiplied, it may result in an *arithmetic overflow*. Arithmetic overflow is a condition that occurs when a calculated result is too large.

- Arithmetic underflow occurs when one floating-point number is divided by another. It is a condition that occurs when a calculated result is too small in magnitude to be represented.

- Any floating-point value may contain an arbitrary number of decimal places, so it is always recommended to use the built-in `format()` function to produce a string version of a number with specific number of decimal places. It can also be used to control the display of strings.

- A raw string does not handle any escape sequences. It is specified by prefixing r or R to the string.

Review Questions

1. Explain the features of Python.

2. Give some applications of Python.

3. What do you understand by the term 'Python character set'?

4. Write a short note on literals in Python.

5. What problems can pop up while dealing with floating-point numbers?

6. With the help of an example, explain the use of `format()` function.

7. What is a string in Python? Explain the different ways in which you can define a string.

8. Differentiate between implicit conversion and type conversion.

9. What is an escape sequence? Give examples. Why are they called so?

10. Write the commands to display the text "I love programming" in a width of 50 characters when the text is left-justified, right-justified and centre-aligned.

11. Write the command to print a string in reverse.

12. Justify the statement, "Python is a free and open-source programming language".

13. Which of the following expressions would result in overflow or underflow error? Justify your answer.
    a. `1.23e+150*4.56e+100`   b. `6.78e-100/4.67e+200`

14. Identify the expressions which will involve implicit conversion and the ones which will involve explicit type conversion.
    a. `5.0+2`   b. `6.5*3.0`   c. `7.0+float(8)`   d. `6.2*5.0`   e. `5.7+int(9.0)`

15. Find and correct the error (if any).
    a. `>>> print('It is Teachers' Day today ')`
    b. `>>> print("Rohan knows "Hindi","English","Punjabi"")`

Fill in the Blanks

1. A _________ in Python is an instruction given to the computer to perform any kind of action.

2. _________ means looking for patterns in the puzzles and categorizing them.

3. Python files are stored with a ______ extension.

4. The ______ function prints one or more literals (or values) followed by a new line.

5. To execute Python script file, ______ key is pressed.

6. ______ are the small units of a programming language.

7. Large floating-point numbers are efficiently represented in _________ notation.

8. ______ denotes that an arithmetic overflow has occurred.

9. _________ function is used to produce a string version of a number with specific number of decimal places.

10. The _____ prefix specifies that the file contains text written in language other than English.

11. A _________ is specified by prefixing r or R to the string.

12. The process of combining two strings is called ___________.

13. The _______ specifies the number of characters to move forward after the first character is retrieved from the string.

State True or False

1. Python is an interpreted programming language.

2. Python is an open-source programming language.

3. Programmers can embed Python programs within their C, C++ codes.

4. Parallel processing can be done in Python.

5. Integers can be specified as octal and hexadecimal numbers also.

6. Arithmetic underflow is a condition that occurs when a calculated result is too large.

7. Strings are immutable in Python.

8. When specifying a string, if a single backslash (\) is added at the end of the line, then it indicates that the string is continued in the next line, but no new line is added otherwise.

9. A Unicode string does not handle any escape sequences. It is specified by prefixing r or R to the string.

10. `format()` function can be used to control the display of strings.

11. The default value of stride is 0.

12. Whitespace characters are also counted as a character in the string.

13. Coding is not a part of computational thinking.

14. \r represents a new line.

15. An escape sequence is treated as a single character.

Multiple Choice Questions

1. Python is a/an ___________ language.
   a. high-level   b. interpreted   c. object-oriented   d. All of these.

2. Python programs work on any of the operating system without requiring any change. This means that Python is _________.
   a. interactive   b. simple   c. portable   d. dynamic

3. Which of the following is not a valid token in Python?
   a. Character set   b. Literals   c. Identifiers   d. Keywords

4. Which of the following is not a valid literal constant in Python?
   a. 1.2   b. 5   c. H5   d. "H5"

5. Which of the following is not a valid number in Python?
   a. 50000000000L   b. 5E10
   c. 5000000000.123455D   d. 3 – 8i

6. The value ______ indicates that an arithmetic underflow has occurred.
   a. –inf   b. inf   c. 0.0   d. All of these.

7. Which of the following is known as the exponentiation operator?
   a. %   b. //   c. **   d. ^

8. By default, the `format()` function uses _____ character to fill the specified width.
   a. blank spaces   b. >   c. <   d. ^

9. A string can be sliced using which of the following operators?
   a. []   b. [:]   c. Both a and b.   d. None of these.

10. The index of the first character is _____ and the index of the last character is _____, where n is the number of characters in the string.
    a. 0, n b. 0, $n-1$ c. 1, n d. 1, $n-1$

11. The index of the last character is ______.
    a. –1   b. 0   c. $n-1$ d. n

12. Which of the following statements is syntactically not correct?
    a. a = input ( )   b. a = input ("enter a number")
    c. a = input (enter a number)   d. a = INPUT ("enter a number")

13. Which of the following statement is correct?
    a. a = 10 * 5   b. 50 = 10 * 5   c. 15 + 60 = y   d. print 3 * 4

14. Identify the invalid string literal.
    a. 'PYTHON'   b. "PYTHON"   c. '"PYTHON"'   d. '""PYTHON""'

15. Identify the valid floating-point value.
    a. 9   b. 23/4   c. 123,456.67   d. 1.2

16. Which of the following is a valid long floating-point value.
    a. 1.2e   b. 1.2e2.3   c. 1.2e01   d. 1,234e9

17. Which of the following is not a valid integer literal in Python?
    a. 0o123   b. 0x123   c. 0X123   d. 0123

Give the Ouput

1.
```python
print("Hello")
print("My Dear Students", end = ' ')
print("Let us learn Python")
print("Programming")
```

2.
```python
>>> format(10**25,'.2e')
```

3.
```python
>>> format(987654321.315978,',.3f')
```

4.
```python
>>> 'PYTHON'
```

5.
```python
>>> "PROGRAMMING IN PYTHON"
```

6.
```python
>>> ''' I ENJOY PROGRAMMING
IN
PYTHON'''
```

7.
```python
>>> 'PYTHON' "PROGRAMMING"
```

8.
```python
>>> print("Python Programming \
is FUN !!!!")
```

9. ```
>>> print(R'It is Teacher's Day today
')
```

10. ```
>>> "I" + 'LOVE' + '''PROGRAMMING'''
```

11. ```
str = "I Love Programming in Python"
print(str[0])
print(str[7])
print(str[-5])
print(str[7:10])
print(str[::2])
print(str[3:11:3])
print(str[:-7])
print(str[-6:])
```

12. ```
>>> print(type(int('10')))
```

13. ```
>>> str(print())+"abc"
```

14. ```
>>> print(print("abc"))
```

15. ```
>>> str(print("abc"))+"xyz"
```

16. ```
>>> print(print("abc",end=" "))
```

17. ```
(10<20) and (20 < 10) or (5 < 30) and
not (15 < 40)
```

## AI Lab Session – Experiments with Google

Google uses ML techniques to help authors create interesting stories with the help of three main tools that can be accessed by clicking on the URL https://experiments.withgoogle.com/collection/aiwriting.

Machine learning models detect meaningful patterns in huge quantities of complex data. ML models can learn from larger patterns of grammar and semantics and use this learning in completely different contexts. The three tools that extensively assist users in creative writing include:

**Between the Lines**  The program takes the first and last line of a story and then uses machine learning techniques to interpolate between the lines and generate an interesting story specifying what would happen in the middle.

**Once upon a Lifetime**  This is a character life story generator in which the user inputs keywords describing the kind of life they want to generate. This is especially important when writing the biography of a character. The program creates the entire life story using the specified keywords.

**Banter Bot**  Banter bot is a character chatbot. Users can input information about what a character is like, and then can converse with it through text. As the user converses, the character evolves by learning from it.

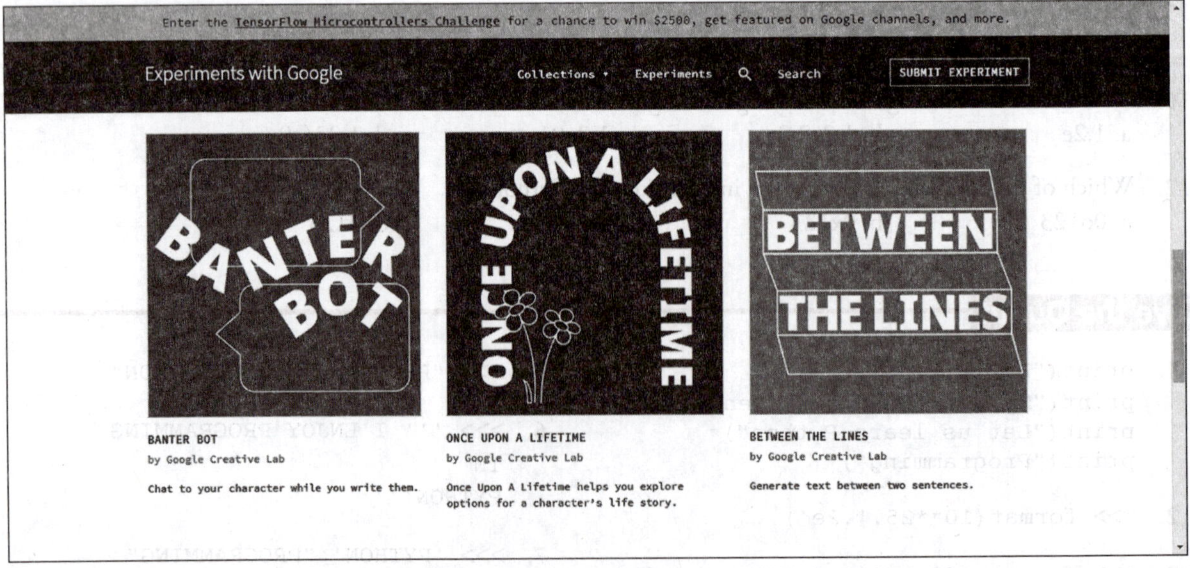
```

Answers

Fill in the Blanks

1. statement
2. Pattern recognition
3. .py
4. `print()`
5. F5
6. Tokens
7. scientific
8. Infinity (inf)
9. `format()`
10. 'U'
11. raw string
12. string concatenation
13. stride

State True or False

1. False
2. True
3. True
4. True
5. True
6. False
7. True
8. True
9. False
10. True
11. False
12. True
13. True
14. False
15. True

Multiple Choice Questions

1. d
2. c
3. a
4. c
5. c
6. c
7. c
8. a
9. c
10. b
11. a
12. c
13. a
14. d
15. d
16. c
17. d

Give the Output

1. ```
   Hello
   My Dear Students Let us learn Python
   Programming
   ```
2. `'1.00e+25'`
3. `'987,654,321.316'`
4. `   'PYTHON'`
5. `'PROGRAMMING IN PYTHON'`
6. `' I ENJOY PROGRAMMING\nIN\nPYTHON'`
7. `'PYTHONPROGRAMMING'`
8. `Python Programming is FUN !!!!`
9. `It is Teacher's Day today`
10. `'ILOVEPROGRAMMING'`
11. ```
    I
    P
    y
    Pro
    ILv rgamn nPto
    o  o
    I Love Programming in
    Python
    ```
12. `<class 'int'>`
13. `'Noneabc'`
14. ```
    abc
    None
    ```
15. ```
    abc
    'Nonexyz'
    ```
16. `abc None`
17. `False`

Python – Building Blocks

11

This chapter allows readers to understand the basic building blocks of Python. The topics listed below are discussed here in detail:

- Variables and identifiers
- Creating, initializing and assigning values to variables
- Multiple assignments that is unique to Python
- Relevance of comments in program code
- Data types, operators and expressions
- Indentation that may change the logic of the program altogether

We have seen that a statement in Python is an instruction that performs an action. A statement may or may not display a value. For example, the statement, sum = 2 + 3, adds two values but does not display any value. But the statement, print(sum) displays the value that we obtain after adding 2 and 3.

In Python, no symbol is used to terminate a statement. The user just has to press the Enter key after typing the statement. Although we can type multiple statements in a single line using semi-colon (;) between the two statements, it is always better to type one statement in a single line for more clarity. So, avoid writing the two statements as,

> A line in Python can contain maximum 79 characters.

```
>>> sum = 2 + 3; print(sum)
5
```

In the last chapter, we had started learning tokens in Python. We had already covered literals. In this section, we will read about other tokens like keywords, identifiers and operators.

11.1 VARIABLES AND INDENTIFIERS

Using just literal constants, nothing much can be done in programs. For developing complex programs, we must store information to manipulate it as and when required. This is where *variables* can help.

Variable, in simple terms, means something that may change. We can store any piece of information in a variable and this information may change. For example, a variable today_temp may have value = 30 today but tomorrow it may be 29 or 31.

Thus, we see that in Python, variable represents a named location that has a value which can be processed as and when required (as for calculating values).

To be identified easily, each variable is given an appropriate name. Variable names are examples of **identifiers**. *Identifiers*, as the name suggests, are names given to identify something. This something can be a variable, function, class, module or other object. For naming any identifier, there are some basic rules that you must follow. These rules are:

- The first character of an identifier must be an underscore ('_') or a letter (upper or lowercase).
- The rest of the identifier name can be underscores ('_'), letters (upper or lowercase), or digits (0–9).
- Identifier names are case-sensitive. For example, myvar and myVar are **not** the same.
- Punctuation characters such as @, $, and % are not allowed within identifiers.

> Python is a case-sensitive language.

Examples of valid identifier names are sum, __my_var, num1, r, var_20, First, etc.

Examples of invalid identifier names are 1num (starting with a digit), my-var (punctuation and special characters not allowed), %check (first character should be an alphabet or an underscore), Basic Sal (space not allowed), H#R&A (special characters not allowed), etc.

11.1.1 Creating Variables

To create a variable in Python, just assign a value to the identifier using the 'equal to' sign (also known as the assignment operator). For example, the following statements create variables with different values in Python.

```
num = 7
float_num = 12.34
ch = 'A'
str = "ABC"
print(num)
print(float_num)
print(ch)
print(str)

OUTPUT
7
12.34
A
ABC
```

When we create a variable, Python creates labels referring to those values as shown in Fig.11.1.

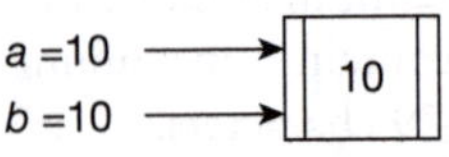
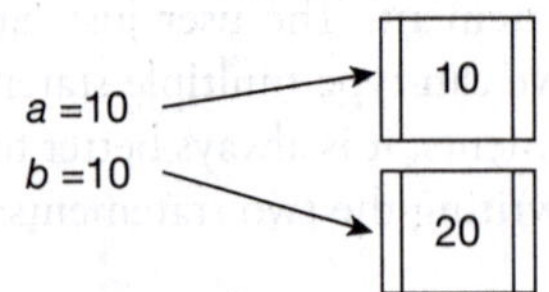
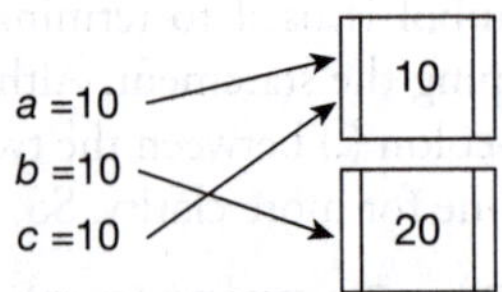

Here, both variables *a* and *b* have the same value. A label with value 10 is created and both variables point to the same label.

Here, the value of variable is changed. Both variables *a* and *b* have different values. A label with value 10 and another with value 20 are created and both variables point to their respective labels.

Here, both variables *a* and *b* have different values. A label with value 10 and another with value 20 are created and both variables point to their respective labels. When the variable *c* is created with same value as that of *a*, it points to the label to which *a* is pointing.

Figure 11.1   Creating labels

Do you know that Python IDLE remembers variables and their values? Just type the following lines in the command console of IDLE and observe the output.

```
>>> x = 10
>>> y = 20
>>> str1 = "HELLO"
>>> print(str1)
HELLO
>>> print(x * y)
200
```

11.2   DATA TYPES OF IDENTIFIERS

In any programming language, data type is a classification that specifies which type of value a variable has. It also specifies the type of mathematical, relational or logical operations that can be applied to it without causing an error. For example, a string data type is used to hold textual data. An integer is a data type that can store whole numbers.

Python has various standard data types that are used to define the operations possible on them and the storage method for each of them. Based on the data type of a variable, the interpreter reserves memory for it and also determines the type of data that can be stored in the reserved memory.

The five standard data types supported by Python include numbers, string, list, tuple, and dictionary. We can even create our own data types in Python (like classes). In this chapter, we will learn about numbers and strings. Other data types will be explored in subsequent chapters.

> Python is a purely object-oriented language. It refers to everything as an object, including numbers and strings.

11.2.1 Assigning or Initializing Values to Variables

In Python, programmers need not explicitly declare variables to reserve memory space. The declaration is done automatically when a value is assigned to the variable using the equal sign (=). The operand on the left side of equal sign is the name of the variable and the operand on its right side is the value to be stored in that variable.

Program to Display Data of Different Types Using Variables and Literal Constants

```
age = 27
salary = 1234567
gender = 'M'
name = "Siva"

print("NAME : " + name)
print("AGE : " + str(age))
print("SALARY : " + str(salary))
print("GENDER : " + gender)
```


OUTPUT

```
NAME : Siva
AGE : 27
SALARY : 1234567
GENDER : M
```

To run this program, type the code in IDLE. Save it with a suitable name with an extension .py. Press F5 or click on *Run*, and then on *Run Module*.

In the code, the program assigns literal constant 27 to the variable age using the assignment operator (=). Similarly, we have assigned literal constants to other variables and then printed their values.

In Python, you can reassign variables as many times as you want to change the value stored in them. You may even store the value of one data type in a statement and then the value of another data in a subsequent statement. This is possible because Python variables do not have specific types; so you can assign an integer to a variable, and later assign a string to the same variable.

Program to Reassign Values to a Variable

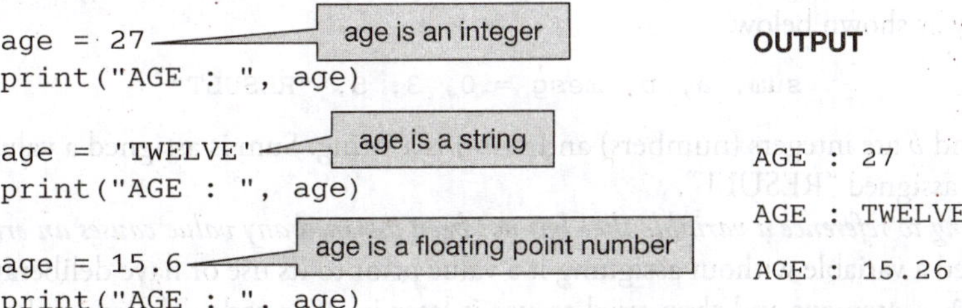


```
age = 27
print("AGE : ", age)

age = 'TWELVE'
print("AGE : ", age)

age = 15.6
print("AGE : ", age)
```

OUTPUT

```
AGE : 27
AGE : TWELVE
AGE : 15.26
```

While re-assigning values to variables, be cautious about ensuring that the right type of value is used in operations. This is very much evident from the code given below.

```
a = 10                   OUTPUT
a = a*10                 100
print (a)                Traceback (most recent call last) :
a = "PYTHON"               File "C : \Python37\try .py" , line 5, in <module>
a = a/10                     a = a/10
print(a)                 TypeError: unsupported operand type(s) for /:
                         ' str ' and ' int'
```

The `type()` Function The `type()` function having the syntax type(object) is used to determine the data type of object. This function should be used to ensure that right type of values is used in the expressions.

```
num = 10                 OUTPUT
print (type (num))       <class 'int'>
val = 3 . 4              <class 'float'>
print (type (val))
ch = ' a'
print (type (ch))        <class 'str'>
str = "abc"              <class 'str'>
print (type (str))
```

lvalue and rvalue As the name suggests, expressions that come on the left side of the assignment operator are known as the lvalue. Correspondingly, expressions that come on the right side of the assignment operator are known as the rvalue.

This means that lvalues are those objects to which values can be assigned. And rvalues are the literals. That is, they are expressions that evaluate a value and they come on the right-hand side of the assignment operator.

Remember that,

- literals or expressions that evaluate a value cannot come on the left-hand side of the assignment operator.
- Variable names can come on the left-hand side of the assignment operator.

Valid lvalue and rvalue	Invalid lvalue and rvalue
a = 10	10 = a
B = 1*20	a*20 = b

11.3   MULTIPLE ASSIGNMENT

Python allows programmers to assign a single value to more than one variable simultaneously. For example,

```
sum = flag = a = b = 0
```

In the above statement, all four integer variables are assigned a value 0. You can also assign different values to multiple variables simultaneously as shown below.

```
sum, a, b, mesg = 0, 3, 5, "RESULT"
```

Here, variable sum, *a* and *b* are integers (numbers) and `mesg` is a string. Sum is assigned a value 0, *a* is assigned 3, *b* is assigned 5 and `mesg` is assigned "RESULT".

Remember that *trying to reference a variable that has not been assigned any value causes an error.* This may happen if you have mistakenly used a variable without assigning it a value prior to its use or have deliberately deleted or removed a variable using the `del` statement and then tried to use it later in your code. The examples given below illustrates this concept.

Also remember that right-hand side expression is evaluated before assignment is done and if there are multiple expressions in a statement separated by commas, then expressions on the RHS are evaluated from *left to right* and assigned in the same order.

```
x,y = 10,20
y,y = y+5, y-20      # last value of y persists
print("x = ",x, " y = ",y)
OUTPUT
x =  10   y =  0
```

Programs to assign and access variables

```
>>> name= "Kartik"
>>> age= 15
>>> print(name)
Kartik
>>> print(grade)
Traceback (most recent call last):
 File "<pyshell#8>", line 1, in <module>
  print(grade)
NameError: name 'grade' is not defined
```

Variable not declared prior to use.

```
>>> name= "Kartik"
>>> age= 15
>>> grade = '0'
>>> print(name)
Kartik
>>>del age
>>> print(age)
Traceback (most recent call last):
 File "<pyshell#14>", line 1, in <module>
  print( age)
NameError: name 'age' is not defined
```

Variable being used after it is deleted.

11.4 DATA TYPE BOOLEAN

Boolean is another data type in Python. A variable of Boolean type can have one of the two values – *True* or *False*. Similar to other variables, the Boolean variables are also created while we assign a value to them or when we use a relational operator on them.

Boolean variables are also created by comparing values using the == operator.

`>>>Boolean_ var =True`
`>>>Boolean_var`
`True`
	`>>> 30 == 50`
	`False`
		`>>>"HELLO" == 'HELLO'`
		`True`

`>>> 10 != 10` `False`	`>>"Python3.7" != "Python3.4"` `True`	`>>> 50 > 80` `False`
`>>> 20 <= 20` `True`	`>>> 13 == 13.0` `False`	`>>> 13 >= 13.0` `True`

11.5 INPUT OPERATION

Real-world programs need to be interactive. By interactive, we mean that you need to take some sort of input or information from the user and work on that input to give the desired result.

To take input from the users, Python makes use of the `input()` *function.* The `input()` function prompts the user to provide some information on which the program can work and give the result. However, we must always remember that the *input function takes the user's input as a string.* So, whether you input a number or a string, it is treated as a string only.

Program to read variables from the user

```
name= input("What's your name?")
age = input("Enter your age:")
print(name+ ",you are" + age + " years old")
```

OUTPUT
```
What's your name? Goransh
Enter your age : 13
Goransh, you are 13 years old
```

To read integers or floating-point numbers using the `input()` **function**, you must use the `int()` and the `float()` function respectively. The `int()` function is used to convert a non-integer value to integer. Similarly, the `float()` function is used to convert a non-floating-point value into a floating-point value. Hence, the output of the `input()` function which returns a string value can be passed to the `int()` or `float()` function to get a numeric value.

```
a = int (input ("Enter a number : "))       marks = float(input("Enter your total marks : "))
a = a + 10                                  avg = marks/5.0
print(a)                                    print (avg)
```

OUTPUT   **OUTPUT**
```
Enter a number : 10                         Enter your total marks : 495
20                                          99.0
```

11.6   COMMENTS

Comments are added in a program to describe the statements in the program code. They make the program easily readable and understandable by the programmer as well as other users who are seeing the code. In Python, a hash sign (#) that is not inside a string literal begins a comment. *All characters following the # and up to the end of the line are part of the comment.*

Program to use comments

```
#Program to find the cost of a dozen pens          OUTPUT
price_ 1 = int(input("Enter the price of 1 pen : "))   Enter the price of 1 pen : 10
price_12 = price_1 * 12  # dozen means 12            Price of a dozen pens = 120
print("Price of a dozen pens = ", price_12)
```

Some important points to remember about comments are:
- Comments are the non-executable statements in a program.
- The interpreter simply ignores the comments.
- When the program is run, comments are not displayed.
- Comments can be either typed in a new line or on the same line after a statement or expression.
- A program can have any number of comments.

11.6.1 Multi-line Comments

In Python, multi-line comments are also known as docstrings. They can be specified in two ways. First, by using three single quotes (or apostrophe). Second, by using three double quotes. They are used when explanation of the statements cannot be sufficiently given in one line. The code given below demonstrates the use of multi-line comments.

```
''' adding two
numbers'''
sum = 2 + 3
print(sum)
""" calculating average
of the two numbers
"""
avg = sum/2.0
print(avg)

OUTPUT
5
2.5
```

Did you notice that comments are not printed?

11.7   RESERVED WORDS

In every programming language there are certain words which have a pre-defined meaning. These words, also known as reserved words or keywords, cannot be used for naming identifiers. Table 11.1 shows a list of Python keywords.

All the Python keywords contain lowercase letters only.

Table 11.1   Reserved words in Python

and	assert	break	class	continue	def	del	elif	else	except
exec	finally	for	from	global	if	import	in	is	lambda
not	or	pass	print	raise	return	try	while	with	yield

11.8   INDENTATION

Whitespace at the beginning of the line is called ***indentation***. These whitespaces or the indentation is very important in Python. In a Python program, the leading whitespace including spaces and tabs at the beginning of the logical line determine the indentation level of that logical line.

The level of indentation groups statements to form a block of statements. This means that statements in a block must have the same indentation level. Python very strictly checks the indentation level and gives an error if indentation is not correct.

In the code below, there is a tab at the beginning of the second line. The error indicated by Python tells us that there is an indentation error. Python does not tell you to arbitrarily start new blocks of statements.

Like other programming languages, Python does not use curly braces ({…}). Therefore, to indicate blocks of code for class and function definitions or for flow control (discussed later in the book), it uses only indentation. *All statements inside a block should be at the same indentation level.*

> Use a single tab for each indentation level.

```
a = 10
    a = a+1      #Indentation Error
print(a)
```

```
a = 10
a = a + 1
print(a)

OUTPUT
11
```

11.9   OPERATORS AND EXPRESSIONS

Operators are constructs that are used to manipulate the value of operands. Some basic operators include +, -, * and /. An expression in a programming language is any valid combination of tokens that represents a value. There are two types of expressions,

Simple expressions in which there are only values. For example, 29.

> Operands are values on which operators are applied to generate a value.

Complex expressions in which one or more operators are used on operand(s) to generate a value. For example, consider the expression sum = 2 + 4. Here, 2 and 3 are operands and + is the operator. 10 * 8 / 2 is another example of a complex expression.

However, expressions can also be classified as arithmetic expressions, logical expressions, string expressions and relational expressions, where,

- Arithmetic expressions consist of numbers and arithmetic operators.
- Logical expressions have literals or variables and logical operators.
- Relational expressions have literals or variables and relational operators.
- String expressions have string operands and string operators (such as * and +).

Different operators supported by Python include:
a. Arithmetic operators   b. Comparison (Relational) operators   c. Assignment operators
d. Logical operators   e. Membership operators

11.9.1 Arithmetic Operators

Some basic arithmetic operators are +, -, *, /, %, ** and //. You can apply these operators on numbers as well as on numeric variables to perform the corresponding operations. For example, if $a = 10$ and $b = 20$, then the result of the operations can be shown as given in Table 11.2.

Table 11.2   Arithmetic operators

Operator	Description	Example	Output
+	Addition – Adds the operands	>>> print(a + b)	30
-	Subtraction – Subtracts operand on the right from the operand on the left of the operator	>>> print(a - b)	-10
*	Multiplication – Multiplies the operands	>>> print(a * b)	200
/	Division – Divides operand on the left side of the operator with the operand on its right. The division operator returns the quotient.	>>> print(b / a)	2.0
%	Modulus – Divides operand on the left side of the operator with the operand on its right. The modulus operator returns the remainder.	>>> print(b % a)	0

//	Floor Division – Divides the operands and returns the quotient. It also removes the digits after the decimal point. If one of the operands is negative, the result is floored (rounded away from zero towards negative infinity):	>>> print(24//5)
		>>> print(24.0//5.0)
		>>> print(-37//4)
		>>> print(-17.0//3)
			4
			4.0
			-10
			-5.0

**	Exponent – Performs exponential calculation. That is, it raises operand on the right side to the operand on the left of the operator.	>>> print(a**b)	10^{20}

11.9.2 Comparison Operators

Comparison operators, also known as *relational operators*, are used to compare the values on its either side and determine the relation between them. For example, assuming $a = 10$ and $b = 20$, we can use the comparison operators on them as specified in Table 11.3.

Table 11.3   Comparison operators

Operator	Description	Example	Output
==	Returns true if the two values are exactly equal.	>>> print(a == b)	False
!=	Returns true if the two values are not equal.	>>> print(a != b)	True
>	Returns true if the value at the operand on the left side of the operator is greater than the value on its right side	>>> print(a > b)	False
<	Returns true if the value at the operand on the right side of the operator is greater than the value on its left side.	>>> print(a < b)	True
>=	Returns true if the value at the operand on the left side of the operator is either greater than or equal to the value on its right side.	>>> print (a >= b)	False
<=	Returns true if the value at the operand on the right side of the operator is either greater than or equal to the value on its left side.	>>> print (a <= b)	True

11.9.3 Assignment and In-place or Shortcut Operators

Assignment operator, as the name suggests, assigns value to the operand. In-place operators, also known as *shortcut operators* that include +=, –=, *=, /=, %=, //= and **=, allow you to write codes like num = num + 10 more concisely, as num += 3. Different types of assignment and in-place operators are given in Table 11.4.

> Remember that <, > operators can also be used to compare strings lexicographically.

Example 11.1 **Application of the += operator on strings**

```
>>> str1 = "PYTHON"
>>> str2 = "PROGRAMMING"
>>> str1 += str2
>>> print(str1)
PYTHONPROGRAMMING
```

11.9.4 Logical Operators

Python supports three logical operators—logical and, logical or, and logical not. As in case of arithmetic expressions, the logical expressions are evaluated from left to right.

Logical and: Logical and operator is used to simultaneously evaluate two conditions or expressions with relational operators. If expressions on both the sides (left and right side) of the logical operator are true, then the whole expression is true; else it is false. For example, (a > b) and (a > c), will return TRUE only if the value of a is greater than the values of b and c.

The and *operator tests the second operand only if the first operand is true.*

Table 11.4 Assignment and in-place operator

Operator	Example
=	c = a, assigns value of a to c
+=	a += b is same as a = a + b
-=	a –= b is same as a = a - b
*=	a *= b is same as a = a * b
/=	a /= b is same as a = a / b
%=	a %= b is same as a = a % b
//=	a //= b is same as a = a // b
**=	a**= b is same as a = a** b

Logical or: Logical or operator is used to simultaneously evaluate two conditions or expressions with relational operators. If one or both the expressions of the logical operator is true, then the whole expression is true. This means that the expression is false only if both the expressions are false. For example, (a > b) or (a != b) will return TRUE if a is either greater than b or less than b. It will return FALSE if a is equal to b.

Table 11.5 Truth table for logical operators

A	B	A and B	A	B	A or B	A	B	A xor B	A	!A
0	0	0	0	0	0	0	0	0	0	1
0	1	0	0	1	1	0	1	1	1	0
1	0	0	1	0	1	1	0	1		
1	1	1	1	1	1	1	1	0		

Logical not: The logical not operator takes a single expression and negates the value of the expression. Logical not produces a zero if the expression evaluates to a non-zero value and produces a 1 if the expression produces a zero. In other words, it just reverses the value of the expression. For example,

```
>>> a = 10
>>> b = not a
>>> print(b)
False
```

> a is non-zero (or TRUE) so b is FALSE

```
>>> a = 0
>>> b = not a
>>> print(b)
True
```

> a is zero (or FALSE) so b is TRUE

It can be noted that the *logical expressions operate in a shortcut (or lazy) fashion and stop the evaluation when it knows the final outcome for sure.* For example, in a logical expression involving logical and, if the first operand is false, then the second operand is not evaluated as it is certain that the result will be false. Similarly, for a *logical expression involving*

logical or, *if the first operand is true, then the second operand is not evaluated as it is certain that the result will be true.*
The truth table for logical operators is given in Table 11.5.

11.9.5 Membership Operators

Python supports two types of membership operators – **in** and **not in**. These operators, as the name suggests, test for membership in a sequence such as strings, lists, or tuples that will be discussed in later chapters and are listed below.

```
>>> str1="HELLO"              >>> str1="HELLO"
>>> 'L' in str1               >>> 'e' not in str1
True                          True
>>> 'T' in str1               >>> 'E' not in str1
False                         False
```

in Operator: The operator returns true if a variable is found in the specified sequence and false otherwise.

not in Operator: The operator returns true if a variable is not found in the specified sequence and false otherwise.

```
>>> a = "r"
>>> str = "Good Morning"
>>> a in str
True
>>> 'R' in str
False
```

11.9.6 Operators Precedence and Associativity

When an expression has more than one operator, then it is the relative priorities of the operators with respect to each other that determine the order in which the expression will be evaluated.

Remember that,

Operators are associated from left to right. This means that operators with same precedence are evaluated in a left-to-right manner.

Parentheses can change the order in which an operator is applied. The operator in parenthesis is applied first even if there is a higher priority operator in the expression.

Priority of operators can be given as shown in Table 11.6

```
>>> 5 * 6 + 3
33
>>> 5 + 6 * 3
23
```

*Has higher precedence than +. Hence, first the operands will be multiplied and then addition will be performed.

Table 11.6	Operator precedence chart
*, /, %, //	**Highest priority**
+ -	
<=, <, >, =>	
!=, ==, <>	
=, %=, /=, //=, -=, +=, *=, **=	
in, not in	
not, or, an	**Lowest priority**

Let us try some more codes to see how operator precedence works in our expressions.

```
>>> (5o + 40) * 10 / 20       >>> ((50+ 40) * 20) / 10      >>> (50+ 40) * (20 / 1o)
45.0                          180.0                         180.0

>>> 50+ (40 * 10) / 20        >>> (False==False) or True    >>> False==(False or True)
70.0                          True                          False

>>> 50*100/5//4               >>> (((50*100)/15)//4)        >>> 50*(100/(5//14))
250.0                         250.0                         5000.0
```

11.10 EXPRESSIONS IN PYTHON

In any programming language, an expression is any legal combination of symbols (like variables, constants and operators) that represents a value. Every language has its own set of rules that define whether an expression is valid or invalid in that language. *In Python, an expression must have at least one operand (variable or constant) and can have one or more operators. On evaluating an expression, we get a value.*

Operand is the value on which an operator is applied. These operators use constants and variables to form an expression. A * B + C – 5 is an example of an expression, where, +, *, - are operators; A, B and C are variables and 5 is a constant. Some valid expressions in Python are: x = a / b, y = a * b, z = a^ b, x = a > b, etc. When an expression has more than one operator, then the expression is evaluated using the operator precedence chart.

An example of an illegal expression can be a+ –b or <y++. When the program is compiled, the validity of all expressions is checked. If an illegal expression is encountered, an error message is displayed.

In Python, we can categorize expressions based on the data type of the result obtained on evaluating an expression. These types of expressions include,

- *Constant Expressions* that involve only constants. Example: 8 + 9 – 2
- *Integral Expressions* that produce an integer result.
  Example:
  a = 10, b = 5
  c = a * b
- *Floating-point Expressions* produce floating-point results. Example: a * b / 2
- *Relational Expressions* return either true or false value. Example: c = a > b
- *Logical Expressions* combine two or more relational expressions and return a value as *true* or *false*.
  Example: a > b and y != 0.
- *Bitwise Expressions* manipulate data at bit level. Example: x = y & z.
- *Assignment Expressions* assign a value to a variable. Example: c = 10.

> Remember that deleted variables can be used again in the code if and only if you reassign them some value.

PROGRAMMER'S ZONE

1. **Write a program to enter a number and display its hex and octal equivalent and its square root.**

```python
num = int(input("Enter a number : "))
print("Hexadecimal of " + str(num) + " :  " + str(hex(num)))
print("Octal of " + str(num) + "  : " + str(oct(num)))
print("Square root of " + str(num) + " : " + str(num**0.5))
```

OUTPUT

```
Enter a number : 17
Hexadecimal of 17  :  0x11
Octal of 17  : 0o21
Square root of 17 : 4.123105625617661
```

2. **Write a program to read and print values of variables of different data types.**

```python
num = int(input("Enter Roll Number : "))
fees = float(input("Enter Fees : "))
grade = input("Enter the grade : ")
name = input("Enter the name : ")
#Print the values of variables
print(ROLL NUMBER = ,num)
print(NAME = ,name)
print(FEES = ,fees)
print(GRADE = ,grade)
```

OUTPUT

```
Enter Roll Number : 1
Enter Fees : 99999
Enter the grade : A
Enter the name : Priya
ROLL NUMBER =   1
NAME =   Priya
FEES =   99999.0
GRADE =   A
```

3. **Write a program to calculate the area of a triangle using Heron's formula.**

   (<u>Hint:</u> **Heron's formula is given as: area = sqrt(S * (S − a)*(S − b)*(S − c)))**

```
a = float(input("Enter the first side of the triangle : "))
b = float(input("Enter the second side of the triangle : "))
c = float(input("Enter the third side of the triangle : "))
print(a,b,c)
S = (a+b+c)/2
area = (S*(S-a)*(S-b)*(S-c))**0.5
print("Area = ",area)
```

   OUTPUT

```
Enter the first side of the triangle : 6
Enter the second side of the triangle : 8
Enter the third side of the triangle : 10
6.0 8.0 10.0
Area =   24.0
```

4. **Write a program to calculate the distance between two points.**

```
x1 = (int(input("Enter the x coordinate of the first point : ")))
y1 = (int(input("Enter the y coordinate of the first point : ")))
x2 = (int(input("Enter the x coordinate of the second point : ")))
y2 = (int(input("Enter the y coordinate of the second point : ")))
distance = ((x2-x1)**2+(y2-y1)**2)**0.5
print("Distance = ", distance)
```

   OUTPUT

```
Enter the x coordinate of the first point : 1
Enter the y coordinate of the first point : 1
Enter the x coordinate of the second point : 5
Enter the y coordinate of the second point : 5
Distance = 5.656854249492381
```

5. **Write a program to perform addition, subtraction, multiplication, division, integer division and modulo division on two integer numbers.**

```
num1 = int(input("Enter two numbers : "))
num2 = int(input("Enter two numbers : "))
add_res = num1+num2
sub_res = num1-num2
mul_res = num1*num2
idiv_res = num1//num2
modiv_res = num1%num2
fdiv_res = float(num1)/num2
print(num1, " + ", num2," = ", add_res)
```

```python
print(num1, " - ", num2, " = ", sub_res)
print(num1, " * ", num2, " = ", mul_res)
print(num1," / ",num2," = ",idiv_res," (Integer Division)")
print(num1," // ",num2," = ",fdiv_res," (Float Division)")
print(num1," % ", num2," = ",modiv_res," (Modulo Division)")
```

OUTPUT

```
Enter two numbers : 25
Enter two numbers : 4
25  +  4  =  29
25  -  4  =  21
25  *  4  =  100
25  /  4  =  6   (Integer Division)
25  //  4  =  6.25   (Float Division)
25  %  4  =  1   (Modulo Division)
```

6. **Write a program that demonstrates the use of relational operators.**

```python
x = 30
y = 10
print(x," < ", y, " = ", x<y)
print(x, " == ", y, " = ", x==y)
print(x," != ",y," = ", x!=y)
print(x," > ",y," = ",x>y)
print(x," >= ",y," = ",x>=y)
print(x," <= ",y," = ",x<=y)
```

OUTPUT

```
30  <  10  =  False
30  ==  10  =  False
30  !=  10  =  True
30  >  10  =  True
30  >=  10  =  True
30  <=  10  =  False
```

7. **Write a program to calculate the volume of a cylinder.**

```python
radius = float(input("Enter the radius : "))
height = float(input("Enter the height : "))
volume = 3.14*radius*radius*height
print("VOLUME = %.2f"%volume)
```

OUTPUT

```
Enter the radius : 7
Enter the height : 14
VOLUME = 2154.04
```

8. **Write a program to print the digit at the one's place of a number.**

```python
num = int(input("Enter any number : "))
digit_at_ones_place = num%10
print("The digit at ones place is : ",digit_at_ones_place)
```

OUTPUT

```
Enter any number : 12345
The digit at ones place of  12345 is 5
```

9. **Write a program to swap two numbers without using a temporary variable.**

```
n1 = int(input("Enter the first number : "))
n2 = int(input("Enter the second number : "))
n1, n2 = n2, n1
print("The first number is = ",n1," and the second number = ",n2)
```

OUTPUT

```
Enter the first number : 6
Enter the second number : 9
The first number is =  9  and the second number =  6
```

10. **Write a program to calculate average of two numbers. Print their deviation.**

```
n1 = int(input("Enter the two numbers : "))
n2 = int(input("Enter the two numbers : "))
avg = (n1+n2)/2
dev1 = n1-avg
dev2 = n2-avg
print("AVERAGE = ",avg)
print("Deviation of first num =",dev1)
print("Deviation of second num =",dev2)
```

OUTPUT

```
Enter the two numbers : 10
Enter the two numbers : 20
AVERAGE =  15.0
Deviation of first num = -5.0
Deviation of second num = 5.0
```

11. **Write a program to convert degrees Fahrenheit into degrees Celsius.**

```
Fahrenheit = float(input("Enter the temperature in Fahrenheit : "))
Celsius = (0.56)*(Fahrenheit-32)
print("Temperature in degrees Celsius = %.2f"%Celsius)
```

OUTPUT

```
Enter the temperature in Fahrenheit : 100
Temperature in degrees Celsius = 38.08
```

Key Terms

Variable: Variable means something that may change. In Python programs, any piece of information can be stored in a variable and the information may change.

Identifiers: Names given to identify a variable, function, class, module or any other object.

Lvalue: Expressions that comes on the left side of the assignment operator

Rvalue: Expressions that comes on the right side of the assignment operator.

Keywords: Reserved words in a programming language that have a pre-defined meaning.

Operators: Constructs used to manipulate the value of operands.

Operands: Values on which the operator is applied.

Expression: An expression in a programming language is any valid combination of tokens that represents a value.

Chapter Highlights

- To create a variable in Python, just assign a value to the identifier using the equal to sign.

- When we create a variable, Python creates labels referring to those values.

- Variables can hold values of different types called data types.

- Based on the data type of a variable, the interpreter reserves memory for it and also determines the type of data that can be stored in the reserved memory.

- The five standard data types supported by Python are – numbers, string, list, tuple, and dictionary.

- In Python, you can reassign variables as many times as you want to change the value stored in them. You may even store the value of one data type in a statement and then a value of another data in a subsequent statement.

- The `type()` function is used to determine data type of object.

- Trying to reference a variable that has not been assigned any value causes an error. This may happen if you have mistakenly used a variable without assigning it a value prior to its use or have deliberately deleted or removed a variable using the `del` statement and then trying to use it later in your code.

- A variable of Boolean type can have one of the two values – True or False.

- Comments are added in a program to describe the statements in the program code. They make the program easily readable and understandable by the programmer as well as other users who are seeing the code.

- To take input from the users, Python makes use of the `input()` function.

- Whitespace at the beginning of the line is called indentation. These whitespaces at the beginning of the logical line determine the indentation level of that logical line.

- A comparison operator, also known as relational operator, is used to compare the values on its either side and it determines the relation between them.

- Python supports two types of membership operators – in and not in. These operators test for membership in a sequence such as strings, lists, or tuples.

Review Questions

1. What are identifiers? List some rules that must be kept in mind while naming an identifier.

2. With the help of a diagram, explain what happens when a variable is created in Python.

3. With the help of an example explain how variables can be re-assigned values in Python.

4. Can we re-assign a value of another data type to a variable? If yes, why?

5. Differentiate between lvalue and rvalue.

6. What do you understand by the term 'multiple assignment'?

7. What are Boolean variables? How are they created?

8. What are comments? How are they written in Python?

9. What is a docstring? How is it defined in a Python program?

10. Why is indentation necessary in Python?

11. Consider the statement, print "Python # Programming". Will it be executed or not? If yes, justify its output.
    Hint: The # is inside a string, so it is just considered as a character and not as comment.

12. Differentiate between = and ==.
    Hint: The = is used to assign value but the == is used to test if two things have the same value.

13. Which data type will you use to represent the following data values?
    a. Number of days in a week.
    b. The circumference of a circle
    c. You school fees
    d. Distance between moon and the earth
    e. Your favorite book
    f. Whether or not you will take the entrance exam of not

14. Which type of value will you use for storing the following information?
    a. Employee ID   b. Employee Name   c. Employee Salary   d. Phone Number

15. Which of the following are correct type conversions?
    a. `int (8.2+6.3)`
    b. `str (5.6 * 6.7)`
    c. `float ("12"+"3.4")`
    d. `str ( 6/4 )`

16. Express the following floating-point numbers in scientific notation:
    a. `123.456789`   b. `0.000123456`   c. `1.234567`

17. Evaluate the following arithmetic expressions using the rules of operator precedence in Python.
    a. `4+5*10`   b. `6+7*2+5`   c. `20//4*2`   d. `5*6**3`
    e. `24//6//3`   f. `4**2**3`   g. `100-(15*3)`   h. `50%7`   i. `-(100/6)+5`

18. Write the following values in the exponential notation.
    a. `1230.4567`   b. `0.00000056009`   c. `7000809.000000000003`

19. Identify the correct arithmetic expression in Python:
    a. `10(13+76)`
    b. `(15*16)(47+18)`
    c. `14*(33-52)`
    d. `15***2`

20. Write the data types of the following:
    a. `type(5+4)`   b. `(20*345)`   c. `type(987/45)`   d. `type(2345//12)`
    e. `type(123%34)`

21. Identify the data types of the following literals: 9, 29.4, 5j, 3+7i

22. Evaluate the following expressions:
    a. `True and False`
    b. `(100<10) and (100>50)`
    c. `True or False`
    d. `(100<10) or (100>200)`
    e. `not(True) and False`
    f. `not (100<10) or (100>50)`
    g. `not(True and False)`
    h. `not (100<10 or 100>50)`
    i. `not True and False`
    j. `100<10 and not 100>50`
    k. `not True and False or True`
    l. `not (100<10 or 50<200)`

23. Which of the following results in True?
    a. `>>>90 == 90 and 11==11`
    b. `>>>31==51 and 71==31`
    c. `>>>72!=12 and 25==25`
    d. `>>>54<51 and 61>86`
    e. `15<20 or 20`

24. Write the following expressions in Python:

$$\frac{-b \pm \sqrt{b^2 - 4ac}}{2a} \qquad \sqrt{a^2 + b^2} \qquad \frac{\pi}{2}rh \qquad x^2 yz \qquad (a-b)^2 = a^2 - 2ab + b^2 \qquad d = a^{mn}/a^{-3} \qquad (e^m)^n = e^{mn}$$

Programming Exercises

1. Write a program to calculate the Body Mass Index (BMI) of a person (BMI = kg/m^2, where kg is the person's weight and m is his/her height in metres).

2. Write a program to perform string concatenation.

3. Write a program to demonstrate printing a string within single quotes, double quotes and triple quote.

4. Write a program to read a character in upper case and then print it in lower case.

5. Write a program to swap two numbers using a temporary variable.

6. Write a program to read the address of a user. Display the result by breaking it in multiple lines.

7. Write a program to calculate simple interest and compound interest.

8. Write a program that prompts users to enter two integers x and y. The program then calculates and displays x^y

9. Write a program that prompts user to enter his first name and last name and then displays a message "Greetings!!! First name Last name".

10. Energy is calculated as, $e = mc^2$, where m is the mass of the object and c is its velocity. Write a program that accepts an object's mass (in kilograms) and velocity (in metres per second) and displays its energy.

11. Write a program that calculates the number of seconds in a day.

12. Write a program to find the area of a parallelogram.

13. Write a program to convert a given distance in metres to kms and vice-versa.

14. Write a program that prompts the user to enter the first name and the last name. Then display the following message.
```
Hello firstname lastname
Welcome to Python!
```

Fill in the Blanks

1. A line in Python can have maximum _____ characters.

2. _____ are used to store values.

3. Names given to identify a variable, function, class, module or any other object are generally known as __________.

4. A variable in Python is assigned a value by using the _________ operator.

5. When we create a variable, Python creates ______ referring to those values.

6. Variables can hold values of different types called _________.

7. _________ are those objects to which values can be assigned.

8. To take input from the users, Python uses the _________ function.

9. The ______ function is used to convert a non-integer value to integer.

10. In Python, multi-line comments are also known as ________.

11. The level of _______ groups statements to form a block of statements.

12. Values on which the operator is applied is called _________.

13. _________ expressions operate in a shortcut (or lazy) fashion and stop the evaluation when it knows the final outcome for sure.

14. 123.45E-9 is equal to ________.

15. ___________ converts an integer to a floating-point number.

16. The ___ operator returns the quotient after division.

17. To find x^y, you will use ______ operator.

18. _________ is a group of characters.

19. Variable names can contain only _________, __________ and ____________.

20. >>>90 != 70 gives output _________.

21. 29%0 = _________.

22. int("10"+"20") will give _______.

23. >>> print (format(12356.265901, '.3f')) will result in the value _______.

State True or False

1. In Python, a semi-colon is used to terminate every statement.

2. Python allows writing multiple statements in a single line.

3. The first character of an identifier must be a dollar sign ($).

4. Python is a case-sensitive language.

5. Based on the data type of a variable, the interpreter reserves memory.

6. While re-assigning values to a variable, the data type must not change.

7. Python variables do not have specific data types.

8. Comments are written to make the program easily readable and understandable.

9. Comments are the executable statements in a program.

10. When the program is run, comments are not displayed.

11. All keywords are written in uppercase characters.

12. Statements in a block must have the same indentation level.

13. Arithmetic operators also known as relational operators.

14. Relational operators can be used to compare strings.

15. INT = 2; print(INT) will give an error.

Multiple Choice Questions

1. Which of the following is a valid identifier in Python?
    a. _AaBb   b. 1A_Bb   c. @AaBB   d. Aa-Bb

2. Which of the following can be the first character of a valid identifier in Python?
    a. #   b. @   c. _   d. -

3. Which of the following is known as the string concatenation symbol?
    a. +   b. *   c. ,   d. -

4. Which function is used to is determine data type of object?
    a. data()   b. type()   c. val()   d. str()

5. A variable can be removed by using the _________ statement.
    a. remove   b. erase   c. del   d. delete

6. Boolean variables are created using which of the following operator(s)?
    a. Equality   b. assignment   c. Both a and b.   d. None of these.

7. The input function takes user's input as a/an _______.
    a. integer   b. floating-point   c. string   d. None of these.

8. All characters following the _______ symbol and up to the end of the line are part of the comment.
    a. #   b. __   c. %   d. @

9. Which operator is used for integer division?
    a. /   b. %   c. //   d.\

10. If both the inputs are 1 then the result is 1, else 0. Identify the logical operator giving this result.
    a. AND   b. NOT   c. OR   d. XOR

11. Which operator returns True if a variable is found in the specified sequence and False otherwise?
    a. is   b. not is   c. in   d. not in

12. Identify valid assignment statements
    a. x = y + 2   b. a = a++   c. x + y = 10   d. x + 10 = y

13. Which line of code produces an error?
    a. "one" + "2"   b. 'one' + 2   c. 1 + 2   d. "1" + "two"

14. abc ="AABBCC"; print(abc*3).
    a. abcabcabc   b. "abcabcabc"   c. ABCABCABC   d. AABBCCAABBCCAABBCC

15. Identify the correct variable creation statement.
    a. my_var =7   b. 123my_var =10   c. my var = 12   d. 10 = myvar

16. Logical operator should not be used on which data type?
    a. Integer   b. float   c. string   d. All of these.

17. Which operator is also known as string repetition operator?
    a. +   b. *   c. &   d. ^

18. The following statement will produce ___ lines of output.
    print('Python \n Programming \n is\n ---Fun')
    a. 1   b. 2   c. 3   d. 4

19. Identify the expression that may result in arithmetic overflow
    a. a*b   b. a**b   c. a/b   d. a+b

20. Which operations do not result in 9?
    a. 95 // 10   b. 130 % 11   c. 3 **3   d. 81 * * 0.5

Give the Output

1.  ```
    x,y,z = 10,20,30
    y,z,x = x+5, y+7, z-3
    print("x = ",x, " y = ",y, "z = ",z)
    ```

2.  ```
    x,y = 10,20
    y,z = x+5, y-20
    print("x = ",x, " y = ",y," z = ",z)
    ```

3.  ```
    >>> 350 + 230 - 170
    ```

4.  ```
    >>> (51 + 9.7 - 4) * 100
    ```

5.  ```
    >>> 110%(95//3)
    ```

6.  ```
    >>> 'Python Programming is fun… '
    ```

7.  ```
    >>> "Python Programming is fun…"
    ```

8.  ```
    >>>'''Python… \n Programming?'''
    ```

9.  ```
    >>> print("Python \n Programmiung")
    ```
    ```

```
10. >>> print("PYTHON !!!!"*3)

11. >>>x = 100 ; x *= 3 ; print(x)

12. >>> s1 = "HELLO"      ;      s1 += "WORLD"      ;      print(s1)

13. days = "Mon Tue Wed Thu Fri Sat Sun"
    months = "Jan\nFeb\nMar\nApr\nMay\nJun\nJul\nAug"
    print("Days are : "+ days)
    print("Months are: "+ months)
    print(""" There's a new dream today.
    I'll tell you some other day.
    Come on, let's enjoy. """)

14. # print ABCD
    Nothing

15. >>>n1 = 20
    >>>n2 = 30
    >>>del num1
    >>>n2 = 40
    >>>n1 = 50
    >>>print(num1 - num2)

16. >>> num1 = "7"
    >>> num1 += "10"
    >>> num2 = int(num1) + 3
    >>> print (float(num2))

17. name = input("Enter a word :")
    print ('HELLO' + name)

18. n1 = 90
    n2 = n1 + 50
    n2 = int(str(n2) + "40")
    print(num2)

19. >>> abs(100-200) * 3

20. >>>float("5678" * int(input("Enter a number:")))

21. >>> int = 2;   print(int)

22. a,b = 10,20
    b,a = a *5, b /2
    print("a = ",a, " and b = ", b)

23. a,b = 10,20
    a,b,a = a*10, b*5,a*20
    print("a = ",a, " and b = ", b)
    a =  200  and b =  100

24. 10 ** 3 ** 2

25. 7 -5 -12 > -5 *3 +8

26. bool('0') and (10 < 20)

27. 23%5 is 23%5
```

28. `10 == 10.0`

29. `10 == int(10)`

30. `str(10)==str('10.0')`

31. `'R' == 'R'`

32. `70/(7-(2+4))or 4<5`

33. `len("abcd") == 30/6 or 30/10`

34. `2 * (5 *(len("007")))`

35. `N = 1 + 1 + 1 == 0.3; print(N)`

36.
```
print(bool(int('0')))
print(bool(str(0)))
print(bool(float('0.0')))
print(bool(str(0.0)))
```

37.
```
a,b,c = 12,13,16
d = a + b *c/b
print(d)
```

38. `"abc" or ""`

39. `'' or ''`

40. `'k' or 'r'`

41. `20 or len(20)`

42. `70/(7-(2+4))or 4<5`

43. `5 < 9 or 60/(10-(6+4))`

Find the Error

1. `>>>10+'20'+30+'40'`

2. `>>>'10'*'20'`

3. `>>>'PYTHON'*7.0`

4.
```
x = 10
print(x)
```

5.
```
x = 123.456
print('%'+x)
```

6.
```
x = 1; y = 2;
print(x+y+z)
```

7. `if = 5; print(if)`

8. `a = 10; b = 20; print(a;b)`

9.
```
x =10
y = x * 30
x = "PYTHON"
z = x/10
```

10.
```
name = int(input("Enter your name : "))
print("HELLO", name)
```

11. `print(len(bool(0)))`

12. `>>> print("HELLO"/2)`

13. `>>> print(type(int("HELLO")))`

AI Lab Session – AI for Music by Google

Visit the link to know about AI applications developed by Google to support music:
https://experiments.withgoogle.com/collection/ai

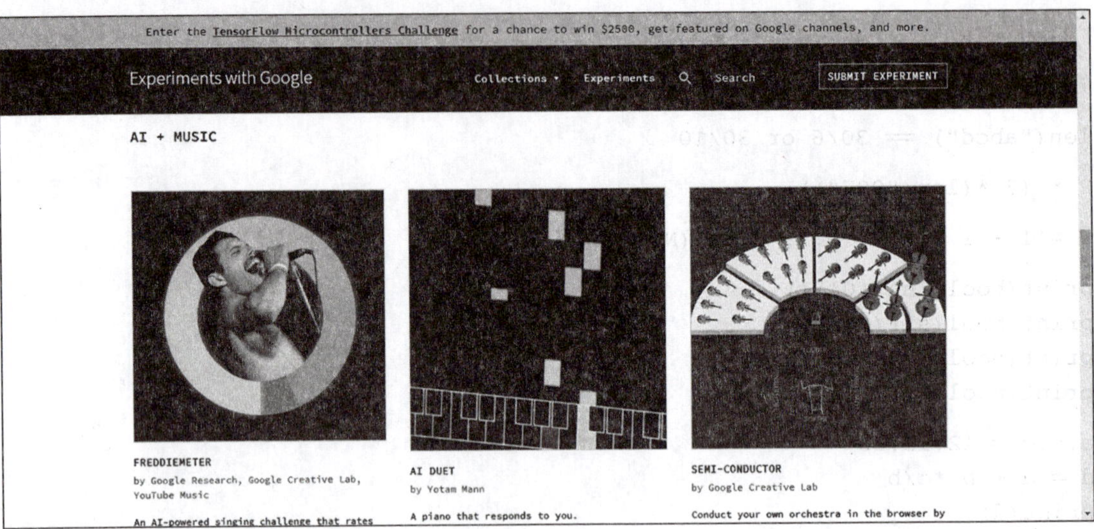

FreddieMeter: It is an AI-powered singing challenge that rates how closely your singing matches the voice of Freddie Mercury. This application uses machine learning models to compare the user's timbre, pitch, and melody with that of Freddie's. Since user's audio is not uploaded to servers for analysis, the vocal information stays private.

Semi-Conductor: This experiment by Google allows users to conduct their own orchestra in the browser just by moving their arms. Movement of the arms creates variation in the tempo, volume, and instrumentation of a piece of music.

AI Duet: It is another AI application by Google that plays a piano based on the inputs given by the user. Users can play some notes, and the computer will respond to the melody. Users may not even know how to play piano. They just have to press some keys and listen to what comes back.

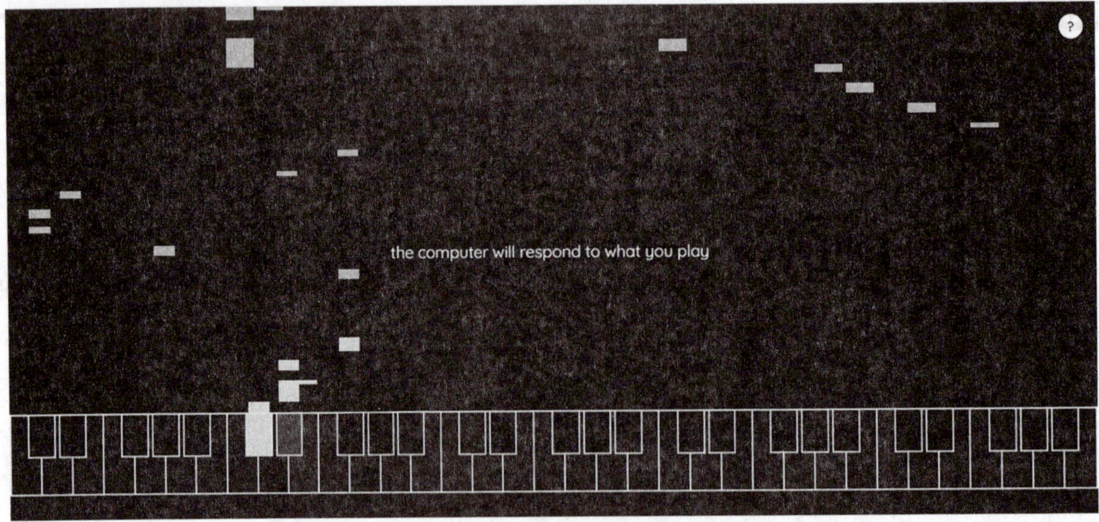

Answers

Fill in the Blanks

1. 79
2. Variables
3. identifiers
4. assignment
5. labels
6. data types
7. lvalues
8. input ()
9. int ()
10. docstring
11. indentation
12. operand
13. Logical
14. 0.00000012345
15. float ()
16. / or //
17. **
18. String
19. underscore, upper case, lower case character
20. True
21. ZeroDivisionError
22. 1020
23. 12356.266

State True or False

1. False
2. True
3. False
4. True
5. True
6. False
7. True
8. True
9. False
10. True
11. False
12. True
13. False
14. True
15. False

Multiple Choice Questions

1. a
2. c
3. a
4. b
5. c
6. c
7. c
8. a
9. c
10. a
11. c
12. a
13. b
14. d
15. a
16. b
17. b
18. d
19. b
20. c

Give the Output

1. x = 27 y = 15 z = 27
2. x = 10 y = 15 z = 0
3. 410
4. 5670.0
5. 17
6. 'Python Programming is fun… '
7. 'Python Programming is fun…'
8. 'Python… \n Programming?'
9. Python
   Programmiung
10. PYTHON !!!!PYTHON !!!!PYTHON !!!!
11. 300
12. HELLOWORLD
13. Days are : Mon Tue Wed Thu Fri Sat Sun
    Months are: Jan
    Feb
    Mar
    Apr
    May
    Jun
    Jul
    Aug
    There's a new dream today.
    I'll tell you some other day.
    Come on, let's enjoy.
14. No output

15. NameError: name 'num1' is not defined
16. 713.0
17. HELLO(input)
18. NameError: name 'num2' is not defined
19. 300
20. inf
21. 2
22. a = 10.0 and b = 50
23. a = 200 and b = 100
24. 1000000000
25. False
26. True
27. True
28. True
29. True

30. False
31. True
32. 70.0
33. 3.0
34. 30
35. False
36. False   True   False   True
37. 28.0
38. 'abc'
39. ''
40. 'k'
41. True
42. 70.0
43. True

Find the Error

1. TypeError: unsupported operand type(s) for +: 'int' and 'str'
2. TypeError:can't multiplay sequence by non-int of type 'str'
3. TypeError: can't multiply sequence by non-int of type 'float'
4. Error! Tab at the start of the line
5. TypeError: cannot concatenate 'str' and 'float' objects
6. NameError: name 'z' is not defined
7. SyntaxError: invalid syntax
8. SyntaxError: invalid syntax
9. TypeError: unsupported operand type(s) for /: 'str' and 'int'
10. ValueError: invalid literal for int() with base 10: 'ABC'
11. TypeError: object of type 'bool' has no len()
12. TypeError: unsupported operand type(s) for /: 'str' and 'int'
13. ValueError: invalid literal for int() with base 10: 'HELLO'

Decision Control Statements

12

The chapter discusses a very crucial set of statements that may alter the sequence of program flow. These statements include conditional branching statements such as:

- The if statement
- The if-else statement
- The nested if statement
- The if-elif-else Statement

We have thus far executed simple statements in Python. Such statements are executed sequentially from the first line of the program to the last. That is, the second statement is executed after the first, the third statement is executed after the second, and so on. This way of execution is known as **sequential control flow**.

However, in some cases we want to either execute only a selected set of statements (i.e., selection control) or execute a set of statements repeatedly (i.e., iterative control). In such cases, decision control system comes into picture.

A *decision control statement* is a statement that determines the flow of control in a program. Flow of control means deciding on which instruction would next be executed. A decision control statement can either skip one or more instructions. The three fundamental methods of control flow in a programming language are *sequential, selection, and iterative control*.

Selection and iterative control are a part of decision control system. Thus, a decision control statement can alter (change) the flow of a sequence of instructions. And this type of conditional processing helps users to extend the usefulness of programs.

Programmers can make programs that determine which statements of the code should be executed and which should be ignored in certain circumstances. Figure 12.1 shows the categorization of decision control statements.

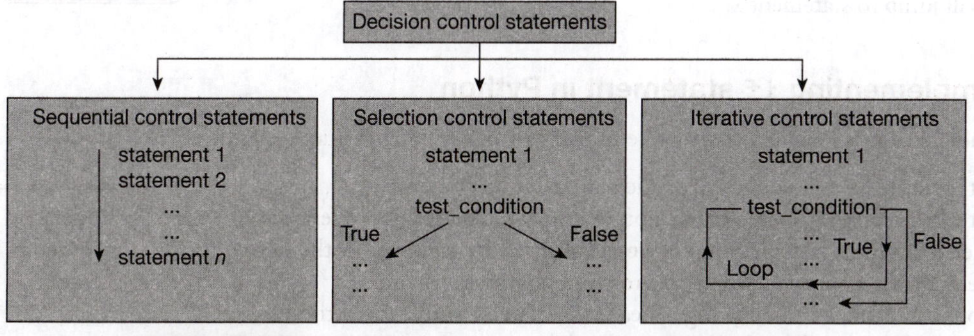

Figure 12.1   Categorization of decision control statements

12.1   SELECTION/CONDITIONAL BRANCHING STATEMENTS

The decision control statements usually jump from one part of the code to another depending on whether a particular condition is satisfied or not. That is, they execute statements selectively based on certain decisions. Such type of decision control statements is known as ***selection control statements*** or *conditional branching statements*. Python language supports different types of conditional branching statements, which are as follows:

- `if` statement
- Nested `if` statement
- `if-else` statement
- `if-elif-else` statement

12.2   `if` STATEMENT

`if` statement is the simplest form of decision control statements that is frequently used in decision making. An `if` statement is a selection control statement based on the value of a given Boolean expression. The general form of a simple `if` statement is shown in Fig. 12.2.

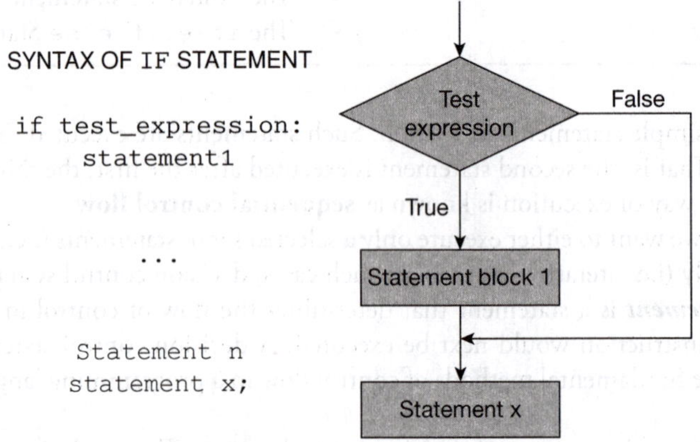

Figure 12.2   **If statement construct**

The `if` block may include 1 or more statements. According to the figure, first the test expression is evaluated. If the test expression is true, the statements of `if` block (statement 1 to *n*) are executed; otherwise, these statements will be skipped and the execution will jump to statement x.

> Python is a case sensitive language. So, `if` is not same as `IF`.

12.2.1 Implementing `if` statement in Python

Always remember the following points while implementing an `if` construct in Python.

- The statement in an `if` block is any valid statement in Python.
- The test expression is any valid expression that may include logical operators.
- **A header in Python is a specific keyword followed by a colon.** In the figure, the `if` statement has a header, "**if text_expression:**" having keyword `if`.
- The group of statements following a header is called a **suite**. After the header, all instructions that are indented at the same level forms a suite.
- While four spaces are commonly used for each level of indentation, any number of spaces may be used.

> Header and its suite are together known as a clause.

Example 12.1   **Program to increment a number if it is positive.**

```
x = 10   #Initialize tbe value of x
if(x>0): #test the value of x
     x = x+1  #Increment the value of x if it is > 0
print(x)  #Print the value of x
```

> Remember to properly indent the statements that are dependent on the previous statements.

OUTPUT
```
x = 11
```

In the above code, we take a variable *x* and initialize it to 10. In the test expression, we check if the value of *x* is greater than 0 or not. If the test expression evaluates to true, then the value of *x* is incremented and is printed on the screen. Note that the print statement will be executed even if the test expression is false.

Python uses indentation to form a block of code. Other languages such as C and C++, use curly braces to accomplish this.

Example 12.2   **Write a program to determine whether a person is eligible to vote.**

```
age= int(input("Enter the age :"))
if(age>=18):
    print("You are eligible to vote")
```

OUTPUT
Enter the age : 35
You are eligible to vote

Example 12.3   **Write a program to determine the character entered by the user.**

```
char= input("Press any key : ")
if(char.isalpha()):
    print("The user has entered a character")
if(char.isdigit()):
    print("The user has entered a digit")
if(char.isspace()):
    print("The user entered a white space character")
```

OUTPUT
Press any key : 7
The user has entered a digit

12.3   `if-else` STATEMENT

Although `if` statement plays a vital role in conditional branching, its usage is very limited. Its simplicity is also its drawback. In the `if` statement, the test expression is evaluated; if the result is true, the statement(s) followed by the expression is executed. But, if the expression is false, nothing useful happens. So, using an `if-else` statement solves our problem. The general form of a simple `if-else` statement is shown in Fig. 12.3.

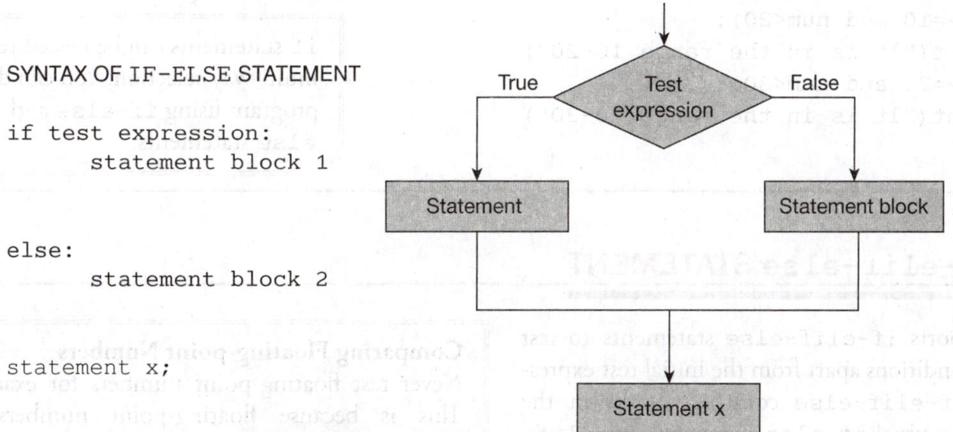

Figure 12.3   `if-else` statement construct

In the above syntax, we have written the statement block. A statement block may include one or more statements. According to the `if-else` construct, first the test expression is evaluated. If the expression is true, statement block 1 is executed and statement block 2 is skipped. Otherwise, if the expression is false, statement block 2 is executed and statement block 1 is ignored. In any case, after the statement block 1 or 2 gets executed, the control will pass to statement *x*. Therefore, statement *x* is executed in every case.

Example 12.4   **Write a program to determine whether a person is eligible to vote or not. If he is not eligible, display how many years are left to be eligible.**

```
age = int(input("Enterthe age : " ))
if(age>=18):
    print("You are eligible to vote")
else:
    yrs = 18 - age
    print("You have to wait for " + str(yrs) +" years")
```

OUTPUT

Enter the age : 10
You have to wait for 8 years

Example 12.5   **Write a program to find larger of two numbers.**

```
a = int(input("Enter the value of a : "))
b = int(input("Enter the value of b : "))
if(a>b):
    large = a
else:
    large = b
print("Large = ",large)
```

OUTPUT

Enter the value of a: 50
Enter the value of b : 30
Large = 50

12.4   NESTED `if` STATEMENTS

A statement that contains other statements is called a ***compound statement***. To perform more complex checks, if statements can be nested, that is, they can be placed one inside the other. In such a case, the inner if statement is the statement part of the outer one. Nested if statements are used to check if more than one conditions are satisfied. Consider the code given below to understand this concept.

Example 12.6   **Program that prompts the user to enter a number and then print its interval.**

```
num = int(input("Enter any number from 0-30: "))
if(num>=0 and num<10):
    print("It is in the range 0-10")
elif(num>=10 and num<20):
    print("lt is in the range 10-20")
elif(num>=20 and num<30):
    print("lt is in the range 20-30")
```

OUTPUT

Enter any number from 0-30: 25
It is in the range 20-30

> if statements can be nested resulting in multi-way selection. You can do the same program using if-else and if-elif-else statements.

12.5   `if-elif-else` STATEMENT

Python supports if-elif-else statements to test additional conditions apart from the initial test expression. The if-elif-else construct works in the same way as a usual if-else statement. if-elif-else construct is also known as **nested-if construct**. The elif (short for else if) statement is a shortcut to if and else statements. *A series of if and elif statements have a final else block, which is executed if none of the if or elif expressions is True.* Its syntax is given in Fig. 12.4.

Comparing Floating-point Numbers
Never test floating-point numbers for exact equality. This is because floating-point numbers are just approximations, so it is always better to test floating-point numbers for 'approximately equal' rather than testing for exactly equal.

We can test for approximate equality by finding the difference between the two floating-point numbers (that are to be tested) and comparing their absolute value of the difference against a very small number, epsilon.

```
SYNTAX OF IF-ELIF-ELSE STATEMENT
if ( test expression 1)
        statement block 1
elif ( test expression 2)
        statement block 2

..........................

elif (test expression N)
        statement block N
else
        statement block x
statement y
```

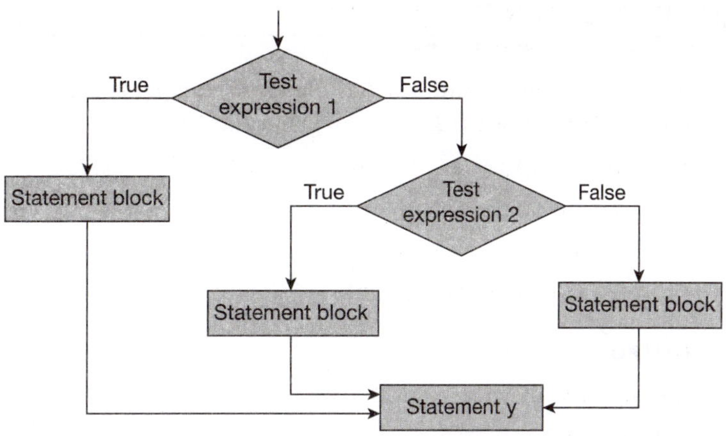

Figure 12.4   if-elif-else syntax

Note that it is not necessary that every `if` statement should have an `else` block as Python supports simple `if` statements also. After the first test expression or the first `if` branch, the programmer can have as many `elif` branches as he wants depending on the expressions that have to be tested. The final `else` block is called if none of the `if` or `elif` expressions is True.

> Remember that the `elif` and `else` part are optional.

Example 12.7   To test whether a number entered by the user is negative, positive or equal to zero.

```
num = int(input("Enter any number : "))
if(num==0):
     print("The value is equal to zero" )
elif(num>0):
     print("The number is positive")
else:
     print("The number is negative")
```

OUTPUT
Enter any number : -10
The number is negative

Example 12.8   Write a program to determine whether the character entered is a vowel or not.

```
ch = input("Enter any character : ")
if(ch=="A" or ch=="E" or ch=="I" or ch=="O" or ch=="U"):
     print ch,"is a vowel")
elif(ch=="a" or ch=="e" or ch=="i" or ch=="o" or ch=="u"):
     print(ch,"is a vowel")
else:
     print(ch, "is not a vowel")
```

OUTPUT
Enter any character: h
h is not a vowel

In the program to test whether a number is positive or negative, note that if the first test expression evaluates a true value then the rest of the statements in the code will be ignored and after executing the `print` statement that displays "The value is equal to zero", the control will jump to return 0 statement.

> Keep the logical expressions simple and short. For this, you may use nested `if` statements.

Python assumes any non-zero and non-null values as TRUE. Similarly, all values that are either zero or null are assumed as FALSE value.

> Use the and/or operators to form a compound relation expression. In Python, the following expression is invalid.
>
> $$if \ (60 \leq marks \leq 75) \ :$$
>
> The correct way to write is,
>
> $$if \ ((marks \geq 60) \ and \ (marks \leq 75) \ :$$

PROGRAMMER'S ZONE

1. **Write a program to find whether the given number is even or odd.**

```python
num = int(input("Enter any number : "))
if(num%2==0):
    print(num,"is even")
else:
    print(num,"is odd")
```

OUTPUT

```
Enter any number : 125
125 is odd
```

2. **Write a program to enter any character. If the entered character is in lower case then convert it into upper case and if it is an upper case character then convert it into lower case.**

```python
ch = input("Enter any character : ")
if(ch >= 'A' and ch <='Z'):
    ch = ch.lower()
    print("The entered character was in upper case. In lower case it is : " + ch)
else:
    ch = ch.upper()
    print("The entered character was in lower case. In upper case it is : " + ch)
```

OUTPUT

```
Enter any character : c
The entered character was in lower case. In upper case it is : C
```

3. **A company decides to give bonus to all its employees on Diwali. A 5% bonus on salary is given to the male workers and 10% bonus on salary to the female workers. Write a program to enter the salary of the employee and sex of the employee. If the salary of the employee is less than Rs 10,000 then the employee gets an extra 2% bonus on salary. Calculate the bonus that has to be given to the employee and display the salary that the employee will get.**

```python
ch = input("Enter the sex of the employee (m or f) : ")
sal = int(input("Enter the salary of the employee : "))
if (ch=='m'):
    bonus = 0.05*sal
else :
    bonus = 0.10*sal
amt_to_be_paid = sal+bonus
print(" Salary = ",sal)
print(" Bonus = ",bonus)
print(" ******************************")
print("Amount to be paid : ",amt_to_be_paid)
```

OUTPUT

```
Enter the sex of the employee (m or f) : f
Enter the salary of the employee : 50000
Salary =  50000
Bonus =  5000.0
*******************************
Amount to be paid :  55000.0
```

4. **Write a program to find whether a given year is leap year or not.**

```
year = int(input("Enter any year : "))
if((year%4==0 and year %100!=0) or (year%400 == 0)):
      print("Leap Year")
else:
      print("Not a Leap Year")
```

OUTPUT

```
Enter any year : 2000
Leap Year
```

5. **Write a program to find the greater of two numbers.**

```
X = int(input("Enter the first number : "))
y = int(input("Enter the second number : "))
if(x==y):
      print("The two numbers are equal")
elif(x>y):
      print(x,"is greater than",y)
else:
      print(x,"is less than",y)
```

OUTPUT

```
Enter the first number : 6
Enter the second number : 3
6 is greater than 3
```

6. **Write a program to find the greatest number from three numbers.**

```
num1 = int(input("Enter the first number : "))
num2 = int(input("Enter the second number : "))
num3 = int(input("Enter the third number : "))
if(num1>num2):
      if(num1>num3):
            print(num1,"is greater than",num2,"and",num3)
```

```
        else:
                print(num3,"is greater than",num1,"and",num2)
    elif(num2>num3):
            print(num2,"is greater than",num1,"and",num3)
    else:
            print("The three numbers are equal")
```

OUTPUT

```
Enter the first number : 13
Enter the second number : 43
Enter the third number : 25
43 is greater than 13 and 25
```

7. **Write a program that prompts user to enter a number between 1–7 and then displays the corresponding day of the week.**

```
num = int(input("Enter any number between 1 to 7 : "))
if(num==1): print("Sunday")
elif(num==2): print("Monday")
elif(num==3): print("Tuesday")
elif(num==4): print("Wednesday")
elif(num==5): print("Thursday")
elif(num==6): print("Friday")
elif(num==7): print("Saturday")
else :
print("Wrong input")
```

OUTPUT

```
Enter any number between 1 to 7 : 5
Thursday
```

8. **Write a program to calculate tax given the following conditions:**

```
If income is less than 1,50,000 then no tax
If taxable income is 1,50,001 - 300,000 then charge 10% tax
If taxable income is 3,00,001 - 500,000 then charge 20% tax
If taxable income is above 5,00,001 then charge 30% tax
MIN1 = 150001
MAX1 = 300000
RATE1 = 0.10
MIN2 = 300001
MAX2 = 500000
RATE2 = 0.20
MIN3 = 500001
RATE3 = 0.30
income = int(input("Enter the income : "))
```

```python
    taxable_income = income - 150000
    if(taxable_income <= 0):
        print("No tax")
    elif(taxable_income>=MIN1 and taxable_income<MAX1):
        tax = (taxable_income - MIN1) * RATE1
    elif(taxable_income>=MIN2 and taxable_income<MAX2):
        tax = (taxable_income - MIN2) * RATE2
    else:
        tax = (taxable_income-MIN3)*RATE3
    print("TAX = ",tax)
```

OUTPUT

```
Enter the income : 2000000
TAX =  404999.7
```

9. **Write a program to take input from the user and then check whether it is a number or a character. If it is a character, determine whether it is in upper case or lower case.**

```python
    ch = input("Enter the character : ")
    if(ch>="A" and ch<="Z"):
        print("Upper case character was entered")
    elif(ch>='a' and ch<='z'):
        print("Lower case character was entered")
    elif(ch>='0' and ch<='9'):
        print "A number was entered"
```

OUTPUT

```
Enter any character : C
Upper case character was entered
```

10. **Write a program to enter the marks of a student in four subjects. Then calculate the total, aggregate and display the grade obtained by the student. If the student scores an aggregate greater than 75%, then the grade is Distinction. If aggregate is 60>= and <75, then the grade is First Division. If aggregate is 50>= and <60, then the grade is Second Division. If aggregate is 40>= and <50, then the grade is Third Division. Else the grade is Fail.**

```python
    marks1 = int(input("Enter the marks in Mathematics : "))
    marks2 = int(input("Enter the marks in Science : "))
    marks3 = int(input("Enter the marks in Social Science : "))
    marks4 = int(input("Enter the marks in Computers : "))
    total = marks1+marks2+marks3+marks4
    avg = float(total)/4
    print("Total = ",total,"\t Aggregate = ",avg)
    if(avg>=75):
        print("Distinction")
    elif(avg>=60 and avg<75):
        print("First Division")
```

> While forming the conditional expression, try to use positive statements rather than using compound negative statements.

```
elif(avg>=50 and avg<60):

     print("Second Division")

else:

   print("Fail")
```

OUTPUT

```
Enter the marks in Mathematics : 90

Enter the marks in Science : 91

Enter the marks in Social Science : 92

Enter the marks in Computers : 93

Total =  366    Aggregate =  91.5

Distinction
```

11. **Write a program that prompts the user to enter three angles. Check whether the angles are that of a triangle or not.**

```
ang1= int(input("Enter the first angle : "))

ang2= int(input("Enter the first angle : "))

ang3= int(input("Enter the first angle : "))

if (ang1 + ang2 + ang3) == 180:

     print("The angles are angles of a triangle")

else:

     print("The angles are not the angles of a triangle")
```

OUTPUT

```
Enter the first angle : 120

Enter the first angle : 40

Enter the first angle : 20

The angles are angles of a triangle
```

Key Terms

Sequential control flow: A programming style in which the statements in a program are executed one after the other.

Flow control: Flow control means control on which statement would be executed next.

Decision control flow: A type of flow control in which either a selected set of statements is executed or a particular set of statements is executed repeatedly.

Selection control statements: Decision control statements that allow the flow control to jump from one part of the code to another depending on whether a particular condition is satisfied or not. Since they execute statements selectively based on certain decisions, such type of decision control statements is known as selection control statements or *conditional branching statements.*

Clause: Combination of header and its suite.

Suite: Group of statements following the header.

Nested (or compound) statement: A statement that contains other statements is called a compound statement.

Chapter Highlights

- A test expression is any valid expression that may include logical operators.
- After the header, all instructions that are indented at the same level form a suite.
- Python uses indentation to form a block of code.
- An `if-else` statement specifies what has to be done if the statement is true as well as when it is false.
- Nested `if` statements are used to check if more than one condition is satisfied.
- A series of `if` and `elif` statements have a final `else` block, which is executed if none of the `if` or `elif` expressions is True.

Review Questions

1. What is flow control?

2. Differentiate between sequential control flow and selection control flow.

3. Why do we need decision control statements?

4. With the help of a flowchart, explain the syntax of the following statements:
   a. if   b. if-else   c. if-el-if   d. nested if

5. What are conditional branching statements? How does Python support such statements?

6. How will you identify the suite of an `if` statement?

7. With the help of an example explain why `if-else` statement is better than a simple `if` statement.

8. What do you mean by a nested `if` statement? How is it implemented in Python?

9. Why should we not use floating-point numbers to test for exact equality?

10. Change the indentation to make the code syntactically correct.
```
if condition1:
statement1
elif condition2:
statement2
elif condition3:
statement3
elif condition4:
statement4
```

11. Under what conditions, Programming will be printed?
```
if a < 10:
   print("Python")
elif a < 20:
   print("Programming")
else:
   print("is fun..")
```

Programming Exercises

1. Write a program to check whether a number is divisible by 10 or not. If the number is not divisible, then print how much should be added to it to make it completely divisible by 10.

2. Write a program to verify whether a candidate is eligible to appear for an exam or not. The minimum and maximum age of a person appearing for the exam is 21 and 35 respectively.

3. Write a program that prompts the user to enter an angle and then prints its quadrant.

4. Write a program that prompts the user to enter a number between 1–12 and then displays the corresponding month of the year.

5. Write a menu-driven program that prompts the user to enter the two sides of a rectangle. The user can then choose from a given set of options, if he/she needs to calculate perimeter, area or diagonal of the rectangle.

6. Write a program that prompts users to enter a character (A, B, C, D, E). Then using `if-elif-else` construct, display Outstanding, Very Good, Good, Average and Fail respectively.

7. Write a program that prompts the user to enter two integers. Divide the greater number with the smaller one and print the remainder and quotient thus obtained.

8. Write a program that prompts the user to enter his/her age (15–18 years) and then display the perfect height and weight for that age.

Age	Weight (kg)	Height (cm)
15	56	170
16	60	173
17	64	175
18	66	176

9. Write a program that prompts the user to enter his/her body temperature. Check and display whether the user has normal body temperature, high fever or low fever.

10. Write a program that prompts the user to enter a number. Display the square root of the number. Remember that square root of negative numbers is not defined.

11. Write a program that prompts the user to enter the lengths of three sides. Check whether these are the sides of a triangle.
    Hint: Sides of a triangle follow the rule, a + b > c. Similarly, b + c > a and a + c > b.

12. Write a program that prompts the user to enter the angles of a triangle. Check whether the triangle is acute-, obtuse- or right-angled.

13. Write a program to check whether a number entered by the user is positive, negative or equal to zero.

14. Write a program that prompts users to enter status code 'S', 'M', 'D', or 'U' and returns the string 'Separated', 'Married', 'Divorced', or 'Unmarried', respectively. In case an inappropriate letter is passed, print an appropriate message.

15. An employee's total weekly pay is calculated by multiplying the hourly wage and number of regular hours plus any overtime pay, which in turn is calculated as total overtime hours multiplied by 1.5 times the hourly wage. Write a program that takes as inputs the hourly wage, total regular hours, and total overtime hours and prints an employee's total weekly pay.

Fill in the Blanks

1. ___________ means which statement would be executed next.

2. _________ is the simplest form of decision control statements.

3. Header and its suite together form a __________.

4. Python uses __________ to form a block of code.

5. A __________ statement contains other statements.

6. A series of `if` and `elif` statements have a final ________ block.

7. ______ and ______ operators are used to form a compound relational expression.

8. ________ is a short form of `else if` statement.

9. Python uses ___________ to form a block of code.

10. A series of `if elif` statements have a final _______ block, which is executed if none of the `if` or `elif` expressions is True.

11. Python assumes any non-zero and non-null values as _________.

12. _________ begin with a keyword and end with a colon.

13.
```
x = 10
y = 20
__x>y__
print print("In if")
________
        print ("In else")
```

14. Fill the blanks to print *Python* on the screen.
```
x = 10
y = 50
if x>10 __ y<100:
___("Python")
```

State True or False

1. A sequential control program can skip one or more statements.

2. In selection control statements, all the statements are executed from the first one to the last.

3. Group of statements following the header is known as a clause.

4. After the header, all instructions that are indented at the same level form a suite.

5. It is mandatory to use four spaces to define each level of indentation.

6. The final else block in an `if-elif-else` statement is executed when none of the `if` or `elif` expressions is True.

7. You can use floating-point numbers for checking for equality in the test expression.

8. Indentation identifies a statement block.

9. Statements within a suite can be indented at different levels.

10. `elif` and `else` blocks are optional.

Multiple Choice Questions

1. Which part of `if` statement should be indented?
   a. The first statement   b. All the statements
   c. Statements within the `if` block   d. None of these.

2. A programming style in which the statements in a program are executed one after the other.
   a. Sequential   b. Decision control
   c. Iterative control   d. None of these.

3. A test expression must have _________ operator.
   a. arithmetic   b. logical
   c. unary   d. assignment

4. In an `if` statement, which of the following headers are optional?
   a. `if`   b. `elif`
   c. `else`   d. Both b and c.

5. Logical expression should not be _________.
   a. simple   b. long
   c. positive   d. Both b and c.

6. Which of the following is placed after the `if` condition?
   a. ;   b. .
   c. :   d. ,

Give the Output

1.
```python
if(5.0 < 9.0):
    print("DONE")
```

2.
```python
years = 99
if(years == 100):
    print("Century")
elif(years == 75):
    print("Platinum Jublee")
elif(years == 50):
    print("Half Century")
elif(years == 25):
    print("Silver Jublee")
elif(years == 10):
    print("Decade")
else:
    print("Long way to go….")
```

3.
```python
years = 99
if years > 30:
    print("30")
if years < 50:
    print("50")
if years == 7:
    print("70")
```

4.
```python
num = int((10*6 + 10 - 20) > 0)
if num == 50:
    print("You win...")
else:
    print("Try Again")
```

5.
```python
num = 3
if (num ** 3) > (5%2 - 3 * 4 /2):
    if (num // 4) >= 2:
        print("You win")
    else:
        print("Try Again")
```

6.
```python
num = 3
if num == 2:
    print("Yes")
elif num == 4:
    print("Yes")
elif num == 8:
    print("Yes")
else:
    print("Number is not an even number")
```

7.
```python
if(10 == 100) and (100 + 200 > 300):
    print("Win Win..")
else:
    print("Oh No !!!")
```

8.
```python
if not True:
    print("WRONG")
elif not((10+10 - 20 * 3) == 30):
    print("Really !")
else:
    print("May Be")
```

9.
```python
if (10 << ((41 - 40 // 2 + 1)%2)) == 60:
    print("WoW")
else:
    print("Gosh")
```

10.
```python
a = 5
b = 70
if not 10 + 10 == b or a == 40 and 70== 80:
    print("Yeah")
elif a != b:
    print("Nope")
```

11.
```python
num = 10
if num > 30:
    if num > 40:
        print("Python")
else:
        print("Programming")
elif num < 20:
    if(num!=0):
        print("is fun..")
print("Isnt it !!!")
```

12.
```python
weather = 'foggy'
if weather == 'sunny':
    print("Take your shades")
elif weather == 'raining':
    print("Take your umbrella")
else:
    print("Stay at home")
```

AI Lab Session – Lip Sync

Go to the URL https://experiments.withgoogle.com/lipsync to launch the lip sync experiment developed by Google. The application uses AI techniques to sync the user's lip to match the song!

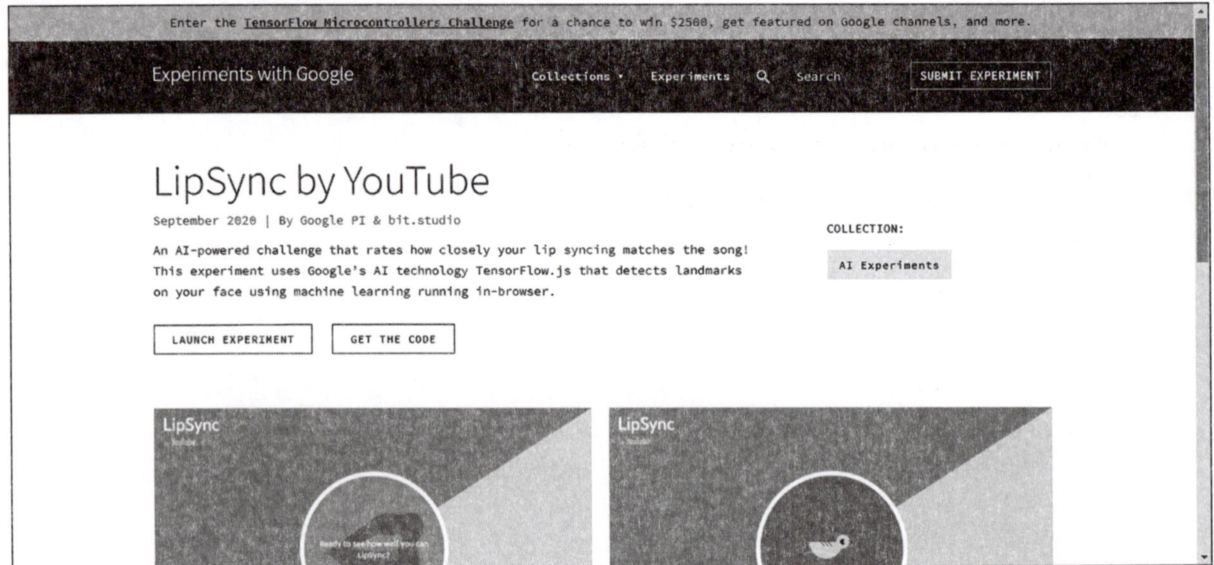

Answers

Fill in the Blanks

1. Flow control
2. `If` statement
3. clause
4. indentation
5. compound/nested
6. `else`
7. `and, or`
8. `elif`
9. indentation
10. `else`
11. True
12. Header
13. `if, :, else:`
14. `or, print`

State True or False

1. False	4. True	7. True	10. True
2. False	5. False	8. True	
3. False	6. True	9. False	

Multiple Choice Questions

1. b	3. b	5. b
2. a	4. d	6. c

Give the Output

1. Done
2. way to go….
3. 30
4. Try Again
5.
6. Number is not an even number
7. Oh No !!!
8. Really !
9. Gosh
10. Yeah
11. is fun..
    Isnt it !!!
12. Stay at home

Basic Loop Structures/Iterative Statements

13

Chapter Objectives

This chapter elucidates the concept of iterative statements in Python. Like decision control statements, the iterative statements may also change the flow of program control. Here, we shall learn about:

- `while` loop
- `for` loop
- The `range()` function
- Nested loops

- The technique to choose an appropriate loop for the given situation
- Path breaking statements like `break`, `continue`, `pass` and `else`

In the last chapter, we read about decision-controlled statements and covered conditional branching statements including `if`, and `if-elif-else` statements. In this chapter, we will study iterative statements through which Python supports basic loop structures. Iterative statements are used to repeat the execution of one or more statements. In Python, iterative statements are implemented through `while` loop and `for` loop.

13.1 `while` LOOP

The `while` loop provides a mechanism to repeat one or more statements when a particular condition is true. Figure 13.1 shows the syntax and general form of representation of a `while` loop.

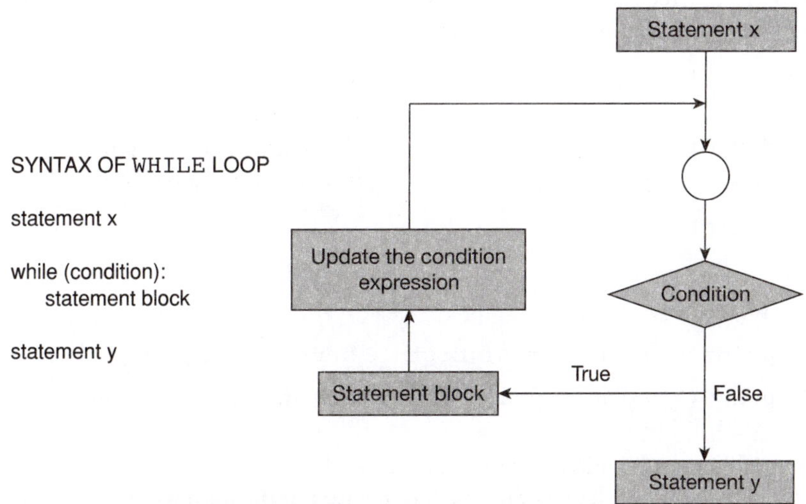

Figure 13.1 The `while` loop construct

Note in the `while` loop, the condition is tested before any of the statements in the statement block is executed. If the condition is true, only then the statements will be executed; otherwise, if the condition is false, the control will jump to statement *y*, which is the immediate statement outside the `while` loop block.

> Iterative statements are used to repeat the execution of a list of statements, depending on the value of an integer expression.

We must update the condition with every iteration of the loop. This is necessary because it is this condition which determines when the loop will end. If we do not update the condition, then it will never become false. This will result in an infinite loop, which is never desirable.

A `while` loop is also referred to as a top-checking loop since control condition is placed as the first line of the code. If the control condition evaluates to false, then the statements enclosed in the loop are never executed. Look at the following example code.

Example 13.1 To print the first 10 numbers using a `while` loop.

```
i = 0
while(i< =10}:
        print(i,end=' ')
        i = i+1
```

OUTPUT

0 1 2 3 4 5 6 7 8 9 10

Example 13.2 Write a program to calculate the sum and average of first 10 numbers.

```
i = 0
s = 0
while(i<=10):
    s = s+i
    i=i+1
avg = float(s}/10
print("The sum of first 10 numbers is : ",s)
print("The average of first 10 numbers is :",avg)
```

OUTPUT

The sum of first 10 numbers is : 55

In the program initially $i = 0$ and is less than 10, that is, the condition is true. So, in the `while` loop the value of i is printed and the condition is updated so that with every execution of the loop, the condition becomes more approachable. Always remember that, when writing a `while` loop,

```
i = 0
sum = 0
avg = 0.0
while(i<=10):
    sum = sum + i
avg = sum/10
print("\n The sum of first 10 numbers=", sum)
print("\n The average of first 10 numbers = ", avg)
```

The infinite loop is a loop which never stops running. Its condition always True.

First, the loop control variable must be initialized before entering the loop.

Second, the test expression that decides whether the statement(s) in the loop will be executed or not, is evaluated.

Third, the statement(s) inside the loop are executed if the test expression is True.

Fourth, the loop control variable is updated.

`while` *loop is very useful for designing interactive programs in which the number of times the statements in loop has to be executed may or may not be known in advance.* Let us look at a program which results in an infinite loop. Though the program is supposed to calculate the average of first 10 numbers, the condition never becomes false, and the desired output is *not* generated. Once you have entered the infinite loop, either press Ctrl + C keys on the keyboard or press the close button of the Python shell window.

13.2 `for` LOOP

Like the `while` loop, the `for` loop provides a mechanism to repeat a task until a particular condition is true. The `for` loop is usually known as a determinate or definite loop because the programmer knows exactly how many times the loop will repeat. The number of times the loop has to be executed can be determined mathematically by checking the logic of the loop.

The `for..in` statement is a looping statement used in Python to iterate over a sequence of objects, i.e., go through each item in a sequence. Here, by sequence we mean just an ordered collection of items. The flow of statements in a `for` loop can be given as in Fig. 13.2.

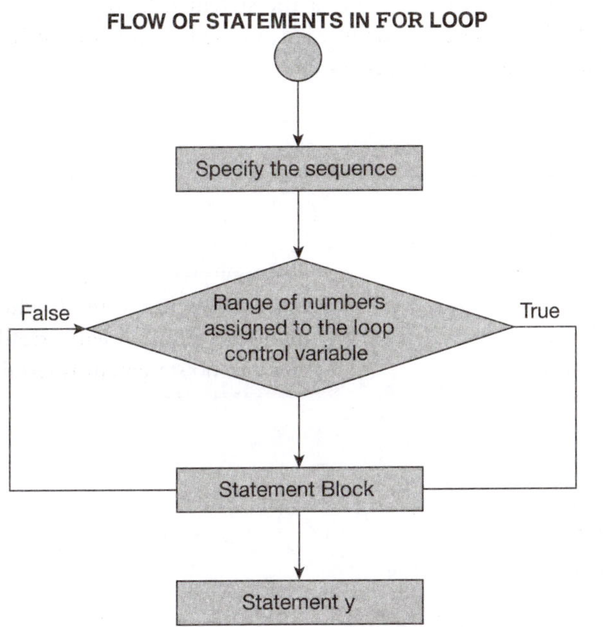

Figure 13.2 `for` loop construct

When a `for` loop is used, a range of sequence is specified (only once). The items of the sequence are assigned to the loop control variable one after the other. The `for` loop is executed for each item in the sequence. With every iteration of the loop, a check is made to ensure if the loop control variable has been assigned all the values in the sequence. If all the values have not been assigned, the statement block of the loop is executed; else, the statements comprising the statement block of the `for` loop are skipped and the control jumps to the immediate statement following the `for` loop body. Note that every iteration of the loop must make the loop control variable closer to the end of the sequence.

Let us print all the characters in a string using the `for` loop. We know that a string is a sequence of characters. So, the `for` loop statement(s) will be executed for each character in the string.

```
for i in "PYTHON":
    print(i, end = ' ')
Ans. P Y T H O N
```

13.3 THE `range()` FUNCTION

The `range()` is a built-in function in Python that is used to iterate over a sequence of numbers. The syntax of `range()` is **range(beg, end, [step])**

The **range()** generates a sequence of numbers starting with **beg** (inclusive) and ending with one less than the number **end**. The **step** argument is optional (hence, written in brackets). By default, every number in the range is incremented by 1 but we can specify a different increment using step. It can be both negative and positive, but not zero.

> Step can be either positive or negative but cannot be zero.

Program to print first *n* numbers using the `range()` in a `for` loop.

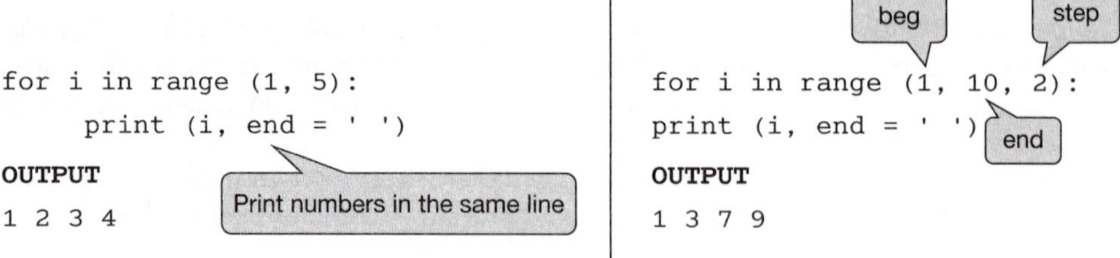


```
for i in range (1, 5):
    print (i, end = ' ')
OUTPUT
1 2 3 4
```

```
for i in range (1, 10, 2):
    print (i, end = ' ')
OUTPUT
1 3 7 9
```

The `range()` function has produced values 1,2,3 and 4. Did you notice that the statement(s) of the `for` loop is executed for each value of the loop control variable (which is *i*, here). Initially, *i* is 1, in the next iteration it is 2, so on and so forth. The loop continues until all the values in the sequence are processed.

PROGRAMMER'S ZONE

1. **Write a program to print 10 horizontal hyphens(-).**

```
i = 1
while(i<=10):
    print("-",end=' ')
    i = i+1
```

> Pass statement is used when a statement is required syntactically but otherwise no statement is required.

OUTPUT

____

2. **Write a program to calculate the sum of numbers from m to n.**

```
m = int(input("Enter the value of m : "))
n = int(input("Enter the value of n : "))
s = 0
while(m<=n):
    s = s+m
    m = m+1
print("SUM = ",s)
```

OUTPUT

```
Enter the value of m : 3
Enter the value of n : 9
SUM =   42
```

3. **Write a program to calculate the average of numbers entered by the user.**

```
s = 0
count = 0
print "Enter -1 to stop...."
num = 0
while(num != -1):
    s = s+num
    num = int(input("Enter the marks : "))
    count  = count+1
```

```
avg = float(s)/count
print "TOTAL MARKS : ",s,"\tAVERAGE MARKS : ",avg
```

OUTPUT

```
Enter -1 to stop....
Enter the marks : 90
Enter the marks : 98
Enter the marks : 97
Enter the marks : 89
Enter the marks : 79
Enter the marks : 96
Enter the marks : -1
TOTAL MARKS :   549   AVERAGE MARKS :   78.4285714286
```

4. **Write a program to find whether the given number is an Armstrong number or not.**
   Hint: **An Armstrong number of three digits is an integer such that the sum of the cubes of its digits is equal to the number itself. For example, 371 is an Armstrong number since 3**3 + 7**3 + 1**3 = 371.**

```
n = int(input("Enter the number : "))
s = 0
num = n
while(n>0):
        r = n%10
        s = s+(r**3)
        n = n/10
if(s==num):
        print("The number is Armstrong")
else:
        print("The number is not Armstrong")
```

OUTPUT

```
Enter the number : 373
373 is not an Armstrong number
```

> Nested loop is a loop placed inside another loop. Although both `for` and `while` loop can be nested, we usually use nested `for` loops as they are easiest to control. In such a case, the inner `for` loop can be used to control the number of times a particular set of statements will be executed and the outer `for` loop can be used to control the number of times the inner loop is repeated.

5. **Write a program to enter a number and then calculate the sum of its digits.**

```
sumOfDigits = 0
num = int(input("Enter the number : "))
while(num!=0):
        temp=num%10
        sumOfDigits = sumOfDigits+temp
        num=num/10
print("The sum of digits is :",sumOfDigits)
```

OUTPUT

```
Enter the number : 456
The sum of digits = 15
```

6. **Write a program to calculate the GCD of two numbers.**

```python
num1 = int(input("Enter the two numbers : "))
num2 = int(input("Enter the two numbers : "))
if(num1>num2):
        dividend = num1
        divisor = num2
else:
        dividend = num2
        divisor = num1
while(divisor!=0):
        remainder = dividend%divisor
        dividend = divisor
        divisor = remainder
print("GCD of",num1,"and",num2,"is",dividend)
```

> To stop an infinite loop, press Ctrl + C keys or close the IDLE.

OUTPUT

```
Enter the first number : 40
Enter the second number : 10
GCD of 64 and 14 is = 10
```

7. **Write a program to print the reverse of a number.**

```python
num = int(input("Enter the number : "))
print("The reversed number is :",)
while(num!=0):
        temp = num%10
        print(temp, end=' ')
        num = num/10
```

OUTPUT

```
Enter the number : 678
The reversed number is : 8 7 6
```

8. **Write a program using for loop to calculate the average of first n natural numbers.**

```python
n = int(input("Enter the value of n : "))
avg = 0.0
s = 0
for i in range(1,n+1):
        s = s+i
avg = s/i
print("The sum of first",n,"natural numbers is",s)
print("The average of first",n,"natural numbers is",avg)
```

OUTPUT

```
Enter the value of n : 10
The sum of first n natural numbers = 55
n The average of first n natural numbers = 5.500
```

9. **Write a program to print the multiplication table of n, where n is entered by the user.**

```
n = int(input("Enter any number : "))
print("Multiplication table of",n)
print("********************************")
for i in range(1,11):
        print(n,"X",i,"=",n*i)
```

OUTPUT

```
Enter any number : 5
Multiplication table of 5
**********************
5 X 0 = 0
5 X 1 = 5
...
5 X 20 = 100
```

10. **Write a program using for loop to print all the numbers from m to n, thereby classifying them as even or odd.**

```
m = int(input("Enter the value of m : "))
n = int(input("Enter the value of n : "))
for i in range(m,n+1):
        if(i%2==0):
                print(i,"is even number")
        else:
                print(i,"is odd number")
```

OUTPUT

```
Enter the value of m : 10
Enter the value of n : 15
10 is even number
11 is odd number
12 is even number
13 is odd number
14 is even number
15 is odd number
```

11. **Write a program using for loop to calculate the factorial of a number.**

```
num = int(input("Enter the number : "))
if(num==0):
        fact = 1
```

```
fact = 1
for i in range(1,num+1):
        fact = fact*i
print("Factorial of",num,"is",fact)
```

OUTPUT

```
Enter the number : 6
Factorial of is : 720
```

12. **Write a program using while loop to read the numbers until −1 is encountered. Also count the number of prime numbers and composite numbers entered by the user.**

```
total_prime = 0
total_composite = 0
while(1):
    num = int(input("Enter no. "))
    if(num == -1):
        break
    is_composite = 0
    for i in range(2,(num-1)/2):
        if(num%i == 0):
            is_composite = 1
            break
    if(is_composite):
        total_composite+=1
    else:
        total_prime+=1
print("total composite : ",total_composite)
print("total prime : ",total_prime)
```

OUTPUT

```
Enter no. 12
Enter no. 17
Enter no. 15
Enter no. 27
Enter no. 39
Enter no. 29
Enter no. 37
Enter no. -1
total composite :  4
total prime :  3
```

13. **Write a program to calculate pow(x,n).**

```
num = int(input("Enter the number : "))
n = int(input("Till which power to calculate?"))
result = 1
for i in range(n):
        result = result*num
print(num,"raised to the power",n,"is",result)
```

OUTPUT

```
Enter the number : 3
Till which power to calculate : 5
3 raised to the power 5 is 243
```

14. Write a program to sum the series – 1+ 1/2 + ... +1/n.

```
n = int(input("Enter the number : "))
s = 0.0
for i in range(1,n+1):
        a = 1.0/i
        s = s+a
print("The sum of 1,1/2......1/"+str(n)+" is "+str(s))
```

OUTPUT

```
Enter the number : 7
The sum of 1,1/2......1/5 is   2.5928571428571425
```

15. Write a program to sum the series - $1/1^2 + 1/2^2 + ... 1/n^2$

```
n = int(input("Enter the number : "))
s = 0.0
for i in range(1,n+1):
        a = 1.0/(i**2)
        s = s+a
print("The sum of series is",s)
```

OUTPUT

```
Enter the number : 7
The sum of series is   1.511797052154195
```

16. Write a program to sum the series – 1/2 + 2/3 + ... n/(n+1).

```
n = int(input("Enter the number : "))
s = 0.0
for i in range(1,n+1):
        a = float(i)/(i+1)
        s = s+a
print("The sum of 1/2+2/3......n/(n+1) is",s)
```

OUTPUT

```
Enter the number : 7
The sum of 1/2+2/3......n/(n+1) is   5.2821428571428575
```

17. Write a program to sum the series – $1/1 + 2^2/2 + 3^3/3 +... n^2/n$

```
n = int(input("Enter the value of n : "))
s = 0.0
for i in range(1,n+1):
        a = float(i**i)/i
        s = s+a
print("The sum of the series is",s)
```

OUTPUT

```
Enter the value of n : 7
The sum of the series is  126126.0
```

18. **Write a program to calculate sum of cubes of numbers from 1 – n.**

```python
n = int(input("Enter the value of n : "))
s = 0
for i in range(1,n+1):
        a = i**3
        s = s+a
print("The sum of cubes is",s)
```

OUTPUT

```
Enter the value of n : 4
The sum of cubes is 100
```

19. **Write a program to find the sum of squares of odd numbers.**

```python
n = int(input("Enter the number : "))
s = 0
for i in range(1,n+1):
        if(i%2!=0):
                term = i**2
        else:
                term = 0
        s = s+term
print("The sum of squares of odd number less than",n,"is",s)
```

OUTPUT

```
Enter the number : 10
The sum of squares of even number less than 10 is 165
```

Key Terms

Iterative statement: Statements that repeat the execution of a block of statements depending on the value of an integer expression.

Definite repetition loop: A counter-controlled loop in which the counter is assigned a constant or a value is also known as a definite repetition loop.

Nested loop: A loop that is placed inside another loop.

Chapter Highlights

- In Python, iterative statements are implemented through `while` loop and `for` loop.
- The `while` loop provides a mechanism to repeat one or more statements when a particular condition is true.
- The value of the loop control variable is updated with every iteration of the loop.
- The `for` loop provides a mechanism to repeat a task until a particular condition is true.

- The `for..in` statement is a looping statement used in Python to iterate over a sequence of objects.
- The `range()` is a built-in function in Python that is used to iterate over a sequence of numbers.

Review Questions

1. With the help of a flowchart, explain the construct of a `while` loop.

2. Why is the value of the loop control variable updated with every iteration of the loop?

3. With the help of a flowchart, explain the construct of a `for` loop.

4. With the help of an example, explain the use of `range()` function.

5. Fill in the blanks to complete the code:
   a. Create a loop that increments the value of *x* by 3 and prints the odd values from 0–100.
   ```
   x = 0
   ___x <= ___
   ___ (x)
   x += 2
   ```
   b. Create a `for` loop that prints only the even values in the range 0-50:
   ```
   ____ i in range(______):
   print(___)
   ```

6. Identify the definite and indefinite loop.

   ```
   n = input('Enter a number: ')        x = 0
   while n != -1:                       while x<10:
        n = input('Enter a number:  ')      print 10**num
                                         n = n+1
   ```

7. Correct the code to produce the desired output.

   ```
   for i in range(10,0):    i=10              i=10 ;  result = 1
       print(i)             while(i>0):       while(i>0):
                                print(i)          result = result + i**2
                                i-1               i = i+1
                                              print(result)
   ```

8. The following `for` loops are written to print numbers from 1 to 10. Are these loops correct? Justify your answer.

   ```
   for i in range(10):      for i in range(10):  for i in range(10):
       print(i)                 num = i+1            print(i)
                                print(num)           i = i+1
   ```

9. Write the following piece of code using `for` loop.
   ```
   i = 20
   while i>0:
       print(i)
       i = i-2
   ```

Programming Exercises

1. Write a function that accepts two positive numbers n and m where m<=n, and returns numbers between 1 and n that are divisible by m.

2. Write a program to convert time in hours into minutes and vice-versa.

3. Write a program to calculate conveyance charges to be paid by the users. Enter the type of car as a character (like s for sedan, p for prime, m for mini) and distance in km. Calculate charges as given below: sedan – 17 Rs per km, prime – 12 Rs per km, mini – 10 Rs per km.

4. Write a program to sum the series $1^2/1 + 2^2/2 + 3^2/3 + \ldots + n^2/n$.

5. Write a program that prints cube of numbers in the range `(1,n)`.

6. Write a program that prompts a user to enter the distance between his/her home and school. If the distance is in kilometers, display it in meters and vice-versa.

7. Write a program that displays Python Programming as
   a. `python programming`
   b. `PYTHON PROGRAMMING`
   c. `pYTHON pROGRAMMING`

8. Write a program that prompts users to enter numbers. Once the user enters -1, it displays the count, sum and average of even numbers and that of odd numbers.

9. Write a program to display the `sin(x)` value, where x ranges from 0 to 360 in steps of 45.

10. Write a program that displays all the numbers from `1-100` that are not divisible by 7 as well as by 11.

11. Write a program that accepts any number and prints the number of digits in that number.

12. Write a program that prints numbers from 100 to 1 in steps of 4.

13. Write a program that reads integers until the user wants to stop. When the user stops entering numbers, display the largest of all the numbers entered.

14. Write a program to generate the Fibonacci series.

15. Write a program to print first 20 even numbers in descending order.

16. Write a program to print the sum of the following series: $-x + x^2 - x^3 + x^4 + \ldots$

Fill in the Blanks

1. ____________ statements are used to repeatedly execute one or more statements in a block.

2. In Python, iterative statements are implemented through _______ and _______ loops.

3. An _________ loop will occur if the condition of `while` loop never becomes false.

4. The `for` loop provides a mechanism to repeat a task until a particular condition is _______.

5. The _______ function in Python is used to iterate over a sequence of numbers.

State True or False

1. The `while` loop repeats one or more statements while a particular condition is false.

2. Iterative Statement repeats the execution of a block of statements depending on the value of an expression that evaluates to an integer value only.

3. In the `while` loop, the condition is tested after statement block is executed at least once.

4. The value of the loop control variable is updated with every alternate iteration of the loop.

5. An infinite loop will occur if the condition of `while` loop is always false.

6. The `for` loop is executed for each item in the sequence.

7. Every iteration of the loop must make the loop control variable farther from the end of the sequence.

8. The step argument in the `range()` function is optional.

9. The number of times the loop control variable is updated is equal to the number of times the loop iterates.

10. In a `while` loop, the loop control variable is initialized in the body of the loop.

Multiple Choice Questions

1. Which keys are not pressed to exit from the infinite loop?

   a. Alt + C   b. Ctrl + C   c. Alt + F4   d. Ctrl + Q

2. The step argument in the `range()` function cannot be _______.

   a. less than zero   b. greater than zero   c. zero   d. none of these

3. `range(1,5)` will generate numbers ________.

   a. 0, 1, 2, 3, 4, 5   b. 0, 1, 2, 3, 4   c. 1, 2, 3, 4   d. 1, 2, 3, 4, 5

4. By default, every number in the range is incremented by _____.

   a. 0   b. 1   c. 2   d. 3

5. In a `while` loop, if the body is executed n times, then the test expression is executed ______ times.

   a. n – 1   b. n   c. n + 1   d. 2n

6.
```
i = 1
while i > 0:
    print("loop")
```
The above loop is best example of _________loop.

   a. nested   b. infinite   c. counter-controlled   d. condition-controlled

7. How many numbers will be printed?
```
i = 5
while i>=0:
        print(i)
        i=i-1
```
   a. 5   b. 6   c. 4   d. 0

8. How many numbers will be printed?
```
i = 10
while True:
        print(i)
        i = i - 1
        if i<=7:
                break
```
   a. 1   b. 2   c. 3   d. 4

9. How many lines will be printed by this code?
```
while False:
        print("Hello")
```
   a. 1   b. 0   c. 10   d. Countless

Give the Output

1.
```python
i=1
while i<=6:
print(i),
i=i+1
print("Done")
```

2.
```python
i=0
while i<10:
   i = i + 1
   if(i == 5):
      print("\n Continue")
      continue
   if(i==7):
      print"\n Breaking"
      break
   print i,
print("\n Done")
```

3.
```python
for i in range(5):
print("hello!", end= " ")
```

4.
```python
for i in range(10):
   if not i%2==0:
print(i+1)
```

5.
```python
for i in range(10,0,-1):
print(i, end = ' ')
```

6.
```python
for i in range(5,25,3):
print(i, end = ' ')
```

7.
```python
for i in "PYTHON":
print(i,'-',end='')
```

8.
```python
for i in range(10):
   pass
print(i)
```

9.
```python
while True:
```
```python
str = input("Enter a string (Bye
to exit) : ")
if str == "bye":
        break
   print(str)
else:
   print("Exiting......")
```

10.
```python
while(4>5):
      print("DONE")
else:
      print("NOT DONE")
```

11.
```python
while(5*2 > 10):
      print("JUST DO IT")
else:
      print("DONE")
```

12.
```python
a = 10; b = 0
while(a>b):
      print(a,b)
      a=a-1
      b=b+1
```

13.
```python
run = True
a = 100
while run == True:
      print(a)
      a = a - 10
      if a < 40:
          run = False
```

14.
```python
for i in range(100,50,-10):
      print(i)
```

15.
```python
for i in range(100,50,-10):
      print(i)
```

16.
```python
x = 10; y = 5
for i in range(x-y*2):
      print("%")
```

Find the Error

1.
```python
while(i<10):
      print(i)
```

AI Lab Session – Touch Type by Google

Touch Type is an interactive type projection application that tracks simple body movements to replicate the effect on the screen. Visit the link to https://pose.yee.gd/ to use the application.

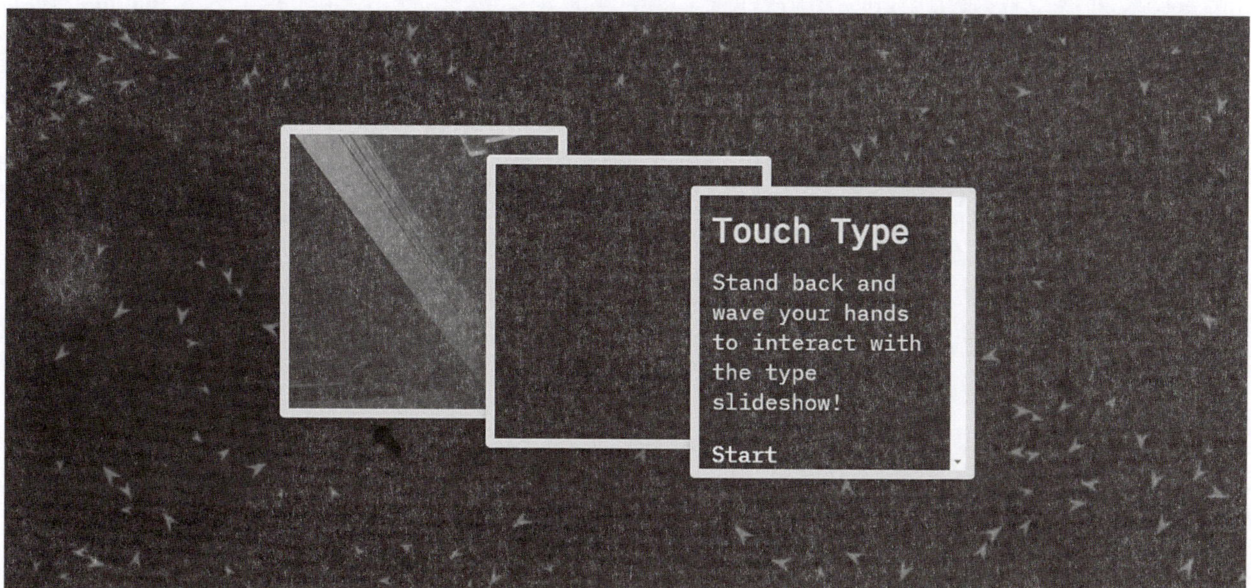

Answers

Fill in the Blanks

1. Iterative

2. `while`, `for`

3. infinite

4. true

5. `range()`

State True or False

1. False

2. True

3. False

4. False

5. False

6. True

7. False

8. True

9. True

10. False

Multiple Choice Questions

1. a

2. c

3. c

4. b

5. c

6. b

7. b

8. c

9. b

Give the Output

1. 1 2 3 4 5 6 Done

2. 1 2 3 4

Continue 6 Breaking Done

3. hello! hello! hello! hello! hello!

4. 2 4 6 8 10

5. 10 9 8 7 6 5 4 3 2 1

6. 5 8 11 14 17 20 23

7. P -Y -T -H -O -N -

8. 9

9. No output when bye is entered.

10. NOT DONE

11. DONE

12. 10 0

13. 100 90 80 70 60 50 40

14. 100 90 80 70 60

15. No output

16. No output

Find the Error

1. `NameError: name 'i' is not defined`

Lists

14

Chapter Objectives

This chapter introduces list as an important and very powerful data structure in Python. The reader will get to learn the following things in this chapter:

- Creating lists
- Accessing and updating its values
- Relational operations
- Nested lists

- The eval() function
- Creating deep copies and shallow copies of a given list
- Difference between list cloning and list aliasing
- List operations and methods

List is a versatile data type available in Python, in which elements are written as a list of comma-separated values (items) between square brackets. Lists in Python are mutable as we can change the value of its elements. This is in striking contrast with strings which are immutable.

The key feature of list is that it can have elements that belong to different data types. The syntax of defining a list can be given as, **List_variable = [val1, val2, …]**

```
list_A = [1,2,3,4,5]
print(list_A)
[1, 2, 3, 4, 5]

list_C = ["HELLO","WORLD")
print(list_ C)
['HELLO', 'WORLD']
```

```
list_B = ['A', 1, 'C', 2, 'E']
print(list_B)
['A', 1, 'C', 2, 'E']

list_D = [1, 'a ', 'HELLO')
print( list_ D)
[1, 'a ', 'HELLO']
```

We can even create an empty list by writing **list_variable = []**. An empty list is equivalent to False when used with logical operators.

```
>>> list = []
>>> list == True
        False
```

14.1 ACCESSING VALUES IN LISTS

Like strings, lists can also be sliced and concatenated. To access values in a list, square brackets are used to slice along with the index or indices to get the value stored at that index. As discussed earlier, the syntax for the slice operation is, seq = List[start:stop:step]

For example,

seq = List[::2] *# get every other element, starting with index 0*
seq = List[10::3] *# get every third element, starting with index 10*
seq = List[-3] *# get third element from the end*
seq = list_A[-3] *# 3rd element from the end*
seq = List[3:] *# get all elements starting from the third index from the beginning*

```
num_list = [2,4,6,8,10,12,14,16,18,20]
print("num_list is:", num_list)
print("First element in the list is",
num_list[0])
print("num_list[2:5] = ", num_list[4:7])
print("num_list[::2] = ", num_list[::3])
print("num_list[1::3] = ", num_list[1::2])
```

```
OUTPUT
num_list is : [2, 4, 6, 8, 10, 12,
14, 16, 18, 20]
First element in the list is 2
num_list[2:5] = [10, 12, 14]
num_list[::2] = [2, 8, 14, 20]
num_list[1::3] = [4, 8, 12, 16, 20]
```

If the start and end values of the slice operation are beyond the size of the list, then all the elements within the specified range are returned. For example, consider the example given below, in which the start and end values are out of range of the size of the list.

```
I = [1,2,3,4,5]          I = [1, 2,3,4,5]
print(l[-9:9])           print(I[-3:9])
OUTPUT                   OUTPUT
[1, 2, 3, 4, 5]          [3, 4, 5]
```

Note that the valid index range of the list is 0–4. Values −9 and 9 are beyond the size of the list; so the entire list is returned, as 0 to 4 lies within the range −9 to 9. But in the second case, when start = −3 and end = 9, −3 lies in the valid range, which is the third element from the end, hence the result.

14.2   UPDATING VALUES IN LISTS

Once created, one or more elements of a list can be easily updated by doing the slice on the left-hand side of the assignment operator. You can also append new values in the list and remove existing value(s) from the list using the append() method and del statement respectively.

Example 14.1

```
num_list = [2,4,6,8,10,12,14,16,18,20]
print("List is : ", num_list)
num_list[5] = 100
print("List after udpation is : ", num_list)
num_list.append(200)
print("List after appending a value is ", num_list)
del num_list(3]
print("List after deleting a value is ", num_list)
```

```
OUTPUT
List is : [2, 4, 6, 8, 10, 12, 14, 16, 18, 20]
List after udpation is : [2, 4, 6, 8, 10, 100, 14, 16, 18, 20]
List after appending a value is [2, 4, 6, 8, 10, 100, 14, 16, 18, 20, 200]
List after deleting a value is [2, 4, 6, 10, 100, 14, 16, 18, 20, 200
```

If you know exactly which element(s) to delete, use the del statement; otherwise, use the remove() method to delete the unknown elements.

Example 14.2

```
num_list = [2,4,6,8,10,12,14,16,18,20] del num_list[3:6] #deletes numbers at
index 3,4,5
print(num_list)
del num_list[:] #deletes all the numbers from the list
print(num_list) # an empty list is printed
```

```
OUTPUT
[2, 4, 6, 14, 16, 18, 20]
[]
```

```
del(num_list)
print(num_list)  # the list no
longer exists
```

OUTPUT
```
Traceback (most recent call last):
    File "C:\Users\Reema\Python\Python37\try.py",
line 5, in <module>
        print(num_list) #the list no loger exists
    NameError: name 'num_list' is not defined
```

Note that when we write `del num_list`, the entire variable is deleted. If you make any attempt to use this variable after the `del` statement, then an error will be generated.

14.3 RELATIONAL OPERATIONS ON LISTS

We can compare two list objects using relational operators like ==, >,<,>=,<=!=, etc. Python compares elements of a list in lexicographical order. Each element of the list is compared with the corresponding element in the other list. However, to use operators like >=,<=,>,<, the two values must be of compatible type; otherwise, an error will be generated.

Example 14.3

```
l1 = [1,2,3]
l2 = [1,2,3]
l3 = [1,[2,3]]
print(l1==l2)
print(l1==l3)
```

OUTPUT
```
True
False
```

```
l1 = [1,2,3]
l2 = [1,3,3]
print(l1>=l2)
print(l1<=l2)
```

OUTPUT
```
False
True
```

```
l1 = [1,2,3,4]
l2 = [1,3,3]
print(l1>=l2)
```

OUTPUT
```
True
```

```
l1 = [1,2,3,4]
l2 = ['a','b','c']
l3 = [1.0,2.0,3.0]
print(l1>=l3)
print(l2>=l3)
```

OUTPUT
```
True
Traceback (most recent call last):
    File "C:\Python37\try.py",line 5,
in <module>
    print(l2>=l3) Type Error: '>=' not
supported between instances of 'str'
and 'float'
```

Example 14.4

```
I =[1,2,3,4,5,6,7,8,9,10)
print(I)
#deleting third element
del I[2]
print(I)
#deleting fourth, fifth, sixth and seventh elements from the list
delI[2:6]
print(I)
#deleting the entire list
print("Deleting List ........ ")
del I
print(I)
```

OUTPUT
```
[1, 2, 3, 4, 5, 6, 7, 8, 9, 10]
[1, 2, 4, 5, 6, 7, 8, 9, 10)
[1, 2, 8, 9, 10)
```

```
Deleting List ....... .
Traceback (most recent call last): File "C:\Python37\try.py", line 12, in
<module> print(I)
NameError: name 'I' is not defined
```

14.4 DELETING ELEMENTS

We can delete one or more elements from the list by using the **del** statement. The syntax to remove a single element from the list is **del list_variable[index]**. And to remove more than one element from the list, we use the syntax, **del[start:stop]**. Finally, to remove the entire list, we need to write **del list_variable.**

14.5 BASIC LIST OPERATIONS

Lists behave in a similar way as strings when operators like + (concatenation) and * (repetition) are used. Common operations on lists are discussed in Table 14.1.

Table 14.1   Operations on lists

Operation	Description	Example	Output
len	Returns length of list	len([1,2,3,4,5,6,7,8,9,10])	10
concatenation	Joins two lists	[1,2,3,4,5] + [6,7,8,9,10]	[1, 2, 3, 4, 5, 6, 7, 8, 9, 10]
repetition	Repeat elements in the list	"Love", "Python"*2	['Love', 'Python', 'Love', 'Python']
in	Checks if the value is present in the list	'a' in ['a','e', 'i','o','u']	True
not in	Checks if the value is not present in the list	9 not in [0,2,4,6,8]	True
max	Returns maximum value in the list	>>> num_list = [1,0,3,7,4,2,4,9] >>> print(max(num_list))	9
min	Returns minimum value in the list	>>> num_list = [1,0,3,7,4,2,4,9] >>> print(min(num_list))	0
sum	Adds the values in the list that has numbers	num_list = [1,2,3,4,5,6,7,8,9,10] print("SUM = ", sum(num_list))	SUM = 55

14.6 LIST METHODS

Python has various methods to help programmers work efficiently with lists. Some of these methods are summarized in Table 14.2.

Table 14.2   List methods

Method	Description	Syntax	Example	Output
`append()`	Appends an element to the list. In `insert()`, if the index is 0, then element is inserted as the first element and if we write, `list.insert(len(list), obj)`, then it inserts obj as the last element in the list. That is, if `index= len(list)` then `insert()` method behaves exactly same as `append()` method.	`list. append(obj)`	`num_list = [1,2,3,4]` `num_list.append(5)` `print(num_list)`	`[1,2,3,4,5]`
`count()`	Counts the number of times an element appears in the list.	`list. count(obj)`	`num_list = [1,2,3,4,3,2,4,6]` `print( num_list. count(4))`	`1`
`index()`	Returns the lowest index of obj in the list. Gives a ValueError if obj is not present in the list.	`list. index(obj)`	`num_list = [1,2,3,4,3,2,4,6]` `print(num_list. index(3))`	`2`
`insert()`	Inserts obj at the specified index in the list.	`list. insert(index, obj)`	`num_list = [1,2,3,4,5]` `num_list.insert(3, 0)` `print(num_list)`	`[1,2,3,0,4,5]`
`remove()`	Removes or deletes obj from the list. ValueError is generated if obj is not present in the list. If multiple copies of obj exists in the list then the first value is deleted.	`list. remove(obj)`	`num_list = [0,1,2,3,4,5]` `num_list.remove(0)` `print(num_list)`	`[1, 2, 3,4,5]`
`reverse()`	Reverses the elements in the list.	`list. reverse()`	`num_list = [1,2,3,4]` `num_list.reverse()` `print num_list`	`[4,3,2,1]`
`sort()`	Sorts the elements in the list.	`list.sort()`	`num_list = [3,5,0,4,1]` `num_list.sort()` `print(num_list)`	`[0,1,3,4,5]`

You must be confused between a method and a function. Observe the above two tables. Clearly, a **function** is a piece of code that is directly called by name. It may or may not accept parameters and may or may not return data. All data that is to be used by a function is explicitly passed (or made global). Example, *len (list1)*.

However, a **method** is a piece of code that is called by name of the object followed by a dot operator and name of the method. Example, *list1.sort()*.

PROGRAMMER'S ZONE

1. **Write a program that creates a list of numbers from 1–20 that are either divisible by 2 or divisible by 4 without using the filter function.**

```
div_2_4 = []
for i in range(2, 22):
    if(i%2 == 0 or i%4 == 0):
        div_2_4.append(i)
print(div_2_4)
```

OUTPUT

```
[2, 4, 6, 8, 10, 12, 14, 16, 18, 20]
```

> The sort() method uses ASCII values to sort the values in the list.

> An error is generated if you try to delete an element from the list or insert an element that is not present in the list.

2. **Write a program to print the index at which a particular value exists. If the value exists at multiple locations in the list, then print all the indices. Also count the number of times that value is repeated in the list.**

```
num_list = [1,2,3,4,5,6,5,4,3,2,1]
num = int(input("Enter the value to be searched : "))
i=0
count = 0
while i<len(num_list):
    if num == num_list[i]:
        print(num, " found at location", i)
        count += 1
    i += 1
print(num, " appears ", count, " times in the list")
```

> It is safer to avoid aliasing when you are working with mutable objects.

OUTPUT

```
Enter the value to be searched : 4
4   found at location 3
4   found at location 7
4   appears  2  times in the list
list_words = []
```

> When using slice operation, an IndexError is generated if the index is outside the list.

3. **Write a program that forms a list of first character of every word in another list.**

```
list1 = ["Hello", "Welcome", "To", "The", "World", "Of", "Python"]
letters = []
for word in list1:
    letters.append(word[0])
print(letters)
```

> The index must be an integer. If you specify a non-integer number as the index, then TypeError will be generated.

OUTPUT

```
['H', 'W', 'T', 'T', 'W', 'O', 'P']
```

4. **Write a program that counts the number of times each word is repeated in a list.**

```python
words =["abc","def","ghi","lmn","lmn","def","pqr","rst","abc","lmn","def","xyz"]
length = len(words)
dups = []
uniq = []
i = 0
for word in words:
    count = words.count(word)
    print(word,count, end = ' ')
    words.remove(word)
```

OUTPUT

```
abc 2    ghi 1   lmn 3    pqr 1   abc 1   def 3
```

5. **Write a program to create a list of numbers in the specified range in particular steps. Reverse the list and print its values.**

```python
num_list = []
m = int(input("Enter the starting of the range : "))
n = int(input("Enter the ending of the range : "))
o = int(input("Enter the steps in the range : "))
for i in range(m,n, o):
    num_list.append(i)
print("Original List :", num_list)
num_list.reverse()
print("Reversed List : ", num_list)
```

OUTPUT

```
Enter the starting of the range : 2
Enter the ending of the range : 30
Enter the steps in the range : 3
Original List : [2, 5, 8, 11, 14, 17, 20, 23, 26, 29]
Reversed List :  [29, 26, 23, 20, 17, 14, 11, 8, 5, 2]
```

> append() and insert() methods are list methods. They cannot be called on other values such as string or integers.

6. **Write a program that prints the largest and the second largest value in a list of numbers.**

```python
list = eval(input("ENter the list elements : "))
length = len(list)
largest = sec_largest = list[0]
for i in range(1,length-1):
    if(list[i]>largest):
        sec_largest = largest
        largest = list[i]
print("LARGEST = ", largest,"SECOND LARGEST = ",sec_largest)
```

OUTPUT

```
ENter the list elements : [9,4,0,2,11,7,6,5]
LARGEST =   11 SECOND LARGEST =   9
```

Key Terms

Immutable data: Data which cannot be modified. Assigning values to elements or slices of immutable data results in a runtime error.

Mutable data value: Data which can be modified.

List: A mutable data structure that can have elements that belong to different data types.

Chapter Highlights

- List is a versatile data type available in Python, in which elements are written as a list of comma-separated values (items) between square brackets.

- Like strings, lists can also be sliced and concatenated.

- Once created, one or more elements of a list can be easily updated by doing the slice on the left-hand side of the assignment operator.

- We can append new values in the list and remove existing value(s) from the list using the `append()` method and `del` statement respectively.

- Lists behave in the similar way as strings when operators like + (concatenation) and * (repetition) are used.

Review Questions

1. What is a list?

2. How can we define a list in Python?

3. With the help of an example, demonstrate how lists can be sliced to access its values.

4. Explain the syntax of the slice operation.

5. What is the role of `del` statement with list variables?

6. Differentiate the use of `del` statement and `remove()` function?

7. Explain the purpose of the following functions:
   a. `sorted()`   b. `sum()`   c. `min()`

8. Name the function or the operator that can be used for the following tasks:
   a. Return length of list
   b. Repeat elements in the list
   c. Join two lists
   d. Check if the value is present in the list
   e. Return maximum value in the list

9. Name the methods that can be used in the following situations:
   a. Append an element to the list.
   b. Count the number of times an element appears in the list
   c. Return the lowest index of obj in the list.

10. Explain the purpose of the following methods in Python:
    a. `insert()`   b. `reverse()`   c. `extend()`

11. Given a list, l = [1,2,3,4,5], write instructions for the following tasks:
    a. Set the third element to 100   b. Insert 200 at the second index
    c. Append 300 to the list   d. Remove the fourth element from the list
    e. Sort the list   f. Reverse the list.

Programming Exercises

1. Write instructions for the following:
   a. Creating a list of first 10 even numbers
   b. Adding second and third items and storing it in fifth position
   c. Delete the fourth element
   d. Add a new value to the list
   e. Divide the seventh value by 5
   f. Swap the value of 4th and 7th position
   g. Print only last two elements
   h. Print the total values in the list.

2. Write a program that creates a list of numbers in the series $2^n - 1$. Display only the even-indexed values in this list.

3. Write a program that prints the elements along with their indices from the start and end of the list.

4. Write a program to calculate the length of a list using `for` loop or `while` loop.

5. Write a program that adds the corresponding elements of two lists.

6. Make a list of first ten letters of the alphabet; then using the slice operation, do the following operations:
   a. Print the first three letters from the list.
   b. Print any three letters from the middle
   c. Print the letters from any particular index to the end of the list

7. Write a program that prints the maximum value of the second half of the list.

8. Write a program that finds the sum of all the numbers using a `while` loop.

9. Write a program that finds the sum of all even numbers in a list.

10. Write a program to find whether a particular element is present in the list, using a loop.

11. Write a program that prompts a number from user and adds it in a list. If the value entered by user is greater than 100, then add "EXCESS" in the list.

12. Write a program that counts the number of times a value appears in the list. Use a loop to do the same.

13. Write a program to insert a value in a list at the specified location using `while` loop.

14. Write a program that creates a list of numbers from 1–50 that are either divisible by 3 or divisible by 6.

15. Write a program to create a list of numbers in the range 1 to 20. Then delete all the numbers from the list that are divisible by 3.

16. Write a program to check whether a given value is present in the list (a) using `for` loop (b) without using any loop.

Fill in the Blanks

1. When using slice operation, ___________ is generated if the index is outside the list.

2. [10,20] < [20,10] will return ________.

3. The `sort()` method uses _________ values to sort the values in the list.

4. Fill in the blanks to create a list and print its second element.
   ```
   List = ___10, 20, 30, 40]
   print(list[___])
   ```

5. Fill in the blanks to create a list, reassign its third element and print the list.
```
List = [1,2,3,4,5__
List[__] = 30
print(__)
```

6. Fill in the blanks to print "Hello" if the list contains 'H'.
```
Letters = ['W', 'G', 'H']
__ 'H'__ Letters:
print("______")
```

7. Fill in the blanks to add 'G' to the end of the list and print the list's length.
```
Letters.____('G')
print(__ ___)
```

8. Fill in the blanks to print the letters in the list.
```
Letters = ['H', 'E', 'L', 'L','O']
___ i __Letters__
print(i)
```

9. Fill in the blanks to print the second element of the list, if it contains an odd number of elements.
```
List =[10, 20, 30, 40, 50]
If ___(list)%2__0__
print(List[__])
```

10. Fill in the banks to print the first two elements of the list.
```
List = [1,2,3,4,5,6]
print(list[0_])
```

11. The range of index values for a list of 10 elements will be _____.

State True or False

1. The index value starts from zero.

2. List is an immutable data structure.

3. Once created, one or more elements of a list can be easily updated.

4. It is possible to edit, add and delete elements from a list.

5. Slice operation can be used to insert items from another list or sequence at a particular location.

6. Items in a list can be deleted by assigning an empty list to a slice of elements.

7. If you specify a non-integer number as the index, then IndexError will be generated.

8. Python sorts the original list with the help of `sorted()` function.

Multiple Choice Questions

1. If `List = [1,2,3,4,5]`, then `List[5]` will result in ______.
   a. 4   b. 3   c, 2   d. Error

2. If `List = [1,2,3,4,5]` and we write `List[3] = List[1]`, then what will be `List[3]`?
   a. 1   b. 3   c, 2   d. 4

3. `type(x)` will print ______.
   a. `<class 'list'>`   b. `<class 'tuple'>`
   c. `<class 'int'>`   d. Error

4. If `List = [1,2,3,4,5,6,7,8,9,10]`, then print `List[8:4:-1]` will give ________.
   a. `[2,3,4,5]`   b. `[9,8,7,6]`   c. `[6,7,8,9]`   d. `[5,4,3,2]`

5. If `List = min([sum([10,20]),max(abs(-30),4)])`, then List = ____.
   a. 10   b. 20   c. 30   d. 4

6. Which slice operation will reverse the list?
   a. `Lists[-1::]`   b. `numbers[::-1]`
   c. `numbers[:-1:]`   d. `List[9:8:1]`

7. If `List = (12,8,7,5)`, then `print(max(min(List[:2]),abs(-6)))` will print ______.
   a. 12   b. 8   c. 7   d. 5

Give the Output

1.
```python
colors = ['red', 'blue', 'green']
print(colors[2])
print(len(colors))
```

2.
```python
list = ['abc', 'def', 'ghi', 'jkl']
print(list[1:-1])
list[0:2] = 'xyz'
print(list)
```

3.
```python
list = ['abc', 'def', 'ghi', 'jkl', [1,2,3,4,5]]
print(list[4][2])
```

4.
```python
list = ['p','r','o','g','r','a','m','m','i','n','g']
print(list[2:5])
print(list[:-5])
print(list[5:])
print(list[:])
```

5.
```python
even = [2,4,6]
print(even + [10, 12, 14])
print(even*2)
even.insert(1,0)
print(even)
del even[2]
print(even)
```

6.
```python
list = ['p','r','o','g','r','a','m']
list.remove('p')
print(list)
```

7.
```python
list = [9,4,3,8,0,2,3,6]
print(list.index(3))
print(list.count(8))
list.sort()
print(list)
list.reverse()
print(list)
print(0 in list)
```

8.
```python
list = [10, 20, 30, 40, 50, 60, 70, 80, 90]
print(list[-4:-1])
print(list[-1:-4])
print(list[-5:])
print(list[-6:-2:2])
print(list[::-1])
```

9.
```python
list = [[10, 20, [30, 40, [50, 60]]]]
print(list[0])
print(list[0][2])
print(list[0][2][2])
print(list[0][0])
print(list[0][2][1])
print(list[0][2][2][0])
```

10.
```python
List = [100, 90, 80, 70, 60, 50]
List[2] = List[1] - 20
if 30 in List:
    print(List[3])
else:
    print(List[4])
```

11.
```python
List = list(range(2, 20, 3))
print(List[5])
```

12.
```python
str = "abcdefghijklmno"
for i in range(0, len(str), 2):
    print(str[i], end = ' ')
```

13.
```python
print([ord(ch) for ch in 'PYTHON'])
```

14.
```python
l1 = [1,2,3]
l2 = ['a','b','c']
l3 = [1.2,3.4,5.6]
l4 = l1 + l2 + l3
print(l4)
```

15.
```python
print([1,2,8,9] < [1,2,8,9,10])
```

16.
```python
l = [1,2,3,4,5,6,7,8,9,10]
print(l[-1])
print(l[l[0]])
print(l[l[-8]])
print(l[l[l[0]+1]]+2)
```

17.
```python
msg = ["PYTHON","is","a",["simple","iterpreted","OOP"],"language"]
print(msg[2:4])
print(msg[2:4][1][2])
print(msg[2:4][1][2][1])
print("im" in msg[2:4][1][2][1])
print(msg[2:4][1][1][3:])
print(msg[1]+msg[4])
```

18. ```
>>> [1,2,3] +[1,2,3] == [1,2,3]*2
```

19. ```
l = [1,2,3]
l * 3 == [1,1,1]
```

20. ```
msg = ["PYTHON","is","a",["simple","interpreted","OOP"],"language"]
print(msg[::2])
print('n' in msg[4])
print(msg[2] in msg[4])
```

21. ```
l = [1,2,3]
print((l + [4,5,6])[3])
```

22. ```
[1,2] == [1,2]
```

23. ```
[1,2] is [1,2]
```

24. ```
L = [1,2,3,4,5,6,7,8,9,10,11,12,13,14]
print(L[::-1])
print(L[-1:-2:-3])
```

## Find the Error

1. ```
list = ['abc', 'def', 'ghi', 'jkl']
print list[2.0]
```

2. ```
even = [2,4,6]
del even
print(even)
```

3. ```
list = [(1, 2), [3, 4], '56', 78, 9.0]
list.remove('abc')
```

4. ```
msg = "Hello"
msg.append("World")
print(msg)
```

5. ```
[1,2,3] + 2
```

6. ```
L = [1,2,3,4]
L.remove(7)
```

7. ```
[1,2,3] * 3.0
```

AI Lab Session – Teachable Snake

Teachable Snake is an interactive web game in which the users have to draw a black arrow on a piece of white paper as controller, and move the snake by turning the paper in different directions in front of webcam.

Visit the URL https://teachable-snake.netlify.app/ to start the game.

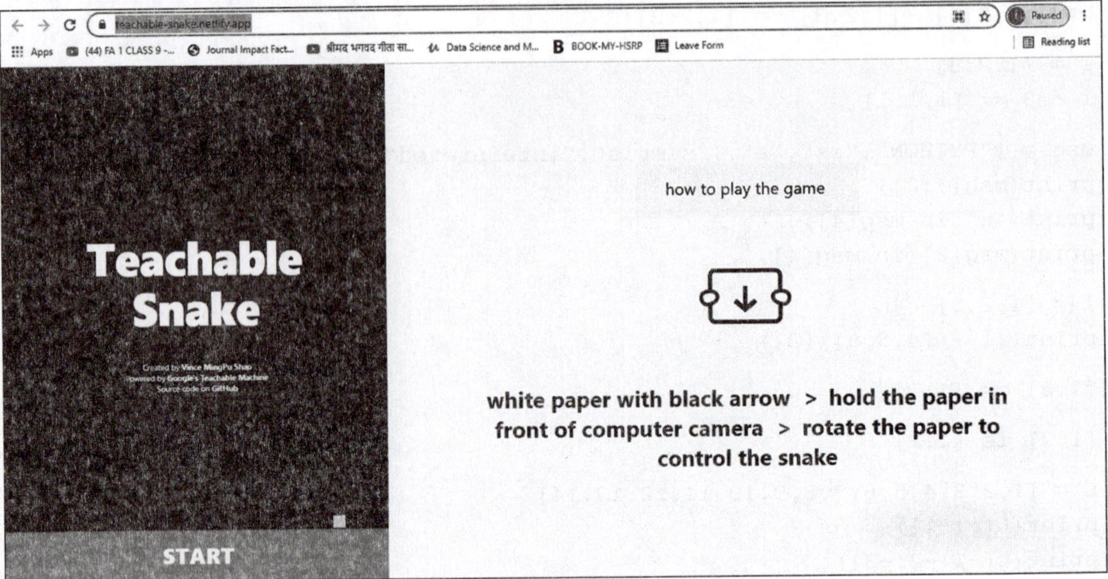

Fun Activity – Fill the Crossword

Down

1. The science involving design, construction, operation, and use of robots.

2. One round of forwarding and backpropagation iteration is known as one training iteration.

3. The process of acquiring data for the project from relevant sources.

4. Rare events or observations that generally do not occur.

5. Any piece of information can be used to store information that may change.

6. Reserved words in a programming language that have a pre-defined meaning.

Across

7. An AI-based software application used to conduct an on-line chat conversation via text or text-to-speech, in lieu of providing direct contact with a live human agent.

8. Huge amounts of data that cannot be stored by any system or analyzed by traditional data management software.

9. Moral principles that govern the behavior and actions of a group or individual.

10. Values on which the operator is applied.

11. Type of data which can be modified.

12. A mutable data structure that can have elements that belong to different data types.

13. A substring of a string.

14. Statements that repeat the execution of a block of statements depending on the value of an integer expression.

15. Names given to identify a variable, function, class, module or any other object.

16. Any valid combination of tokens that represents a value.

Answers

Fill in the Blanks

1. IndexError
2. True
3. ASCII
4. [, 1
5.], 2, List
6. if, in, Hello
7. append, len, (, Letters,)
8. for, in, :
9. len, !=, :, 1
10. :2
11. 0–9

State True or False

1. True
2. False
3. True
4. True
5. True
6. True
7. False
8. True

Multiple Choice Questions

1. d
2. c
3. c
4. b
5. c
6. b
7. b

Give the Output

1. green, 3
2. ['def', 'ghi']
   ['xyz', 'ghi', 'jkl']
3. 3
4. ['o', 'g', 'r']
   ['p', 'r', 'o', 'g', 'r', 'a']
   ['a', 'm', 'm', 'i', 'n', 'g']
   ['p', 'r', 'o', 'g', 'r', 'a', 'm', 'm', 'i', 'n', 'g']
5. [2, 4, 6, 10, 12, 14]
   [2, 4, 6, 2, 4, 6]
   [2, 0, 4, 6]
   [2, 0, 6]

6. ['r', 'o', 'g', 'r', 'a', 'm']

   o

   ['r', 'g', 'r', 'a', 'm']

   m

   ['r', 'g', 'r', 'a']

7. 2

   1

   [0, 2, 3, 3, 4, 6, 8, 9]

   [9, 8, 6, 4, 3, 3, 2, 0]

   True

8. [60, 70, 80]

   []

   [50, 60, 70, 80, 90]

   [40, 60]

   [90, 80, 70, 60, 50, 40, 30, 20, 10]

9. [10, 20, [30, 40, [50, 60]]]

   [30, 40, [50, 60]]

   [50, 60]

   10

   40

   50

10. 60

11. 17

12. a c e g i k m o

13. [80, 89, 84, 72, 79, 78]

14. [1, 2, 3, 'a', 'b', 'c', 1.2, 3.4, 5.6]

15. True

16. 10   2   4   6

17. ['a', ['simple', 'iterpreted', 'OOP']]

    OOP   O   False   rpreted   islanguage

18. True

19. False

20. ['PYTHON', 'a', 'language']

    True

    True

21. ['PYTHON', 'a', 'language']   True   True

22. True

23. False

24. [14, 13, 12, 11, 10, 9, 8, 7, 6, 5, 4, 3, 2, 1]

    [14]

Find the Error

1. ```
TypeError: list indices must be integers, not float
```
2. ```
NameError: name 'even' is not defined
```
3. ```
ValueError: list.remove(x): x not in list
```
4. ```
AttributeError: 'str' object has no attribute 'append'
```
5. ```
TypeError: can only concatenate list (not "int") to list
```
6. ```
ValueError: list.remove(x): x not in list
```
7. ```
TypeError: can't multiply sequence by non-int of type 'float'
```
```